FIFTH EDITION

Marketing
Practices and Principles

Ralph E. Mason

Instructor of Marketing
Maysville Community College
Maysville, Kentucky
Professor Emeritus
School of Business
Indiana State University,
Terre Haute, Indiana

Patricia Mink Rath

Marketing Education Consultant
Professor of Merchandising Management
The International Academy of Merchandising and Design, Ltd.
Chicago, Illinois

Stewart W. Husted

Donaldson Brown Distinguished Professor of Marketing
Lynchburg College
Lynchburg, Virginia

Richard L. Lynch

Professor and Director
School of Leadership and Lifelong Learning
University of Georgia
Athens, Georgia

 **Glencoe McGraw-Hill**

New York, New York   Columbus, Ohio   Woodland Hills, California   Peoria, Illinois

Glencoe/McGraw-Hill

*A Division of The **McGraw·Hill** Companies*

Send all inquiries to:
Glencoe/McGraw-Hill
21600 Oxnard Street, Suite 500
Woodland Hills, CA 91367

ISBN 0-02-635601-5 (Student Edition)
ISBN 0-02-635602-3 (Teacher's Annotated Edition)

Printed in the United States of America.

6 7 8 9 10 11   027   02 01 00 99 98

About the Authors

Ralph E. Mason, former chair of the Department of Administrative Services and Business Education, School of Business at Indiana State University until 1984, began his career in business and marketing education in 1940 in the public schools of Illinois. He worked in several school systems, first as a teacher coordinator of marketing education for ten years, then as a director of adult and vocational education. In 1956, he joined the staff of the University of Illinois as the state's first full-time teacher educator in marketing education.

Mason is the former president of the National Council for Distributive Teacher Education, the Illinois Business Education Association, the Illinois Vocational Education Association, and the Indiana Business Education Association. He was a member of the Task Force on Standards and Evaluation Criteria for Distributive Teacher Education.

He has contributed much to the growth of marketing education through his teaching and publications, which include several magazine articles and popular professional books. He was presented a Distinguished Teaching Award in 1983 by Indiana State University and a Distributive Education Professional Development Award in his name in 1985. He continues to consult and write and is currently an instructor of marketing at Maysville Community College in Kentucky.

Patricia Mink Rath is a marketing education consultant and professor of Merchandising Management at The International Academy of Merchandising and Design, Ltd., Chicago, Illinois. In addition to teaching marketing, fashion, and management courses, she is a member of the college's Institutional Planning Committee.

Rath has extensive marketing experience with several fashion merchandising businesses and has written educational materials used by businesses as well as schools. A former state supervisor of business and distributive education, she has taught both adult and high school business programs. She is a member of the American Marketing Association and the Marketing Education Association, a life member of the American Vocational Association, and past president of the National Association of State Supervisors of Distributive Education. Her post-Master's study was done at Northwestern University; her Master's Degree was earned at the Prince School of Retailing, Simmons College; and her undergraduate degree is from Oberlin College.

Stewart W. Husted is the Donaldson Brown Distinguished Professor of Marketing at Lynchburg College in Virginia. Husted previously taught business and marketing courses at Indiana State University (1976–1989) where he was Professor of Business, the Program Coordinator, and teacher educator for Marketing Education. He has also taught at the high school and community college levels.

Husted has published extensively in business and marketing education and has served as consultant or trainer to a variety of profit and nonprofit organizations.

Husted has served as President of the Blue Ridge Marketing Association (American Marketing Association affiliate), as a national board member (Sales & Marketing Division) of the American Society of Training & Development, and as a member of the MarkED Board of Trustees. He has received Outstanding Service Awards from Indiana and Virginia DECA (1989 and 1993), the Indiana Vocational Association (1980), and Indiana State University (1989). Husted has earned degrees from Virginia Tech (B.S.), University of Georgia (M.Ed.), and Michigan State University (Ph.D.).

Richard L. Lynch is Professor and Director of the School of Leadership and Lifelong Learning at The University of Georgia. Lynch has many years of experience in marketing occupations and in marketing education. He has been employed in retailing, marketing research, hotel operations, and in purchasing. He has been a high school marketing teacher coordinator and postsecondary marketing instructor in Milwaukee, Wisconsin, and professor of marketing education at Indiana University and Virginia Polytecnic Institute and State University. He is currently Professor and Director of the School of Leadership and Lifelong Learning at The University of Georgia.

Lynch is a frequent speaker at conferences and workshops for teachers of marketing and other educators. He has written materials and conducted training sessions for organizations such as DECA, Phillips Petroleum Company, IBM, Menswear Retailers of America, the United States Department of Education, the United States Department of Labor, and the National Center for Research in Vocational Education. He has authored and served as consulting editor on several marketing texts. He is a member of a number of marketing and professional education associations and has received several honors and awards for his research, teaching, and professional service activities. Lynch received his BA degree in Business Education from the University of Northern Iowa, an MA degree in Marketing Education from the University of Minnesota, and an EdD degree in Vocational Education from Indiana University. He completed postdoctoral study at Ohio State University.

Reviewers and Consultants

Carolyn Partain Lecocke
Marketing Coordinator/Instructor
Clark High School
Northside Independent School District
San Antonio, Texas

Debbie Leinweber
Marketing Education Teacher/Coordinator
Westwood High School
Round Rock Independent School District
Austin, Texas

Pam McKenney
Marketing Education Consultant
Phillips Ranch, California

Don Meek, Jr.
Marketing Education Coordinator
W. B. Ray High School
Corpus Christi Independent School District
Corpus Christi, Texas

Gay Morrison Sabom
Marketing Education Coordinator
Northbrook High School
Spring Branch Independent School District
Houston, Texas

Clifton L. Smith
Associate Professor and Program Leader
Marketing Education
University of Georgia
Athens, Georgia

Dana J. Witmer
Marketing Education Coordinator
North Central High School
J. E. Light Career Center
Washington Township Schools
Indianapolis, Indiana

Table of Contents

▮ UNIT 4: *Marketing Research* 160

█ UNIT 5: *The Product*................................ 200

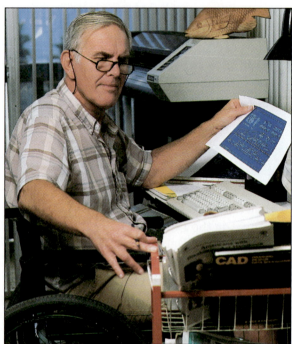

Chapter 19   *Credit as a Customer Service*   240

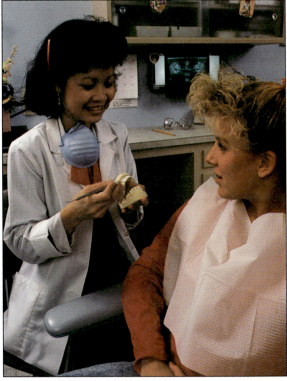

Chapter 20   *The Marketing of Services*   252

■ UNIT 6: *Pricing* 266

Chapter 21   *The Elements of Pricing*   268

UNIT 8: *Promotion* 370

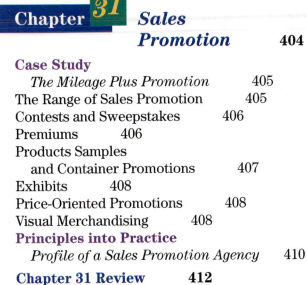

UNIT 1

The World of Marketing

Chapters ▼

Marketing in Modern Society

Terms to Know

product
goods
services
customer
consumer
marketing
marketplace
market
micromarketing

macromarketing
profit
nonprofit marketing
marketing concept
ethics
marketing ethics
marketing mix
promotion

Chapter Objectives

After studying this chapter, you will be able to:

- define *marketing*;
- explain how marketing serves people;
- give examples of marketing in everyday experiences;
- explain the difference between macromarketing and micromarketing;
- discuss the marketing concept;
- discuss the importance of marketing ethics;
- identify the four Ps of marketing and explain how they relate to the marketing concept; and
- tell why the field of marketing is called *dynamic*.

Case Study

We All Scream for Ice Cream

Peek inside your freezer. You will probably agree: ice cream has become more American than apple pie. It is so American, in fact, that Congress has declared July National Ice Cream Month.

The passion is long-standing. President James Madison's wife, Dolly, popularized the French dessert nearly 200 years ago when she served it at White House parties. Ever since then, Americans have enjoyed, craved, and demanded frozen treats. Today, that demand has been transformed into hundreds of different products.

In a well-stocked supermarket, people who eat ice cream daily can find five-gallon tubs. Gourmets can select from pricey pint-sized delights. Dieters can choose from "light" ice cream, ice milk, frozen yogurt, tofu-based ice cream substitutes, and products made with low-calorie sweeteners and artificial fat.

In addition to these, there are specialty products, such as single-serving frozen desserts, ice cream sandwiches, rocket-shaped ice pops, and hand-dipped chocolate bars. The most growth recently has come from the super-premium ice cream which is ice cream containing more than 14 percent butterfat.

It is easy to see why the United States is the world's largest consumer of ice cream. Each person in the United States eats an average of 14 quarts each year. In fact, ice cream is so popular that 98 percent of all households in the country have some in their freezers right now.

How did the freezer get so crowded? In a very real sense, our individual tastes stocked those shelves. We voted for (or against) each product whenever we bought (or passed up) a new temptation. Successful products made money. The duds disappeared. The commercial marketplace is serving Americans their just desserts.[1, 2, 3]

What Is Marketing?

People have wants and needs that they satisfy by products. A **product** is all the physical features and psychological satisfactions received by the customer. Marketers use the term *products* to refer to both goods and services.

Goods are products grown or manufactured and prepared for sale. They are *tangible*, which means they can be physically touched. Books, magazines, automobiles, staplers, and cameras are all goods. **Services** are benefits or satisfactions that improve the personal appearance, health, comfort, or peace of mind of their users. Services are *intangible*, which means they cannot be physically touched. Services include haircuts, insurance, and health care. Services cannot be separated from the organization or person giving the service. For example, you cannot buy a haircut from an airline.

A **customer** is anyone who buys or rents goods or services. A **consumer** is the person who uses the goods or services. Often, the customer and the consumer are the same person. For example, if you purchased the pencils and paper you use in school, you are both customer and consumer.

Sometimes the customer and the consumer are separate people. When parents buy baby food and infants' clothing, for example, they are the customers but their children are the consumers. Customers and consumers may be individuals, like the parents and their children, or institutions, such as schools, hospitals, and governments. They may even be other businesses. In marketing, these terms are often used interchangeably to mean buyers and users of goods and services.

The American Marketing Association (AMA) defines **marketing** as the process of planning and executing the conception, pricing, promotion, and distribution of ideas, goods, and services to create exchanges that satisfy individual and organizational objectives. Marketing moves goods and services from conception to consumption using a step-by-step process in the marketplace. The **marketplace**

■■■ *Some organizations, such as the Salvation Army, do not have profit making as their goal. What might be the goal of this organization?*

Nonprofit organizations also have financial concerns and thus need to raise money for their purposes. When they take in more money than they spend, these profits are used to further the organization's goals. A hospital, for example, will buy more medical equipment. A museum will add to its collection. A zoo will improve housing for its animals.

Both profit and nonprofit organizations use the marketing process. It helps them to plan, price, promote, and distribute their products and ideas.

The Marketing Concept

As you know, successful businesses focus on satisfying customers' wants and needs. They ask themselves, What do our customers want that we can best supply and make a profit? The idea of fulfilling the wants and needs of customers at a profit (or other gain for a nonprofit organization) is the **marketing concept**.

A business that applies the marketing concept first determines the customers it is best equipped to serve and then works to meet their needs. Instead of trying to sell one product to everybody, the firm markets its products to the customers most likely to buy them. For example, Levi Strauss & Company markets its 501 jeans to young people and its Levi's Dockers to mature customers.

Organizations employing the marketing concept create win-win exchanges: both buyers and sellers come out ahead in the transaction. For example, Ford created a win-win situation with the Taurus. The design grew out of extensive research to learn precisely what customers wanted in a mid-priced American car. When the company produced the car its customers wanted, the customers responded by buying it in record numbers.

Nonprofit organizations use marketing concepts, too. When the New England Aquarium in Boston learned how frequently visitors came to the exhibits, for example, it developed new exhibits and programs for them. The Aquarium patrons enjoyed a greater variety of experiences. The Aquarium itself received more financial and community support. This win-win situation enabled the Aquarium to continue to maintain its good reputation—and thus draw more people.

Ethics and the Marketing Concept

Ethics are guidelines for good behavior that benefit everyone in society. **Marketing ethics** are guidelines of behavior designed for organizations and their employees in their role as marketers. Some rules of ethical behavior are enforced by law. For example, laws can enforce promises that are clearly documented as part of a contract. If you and an employer sign a contract and the employer does not pay you for the work you have done, the employer is acting unethically. By law, you must be paid money in exchange for your services.

The law also protects a person's inventions from theft, thus assuring reward for creative effort. The inventors of a pocket telephone, for instance, can register their unique technology with the U.S. Patent Office. The inventors alone can choose to sell their product or hire someone to do it for them.

Unfortunately, the law cannot assure fairness and ethical behavior when verbal agreements have not been written into formal contracts. If you agree to work for someone at $11 per hour but you fail to sign an employment agreement, you do not have written proof of the hourly wage. An ethical person would pay you the $11 per hour. An unethical person might pay you less or not at all!

When implementing a marketing concept, a business should be guided by the standards of marketing ethics. This means that the transactions should benefit everyone fairly. The general rules of good ethical behavior are the basis of the American Marketing Association's "Code of Ethics." (You will look at this further in Chapter 37.) A good measure of sound marketing ethics is the Golden Rule: treat others as you would like to be treated.

Applying good marketing ethics to the marketing concept can lead to long-term satisfaction for the business, the customers, the consumers, and the community. Thus, sound marketing ethics, such as producing safe products, contribute to a marketer's own sales and profits in the long run.

In recent years, ethical issues in marketing have received a great deal of attention and have been the subject of much debate. Is it ethical, for example, to market tobacco and liquor as masculine, feminine, or glamorous? We will be looking at ethical questions such as this throughout this text.

The Marketing Mix

To achieve its goals, a business creates a marketing program. Four major elements of a marketing program are:

- planning and developing the product idea;
- deciding how to price the product;
- placing the product conveniently for customers; and
- promoting the product.

Product, price, place, and promotion are called the four Ps of marketing. They make up what is known as the **marketing mix**—the core of a company's marketing system. Each element of the marketing mix is used to target a market in order to make a profit. All four elements are interrelated. (See Figure 1–1.) Let's take a closer look at each of these elements.

Product

When marketers make decisions about products, they ask themselves what product to make, when to make it, what level of quality to produce, how many to offer for sale, and how to package and label it. To do all of these things, marketers must anticipate their customers' present and future needs. For example, Apple Computer Inc. developed the Macintosh computer for businesses that needed a

■■■ *Figure 1–1 The Marketing Mix*
The marketing mix is the core of a company's marketing system. It is made up of a combination of decisions about product, price, promotion, and place. What is the purpose of the marketing mix?

computer that was easy to operate, yet capable of rapidly processing a greater volume of work than the Apple II.

When automobile manufacturers bring out a new line of cars, they often ask their most recent customers for their opinions of the latest models. The company will continue to offer features that customers like, such as sunroofs. Less popular features will be discontinued. Suggestions for new features are carefully noted. (You will look further at this type of Marketing Research in Unit 4.)

Hair salons will often survey their customers to see which services they would pay for in addition to haircuts. Based on customer preferences, they may add such services as manicures or makeup consultations. (You will explore how services are marketed in Unit 5.)

Price

The price a customer is willing to pay and the price at which a marketer is willing to offer a product determine whether or not an exchange will occur. Many things influence prices, including the number of suppliers, the number of customers, and the availability of the product.

Sometimes, customers are willing to pay high prices for something they want, such as a luxury automobile, a piece of jewelry, or tickets to the Super Bowl. At other times, due to seasonal changes or a large supply of an item, marketers must lower prices on products to encourage sales. For example, a car dealership usually reduces prices at the end of the year to move old models and make room for newer ones.

Prices also may be set low when a new product is introduced to encourage people to try it. (Unit 6 will give you more information about pricing.)

Place

When marketers make decisions about place, they base them on how their products will get from producers or manufacturers to the people who will use them (the ultimate consumers). They may decide to market their products directly to the consumers. Or they may decide to market through intermediaries, that is, wholesalers and retailers.

Consider Ben & Jerry's Homemade, Inc. This Vermont ice cream company was founded in 1978 by Ben Cohen and Jerry Greenfield, friends and avid ice cream eaters from childhood. When Ben and Jerry decided to manufacture and market their brand of super-premium ice cream, they began by selling it in their own Burlington, Vermont, shop. Before long, they decided they could reach more customers by placing their ice cream in restaurants and supermarkets and by opening new ice cream shops.

Getting the product to the customer as quickly and conveniently as possible is an essential aspect of the marketing mix. Figure 1–2 on page 12 shows how marketing serves in creating ice cream from raw ingredients to placing it most conveniently for consumers. Place marketing may involve several ways of reaching customers. You will explore it further in Unit 7.

Promotion

Promotion includes all the activities designed to bring a company's goods or services to the favorable attention of customers. When marketers promote products, they educate potential customers about them through promotional activities such as newspaper, radio, television, or magazine advertisements. To see how marketers promote their products, you have only to look around your town.

THE FUTURE IS NOW

Lights, Computer, Action!

Multimedia magic is bringing the glitz and glamour of Hollywood to local ad agency conference rooms. Macintosh computer operators project digitalized client presentations onto "big-screen" monitors, import customer images and animation, then add SurroundSound audio to create a *Star Wars*-style production in-house. Agencies are able to wow clients at a fraction of the cost and production time of a major studio production.

Ben & Jerry's Homemade, Inc.

Ben Cohen and Jerry Greenfield wanted to be in a business that serves people. They also wanted to make and sell something that they and others would love. They hit upon the ice cream business because it seemed like fun and a risk they could handle.

They began their venture by enrolling in a $5 correspondence course from Penn State University on how to make ice cream. Scraping up $12,000 from savings and borrowing from others, they converted an old Burlington, Vermont, gas station into an ice cream shop. Before long they were known for such funky flavors as New York Super Fudge Chunk, Dastardly Mash, and Cherry Garcia (named after the rock star Jerry Garcia). Soon, the new company began to market to restaurants and then supermarkets and opened other ice cream stores throughout the country. By the 1990s, sales had soared to over $58 million.

The company is famous for its off-the-wall approach to marketing. For example, one of Ben & Jerry's early promotions was to tour the country in an ice cream truck called the cowmobile with samples of their ice cream.

At one time a large competitor tried to squeeze Ben & Jerry's ice cream off of supermarket shelves, insisting that stores carry only their own brand of super-premium ice cream. Ben and Jerry considered this an unfair trade practice. Let the customers decide which ice cream they liked!

They took on the corporate giant with a publicity campaign which included printing T-shirts that asked what the much larger competitor was afraid of when it sought to keep Ben & Jerry's ice cream out of supermarkets. Jerry even stood as a one-man picket outside the competitor's corporate headquarters. Public sympathy went to Ben & Jerry's ice cream. As a result, it was stocked in more supermarkets than ever before.

Ben & Jerry's believes that businesses have a social responsibility, that is, an obligation to people.

The company's three-part mission is to make the finest products, recognize the responsibility of business in improving the quality of life everywhere, and operate the company soundly to improve its growth and value to its owners.

To carry out its mission, Ben & Jerry's has done some innovative things. Each year it sets aside 7½ percent of its pretax net income for donations to nonprofit groups. (Most companies contribute only 1 to 2 percent to worthy causes.) It does this through the Ben & Jerry's Foundation. The issues that the foundation focuses on include the environment, world peace, children and families, and disadvantaged citizens. Some of the organizations receiving help include a street library for New York children in a disadvantaged area, a job training program for people on public aid in San Francisco, and a group of recycling education programs for schools and communities.

To raise money to build its first factory, the company sold shares of stock to Vermont residents. Now part of the company mission is to reward stockholder loyalty by operating the company so that it will grow and be profitable to those owners.

To encourage employee cooperation toward company goals, Ben & Jerry's has a policy that the highest-paid executive earns no more than seven times the wages of the lowest-paid employee. This helps attract people who are less concerned with money than they are with the social consciousness Ben & Jerry's promotes. [4, 5, 6]

1. Is Ben & Jerry's selling a good or a service?
2. What changes did Ben and Jerry make in placing their product over the years?
3. Discuss one nonmonetary reward of working for Ben & Jerry's.

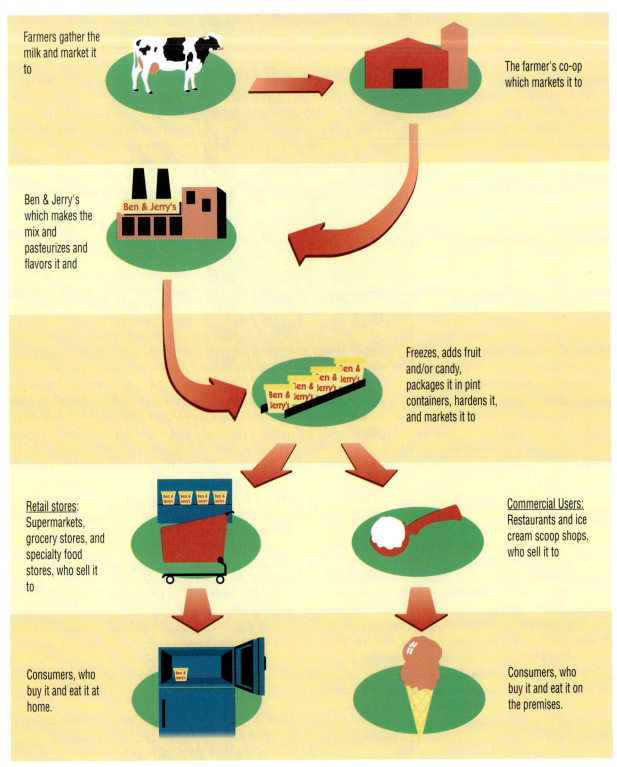

Farmers gather the milk and market it to

The farmer's co-op which markets it to

Ben & Jerry's which makes the mix and pasteurizes and flavors it and

Freezes, adds fruit and/or candy, packages it in pint containers, hardens it, and markets it to

Retail stores: Supermarkets, grocery stores, and specialty food stores, who sell it to

Commercial Users: Restaurants and ice cream scoop shops, who sell it to

Consumers, who buy it and eat it at home.

Consumers, who buy it and eat it on the premises.

■ ■ ■   *Figure 1–2   The Path of Ben and Jerry's Ice Cream from Producer to Consumer*
To get the product to the customer, where does Ben and Jerry's place its ice cream?

Global MARKETPLACE

Is Anyone Up There Listening?

Boeing Aircraft Company is. Over the whine of jet propulsion engines, Boeing, the largest international supplier of commercial airplanes, employs the valuable marketing concept of listening to the needs of its global customers. But it doesn't stop there. The company then responds to customer input by endlessly testing new designs and materials aimed at meeting the needs and demands expressed by its ever-progressive, aerospace clientele. The result: Boeing is among the nation's major exporters.

Billboards encourage you to wear Reebok shoes or visit Disney World. Attractive displays in store windows invite people to shop. Posters proclaiming the daily specials are splashed across supermarket windows. Turn on your radio or television and you will hear commercials for everything from retail stores to automobiles. Step inside a large airport and you may see a display of a new boat revolving under a spotlight that highlights its best features. Buy a newspaper or magazine and you will see that it contains a wide variety of advertising. Visit a computer store and allow a well-informed salesperson to show you how various computers work and answer your questions about them.

As you can see, many forms of promotion are an essential part of marketing. By putting customers' needs at the center of marketing planning, marketers can develop the most effective marketing mix. They can create the best combination of the four Ps of marketing—product, price, place, and promotion.

You Are a Part of Marketing

There is hardly anything you do that does not put you in touch with marketing or influence marketing activities. You are already familiar with the role of the customer and the consumer. When you buy something—a pair of jeans, notebook paper, a videotape, or a magazine—you have taken the last step in a vast and complicated process. Business has done a great deal of planning and spent huge sums of money to get you to take that step. In doing so, they fulfill the marketing concept.

As you proceed through this text, you will learn the many roles involved in serving people through the marketing process. By anticipating and meeting customers' needs and by serving them efficiently, marketing adds to the quality of people's lives and to the quality of nations.

As a person considering a career in marketing and also as a customer and consumer, you have an important role to play. Never have the opportunities been so challenging for those who want to work in marketing.

Successful large businesses, such as Ford, Disney, and Levi Strauss, are developing new products and marketing them throughout the world. At the same time, the greatest number of new job openings are appearing with small businesses. The field of marketing has never been more dynamic than it is now. *Dynamic* means energetic, alive, forceful, changing—and there is no better term to describe marketing!

CHAPTER NOTES

1. Lisa H. Towle, "What's New in Ice Cream?" *New York Times*, 17 July 1988, p. 17.

2. Kevin Maney, "Ice Cream Sellers Scoop Up Business," *USA Today*, 23 June 1987, p. 1.

3. International Ice Cream Association, *Latest Scoop* (Washington, D.C.: International Ice Cream Association, 1989). Telephone conversation with the Association, 25 May 1990.

4. Ben & Jerry's Annual Reports 1988 and 1989 and other Press Kit items.

5. Geoffrey Stokes, "Ice Cream Socialists," *The Village Voice*, 27 February 1990.

6. Carol Clurman, "Bosses for the '90's," *The Boston Herald, USA Weekend Magazine*, 19–21 January 1990, p. 4ff.

Chapter *1* Review

Chapter Summary

- Marketing is the process of planning and executing the conception, pricing, promotion, and distribution of ideas, goods, and services to create exchanges that satisfy individual and organizational objectives.
- Marketing serves people by supplying them with goods and services that satisfy their needs and wants.
- Micromarketing is how products are conceived, promoted, priced, and distributed in individual marketing situations.
- Macromarketing is the process that directs the flow of goods and services in an economy.
- The idea of fulfilling the wants and needs of customers at a profit is the marketing concept.
- Marketing ethics assure that transactions in the marketplace will benefit everyone fairly.
- A company's marketing program focuses on the customer and contains the four elements of the marketing mix: product, price, place, and promotion.
- Marketing is a dynamic field—exciting, challenging, and growing.

Building Your Marketing Vocabulary

On a separate sheet of paper, define the terms below. Then write a sentence or two for each set of terms, using them in a way that shows you understand the difference between them.

- goods—services—product
- customer—consumer—ethics
- micromarketing—macromarketing
- marketing concept—marketing mix—promotion
- marketing—marketplace—market
- marketing ethics—profit—nonprofit marketing

Questions for Review

1. Tell one way in which goods are different from services.
2. How do customers and consumers influence marketers?
3. Explain why the sale is the central transaction of the marketing process.
4. Explain the difference between macromarketing and micromarketing.
5. Give one possible goal of a nonprofit organization.
6. Why are nonprofit organizations using marketing practices? Give an example of a marketing activity conducted by a nonprofit organization.
7. When applying the marketing concept, what is the first thing a business determines?
8. What are ethics?
9. Identify each of the four Ps of the marketing mix, and explain its function.
10. Why is the field of marketing dynamic?

Critical Thinking

1. Describe how you might be both a customer and a consumer.
2. Give an example of a good and service.
3. Give an example of marketing taking place in your neighborhood.
4. Can marketing take place if no money is exchanged? Explain your answer.
5. Give one example of how you would promote a lawn mowing service.
6. Explain how marketing ethics can contribute to a company's success.

Discussion Questions

1. Do you think a company can create a need for its product? Explain.

2. A business markets its products to the customers most likely to buy them. Name three products and the customers they are designed to serve.

3. Is any one of the four Ps more important than the others? Explain.

4. Is it ethical for marketers to promote cigarette smoking as glamorous? Explain.

Marketing Project

Distinguishing Between Marketing Businesses

Project Goal: Given a group of businesses, distinguish between those that market goods and those that market services.

Directions: As you complete each project in this book, you will be acquiring skills and knowledge that will help you achieve your career goal. Whenever you begin a project, prepare a form like the one below. Give the completed form to your teacher along with your finished project.

_____

Project Number _____

Name _____ Date Assigned _____

Career Goal _____ Date Completed _____

_____

Select an area in your local business district, such as a block or a shopping center containing at least five businesses. Draw a map of that area and identify each business. In a written report, state briefly what each business does. Does it provide goods or services? Does it market to customers or to other businesses?

Applied Academics

Language Arts

1. Ask one relative and one businessperson what role marketing plays in their lives. Write your findings in a 100-word paragraph.

Math

2. Ben & Jerry's sets aside 7½ percent of its pretax net income for nonprofit groups each year. Suppose pretax net income for the year is $58,000,000. How much money is set aside?

3. Colony Candy Company spent $45,000 on promotions last quarter. Seven percent of this was spent on radio ads. How much money did it spend on radio ads?

Social Studies

4. For each social rule listed below, write out a way that marketers might follow that rule in their business.
   a. Do good.
   b. Be truthful and honest.
   c. Do not knowingly harm others.
   d. Consider the consequences of your actions.

Marketing and Multiculturalism

The United States is recognizing the dramatic shift from a predominately Caucasian society to a multicultural society. Signs of this transition are seeping into the marketplace. Walk down the aisle of your local supermarket and you will likely find shelves lined with ethnic foods such as burritos, sushi, and couscous. Some stores are including shelf labels in languages other than English that describe common foods and their uses. As American society continues to become increasingly multicultural, there will be ample opportunity for marketers to satisfy ethnic tastes.

1. How does this recognition of a multicultural society provide marketers with a potential for profit?

2. Name two products supermarkets might offer to take advantage of the changing ethnic marketplace.

3. Tell one way a marketer would determine which ethnic foods to put in a store.

4. As a customer, how might you personally influence a supermarket's decision to market ethnic food?

5. Name one way marketers might promote ethnic foods in the supermarkets.

Marketing and Our Economic System

Terms to Know

resources
capital
economic system
   (economy)
planned economy
private enterprise
   (capitalism)
production

competition
risk
socialism
communism
monopoly
supply
demand

Chapter Objectives

After studying this chapter, you will be able to:

* list a nation's economic decisions;
* describe the private enterprise system and compare it to socialism and communism;
* discuss the effects of risk, profit, and competition in the private enterprise system;
* describe the government's role in private enterprise; and
* describe the consumer's role in private enterprise.

Case Study

Nike and Reebok Run for the Money

Take a look at your feet. The odds are that you are wearing a pair of athletic shoes. The extremely competitive market for athletic shoes is dominated by Nike and Reebok. From its founding in 1964 until 1985, Nike was the market leader in the athletic shoe industry. However, Nike management did not expand its product line beyond its successful Air Jordan shoe.

Consequently, this gave Reebok the opportunity to expand its market of stylish aerobic shoes. Reebok sales skyrocketed from $66 million in 1984 to $1.8 billion in 1990. Reebok had taken over as the athletic shoe industry leader.

To beat Reebok at its own game, Nike substantially increased its marketing budget and marketing research activities. It geared up its Far Eastern manufacturing facilities to turn out shoes at a rapid clip. To better control inventory, Nike pressured retailers to order six months in advance.

Nike rolled out an ad campaign to promote its "air" technology shoe construction. It signed football and baseball star Bo Jackson as celebrity spokesman.

Nike supported its marketing effort with a variety of sales promotion activities. These included sponsoring summer leagues for college players in 25 cities; paying high school and college coaches $5,000 to $20,000 for having their teams wear Nike shoes; and cosponsoring the Dapper Dan Roundball Classic all-star game. All the while, the company continued to produce athletic shoes in the designs, colors, names, and price ranges that research showed consumers wanted.

By 1989 Nike had regained its lead over Reebok, taking a 26 percent market share of the $5.5 billion industry. Reebok ran close behind with 23 percent of the market.

The very nature of the U.S. private enterprise system allows competitive forces such as Nike and Reebok to act freely. Unlike some economic systems, U.S. business owners, workers, and consumers decide what should be produced, how it should be produced, and how it will be distributed. Companies like Nike and Reebok take risks each time they introduce new products.

The competitive strategies used by Nike and Reebok were incredibly successful. As you well know, athletic shoes are now a fashion statement that often has nothing to do with athletics.[1,2,3,4]

Marketing and Our Economic System

Resources are the means to accomplish a goal. For example, wages and salaries are the means or resources we use to buy goods and services. *Productive resources* are the means of producing goods and services. There are three basic types of productive resources: natural resources such as coal and trees, the labor force, and capital. **Capital** is all the money and tools (such as machinery and factories) that are used in an organization's operation. (You will look further at productive resources in Chapter 3.)

Each nation has a variety of productive resources. The way a nation chooses to use its productive resources to produce and market goods and services is called an **economic system**, or an **economy**.

An Economic Problem

Any nation's productive resources have limits. Each country has only a certain amount of land, a certain amount of minerals and water, a certain number of people, and a certain amount of capital. Therefore, the amount of goods and services a nation can produce is limited. But human wants are endless. Whenever some of our wants are satisfied, others take their place. Even the richest nations cannot supply everything their people want. They have to decide how to get the greatest benefit from their resources. Every country, however large or small, must make this decision. How it decides to get the greatest benefit from its resources determines the form of its economic system.

The Basic Decisions

Every economic system must deal with three basic questions.

1. What goods and services should be produced?
2. How should they be produced?
3. How should they be distributed?

In a **planned economy**, such as in North Korea, the government decides the economic questions. In a **private enterprise,** or **capitalist,** system, such

as in the United States or Japan, the people—consumers, business owners, and workers—make the economic decisions. These decisions interact in the marketplace and create our changing economy. This change in our economy is possible because the bulk of capital is privately owned by people themselves, not by the government. The decisions of the marketplace, however, are subject to laws and regulations of our government. Here is a closer look at the three basic economic decisions.

What Should Be Produced?

Should a country use its resources to produce video cameras, barbecue grills, dishwashers, space shuttles, parks, or schools? In a planned economy, the government decides. In private enterprise, the choices of the people, as consumers and producers, determine the goods and services to be produced.

In the United States' private enterprise system, however, the people's choices are restricted to some extent. Certain products, such as some narcotics, cannot be legally produced. The production of some products, such as medicine and cars, is regulated for safety by the government.

How Should It Be Produced?

Production is the process of creating or improving goods and services. An economic system must decide how to produce goods efficiently, and thus make the best use of its resources.

A method of production that uses only a little of one resource might use too much of another. For example, a production method might require a great deal of hand labor but only a little capital. If the hand laborers were replaced by machines, there would be a savings in one resource (labor) but increased spending of another resource (the capital required to buy the machines).

In a planned economy the government either owns the means of production or decides who will own them. It also decides how to use the nation's resources.

In a private enterprise system, businesspeople decide which resources they will employ, although they are not always free to make such decisions. Safety laws, for example, might prevent them from using less expensive but more hazardous equipment in the workplace.

■■■ *Every economic system has the economic problem of determining how to use its natural resources. In the private enterprise system, natural resources, such as oil, are used to produce goods and services. What are two other natural resources available in the United States?*

The Climate of a Private Enterprise System

A marketer doing business in a private enterprise system expects certain privileges, certain risks, and certain government control. Freedom of business ownership will be somewhat regulated. There will be competition to face and economic risks to take. Success will be measured mainly by net earnings, or profit. These elements—regulated freedom of ownership, competition, risk, and profit—are characteristics of businesses that operate in a free enterprise system. Today's marketer must be prepared to deal with all of them.

Freedom of Ownership

In some countries, personal belongings such as clothes, books, and toothbrushes are the only things that people are allowed to own. Everything else, such as forests, factories, and machinery, is owned by the government. The government owns all of the productive resources of the country, so it can easily control what is produced.

However, in a private enterprise system such as in the United States, people may own land and other natural resources as well as buildings, tools, and equipment. There are some restrictions on the use of property. For example, a law may prohibit the building of factories on land reserved for private housing. But, in general, people are free to lease, sell, or give their property away. Or they may decide to put it to work to earn an income; that is, they may decide to use it to start a business. These property rights are preserved by law.

■ ■ ■ *In a private enterprise system, producers must respond to consumer choices in deciding what to produce. Besides determining what is produced, what are two other questions they must address?*

How Should It Be Distributed?

Division of available goods and services is important to a sound economy. Who will get the video cameras and barbecue grills? If there are not enough to go around, who will be left out? What will business owners get in comparison to workers?

In a planned economy, the government decides who gets what and how distribution is to be made. In private enterprise, goods and services are distributed according to personal income. The more you earn, the more you can buy. Taxes are used in part for such programs as welfare and social security which help provide the poor with goods and services.

Competition

The struggle of each business to obtain a share of the market is known as **competition**. It is an essential ingredient in the private enterprise system. It accounts for fair prices and a constant improvement in goods and services. Competing businesses strive to offer better goods and services at lower prices than the products already available in the marketplace.

In a private enterprise system, any person can start a business of his or her choice. Many people operate the same kind of business. In one community, there may be a half-dozen places where people can buy a pair of shoes, go to lunch, get a haircut, buy their groceries, and have their clothes dry-cleaned. Each of these businesses must compete to obtain customers.

Suppose there was only one place in your community where you could buy a pair of shoes. Unless you were willing to go to the trouble and expense of traveling to stores in other communities, you would have to settle for the selection this store had to offer. You would be forced to pay whatever price the store asked. You might have to settle for a pair of shoes that did not fit properly.

A shoe store without competition could offer you only a minimum of service. It could refuse to sell on credit, to make an exchange, or even to show you its complete line of products. A shoe store that has competition, however, is more likely to offer you a wide selection, courteous service, and a fair price. It will do everything it can to win your business from the competition.

Risk

Some 1,000 new businesses are started every day in the United States. Some are small, such as a lunch wagon. Others are big, such as a discount department store. No matter how large or small the business, each business opening involves risk. **Risk** is the possibility of loss or failure.

No one who opens a business can be absolutely sure of success. About one out of every three new businesses fails within the first year of operation. Only one in two lasts as long as two years. Table 2–1 shows the number of businesses that failed in each industry in one year.

One of the major reasons for business failure is poor management. Every business—even an established one—must stay alert to changing economic conditions. The difference between success or failure may rest on such decisions as whether to take on a new product line, to build a new building, to lower prices, to give easier credit terms, or to expand the facilities. Other reasons why businesses fail include poor record-keeping, lack of education and training, inadequate inventories, insufficient cash reserve, and poor financial management.

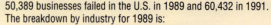

50,389 businesses failed in the U.S. in 1989 and 60,432 in 1991. The breakdown by industry for 1989 is:

Mining	346
Agriculture, forestry, and fishing	1,438
Transportation and public utilities	2,052
Finance, insurance, and real estate	2,839
Wholesale trade	3,636
Manufacturing	3,915
Construction	6,959
Retail trade	10,982
Services	17,495

Source: 1992 *Britannica Book of the Year*, p. 726; *Statistical Abstract of the United States*, 1991, p. 537.

■ ■ ■ ***Table 2–1 Business Failures***
This table illustrates the risk involved in creating a business. What is one reason so many businesses fail?

Every business faces daily risks. If expenses are high, operating costs must be reduced and some services eliminated. Or, prices must be increased. Any of these actions may result in business lost to competitors. The business owner's need to reduce risks may help to explain why he or she carefully watches expenses and expects employees to work hard.

Profit

If the risk of going into business is so great, why are so many people so eager to start a new business or invest their money in an existing one? The answer is that they hope to earn a profit. As you learned from Chapter 1, a profit is the difference between the money a business brings in and the amount it spends. Generally, profits range from 1 to 5 percent of sales. Profits are the driving force behind our economic system.

Of course, a profit cannot be earned without customers. And customers expect to buy what they want at reasonable prices. Thus, for successful marketers, realizing a profit and satisfying the needs of customers are related goals.

Alternative Economic Systems

Capitalistic nations such as Japan, Germany, South Korea, and Brazil have systems similar to ours. But, as you know, not every country operates within a private enterprise system. Many other nations live within socialist or communist economic systems.

Socialism

Socialism is an economic system that depends heavily on the government to plan and make economic decisions. Under socialism, the government owns and controls important economic resources and industries, such as communications, transportation, minerals, utilities, and major manufacturing. Classic examples of socialist nations are Holland, Spain, New Zealand, Norway, Ireland, and Australia.

Socialists claim that there are several advantages to their economic system. First, they say their system distributes personal income more equally and thus provides the masses with a higher standard of living. For example, a visitor to Denmark would be hard pressed to find slums.

Socialists also claim that a socialist government can better care for the people's welfare. In a socialist system, many things such as college education, health care, public transportation, and housing are offered free or more cheaply than in a capitalist system. Nevertheless, as economist Milton Freidman explains, "There is no such thing as a free lunch."

While a free college education might seem nice, someone must pay the price. In many socialist nations, the average personal income tax rate exceeds 45 percent. (The highest personal income tax in the United States is about 36 percent.)

Socialism, as we have known it the past 50 years, is dying. Today, all major developed democracies and many smaller ones have rejected political candidates who do not believe that market forces and entrepreneurship spur economic growth. Led by Great Britain, many state-owned companies on every continent were sold in the 1980s. Thousands of companies were marked for sale by the early 1990s. These include Britain's electricity industry and large chunks of France's insurance industry. While tax rates are also headed down, economists believe the welfare portion of socialism is likely to provide greater public assistance rather than less.

Communism

The term **communism** describes a socialist economy ruled by a single political party where all industries and resources are owned by the government. Communism is based on the economic and political doctrines of Karl Marx, a German political philosopher who died in 1883. His goal was to create a classless society.

In contrast to capitalism and socialism, communism offers people few economic freedoms. (Figure 2–1 shows the range of economic systems.) North Korea, Cuba, and Vietnam are communist nations.

Led by the former Soviet Union and China, many communist nations are presently undergoing massive reforms of their economic systems. These reforms have and will continue to have an impact

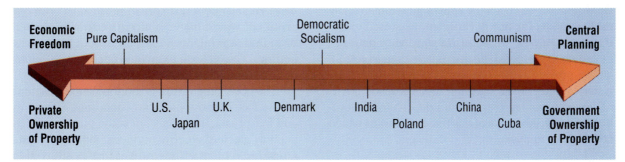

■■■ *Figure 2–1 The Range of Economic Systems*
Economic systems differ according to the direct involvement of government in each economy. In which system does government planning dominate?

Global
MARKETPLACE

Rollerblades in Russia?

How do you market Rollerblades—or anything else—to customers in Russia? They speak many different languages and face different cultural, social, and economic realities. Other challenges in this marketplace include a limited distribution system, high inflation, and a customer who does not recognize many Western-culture brand names. So much for one-size-fits-all marketing. You'd better sit down with a bowl of borscht and brainstorm!

on our world economy. For example, businesses will integrate themselves into the world economy through economic alliances within other nations. People who had limited freedom to make economic choices in the past will have a stronger influence on economic decisions in the future. There will be fewer trade barriers among countries and more changes in international politics and policies. (See the Principles into Practice for more information on capitalistic reform in the Soviet Union.)

The Role of Our Government

The difference among the three economic systems we discussed has been the role of government. The earliest goals for our government as stated in the Preamble of our Constitution were very general, including to "establish justice, insure domestic tranquility, provide for the common defense, promote the general welfare, and secure the blessings of liberty...."

As our country grew, so did the role of government. Today, government has five major roles which are specific to business:

- regulator;
- promoter of growth and self-development;
- protector;
- competitor; and
- supporter.

Let's look further at each one.

Regulator

The founders of our nation believed that individuals and businesses should be free to advance their interests as long as their actions advanced the welfare of the whole society. The government acts like an umpire, calling "foul" on the few who hurt the entire economy for their personal gain.

The government would like individuals and groups to regulate themselves, but some can't or won't. The government must control these by using laws and agencies to protect the public safety, health, and morals, and to promote the general welfare.

When properly directed and practiced, regulation can benefit everyone. Today, the U.S. government has more than 60 federal agencies to regulate industry. These include such agencies as the Federal Trade Commission, the Food and Drug Administration, the Consumer Product Safety Commission, and the Environmental Protection Agency.

The government also prevents unfair competition. One example of unfair competition is a **monopoly**, that is, a market structure where one producer controls the industry. That producer could set prices, control production, and thus force others out of business.

Imagine that one oil company became so successful that it could buy most competing companies, thus becoming a monopoly. Because of its size, it could prevent oil drill makers from supplying the remaining competitors. It could lower prices for a while and force its competitors to go out of business. Then it could raise prices and make enormous profits. It would have no incentive to work better, or to find new oil, because there would be no competitors. The oil business would become inefficient, supplies would be low, and prices would be high.

The government forces monopolies to disband, so the free marketplace can encourage efficiency and fair prices. In the case of some public utilities, such as gas and electric services, monopolies are considered most efficient. A utility is allowed to operate in a given area, but it is regulated by the government to be certain that its services and prices are reasonable.

People the world over are asking the same question: "Is the former Soviet Union really embracing capitalism?" The answer is not a simple yes or no. But it is true that the Soviets and other Eastern European nations are currently restructuring their economies so their economic systems are more responsive to the needs of consumers.

An overhaul was necessary because Soviet and Eastern European citizens were angry over critically short supplies of food and other consumer goods. Shortages were so bad that in some areas even milk was sold only by a doctor's prescription or to nursing mothers.

The economic reform in the Soviet Union is called *perestroika*. It began in 1986 when the Supreme Soviet, the nation's nominal parliament, passed the first law allowing people to be legally self-employed. Twenty-nine types of services were allowed, including shoe and appliance repair, sewing and tailoring, furniture making, music and language lessons, production of makeup, photography, translation, and tourist services.

It was illegal to hire another person to work as a subordinate. The Soviet state had a monopoly on employment, and considered other forms of employment to be exploitation of labor.

Another breakthrough for the economy came in 1989. The Central Committee, led by Soviet President Mikhail Gorbachev, chose to allow Soviet farmers the right to lease state-owned land for up to 50 years, and to pass those leases on to their heirs. In the past, these farms have produced 23 percent of all food on just 5 percent of the arable land.

To further encourage private enterprise at home, the Soviets invited hundreds of entrepreneurs to the Soviet Union with the hope of economic cooperation. Deals made with companies such as petrochemical plants, McDonald's, and even Ben & Jerry's Homemade Inc., introduced the Soviets to American style capitalism.

Restructuring the Soviet Economic System

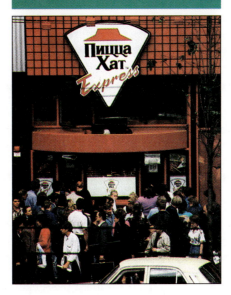

On August 19, 1991, the communist system broke in the Soviet Union after 40 years of rigidity and repression. An unsuccessful coup against Mikhail Gorbachev quickly led to the breakup of the Soviet Union. By October 18, 1991, 8 of the 12 Soviet republics signed a treaty of cooperation. It endorsed such principles as private property, free-market economy, a single banking system, and free movement of goods and services.

On December 25, 1991, Gorbachev formally resigned as president of the Soviet Union because the nation he once governed no longer existed. The Commonwealth of Independent States (CIS) was formed to include 11 of the 12 former Soviet republics. Boris Yeltsin, premier of the Russian Republic, became president of Russia and began the slow process of transforming Russia into a free-market system. In January 1992, most prices in Russia were set free and the government launched a sale of state-owned businesses.

Other notable changes occurred in the Eastern European nations of the former East Germany, Poland, Hungary, Czechoslovakia, and Romania. While genuine democracy is now reality in some former communist nations, others like North Korea and Cuba are still struggling under economic systems that fail to deliver food and consumer goods in sufficient quantity or quality. [5, 6, 7, 8]

1. In capitalist countries, there are usually a variety of goods and services available to consumers. In communist countries, people historically have had few goods and services from which to choose. If you wanted to open a business in Russia today, what goods and services could you offer that consumers might not have been able to get prior to this?

2. What would be your incentive for going into business in Russia today?

Promoter of Growth and Development

The second important role of government is promoting growth and development of business. This can be accomplished in a variety of ways.

For example, the federal government provides millions of dollars in urban renewal funds to cities to redevelop their downtown business districts. Detroit, for example, has used this money to transform its deteriorating urban center into a "Renaissance City."

The government promotes business in many other ways. The Small Business Administration provides direct and guaranteed loans to businesses and farmers. The Joint Training Partnership Act (JTPA) provides jobs and training for hundreds of thousands of Americans. The Federal Trade Commission places tariffs on foreign imports to protect and promote domestic producers. The Department of Commerce encourages foreign trade by a variety of activities and projects. These are but a few of many examples of how government promotes business.

Protector

Many laws and agencies exist to protect businesses. For example, trademarks, copyrights, and patents registered with the U.S. Patent and Trademark Office are protected by law. No other company can use or duplicate these protected names, symbols, or products without getting permission and/or paying a fee or royalty for the use.

As competition in certain markets intensifies, patent infringements and undercover attempts to pirate new technology have become more common. In these cases, the government must be ready to protect a company and its property from business thieves. Such was the case when the government stepped in to prevent several well-known Japanese firms from acquiring trade secrets from IBM.

The government also regulates trade with foreign nations. (You will look at this further in Chapter 12.) The government might limit imports (goods purchased from other countries) or tax them to protect U.S. industries. In addition, government may regulate trade to prevent a military conflict of interest. That is, if goods are sold to a country which then uses the goods for military purposes we oppose, the federal government may restrict trade.

Trade restrictions can hurt business and consumers in the long run. Curtailing foreign imports through trade restrictions takes out the competitive nature of business. For example, if trade restrictions regulate foreign trade in the automobile industry, U.S. manufacturers would not feel the pressure of their foreign counterparts and may not try to improve the existing automotive technology.

Competitor

The government has also been forced into the role of competitor. During the Depression in the 1930s, for example, the government was forced to establish the Tennessee Valley Authority (TVA) to produce electric power for certain parts of the rural South because private power companies were unwilling to risk investment in this area.

Today the government also owns and operates the U.S. Postal Service and Amtrak, a nationwide passenger rail service. The government established Amtrak under the Rail Passenger Act of 1970 after existing private rail line owners decided to withdraw their passenger service.

Supporter

In some cases, the government has given direct support to an industry or to a company. For instance, when the Chrysler Corporation faced bankruptcy, the government guaranteed loans to Chrysler, thus enabling the company to recover. Thousands of jobs were saved, and Chrysler repaid the loans. The government has also supported the farm industry, which faces weather and market risks that could ruin most small businesses.

Some people feel that support interferes with competition and hurts the economy, though. They argue that businesses that fail deserve to fail, and that good businesses will succeed in their place.

The Role of the Consumer

Approximately two-thirds of our nation's total economic output consists of goods and services bought by individuals and households for the consumer's personal use. The remaining one-third is

■■■ *The U.S. Postal Service competes with private business such as UPS and Federal Express. What other business does the government run?*

bought by business and government. It is easy to see why ours is a consumer-oriented economy.

Each of us has an economic vote. Dollars are ballots. How you spend your money determines who will stay in the market and who will not. The manufacturer who gets the most votes (that is, the most money) can make the most profit. Furthermore, when we don't cast our vote (or spend our money) for certain goods and services, the economy is affected.

This free-market concept holds that each person is free to sell goods or services at any price and to anyone willing to pay that price. Supply and demand regulate the system. **Supply** is the quantity of a product offered on the market at a specified price. **Demand** is the amount of a product that consumers are willing and able to purchase at a given price. The supply of a good or service will increase as the demand for it increases.

When the supply of a product is plentiful and available, people are not willing to pay as much for it. You would probably not be willing to pay $3 for a cheeseburger, for example, if you could get the same quality of cheeseburger for $1.50 at three or four other restaurants close by.

On the other hand, if the demand for a product is great but the supply is short, then consumers will generally pay more for it. For example, NCAA Basketball Tournament tickets are very expensive because the demand exceeds the supply.

Generally, the supply of a product is affected by the demand. If demand for a product decreases, the supply of the product decreases, too. You can see, then, why demand affects the efficiency of producers. Most of us look for good values in the products we buy. We seek products that are safe and reliable. Our selection process (that is, the way we spend our money) rewards those efficient producers who keep quality up and prices down. The process penalizes the inefficient producers who produce inferior products. To succeed, producers must continue to offer products that consumers want. Chapter 3 discusses the role of the producer in further detail.

CHAPTER NOTES

1. J. B. Strasser and Laurie Becklund, *Swoosh* (New York: Harcourt Brace Jovanovich, 1991).

2. Barbara Buell, "Nike Catches Up with the Frontrunner," *Business Week*, 24 October 1988.

3. Tom Murray, "The Wing at Nike's Back," *Adweek*, 14 November 1988.

4. Curry Kirkpatrick, "The Old Soft Shoe," *Sports Illustrated*, December 1988.

5. Robin Knight, "Cracks in the Bloc," *U.S. News & World Report*, 27 March 1989, pp. 35–38.

6. Clemens P. Work, "All That's Glasnost Does Not Glitter," *U.S. News & World Report*, 4 April 1988, pp. 50–53.

7. Barry Newman, "Russians Want Stuff to Spend Money On," *The Wall Street Journal*, 17 June 1988, p. 1.

8. *1992 Britannica Book of the Year* (Chicago: Encyclopedia Britannica, 1992), pp. 22–29.

Chapter 2 Review

Chapter Summary

- Every economic system must deal with three basic questions: what goods should be produced, how they should be produced, and how they should be distributed.

- Americans live in a private enterprise system which allows consumers, business owners, and workers to make the basic economic decisions. Socialism relies heavily on government to plan and make economic decisions. Under socialism, major industries and resources are owned by the government. Communism not only plans the economy, but also owns all industries and resources.

- Marketers in the private enterprise system expect competition, certain risks, and a certain amount of government control in return for the right to earn a profit.

- The U.S. government has five major roles which are specific to business: regulator, promoter of growth and development, protector, competitor, and supporter.

- The United States operates a consumer-driven economy. Each consumer has an economic vote to accept or reject products which are offered in the marketplace. Those products which get enough votes (units sold at the best price) continue to serve the people's needs.

Building Your Marketing Vocabulary

On a separate sheet of paper, define each of these marketing terms. Then, using the terms, write a paragraph or two on marketing and our economic system.

resources	competition
capital	risk
economic system (economy)	socialism
	communism
planned economy	monopoly
private enterprise (capitalism)	supply
	demand
production	

Questions for Review

1. What three decisions must every economic system make?
2. What is the fundamental difference between a planned economy and a private enterprise or capitalist system?
3. Name four characteristics of a private enterprise business.
4. Explain why competition is important to the successful functioning of a private enterprise system.
5. Identify the effects of competition on buyers and sellers.
6. Name the major reasons why so many new businesses fail each year.
7. Explain why profit is an essential part of the private enterprise system.
8. Describe the role of the government in the private enterprise system.
9. Describe the role of the consumer in the private enterprise system.
10. Explain the relationship between the supply and demand of a product.

Critical Thinking

1. How might the economic decisions made in Cuba differ from those made in the United States?
2. Explain how lack of competition may affect the consumer in a planned economy.
3. Tell why it may be more efficient to have monopolies in the case of some public utilities.
4. Discuss how supply and demand affect the sales of NCAA Basketball Tournament tickets.

Discussion Questions

1. How can decisions regarding how a product is produced affect competition?
2. Discuss the pros and cons of the three types of economic systems: capitalism, socialism, and communism. Which would you prefer to work under? Why?
3. Visualize a company with no competition. What may influence it to offer quality products?

4. Should the government be allowed to determine prices for a company that has a monopoly? Explain.

5. Some people feel the government should not support failing businesses. Do you agree or disagree? Why?

Marketing Project

Analyzing Economic Systems

Project Goal: Given three nations that have different economies, determine whether their economies are capitalistic, socialistic, or communistic. State the advantages and disadvantages of each type of economy.

Directions: Prepare a form like the one below. In the left column, list Singapore, Holland, and Cuba. Research the type of economic system that exists in each nation, and then list the advantages and disadvantages of each.

Nation	Advantages	Disadvantages

Applied Academics

Language Arts

1. Working with your teacher, use sources such as your local Chamber of Commerce or other governmental agencies to find students in other countries. Write letters to the students explaining your country's economic system. Ask them to write back explaining theirs. As an alternative, you may wish to invite a foreign exchange student to your class to discuss the economic system of his or her country.

2. Read a current article about the Commonwealth of Independent States to find out what economic changes have taken place recently. Write your findings in a 100-word paragraph.

Math

3. If Nike has 26 percent market share of the $5.5 billion athletic shoe industry, what is its share in dollars?

4. Jackie decided to take part in the free enterprise system of the United States by opening her own business. Using the figures below, determine whether there is a profit or loss at the end of her first year.

Income Statement for the Month Ending December 31, 19—–

Revenue:		
Sales		$1,600
Expenses		
Insurance Expense	$ 15	
Miscellaneous Expense	370	
Rent Expense	900	
Supplies Expense	500	
Utilities Expense	75	
Total Expenses		
Net Loss or Profit		

Social Studies

5. Interview two people in business. Ask them how they feel about working in a free enterprise system. Would they like to see less government control? Report your findings to the class.

Marketing and Multiculturalism

In a private enterprise system, the consumer cannot be ignored. In order to survive, marketers must meet the needs of their consumers. That is why it is important for marketers to keep a close eye on the changes taking place in the marketplace. For instance, during the 1980s the Hispanic population rose 53 percent. By the year 2000, there is expected to be more than 31 million Hispanics in the United States. The Hispanic market has tremendous buying power and in 1990 alone spent $171 billion. This number is expected to double in the next decade.

1. In a private enterprise system, how does Hispanic buying power influence a company's economic decisions on what goods should be produced?

2. Why would Hispanic buying power not have the same influence on economic decisions in a communist country as it does in the United States?

Chapter 3

The Economic Environment of Marketing

Terms to Know

business
entrepreneurs
gross national product
    (GNP)
sole proprietorship
partnership
corporation
cooperative

franchise
business cycles
expansion
peak prosperity
recession
depression
inflation
consumerism

Chapter Objectives

After studying this chapter, you will be able to:

- describe the role of business in the economy and the factors contributing to production;
- explain the relationship between the gross national product (GNP) and the standard of living;
- list examples, characteristics, and advantages of three forms of business ownership;
- name the phases of a typical business cycle and describe the characteristics of economic growth, prosperity, recession, and inflation; and
- explain how economic, political, social, and technological factors influence business conduct.

Case Study

Just a Phone Call Away

Caught in the late-afternoon traffic driving home from work, Lisa picked up her car telephone and dialed her husband.

"Hi Mark!" she exclaimed when he answered. "I've left the office but the traffic is fierce. I'll pick up Susie from the day-care center. Can you delay dinner 20 minutes?"

"Sure, Lisa. I'll reprogram the microwave from here. I'm almost home. Where are you?"

"Just passed Armitage. See you soon."

Even though Mark and Lisa are each in their own cars heading home from separate jobs, they are able to get in touch en route because they each have cellular telephones—portable phones—in their cars. Cellular phones have become indispensable to many businesspeople. They're also useful to busy families like Mark and Lisa's. In 1983, Ameritech Mobile Communications became the first telephone company to offer commercial cellular service. Five years later, it had 22 cellular markets in major Midwestern cities, each with thousands of customers and potential for many more. Improved technology allowed the company to lower the cost of its cellular phones and increase the number of customers.

To make cellular phones readily available to Ameritech's Midwestern customers, the company marketed them through retail stores. As customers became familiar with cellular phones, more people became interested in owning them.

There was a time when life was simpler and families provided for their own needs. Families worked their farms, growing food and making their own clothes. Parents could teach children the skills they would need when they grew up.

Now, life is more complex. People work away from home. We want things that we cannot produce ourselves: automobiles, VCRs, cellular phones, a variety of food products, and services such as specialized medical care and higher education. To satisfy these needs, we turn to business and its marketing activities. As we demand more, business seeks to anticipate and respond to our needs.[1]

The Role of Business in the Economy

To understand marketing and its role in our economy, we must first understand the term *business*. **Business** is all the activities of an individual or a group of individuals involved in producing and distributing goods or services to customers. The intent of business is to create satisfying exchanges. Business involves production and marketing.

Production

As you learned in Chapter 2, production is the process of creating or improving goods and services. Mining, manufacturing, and agriculture, for example, are part of the production process. Production requires four ingredients: *natural resources*, *labor*, *capital*, and *entrepreneurs*.

Natural Resources

Natural resources such as fertile soil, water, minerals, and favorable climate are vital to a country's well-being and productivity. Soil is needed for raising grain, fruits, and vegetables. Water must be available for power, drinking, and transportation. Oil is needed for operating and lubricating machinery.

The United States is fortunate to have abundant natural resources. The temperate weather favors agriculture. The lakes and rivers provide a supply of water. Without adequate natural resources, it would be difficult to produce goods in quantity.

However, even this country's vast resources are limited and must be conserved. Through ecology—the study of our relationship to the physical environment—we are learning how to preserve our natural resources.

Some of the means used by various businesses to conserve natural resources include: controlling the dumping of industrial waste products into lakes and rivers; marketing unleaded gasoline to combat

■■■ *America's high production rate can be traced in part to its natural resources, such as water and forests. What other factors contribute to the production rate?*

air pollution; improving packaging materials so that they can be disposed of safely; and recycling such things as paper, plastic, and glass.

Labor

Labor is all the human activity that goes into producing goods and services. It refers to both part-time and full-time employees and to managers. There are some 125 million people employed in the United States today. Many groups of people with wide ranges of talents and interests contribute to production through their work efforts.

Capital

Natural resources and labor alone cannot meet the needs of production. Capital is also necessary. As you know from Chapter 2, *capital* is all the tools (such as factories and machinery) and the money that are used in an organization's operation.

When people own their own businesses, they put their own capital and labor into the business. Henry Ford, for example, invested his own capital along with funds from others in what was to become Ford Motor Company. Estée Lauder used capital from her family to start her cosmetics company.

Sometimes people and organizations put capital into a business without becoming involved in its daily operation. For example, people who invest in a business by buying shares of stock in the company become part owners but do not go to work for that business. The capital that owners and investors provide helps a business operate and expand.

Entrepreneurs

People who take the risk and provide the capital to start and operate their own business are **entrepreneurs**. Famous American entrepreneurs include John D. Rockefeller (Standard Oil), Richard Sears (Sears, Roebuck & Co.), John Johnson (Johnson Publishing, publisher of *Ebony*), Liz Claiborne (clothing), and Bill Gates (Microsoft).

These people's creative business ideas and business efforts created some of the world's best-known organizations. But entrepreneurial spirit is not limited to large companies. Ninety-five percent of all U.S. businesses are small businesses.

In an effort to capitalize on the entrepreneurial spirit, many large and forward-thinking companies promote creative approaches internally. Known as *intrepreneurship*, the process involves the development of new methods and ideas within a larger company in a free-wheeling manner similar to that of entrepreneurship.

Such companies encourage their employees to be *intrepreneurs*—that is, to put their creativity to work by helping the company develop such things as new or improved products, better marketing strategies, and improved management practices. Employees are often rewarded for their contributions with bonuses or some other kind of incentive, or perhaps with a new position within the company.

In intrepreneurial situations, everyone wins. Intrepreneurs have the satisfaction of making a contribution to the company and having it recognized and implemented. Companies have increased productivity that will more than likely be reflected in increased profits.

Gross National Product

Production is so important that we measure the health of our entire economy by the amount of goods and services produced each year. The total value of the final goods and services produced in the nation over a specified period (usually a year) is its **gross national product**, often referred to as GNP. GNP is expressed in dollars. The GNP of the United States is more than $4.9 trillion and is expected to exceed $5.8 trillion by 2005.

Closely tied to the GNP is the *standard of living*, or how well the people in a given nation live. This standard is measured by the number and kinds of goods and services the people in a nation have. The standard of living can be determined by dividing the GNP by the nation's population. This figure is called the per capita GNP. The more goods and services a nation produces in proportion to its population, the higher its standard of living (unless it exports most of those goods and services).

Purchasing power is the dollars used to buy the things people need and want. When people have more purchasing power, a higher standard of living often results. Circumstances such as a slowdown in business activity, high unemployment, and inflation contribute to lowering the people's purchasing power and a nation's standard of living.

Purchasing power creates the sales transactions that turn the wheels of marketing in the economy and increase the GNP. Fortunately, Americans are free to make the kinds of business decisions that can lead to a higher GNP and standard of living.

Forms of Business Ownership

In the private enterprise system, people are free to determine their form of business ownership. In the United States, there are three basic forms of business ownership: *sole proprietorship*, *partnership*, and *corporation*. *Cooperatives* and *franchises* are associated with corporations but have unique characteristics of their own. Each form of ownership has its own risks and rewards.

Sole Proprietorship

A business owned by one person is a **sole proprietorship**. Seventy percent of all businesses in the United States fall into this group. In a sole proprietorship, the owner invests his or her money, makes all decisions, and receives all profits.

Owners in a sole proprietorship, however, may have more difficulty than larger organizations obtaining loans. More significantly, sole proprietors are personally liable for their debts if their businesses fail. In addition, most sole proprietors work long hours. They may do all the buying, promotion, hiring and supervising of employees, budgeting, and record-keeping.

Partnership

A business owned by two or more people is a **partnership**. Some global firms contain hundreds of partners. Partnerships are the least common form of business and represent only 10 percent of total businesses in the United States.

The partners share the responsibility for financing, operating, and managing the business. They also share the profits. Usually, the profits are divided in proportion to the amount of money that each partner has invested in the business.

One advantage of a partnership over a sole proprietorship is that two or more people share the risks and management. Also, it is usually easier for two or three people to raise capital than it is for one to do so. Thus, a partnership usually has more funds to draw on than a sole proprietorship does.

There are disadvantages to partnerships, however. Like sole proprietors, partners are personally liable for their business dealings. An added drawback of a partnership is that each partner is responsible for the actions of the others. One partner may make foolish decisions, shirk duties, or even cheat the other partners. Even though the partnership agreement is usually in the form of a written contract, there is no assurance that one partner will not bankrupt the business.

Partnerships are built on mutual trust. As you look around your community, you will find many thriving partnerships. They are often found in real estate, insurance, finance, and professional services such as the law, medical, and accounting professions.

Corporation

A **corporation** is a business organization with many owners that operates under a government charter. A *charter* is a legal document granted by a state or the federal government setting forth the rules of operation. The charter includes the legal name of the business and the number of shares of stock to be issued.

The owners of a corporation (often as many as several thousand) hold stock or shares in the corporation and are called stockholders or shareholders. (AT&T at one time had 3 million shareholders.) Most corporations entitle stockholders to one vote on business and management affairs for each share of stock owned. Thus, the more shares a stockholder owns, the greater that stockholder's influence.

A corporation's stockholders periodically elect a board of directors to manage the corporation. The directors, however, are not personally responsible for the debts of the corporation. That is, they cannot be forced to pay the corporation's debts.

Corporations are especially important to our economy. Ninety percent of the annual receipts and 74 percent of all net profits are generated by corporations. In addition, they employ 70 percent of all U.S. workers. Most of the familiar names in television commercials and in other advertising—Chrysler, Pepsi-Cola, and Quaker Oats—are corporations.

Some corporations are multinational. They exist and do business in more than one nation. Our economy is becoming increasingly international. Some examples of multinational organizations are Coca-Cola, Kellogg, and Procter & Gamble.

Some corporations are acquired by others to become part of a *conglomerate*—a business organization made up of a group of firms in unrelated industries. Two well-known conglomerates are International Telephone & Telegraph Company (ITT) and International Business Machines (IBM).

Another conglomerate is Mobil, which counts among its diverse holdings Mobil Container Corporation, the largest maker of paperboard containers; Mobil Chemical, maker of plastic products such as Hefty trash bags; and W. F. Hall Printing, which prints *Ebony* and *National Geographic*.

Conglomerates are important to marketers because the corporations within the conglomerate can provide money and other resources when needed. For example, Mobil owned the retail organization Montgomery Ward and Co., and loaned it $355 million when Ward's was close to bankruptcy. Of course, conglomerates may sell companies that operate unprofitably for them. Mobil, for example, later sold Montgomery Ward to Ward's own management which then set out to turn the company around.

Cooperatives

A **cooperative**, or co-op, is a group of people or small businesses in similar fields who together organize a business in order to benefit from its services. The members of a cooperative have shares of ownership in the new corporation (the cooperative) which provides its services to them virtually at cost.

For example, Sunkist-Agway is a marketing co-op formed by farmers. Instead of selling their crops to a food processing company, which makes its own profit, the farmers send them to their own co-op and later receive the profits themselves.

Similarly, a group of customers buys large quantities of food at wholesale prices. Another example is a credit union, where members can borrow money at less interest than they would pay at a commercial bank.

Franchises

A **franchise** is an agreement between a well-known corporation and an independent individual or group who wishes to operate the business locally. Franchising is one way corporations may expand. The independent local operator signs a franchise agreement stating that the business will be run according to the corporation's standards.

Franchising has several benefits. It helps corporations to expand. The franchisee can start a business with limited capital and benefits from the corporation's experience and reputation. Franchisees are usually more highly motivated than salaried employees because of their personal investment in the business. Therefore, they work harder to make the franchise successful.

One drawback of franchising is that franchisees do not have complete freedom to run the franchise. They must comply with the corporation's standards. Difficulties can arise when the franchisee and the franchisor disagree on how the franchise should be run.

Many well-known businesses are franchises; the names of McDonald's, Dairy Queen, and Long John Silver's are among those franchises dominating the fast-food field. Franchises are growing in other industries. For example, Holiday Inns, General Motors dealerships, and Benetton stores worldwide are franchises.

The Fed Smooths the Way

In the United States, business is not left to cope alone with shifting business cycles. The Federal Reserve System, known as "The Fed," is the bank of some 6,000 of the nation's major commercial banks (including, possibly, your bank) and of the U.S. Treasury.

One of The Fed's jobs is to control the supply of money loaned to businesses and individuals. By regulating the amount of money in circulation, The Fed encourages or discourages marketing transactions. It brings money into the economy to stimulate business in times of recession and pulls money out to discourage sales and borrowing when inflation skyrockets prices.

The Fed controls the money supply in four ways:

- It requires member banks to keep some money on reserve and not lend it all out. The Fed may raise that reserve requirement to keep banks from lending or lower it to encourage lending.
- It can raise or lower the rate of interest that banks must pay when they want to borrow money from The Fed.

- It can buy or sell U.S. Treasury Notes and bills. Buying puts money into the economy; and selling pulls it out.
- It can raise or lower requirements on the amount of money stockbrokers can lend to their clients who borrow from them when buying stock.

These controls of The Fed have the effect of making more money available when business is slow and the economy needs it and less available in times of inflation when prices shoot up.

1. How does the Federal Reserve System's controlling the money help the economy?

2. In the early 1990s, the United States experienced a recession. Consumers were unsure of the economy. Consequently, spending decreased and savings increased. Based on the information you have just read about the Federal Reserve System, what steps do you think The Fed took in order to increase spending?

The Business Environment

Businesses operate in an uncertain world, coping with many forces beyond their control. As you learned in Chapter 2, the private enterprise system encourages competition. This in turn provides consumers with a wide product selection. While businesses may battle each other with production, pricing, promotion, and distribution strategies, they must also react to changes in the economic, political, social, and technological environment. Let's take a closer look at each of these areas.

Economic Factors

The goals of any healthy economy include high productivity, high employment, high income, and stability. For a number of years after World War II, the United States enjoyed such an economy. Many things can happen to prevent a society from maintaining its economic standards. These include war, inflation, failure to maintain productivity, and severe, unfair competition.

An economy typically does not rise steadily upward but goes through alternating periods of growth and inactivity called **business cycles**. The four phases of a business cycle are:

- expansion;
- peak prosperity;
- recession; and
- depression.

Expansion is characterized by a growth in business activity, increased sales, construction, and business expansion, with a rise in employment. During times of expansion, many marketers look to enlarge their businesses because they have or can borrow the money to do so.

Peak prosperity is a period of high sales and income. Individuals and businesses are confident and willing to take risks to maintain prosperity. For example, in peak prosperity an automobile dealer will carry a heavier inventory, or a boutique owner will buy a more trendy line of apparel.

A **recession** is a decline in the gross national product for six months. Business slows down during a recession. People do not buy goods, perhaps due to high prices or unemployment. Prices then drop and so do wages.

A **depression** is an extended recession with high unemployment. A depression does not always follow each recession. The economy may begin to rise again after a recession. This has been the case in recent decades.

These phases, which are shown in Figure 3–1, are of uneven length. For example, the United States has not known a severe depression since the 1930s.

Another condition the economy may face is inflation. **Inflation** is a general rise in prices. It can occur at any phase of the business cycle.

A price increase below 5 percent a year can be normal. High inflation, however, can damage an economy. Since all prices rise, each dollar buys less. For instance, during times of inflation when prices rise 15 percent or more, you might hope to buy two good sweaters and then find that you can only afford the price of one.

During inflation retired people and people on fixed incomes find their money worth less and less. Although the amount of money spent is high, many

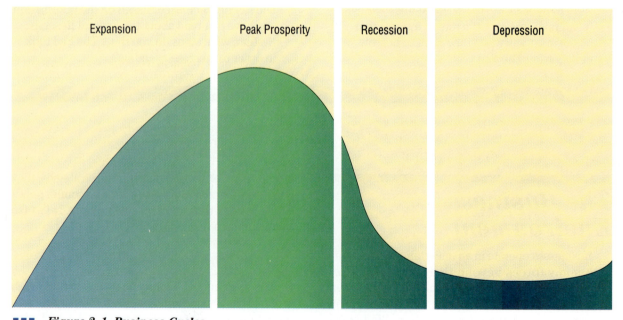

| Expansion | Peak Prosperity | Recession | Depression |

■■■ *Figure 3–1 Business Cycles*
Business cycles are of uneven length. What happens to the GNP during periods of expansion?

businesses cannot expand because the cost of borrowing money (that is, the interest rate) is too high. Inflation can stimulate production and employment for a while, but it often leads to economic slowdown.

In contrast to recession and inflation, a healthy economy is marked by growing production, stable prices, more jobs, higher incomes, and more personal spending. Businesses often plan expansions to match the business cycle. Business maintains close watch on the economy to see how best to react to changing economic conditions. Prompt response by a business can mean the difference between a profit and a loss.

Political Factors

Because our business system is not perfect, citizens have had the government establish laws to ensure fair treatment to people involved in business activities. For example, there are laws established to:

- maintain equal opportunity for access to advancement in jobs;
- ensure fair competition among businesses;
- forbid price discrimination and other deceptive practices;
- make sure customers can buy only pure food, drugs, and cosmetics;
- provide equal employment opportunities among all people;
- protect the safety of employees on the job once they are hired;
- safeguard the funds of investors in bank deposits and owners of corporations; and
- help maintain our environment and discourage business from polluting it.

These laws and other activities of the government influence the way business is conducted.

Social Factors

The social environment directly influences the way people live and how they spend their money. For this reason, businesses learn the latest trends and what is important to people.

Later in this text, you will study consumer buying behavior. You will learn what marketers look for

when they attempt to analyze and understand what motivates people to buy. For now we will limit our discussion to three major social trends that affect business operations in the United States today:

- changes in the work force;
- the diverse population; and
- the voice of special interest groups.

Changes in the Work Force

Perhaps the greatest social and economic influence in the country today is the changing work force. Between 1989 and 2000, 29 percent of those who enter the work force will be members of racial or cultural minorities.

Women now compose 45 percent of the labor force. Today, women have greater responsibilities at work and earn more money than in past decades. They are also beginning to close the income gap between themselves and men.

In addition, there are more families headed by a single working parent. Even in households with two parents living at home, both tend to be employed. The growing number of employed people has increased the demand for many consumer goods and services.

Businesses are tuning in to the needs of these consumers in the work force. For example, clothing stores, such as The Limited and Casual Corner, expanded their focus to include not only young sportswear but also career wear. Supermarkets, gourmet food stores, and delis are providing quick carry out dinners for working families. Child care facilities, housecleaning services, and lawn care services are in greater demand.

Another trend businesses are facing is the aging of America. This means that the number of elderly is rising. Also, there are fewer people in their early twenties just entering the work force.

Changes in the work force mean that organizations have to market themselves to employees and prospective workers, too. For example, Fel-Pro, a Skokie, Illinois, gasket-maker, provides an on-site day-care center, a family vacation camp, and a learning center to tutor employees' children. American Express and other companies offer flexible work schedules, paid maternity leave, and financial help to employees adopting children.[2] Employers who promote employee well-being are likely to attract and keep loyal workers.

As changes in our world economy occur, global changes in the work force will also occur. Businesses may deal with the massive relocation of workers. Loosening of immigration policies will result in a worldwide labor pool and improved labor productivity. As a result, companies and countries may have to compete for trained human resources on a worldwide basis.

The Diverse Population

There really is no single mass market for all goods and services. In the United States, there are many individuals and groups with a wide range of consumer needs. Factors such as education, income, religion, and ethnic background have an effect on what people buy. Many people have special activities and hobbies that influence their spending.

These diverse interests create many markets for goods and services. Business must stay alert to these needs in order to satisfy them at a profit. For example, the *Los Angeles Times* publishes a monthly, bilingual section called "Nuestro Tiempo." It is geared to meet the needs of Spanish-speaking residents in Los Angeles.[3]

The Voice of Special Interest Groups

Increasingly, people are organizing to effectively voice their opinions as consumers. As a result, a movement called consumerism has emerged. **Consumerism** is the effort to protect consumer rights by putting pressure on businesses to produce products that are

- safe;
- labeled honestly with respect to ingredients;
- advertised ethically; and
- produced with regard to environmental concerns.

Individual consumers, consumer groups, government, and business leaders all share in the effort on consumerism.

Consumerism is healthy for both consumers and marketers. When consumers let business know what they want, then marketers can supply it. An early leader in consumerism was Ralph Nader. The work of his Public Citizen organization on automobile safety led to improved automobiles and new safety laws.

Some special interest groups such as Greenpeace work to protect the environment. Others, such as SADD, support young people in combating drinking while driving. The League of Women Voters provides citizens with information on issues such as controlling land, water, and air pollution. The information helps voters make informed choices.

Businesses often take the concerns of special interest groups into consideration when developing their production plans. For example, to cut down on waste, the Kellogg Company estimates that more than half of its packaging is recycled cartonboard.[4]

■■■ *Our diverse population calls for products such as Maybelline's Shades of You, geared to its interests. How have marketers responded in this case?*

THE FUTURE IS NOW

Come in, Dick Tracy

Just when you thought you could get away from your parents, your wrist starts chirping. No longer will the "I didn't know what time it was" excuse get you off. Now your watch, the one that you're careful not to look at around curfew time, is going to beep at you. That's right, it's those parental timekeepers calling you on your new *Piepser* (German for "Beeper") wristwatch. It can be programmed to receive beeps from four telephone numbers. There is one last hope. You can forget to turn it on.

■ ■ ■   *Businesses must cope with forces beyond their control. What economic and technical forces has the owner of this Asian fishing vessel not coped with?*

Technological Factors

Technology is the combination of all tools, machines, and methods used to provide goods and services. Technology includes hand crafting and personal service, as well as the newest uses of scientific discoveries. Business and industry use technology to create and deliver better products.

Constant improvement in basic machinery over the years led to mass production—the efficient and rapid production of large quantities of standardized goods. The invention of the light bulb led to the development of the power generation system that supplies electricity to air conditioners, computers, and all appliances plugged into wall outlets. The steam engine and the expansion of the railroads—and later trucks and the growth of highways—made possible the mass marketing of these new goods. Radio and television advertising helped sell them.

Advances in technology support the economy by determining how resources will be used. For example, because of advances in technology, factories make microprocessors or computers on a chip. These chips become components in many products: smart cameras, irons that turn themselves off when not in use, and even greeting cards that play music.

Marketing introduces new technology to society, which changes the way people live. For example, microprocessors have already revolutionized our communications system. For instance, while riding in our cars we can transmit data signals using the telephone to turn our lights on at home.

With new technology, consumer and business needs change and create needs for other new technology. People like Lisa and Mark in this chapter's opening vignette who want to start dinner from car telephones now need the ovens and other appliances capable of responding to those commands.

Technological changes also lead to changes in the way businesses produce goods. For example, factories make cars and other products using robots, lasers, and computer-aided manufacturing (CAM) techniques.

Investments in research and development bring about new technologies which improve products and affect consumer choices. In a high-technology environment, business constantly deals with new products and changing customer demand.

Successful marketers seek out the new applications of such new technologies as shopping by computer and 24-hour banking. They then interpret these changes and innovations to customers.

CHAPTER NOTES

1. Ameritech Annual Report, Chicago, IL, 1988, p. 18.

2. *CEP Research Report*, Council on Economic Priorities, February 1990, p. 2.

3. *Marketing News*, 29 March 1989, p. 5.

4. *CEP Research Report*, Council on Economic Priorities, New York, February 1990, p. 4.

Chapter Summary

- Business includes all of the activities of an individual or group involved in producing and marketing goods and services to consumers.

- Production is the process of creating or improving goods and services. Production requires four ingredients: land, labor, capital, and entrepreneurs.

- Production is measured by the GNP—the total value of goods and services a nation produces in a certain time, usually a year. Dividing the GNP by the nation's population determines the standard of living (per capita GNP).

- There are three forms of business ownership: the sole proprietorship, owned by one person; the partnership, owned by two or more people; and the corporation, owned by its stockholders. A special form of corporation is a cooperative, an organization owned by its members. A franchise is an agreement between a well-known corporation and an independent individual or group that wishes to operate a business in the name of the recognized corporation.

- The four phases of a business cycle are expansion, peak prosperity, recession, and depression.

- Business is conducted in an uncertain environment and is continually influenced by many factors. Among these are economic, political, social, and technological factors.

Building Your Marketing Vocabulary

1. Write a paragraph using the terms below. Use the terms in a way that shows you understand the difference between them.
   - sole proprietorship — partnership— corporation
   - cooperative — franchise
2. Using the following terms, write a paragraph or two describing how each term relates to the economic environment of marketing.

business
entrepreneurs
gross national product (GNP)
business cycles
expansion
peak prosperity
recession
depression
inflation
consumerism

Questions for Review

1. Define business and its purpose.
2. Describe the contribution of each of the four factors of production.
3. Tell how production is measured.
4. Describe the relationship between the GNP and the standard of living.
5. Describe the relationship between people's standard of living and their purchasing power.
6. What is a cooperative and how does it benefit its members?
7. List the four phases of a business cycle and their characteristics.
8. Name three types of laws that ensure fair treatment of people involved in business activities.
9. Name three social trends that have an effect on business.

Critical Thinking

1. Explain how each of the four factors of production might be involved in the production of chocolate candy bars.
2. Compare the risks and rewards of a partnership and sole proprietorship.
3. Suppose you want to open a computer store. During which phase of the business cycle would it be best to do this? Why?
4. Give an example of how a food store might react to a recession.
5. Why is it important for marketers to be aware of new technologies?

Discussion Questions

1. What do you feel is the most important factor to successful production?

2. Suppose you decide to open a video rental store. Discuss the form of business ownership you would select. Would the fact that your best friend is willing to run the business with you influence your choice of ownership? Give your reasons.

3. Discuss how different national businesses have been influenced by economic, political, social, and technological factors. Give examples for each type of factor.

4. As a member of a special interest group that lobbies for the protection of animals, discuss the concerns you would voice to a business that produces cosmetics.

5. Name products recently introduced to the market and made available because of advances in technology.

Marketing Project

Comparing Forms of Business Ownership

Project Goal: State the advantages and disadvantages of the four forms of business ownership.

Directions: Prepare a form like the one below. In the left column, list the various forms of business ownership. Talk with several businesspeople to learn their views of the advantages and disadvantages of each form of ownership. Then write your findings in the appropriate columns.

Form of Ownership	Advantages	Disadvantages

Applied Academics

Language Arts

1. Read a magazine article about the current makeup of the U.S. labor force. Write a 150-word paragraph on your findings.

Math

2. If the population in the United States is 250 million and the GNP is $4.9 trillion, what is the per capita GNP which indicates the standard of living?

Science

3. Through ecology we are learning how to preserve our natural resources. Choosing either fertile soil, air, water, or a useful mineral, describe steps that are currently being taken to preserve and protect it.

Social Studies

4. Special interest groups voice their opinions, concerns, and questions to businesses. Write a paragraph telling how special interest groups benefit society.

Marketing and Multiculturalism

Who says there's no such thing as a free lunch? In Austin, Texas, with only $5,000 of start-up capital and no budget for advertising, Hispanic-American entrepreneur Benjamin Castelan promoted the opening of his new, 25-seat Mexican restaurant, Peso's, by giving free lunch samples to nearby businesspeople. Peso's was so popular that within the first year Castelan had moved it to a larger, 85-seat location, broadened the menu, and earned $300,000 in sales. Two years later, Castelan opened a second restaurant and projected an estimated $1.4 million in sales between the two sites.

Castelan attributed his success to providing an ethnic menu that met the tastes of the culturally diverse Central Texas population and hiring a work force of 60 people, primarily Hispanic, who are experienced in Mexican food preparation.

1. Which business cycles would provide the best financial climate for Castelan's restaurants?

2. Peso's is an example of what kind of business ownership?

3. Why might a primarily Hispanic employee base benefit Peso's?

4. How did the trends discussed in the chapter affect the operation of Castelan's business?

Chapter 4

The Functions of Marketing

Terms to Know

target market

market segmentation

utility

form utility

time utility

place utility

possession utility

information utility

advertising

value added

marketing strategy

Chapter Objectives

After studying this chapter, you will be able to:

- define the term *target market* and explain how it relates to the marketing concept;
- describe five utilities and other benefits that are added to products;
- illustrate the cost and value added by marketing;
- identify and describe three categories of marketing functions;
- identify eight functions of marketing and how to explain each briefly; and
- define the marketing strategy and relate it to the marketing mix.

Case Study

Sam Walton's Secret to Success

"There is only one boss, and whether a person shines shoes for a living or heads up the biggest corporation in the world, the boss remains the same. It's the customer!

"The customer is the person who pays everyone's salary and who decides whether a business is going to succeed or fail. In fact, the customer can fire everybody in the company from the chairman on down, and he can do it simply by spending his money somewhere else."

These are the words of Sam M. Walton, founder and chairman of Wal-Mart Stores, Inc. Among other things, Sam Walton was famous for bringing home one of the biggest paychecks in the United States, thanks to the success of his very profitable discount chain, Wal-Mart Stores, Inc.

After working for years with J. C. Penney and the Ben Franklin Stores, he opened his first Wal-Mart store in Arkansas in 1962. Now there are more than 1,720 Wal-Mart stores plus a number of Sam's Wholesale Clubs scattered across the country with sales and profits rising every year. Wal-Mart is the largest retailing company in the world, with more than $44 billion in annual sales.

What accounts for Wal-Mart's success? Sam Walton put the marketing concept to work. As you remember, according to the marketing concept, businesses are successful when they can supply what customers want at a profit. Sam Walton's statement that the customer is the boss was his version of the marketing concept. Consider what his statement says:

1. The focus of the business is the customer.
2. All of the activities of the business must focus on the customer.
3. The business stays in business as long as the customer supports it.[1,2]

The Target Market

Although businesses focus on serving their customers' wants and needs, no business can serve everyone. In fact, most successful businesses first try to determine their **target market**—the customers that they can serve best.

To identify their target market, businesses use **market segmentation**—a process of subdividing the market according to customer needs and characteristics. For instance, a marketer may segment a market according to the special needs of young families, high school students, or Hispanics in the Southwest. You will explore market segmentation further in Chapter 6.

Some organizations target individuals. Others target businesses. For example, one accounting firm might specialize in serving sole proprietors and partnerships. Another firm might seek medium-size retailers or manufacturers as its primary clients.

Nonprofit organizations determine their target markets, too. For example, the Public Museum in Milwaukee seeks families with children to view its lifelike exhibits. The Santa Fe Symphony caters to educated music-lovers with above-average incomes.

Once a company identifies its target market, its activities can be guided by the marketing concept. For instance, Wal-Mart first began focusing on the needs of moderate-income families who live in Southern and Midwestern rural areas. To meet the needs of these customers, Wal-Mart offered:

- convenient locations in easy-to-reach malls on highways serving a local community and nearby towns;

- a number of departments for one-stop family shopping, such as clothing and accessories, household goods, electronics, and toys;

- everyday low prices;

- the option to buy on credit; and

- a liberal return policy.

Let's take a closer look at how marketers use the marketing process to serve the target market.

How Marketing Serves Customers

The processes of both production and marketing add utility to goods and services. In marketing, **utility** means usefulness to consumers.

To serve customers, businesses add five basic kinds of utility to products. The production processes add *form utility*. Marketing processes add four other utilities to products: *time utility*, *place utility*, *possession utility*, and *information utility*. These are illustrated in Figure 4–1.

Form Utility

Form utility is the increased usefulness of a product to a consumer by causing a change in the basic material through production. For example, steel, glass, and chrome combined to form an automobile are more useful to consumers than they are as raw materials.

Time Utility

The increased usefulness that a marketer gives a product by making it available to the customer at the right time of year and most convenient time of day is called **time utility**. Marketers buy and store products so they will be available when customers need them. Months before the Christmas season begins, for example, marketers prepare to offer customers the merchandise they expect to see: toys, greeting cards, decorations, gift items, gift wrappings, and tree ornaments.

Months in advance, marketers plan other events that take place during the year, such as Mother's Day, Halloween, and Valentine's Day, so that customers will have the things they want when they want them. For example, store buyers purchase back-to-school clothing in March and April to reach the stores in July and August. This allows families to buy before school opens in the fall. Sporting goods stores are ready in August with a full array of football, soccer, and other fall sports equipment. Different clothing is made available to meet the needs of each season.

Marketing provides goods not only at the time of year customers want them but also at the time of

■ ■ ■ *Marketers add time utility to products such as greeting cards by offering them to customers at the right time of the year. Name two other products to which marketers add time utility.*

day that is most convenient for them to shop. Many stores are open six nights a week so that a person who works all day can shop after work.

Place Utility

Place utility is the increased usefulness of products because of location. Marketers add place utility to products by offering convenient selling locations and by shipping products to these locations. For example, marketers add place utility by locating their products in shopping centers that are easily accessible to customers. The modern shopping center provides numerous retail stores and service establishments with ample parking so that customers can easily satisfy their needs at one location. Customers may buy a jacket, pick up their clothes at the dry cleaner, get a haircut, and have a picture framed all at one location. They may also stop at the supermarket and buy oranges from California, poultry from Arkansas, cheese from Wisconsin, and blueberries from Maine.

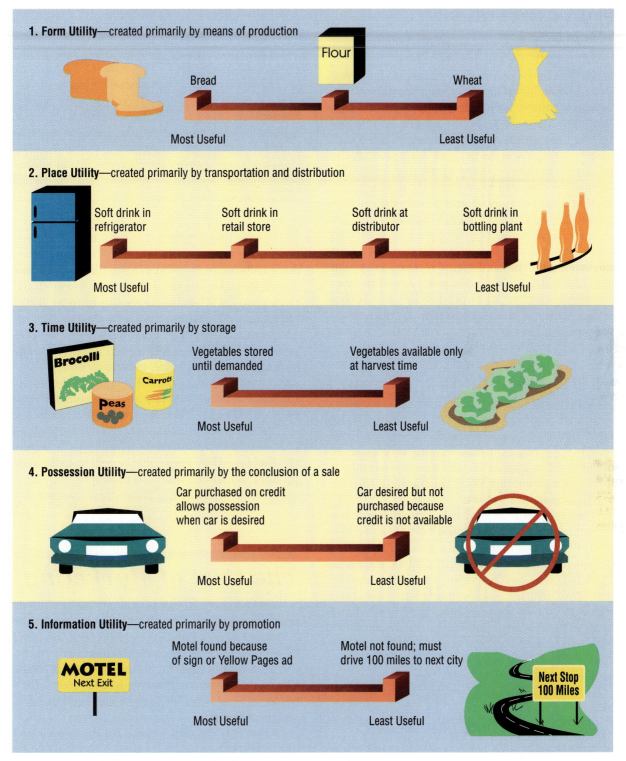

1. **Form Utility**—created primarily by means of production

Flour

Bread — Most Useful ... Wheat — Least Useful

2. **Place Utility**—created primarily by transportation and distribution

Soft drink in refrigerator — Most Useful ... Soft drink in retail store ... Soft drink at distributor ... Soft drink in bottling plant — Least Useful

3. **Time Utility**—created primarily by storage

Brocolli / Peas / Carrots

Vegetables stored until demanded — Most Useful ... Vegetables available only at harvest time — Least Useful

4. **Possession Utility**—created primarily by the conclusion of a sale

Car purchased on credit allows possession when car is desired — Most Useful ... Car desired but not purchased because credit is not available — Least Useful

5. **Information Utility**—created primarily by promotion

MOTEL Next Exit

Motel found because of sign or Yellow Pages ad — Most Useful ... Motel not found; must drive 100 miles to next city — Least Useful

Next Stop 100 Miles

■■■ *Figure 4–1 Utility Added to Products*
There are five kinds of utility that are added to products. How does transportation create place utility?

Possession Utility

Even if goods were brought to a convenient location at a time when the customer wanted them, they would be useful only if the customer could have them. The ability of marketers to aid customers in owning goods is known as **possession utility**. Marketers may add possession utility by offering credit or accepting checks. For example, if a customer cannot or will not pay cash for a product, the seller adds possession utility by offering credit. This enables the customer to purchase the product.

Marketers may also add possession utility by offering a payment plan or a partial trade. For example, a car dealer may accept a customer's old car as part of a trade-in on the purchase of a new car. In addition, the car dealer may set up a payment plan that helps facilitate the purchase of the car. Possession utility takes place when marketing activities help to provide the customer with possession and legal ownership.

Information Utility

Information utility is the usefulness added to a product through communication. For example, **advertising**—any sales message paid for by a sponsor and appearing in media—may inform customers of the benefits, availability, and prices of a product. A billboard promoting Mobil Oil informs a traveler of a nearby service station.

Packaging and labeling may simplify shopping by identifying the qualities and best uses of products. Cereal packages contain information on ingredients, vitamins and mineral content, and more. The label on a Gore-Tex jacket tells consumers the benefits of breathable, waterproof fabric. Labels and warnings on cold medicine contribute to relief and safety. The directions that come with a microwave oven tell the user how long to heat certain foods. By communicating with the public, marketers make products more useful.

Other Benefits of Marketing

In addition to time, place, possession, and information utility, marketing provides other customer benefits. People enjoy more conveniences and luxuries because marketing has made them possible.

THE FUTURE IS NOW

What You See Is What You Get

Until now, autofocus cameras required that you point at your subject, focus, and then frame your shot. Not anymore. Now there's a camera that thinks like you do. The new Canon A2E uses infrared sensors to determine where your eye is looking and focuses accordingly as you click the shutter.

By creating a demand for goods, marketing encourages greater production. When goods are manufactured in large quantities, the costs of producing them drops. Prices can then be lowered, and more people will buy the goods. The introduction of personal computers provides a typical example.

Originally, personal computers were very expensive. Marketing information convinced many people of the educational, entertainment, and personal uses of this product. The increased demand for computers allowed large-scale production and encouraged competition from other producers.

Prices came down, and marketers informed the public again. Demand increased further, as more people discovered how they could benefit from this new product. By adding utility to products, marketers increase the well-being of the entire marketplace.

The Cost of Marketing

Marketing costs represent about half the selling price of most items. Thus, a ballpoint pen selling for 1 dollar may cost the marketer 50 cents; the other 50 cents is the cost of marketing including profit. Figure 4–2 shows typical marketing costs involved with selling a product such as Ritz Crackers. Let's try to find out whether these costs need to be as high as they are.

When Ritz Crackers come off the production line, workers must package them. They will encase them in a plastic wrapper. They will then place them in a cardboard box that has the manufacturer's name and nutritional information written on it.

The boxes of crackers must be packed into cartons and loaded onto delivery trucks. The destination of the trucks may be a large warehouse. The warehouse provides storage for the cartons until they are sold. Salespeople from Nabisco, the manufacturer of the crackers, will call on retail store owners to interest them in stocking Ritz Crackers in their stores. The warehouse ships the resulting orders to the various retailers buying the crackers.

Advertising occurs all along the line, from the Nabisco factory to the retail store, to bring the crackers to the consumer's attention. Nabisco may advertise in trade journals, in national consumer magazines, and on radio and television. Retail store owners may advertise in local newspapers.

Each of these activities—the printing, design, and making of the package; the packing operation; loading, shipping, and storage; selling; and advertising—is a marketing cost. Each one is a necessary step in Ritz Crackers' long journey to the customer.

In addition, the people or businesses performing these various marketing functions want to earn a profit for their efforts. This profit adds to the cost of manufacturing and marketing. Profit is necessary,

however, to improve goods and services and ways of marketing them.

Product Modifications

Another factor contributing to marketing costs is the customer's desire for more convenience and service. Consider green beans, for example. Locally grown green beans may be sold when in season with no extra processing. However, if customers want beans year round and live in areas where no beans are grown, fresh green beans must be shipped long distances in special trucks or train cars.

Customers may also want different varieties of beans. So, marketers make frozen green, wax, and lima beans available. Trimming, cleaning, cooking, canning, freezing, packaging, shipping, and storing each contribute to the cost of the final product.

The Human Factor

Some critics claim that marketing is inefficient compared with production. Although the cost of producing an article gets lower and lower because of

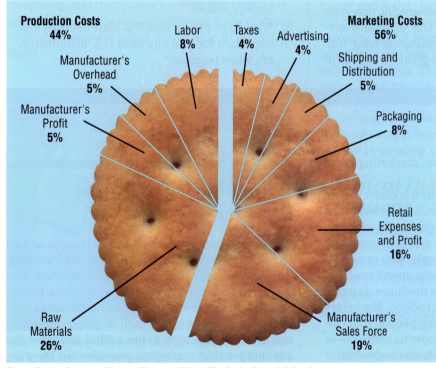

Source: David J. Rachman, *Marketing Today*, 2nd Edition (The Dryden Press, 1988), p. 9.

■ ■ ■ *Figure 4–2 Costs of Producing and Marketing Ritz Crackers*
Marketing costs make up about half the selling price of most items. Could most customers obtain this product without the costs of marketing? Why or why not?

The Domino Effect

"Domino's Pizza Delivers" is not just another advertising slogan. Founded in 1960, this retail chain guarantees delivery within 30 minutes or customers receive a $3 refund.

The idea for fast pizza delivery was the brainchild of Tom Monaghan. While an architecture student at Eastern Michigan University, Monaghan purchased a tiny Italian restaurant with $500 down on the nearby campus of Eastern Michigan University. He then started delivering pizza to college students. Less than a year later, he opened other stores near the University of Michigan and Central Michigan University.

Monaghan soon found himself in trouble. His expenses were too high, and his guarantee was too generous. His customers did not always pay their bills. His business was in debt.

Believing that his restaurant operation had little promise, Monaghan decided to specialize in home delivery. About the same time, he began to franchise his operation, selling his business expertise to others. Unfortunately, he soon found that he could not keep up with the demands of his franchises. A less savvy entrepreneur may have lost the business to his creditors, but Monaghan worked with his backers to refocus Domino's market, product, and operations.

By 1971, Monaghan was out of debt and rebuilding the Domino's Pizza chain. He continued to focus on free delivery but began targeting the residential market. To help insure customer loyalty, Domino's added a product guarantee and a $3 discount if the pizza was not delivered within 30 minutes. This marketing strategy seems to work. Domino's sells more than 275 million pizzas annually and accounts for 53 percent of all pizza delivered in the United States.

Continuously meeting this commitment to 30-minute pizza delivery requires a high degree of employee devotion. How does Domino's achieve this goal? One answer is its $5 million a year expenditure for a performance-based employee incentive program. Monaghan offers a variety of rewards to employees ranging from cash bonuses to vacations. Another popular incentive program is the Domino's Distribution Olympics that awards medals and prizes for excellence in job assignments such as dough making, driving, and vegetable slicing.

Since those early days, the company has grown to more than 5,000 outlets. Monaghan's goal is 10,000 outlets. To meet this goal, Domino's uses a little creativity. For example, in 1987 it added nautical delivery to its chain at the Lake of the Ozarks in Missouri. The outlet uses a fleet of ten 19-foot Bayliner boats. To help meet its deadlines, the outlet limits its deliveries to an 11-mile section of the resort lake. So far, only 3 percent of its deliveries are delayed. Most of the delays are due to mechanical problems or storms.

Despite its efficiency, some people criticize Domino's 30-minute pizza delivery guarantee. They feel that it encourages speeding and reckless driving. One city council in Lafayette, California, refused to license a Domino's franchise, citing the company's high rate of traffic accidents. In 1989, Domino's drivers were involved in about 100 accidents. In 1988, 20 people were killed in accidents involving Domino's vehicles.[1,2,3,4,5,6]

---

1. How did Tom Monaghan apply the marketing concept to his business?

2. Based on this case and on your own experience, describe Domino's marketing mix in terms of
   a. product;
   b. price;
   c. place; and
   d. promotion.

3. Compare Domino's marketing mix to that of a local pizza business in your area.

4. What aspects of the marketing mix might Domino's have to reconsider before going into business in Russia today?

5. What types of utility does marketing create for Domino's? Explain.

6. Is Domino's policy of guaranteeing delivery within 30 minutes a socially responsible one? Explain.

CASE NOTES

1. John Hilkirk, "Domino's Service No Game," *USA Today*, 21 July 1987, p. B-7.

2. "It's Anchovies Aweigh as Delivery Shoves Off," *Insight*, 20 July 1987, p. 43.

3. David M. Roth, "How Domino's Dominates," *Venture*, February 1988, p. 21.

4. Bernie Whalen, "People-Oriented Marketing Delivers a Lot of Dough for Domino's," *Marketing News*, 15 March 1984, p. 4.

5. "Domino Pizza to Stress Safety Over Speed," *Washington Post*, 18 December 1989, p. D4.

6. Chip Johnson, "Domino's Craps Out as a Suburb Refuses to Gamble on Safety," *The Wall Street Journal*, 4 September 1990, p. A3.

UNIT 2

The Consumer Market

Chapter 5

The Changing Consumer Market

Terms to Know

consumer market

consumer products

demographics

income

national income

personal income

disposable income

discretionary income

spending patterns

Chapter Objectives

After studying this chapter, you will be able to:

- describe the consumer market;
- describe demographic factors that affect marketing;
- explain why marketers study types of income; and
- describe factors that influence spending patterns.

Case Study

Kellogg Meets the Tastes of the Adult Market

In 1983 a prominent Wall Street analyst described the Kellogg company as "past its prime." At that time the Company had 36.7 percent of the market. Its primary consumers had been 80 million baby-boomers who had finally reached adulthood.

As this market aged, its tastes changed, too. Unfortunately for Kellogg, research revealed that adults didn't care much for many of its products. Let's face it, sugar-coated Froot-Loops just don't appeal to most adults!

Kellogg decided to address the adult market with the development of Mueslix, a nutritional cereal made of dense, crispy flakes mixed with dried fruit and nuts. Kellogg launched the product with a $33 million marketing budget, which was an industry record. TV commercials featured Swedish actor Max Von Sydow, who touted the cereal as a centuries-old balance of healthy ingredients.

Kellogg's success was clear. Sales of Mueslix ran close to $100 million annually. This was twice what Kellogg forecasted. Repeat purchases ran 25 percent higher than the average for new cereals. Loyal customers and new ones lifted Kellogg's profits 24 percent.

The company plans to continue producing new, high quality cereals for the U.S. market. In the early 1990s, adults from ages 25 to 49 ate 26 percent more cereal than in 1983. However, future projected growth will come from foreign markets. On the average, the people of Ireland, Australia, and Britain eat more cereal than Americans do.[1]

The Consumer Market

To fulfill their customers' needs and still make a profit, marketers must thoroughly understand the characteristics of their various markets. As you know from Chapter 1, a market is all the potential customers for a product. There are two primary types of markets: the consumer market, which we will look at in this chapter, and the industrial market, which we will look at in Chapter 9.

The **consumer market** is all the potential customers for goods and services sold for personal use. It includes people like you and your family: people who buy such things as clothes, wristwatches, auto insurance, food, notebook paper, dry-cleaning services and televisions for their own use and enjoyment. These are **consumer products**—goods and services intended to satisfy the needs and wants of the individual consumer.

The consumer market in the United States is tremendous. There are more than 250 million people in the United States, and the population is constantly growing. It is also constantly changing. For example, every year:

- people get jobs for the first time and begin to earn their own money;
- new consumer goods and services are introduced;
- thousands of individuals and families move to different parts of the country;
- the average earnings of the average person can increase or decrease with fluctuations in the economy; and
- thousands of people retire and completely change the patterns of their lives.

Statistics about population patterns such as age, gender, ethnic background, income, education, and occupation are called **demographics**. Demographic changes affect which products are developed and how products are marketed. For example, an increase in population could result in a greater demand for the development of certain goods and services. Or it could mean that existing products have to be marketed differently to reach a larger or a more diverse audience. Increases in average income could mean an increase in spending.

The three areas of change in the consumer market that most affect marketers are:

- the size and characteristics of the population;
- the amount of money people have available to spend; and
- the way people spend their money.

Thus, you can see why marketers seek data on population, income, and spending patterns. This information helps them develop and sell the goods and services that society needs and wants.

Population

The U.S. Census Bureau expects that more than 268 million people will be living in this country by the year 2000. In addition, the world population, which is increasing by a growth rate of 1.7 percent, is expected to reach 6 billion by 1998. This means the national and international consumer market will be larger than it is today.

By the turn of the century, the characteristics of the U.S. population also will have changed. Various groups within the population will increase or decrease. Such changes in the characteristics of the consumer market will present marketers with new challenges and new opportunities.

Size

Data from a 1992 Census projection report predict that if the U.S. birth and immigration rates and longevity continue to surge at the current 7.8

percent rate, the U.S. population will reach 383 million in 2050. Figure 5–1 gives a projected forecast for the U.S. population.

The birth rate in the United States rose from 1.8 children per woman (ultimate lifetime births per woman) in the 1980s to 2.1 in 1992. This resulted in a half million extra births in 1992. A number of these births were to married women in their 30s, many of whom are college-educated managers and professionals.[2] This is significant because these women who have delayed childbearing are more affluent and have more purchasing power in the children's market. While the current birth rate is projected to drop by 2000, the Census Bureau projects the share of population growth due to immigration will rise to 880,000 per year in 2050.

Life expectancy is also predicted to increase. The average person born in the United States today is expected to live to 82.1 years.[3] This means that the average person will be a part of the consumer market for a steadily increasing span of time. (See Table 5–1).

Characteristics

Think about your own neighborhood for a minute. If you have lived there for a number of years, you have probably noticed some changes. Perhaps the neighborhood used to be made up mainly of young couples and their children. Now the couples are older, their children are almost grown, and many new people have moved into the neighborhood.

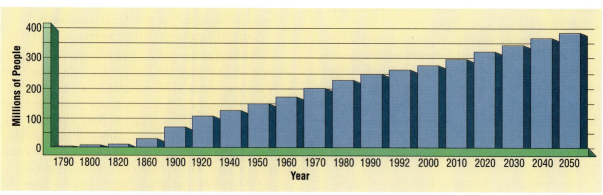

Source: *Population Projections of the United States*, The Census Bureau, December 1992.

■■■ *Figure 5–1 U.S. Population*
This graph projects the U.S. population growth through 2050. Why would this information be important to marketers?

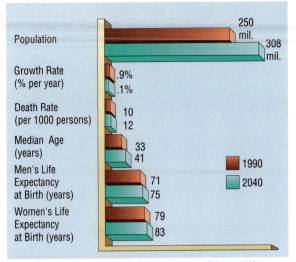

Source: Based on official U.S. Census Bureau projections, February 1989.

■■■   **Table 5–1 U.S. Population: 1990 and Projections for 2040**
Changes in population characteristics affect marketers. What marketing changes might you expect to see as a result of the rise in the median age of Americans?

Perhaps new apartment buildings or houses have been built or old ones have been torn down.

Such changes in the characteristics of the population are occurring throughout the nation. The changes that will probably most affect marketers in the next ten years are:

- the number of households, their size, and the number of household wage earners;
- the sizes of various age groups; and
- the geographic distribution of the population.

Households

A *household* is a social unit that consists of one or more people, who may or may not be related, living in the same dwelling place. A *family*, another important population measurement, consists of two or more related people living together.

The number of households in this country is increasing more rapidly than the size of the population. For example, between 1980 and 1990, the population grew by 10 percent while the number of households grew by 14 percent.

Information on the growth in households is important to marketers because the market for consumer goods and services—such as home

furnishings and electrical appliances—is more closely related to the number of households in the country than to the number of people. An increase in the number of households means an increase in sales opportunities.

Although the number of households is growing, the average size of a household is getting smaller. The number of households with married couples who have no children exceeds the number of households with married couples who have children. In one-fourth of U.S. households, people live alone. One way in which marketers have responded to the downsizing of households is by offering smaller size packages of food and household products.

Many households now include two or more wage earners. This means that adults are spending less time in the household. As a result, there is an increased demand for convenience products such as microwave dinners, day-care centers, and house-cleaning services. Marketers constantly assess such changing household characteristics to offer consumers products that match their needs.

Age Groups

For years young people dominated this country's culture and heavily influenced attitudes toward how products should be marketed. Now, slowly but surely, the age of the average American is creeping up from 33 years in 1990 to an expected 42 by the year 2030.

As shown in Figure 5–2 on page 60, almost one-third of the U.S. population is expected to be at least 55 by 2020. One major reason for this upward age swing is that people are living longer (mostly because of advances in medicine).

There are more people aged 65 and over in the population than there are teenagers. In 1992 the number of citizens over the age of 55 surpassed 52.6 million. Although the teenage population shrank to 23 million, it is expected to increase to 29 million by 2004.

This aging of the United State's population will result in profound marketing changes, a few of which can be seen already. For example, a recent national study of people 55 or older found that 80 percent of the respondents were dissatisfied with the way companies marketed goods and services to them. Seventy percent of the respondents said they found bottles and packages difficult to open. Sixty percent said the lettering on the labels was too small

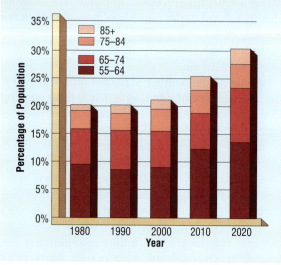

Source: U.S. Census Bureau

■■■ *Figure 5–2 Aging of America*
The average age of Americans is rising. What is one reason for this change?

to read. As a result of this research, marketers improved their packaging and labeling.

Geographic Distribution

In comparison to people in other countries, Americans move often and in great numbers. This trend is expected to continue. In general, the population has been moving away from the central part of the country and toward the southern and southwestern Sunbelt states. As a result, the population in these states is growing four times faster than the rest of the country.

Also, people are moving away from major cities to the suburbs and nonmetropolitan areas 75 to 100 miles outside the urban areas. Except for the Northeast and parts of the Midwest, our cities are still growing. But, for the first time in many years, they are growing less rapidly than the nonmetropolitan areas around them.

People are moving to all parts of the West and South. A recent Census report indicates that by 2010, California, Texas, and Florida will account for more than one-half of the total population growth in the United States. Wyoming is projected to have the lowest population. The most crowded states are still in the North and East. However, the majority of Americans live in the South and West.

Mobility—the ability of people to move from place to place—is significant to marketers. For example, the move from rural areas to the suburbs means a loss of customers for rural retailers and an increase in customers for suburban retailers. It may mean an increase or decrease in sales opportunities for those marketers whose goods have particular appeal in specific geographic regions.

Those people starting a business must know the potential market in a geographic area for goods and services. That is, they must know whether there are enough possible customers for the business to be profitable.

Income

To be a customer, a person must have money to spend. The money that a person receives or earns is usually called **income**. In marketing, income is divided into four types: *national, personal, disposable,* and *discretionary.*

National income is the money measurement of the annual flow of goods and services in a nation. National income consists of income such as employee earnings and corporate profits. **Personal income** is the amount of money that a person earns or receives before any taxes are deducted. **Disposable income** is the amount of money that people have for spending and saving. It is the money they have left after paying taxes. **Discretionary income** is the amount of money that people have left to spend as they choose after they have paid for the basic costs of living. Thus, discretionary income is disposable income minus the money spent for such necessities as food, shelter, clothing, transportation, and medical expenses. The word *discretion* means freedom to decide, so discretionary income is the part of a person's income that may be spent on anything a person wants.

In analyzing income, marketers must find answers to these three questions.

1. How much income do consumers have to spend?
2. Where is that income geographically located?
3. How is it distributed among the population?

Amount of Available Income

Marketers are interested in trends in disposable income and discretionary income. Both types of income determine how much money consumers have available to spend on goods and services (although, of course, they may put some of their income into savings or investments).

All marketers want to know how much disposable income consumers have and whether that amount is increasing. Disposable income is of special interest to the marketers who supply the necessities of life, such as food, housing, and clothing. The success of their businesses depends on how much disposable income people use to buy the goods or services that will satisfy their basic needs.

The average person has more disposable income than ever before. Per capita disposable income (amount of available disposable income per person) rose from $3,390 in 1970 to $22,400 in 1991. It is still rising.

Nearly every type of marketer is interested in trends in discretionary income. Discretionary income is spent on luxuries rather than on necessities. Therefore, marketers who make and sell so-called luxury goods, such as speed boats, jewelry, and video cameras, are especially interested in this type of income.

Although discretionary income is increasing, it has not increased as rapidly as disposable income did. A few goods and services that had been considered luxuries such as VCRs and microwaves were added to the necessities list. Many people do have considerable discretionary income. Even with rising inflation, this should mean more business for all types of marketers.

Location of Income

Information on income level in various geographical areas helps a marketer determine whether to try to sell in a particular area and what kind of marketing effort to use. Income levels can be figured for a large region, for a city, or even for a neighborhood. (See Figure 5–3.)

At present, some of the highest levels of income in the United States are found along the Atlantic Coast and in the Great Lakes region. However, great growth in income level is occurring in areas of the West and South because of growth in population, industry, and business.

In general, marketers use this information to target potential markets. A distributor of fine jewelry, for example, might advertise its best and most expensive lines to East and West Coast customers in major urban areas where discretionary income is higher. A home furnishings manufacturer might decide to start promoting a higher-price line in West Coast outlets.

Distribution of Income

Poverty is and will continue to be a serious problem in the United States. Today, experts predict that we are rapidly becoming a nation of rich and poor. More families are earning incomes that place them in the upper-income brackets. Conversely, more families find themselves in the low-income bracket.

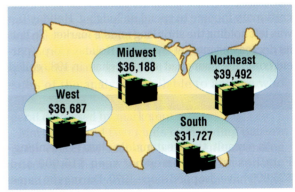

Source: *Statistical Abstract of the United States 1992*, p. 45.

■■■ **Figure 5–3 Median Family Income in 1990**
Disposable income varies according to the region of the country where you live. How might marketers use the information here?

	Middle Income ($20,000 to $25,000)		Highest Income ($50,000 and above)	
	Amount	Percent	Amount	Percent
Total Spending	$23,290	100	$48,718	100
Food	$ 3,545	15.2	$ 6,071	12.5
Housing	$ 7,051	30.3	$14,434	29.6
Transportation	$ 4,882	21.0	$ 9,158	18.8
Clothing, Services, and Personal Care	$ 1,356	5.8	$ 3,025	6.2
Health Care	$ 1,286	5.5	$ 1,550	3.2
Entertainment, Reading, and Education, etc.	$ 3,326	14.2	$ 8,351	17.1
Life Insurance	$ 256	1.1	$ 730	1.5
Social Security, Retirement, and Pensions	$ 1,588	6.8	$ 5,399	11.0

Source: *Statistical Abstract of the United States 1991.*

■■■ **Table 5-2 Household Spending by Income**
Shown here are the spending habits of middle-income and highest-income households. Which industry stands to benefit the most from these spending habits?

Spending Patterns by Income Levels

Reports from the Bureau of Labor Statistics show that higher-income households spend more money in all categories. This is not surprising, but the amounts spent are useful to marketers. Statistics also show the proportion of a household budget represented by each spending category. These proportions differ by income level, too.

Let's compare the spending habits of middle-income and highest-income households. Table 5–2 compares the amounts spent by those two groups in a year. Notice that the high-income household spent $7,383 more on housing, $4,276 more on transportation, $1,669 more on clothing and personal

services, and $5,025 more on entertainment, reading, and education.

Percentages show the part of each total budget represented by an amount. For instance, we see that the middle-income household spent $3,545 on food, which was 15.2 percent of all its spending. The high-income household spent $6,071 on food, but that was only 12.5 percent of its budget.

Government studies on consumer spending reveal several patterns:

- The proportion of the budget spent on food decreases as income rises.

- The proportion of the budget spent on housing (including home furnishings and utilities) decreases sharply from low to middle incomes but remains about the same across middle- and highest-income levels.

- The proportion of the budget spent on clothing and services is similar for low- and middle-income levels but higher for the high-income households.

- The proportion of the budget spent on transportation increases sharply from low to middle income but declines at the highest levels.

These patterns have little meaning to the owner of a small store, but they are useful to large retailers and manufacturers. A large retail chain, for example, can use the patterns to help determine the probable sales volume when opening a store in a new area. A large manufacturer can use them to help figure out how a shift in national income level is going to influence the general market demand for certain products.

Patterns in Product Demand

Consumer spending keeps on rising, with the largest amounts being spent on housing and food. How people divide the amount they spend changes from year to year. While every category of consumer spending is increasing, some are increasing more rapidly than others.

A major change in the amount spent on food is the rising amount spent on meals away from home—approximately 43 cents of every food dollar. This rapid rise reflects generally rising prices as well as trends such as more two-wage earner families and more one-person households.

Table 5–2 shows the following major categories of household spending:

- food, eaten both at home and away;
- housing, including home furnishings and household operations;
- transportation, including car purchase and operation;
- clothing, dry cleaning, and laundry;
- health care;
- entertainment, education, and reading material;

- personal life insurance; and
- retirement, pensions, and social security.

If these patterns persist and there is no leveling off in demand, they will mean important opportunities for marketers. They will mean good news to the housing, travel, and amusement industries; to retail stores; and to insurance companies.

Regular government surveys estimate family spending patterns. Results are based on information collected by the U.S. Bureau of Labor Statistics and the U.S. Bureau of the Census. Thousands of families participate in the data collection process. Some are interviewed, and some keep diaries of their spending.

Information in the survey is organized by family income, size, geographic location, age, sex, and type of employment. Because of the number of people taking part and the detailed information gathered, these survey results are used by marketers of all kinds of goods and services.

Marketers watch changes in the consumer market carefully to better serve the people who are buying their goods and services. The marketers who best adapt their operations to changes in demand usually win the major share of the consumer market.

CHAPTER NOTES

1. Patricia Sellers, "How King Kellogg Beat the Blahs," *Fortune*, 29 August 1988, pp. 54–64.

2. Joseph Spiers, "The Baby Boomlet Is for Real," *Fortune*, 10 February 1992, pp. 101–104.

3. "Census Bureau Lifts Population Forecast, Citing Fertility, Immigration, Longevity," *The Wall Street Journal*, 4 December 1992, p. B1.

4. John Helyar, "The Holiday Inns Trip: A Breeze for Decades, Bumpy Ride in the '80s," *The Wall Street Journal*, 11 February 1987, p. 1.

5. Joe Agnew, "Hotel Industry Focusing on High-quality Rooms," *The Marketing News*, 1 February 1988, p. 1.

6. Michele Manges, "Hotels Change Pitch to Businesswomen," *The Wall Street Journal*, 1988, p. B1.

7. Greg Foster, "Innkeeper to the World," *Brandweek*, 9 November 1992, p. 16–19.

8. "Wake-Up Call For the American Dream," *U.S. News & World Report*, 27 April 1992, p. 13.

Chapter Summary

- Marketers are most interested in three characteristics of the consumer market: the size and characteristics of the population; the amount of money people have available to spend; and the way people spend their money.

- Marketers study population patterns (demographics). Statistics on population size and its characteristics as related to households, age groups, and geography are all keys to market analysis.

- Income may be classified four ways: National, personal, disposable, and discretionary. In analyzing income, marketers must find answers to three questions: How much income do consumers have to spend? Where is the income located geographically? How is it distributed among the population?

- Spending patterns vary according to the amount of income earned.

Building Your Marketing Vocabulary

On a separate sheet of paper, define each of these marketing terms using your own words. Then write a 250-word paper on the consumer market using each term.

consumer market
consumer products
demographics
income
national income

personal income
disposable income
discretionary income
spending patterns

Questions for Review

1. Identify and describe three changes in population characteristics that will probably most affect marketers in this decade.

2. What do the marketers who supply the necessities of life want to know about disposable income?

3. Identify the marketers who are most interested in trends in discretionary income and explain why.

4. Name four sources that marketers use to get information on spending patterns.

5. Identify the three questions most marketers must ask when analyzing income.

6. Explain why spending patterns vary at different income levels. Give some examples.

7. Explain the importance of population mobility to marketers.

8. Identify six factors that cause changes in spending patterns.

9. Explain the impact that two-family incomes have had on redefining the U.S. middle class. Give examples of how retail stores in your community have reacted to those changes.

Critical Thinking

1. How might a marketer of cars respond to a growing lower-income population with a declining disposable income?

2. The growth rate in the United States is expected to drop from .9 percent in 1990 to .1 percent in 2040. What types of marketers will be affected by this drop? Why?

3. What type of demographic changes would be especially encouraging to a pool manufacturer?

4. What demographic change might cause sales to decline in general department stores and rise in discount department stores?

5. Why might grocery stores do equally well in both high- and low-income areas?

Discussion Questions

1. Select a business in your neighborhood and discuss how demographic changes in the consumer market would affect this business.

2. How could the business you selected in the first discussion question take advantage of a rise in the teenage population in your area?

3. What demographic changes would have a negative effect on the business you selected in the first question?

4. What changes could your selected business make in order to survive the negative demographic changes you listed in question 3?

5. What types of businesses in your area are least affected by changes in income levels? Why?

Marketing Project

Distinguish the Difference Between Disposable and Discretionary Income

Project Goal: Given a list of goods and services, determine whether it is a disposable or discretionary expenditure.

Directions: Determine whether the following items are a disposable or discretionary expenditure: food, housing, transportation, clothing and personal care, health care, entertainment, reading and education, insurance and pension, contributions, and miscellaneous services and materials.

Prepare a form like the one below. In the left columns, write the expenditures listed in the preceding paragraph. Then place a check mark in the appropriate column to indicate whether the expenditure is disposable or discretionary. (Note that an expenditure may be partly disposable and partly discretionary.)

Expenditure	Disposable	Discretionary
Contributions		✓

Applied Academics

Language Arts

1. Write a 250-word report that identifies five changes in the characteristics of the consumer market that are currently occurring. Explain how you feel these changes will present challenges and opportunities to marketers.

Math

2. If there are 250 million people in the United States and the population is expected to reach 268 million in 2000, by what percent will the population increase?

Science

3. Research then write a 250-word paper on the advances in science and technology that allow people to live longer and therefore contribute to the upward age swing in our society.

Social Studies

4. Examine the graph below. Discuss the changes that will take place in the age of our population between 1992 and 2000. How will these changes affect marketers?

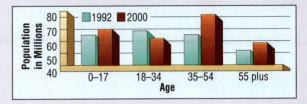

Marketing and Multiculturalism

Demographics show a tremendous change taking place in the African-American market. The African-American population increased 13 percent during the 1980s. The combined annual income rose to $270 billion, which is six times what it was during the 1970s. The percentage of African-American families in the United States with incomes over $50,000 rose from 10.9 percent in 1980 to 14.5 percent in 1990. In addition, demographics show that the African-American population will spend a greater percentage of its income on consumer products than the Caucasian population and will also venture money on new products.

1. How will these demographic changes affect marketers of clothing?

2. How might marketers use the information on income in developing products?

3. What might the information on spending behavior indicate to marketers?

4. What additional demographic information will aid marketers as they begin to focus on the growing market potential of the African-American population?

5. What affect will a growing multicultural consumer market have on marketers?

Market Segmentation

Chapter Objectives

After studying this chapter, you will be able to:

* describe the four types of variables used by marketers to segment a market;
* discuss the benefits of using demographics to segment a market by gender, education, occupation, and ethnic background;
* define and explain the importance of geographic segmentation;
* describe the information marketers use about potential customers' life-styles to segment a market;
* describe the behavioristic variables marketers use to segment a market; and
* tell why marketing segmentation has its limits and determine when it should be used.

Case Study

Targeting American Markets

Is your family knee-deep in direct-mail catalogs from companies such as L.L. Bean, Talbots, Burpee, Lands' End, or Lillian Vernon? Or does your household receive dozens of offers to visit vacation properties or to apply for VISA, MasterCard, or American Express cards? If so, the odds are that you and your family have been targeted to receive such mail based on your zip code.

Marketing research companies such as the Claritas Corporation supply zip code statistics to marketers. Claritas uses Census Bureau data and a host of other consumer surveys and public opinion polls to isolate even the most unusual customer or market profile.

Claritas devised life-style portraits of America's 250,000 neighborhoods (including 36,000 zip codes). Every neighborhood block was classified into one of 40 clusters. Clusters have descriptive names such as Blue Blood Estates, Middle America, Shotguns and Pickups, Bohemian Mix, and Tobacco Road.

The Tobacco Road cluster, for example, is composed of rural southern, low-income families. In contrast, the Blue Blood Estates cluster is made up of households of older couples, with no children at home, who are influential and come from old money backgrounds. Scarsdale, New York, is an example.

Armed with this information, corporations, political parties, and others can draw a portrait of residents in each cluster. Identification tells marketers where consumers work, how they spend their money, which cars they drive, what they read, what TV programs they watch, and even who they vote for.

Every community in America has a unique makeup. For instance, marketers know that Los Angeles is rich in Hispanics and many other ethnic groups. The city contains many Blue Blood Estates in areas such as Beverly Hills, and many Money and Brains neighborhoods in areas near the city's many universities and colleges where wealthy professionals and scholars prefer to live.

People from the above Los Angeles' neighborhoods are more likely than other people in the country to own a convertible, have a brokerage account, enjoy sailing, attend the theater, and drink imported wine at dinner. On the other hand, they have little interest in woodworking, driving a pickup, or buying from catalogs. By using market clusters, such as the one found in Los Angeles and in other cities, marketers can segment the population into groupings of individuals who are likely to make similar purchases.[1,2,3]

Market Segmentation

As you know from Chapter 4, the process of subdividing the market into segments (groups) according to customer needs and characteristics is market segmentation. Thinking in terms of market segmentation helps marketers sell more efficiently. Only when marketers identify and understand the various groups of possible customers can they tailor their offerings to meet the exact needs of one or all of these groups. For example, the automobile industry has grown to its present size and diversity because auto manufacturers recognize and try to meet the needs of the many different segments within the total auto market.

Let's take a look at the market for blue jeans. Instead of aiming at the total market for blue jeans, a manufacturer such as Lee divides the total market according to gender, age level, or intended use of the product. It offers heavy-duty jeans for work, casual jeans for sportswear, and brightly colored jeans for children. Thinking in terms of these market segments continues throughout the company's pricing, promotion, and distribution of a product.

Market segmentation is just as important to retailers and wholesalers as it is to manufacturers. For example, a department store and a discount store may offer the same television set. However, their ways of pricing (higher vs. lower), promoting (newspaper vs. TV), and distributing the television set may be very different because they are tailoring their

Regional Distribution

Every geographic change in the population produces at least one change in the consumer market. If you moved from the Northeast to the West Coast, there would be one less consumer in the Northeast and one more consumer on the West Coast. And because people in the Northeast buy more overcoats than do West Coast people, your moving away would mean a slight decrease in the size of the potential market demand for outerwear.

However, people on the West Coast tend to buy more barbecue equipment. So your move would mean a slight rise in the size of the potential market demand for barbecue equipment.

Some national magazines, such as *Newsweek* and *Time*, publish separate editions for different geographic market segments. These separate editions help advertisers such as barbecue manufacturers to aim messages at, say, the Western market segment and to avoid advertising in nonmarket areas.

Furthermore, makers of such consumer goods as coffee or cars are attaching new importance to regional marketing strategies. Companies such as

General Foods and the Campbell Soup Company are supplementing or replacing marketing to the entire market with custom-tailored approaches. These include not only specially targeted ads and promotions but also new products that cater to regional preferences.[14]

Statistical Reporting Areas

The federal government tracks population changes to ensure fair voter representation and to determine where its services are needed. A **statistical reporting area** is a geographic unit used to measure population characteristics. Data are collected for a number of statistical reporting areas: 23 major metropolitan regions, 78 major cities within these regions, and 257 smaller cities which stand alone. Figure 6–3 shows the population shift in major statistical reporting areas. Marketers use this valuable public information to get a detailed picture of the areas they serve.

A clear picture of an area can help a marketer anticipate shifts in demand and locate new business. For example, a health care corporation planning to open new hospitals will seek metropolitan areas that

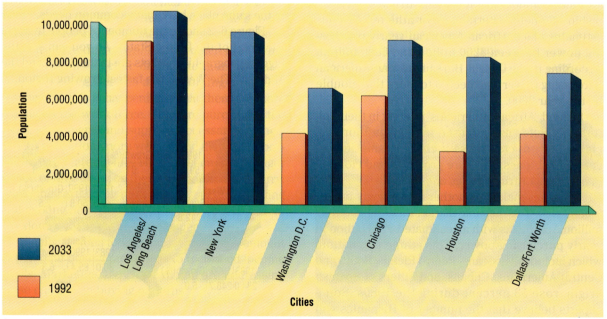

Source: *U.S. News & World Report.*

■ ■ ■   *Figure 6–3 Metropolitan Area Populations*
Statistical reporting areas such as these major metropolitan regions provide marketers with detailed information on population shifts in demand. Why is this information important to marketers?

have a strong population of people at a certain age and income. A shoe manufacturer planning shipments and promotions will take population changes into account when targeting areas according to past sales.

Although two reporting areas have the same number of people, one area may account for many more sales because of its population characteristics. For example, department stores want to locate in areas of population density since they must attract a large number of customers. They will also track the changes in their selling areas so that they can stock the right mix of products.

Psychographic Variables

Information about people such as their personality characteristics and life-style is called **psychographics**. When marketers segment a market according to **life-style**, they consider people's typical way of life. They take into account their family life cycle and the attitudes and values that determine their life-style.

Life Cycle

Part of an individual's life-style is determined by where that person is in the family life cycle, or stage of life. Marketers use life cycle information when segmentation by age and sex is not enough.

For example, families with children need to buy different kinds of products and household appliances than do people the same age living alone. A busy parent with small children, for example, may prefer to buy such things as catsup and mustard in squeeze bottles that are easy for kids to use. An adult with no children may prefer catsup and mustard from traditional jars.

The five major segments according to family life cycle are:

- young single people;
- young couples with no children;
- families with children at home;
- older couples with no children living at home; and
- older single people.

The buying needs of each of these groups vary from those of the others. By segmenting markets according to family life cycle, marketers can pinpoint possible customers more accurately.

For example, the manufacturers of children's furniture advertise to families with children at home through family-centered magazines. Retirement community developers, on the other hand, direct their marketing efforts to older couples and singles through mailings to retirement clubs.

Attitudes and Values of the Individual

Values or attitudes about what is important in life influence an individual's life-style. Over the past 35 years, people have changed their attitudes and values in several areas vital to marketers.

In the 1950s, the traditional nuclear family was the center of attention. The crowning achievement of most young people was to get married and raise children. Along the way the couple hoped to acquire a home, a car or two, and a host of other goods including appliances and home furnishings. In many cases, men worked outside the home; women worked in it.

Today, however, individual values and attitudes about personal priorities have changed. Fewer and fewer people are part of a traditional nuclear family. Both men and women work outside the home. Many people today are choosing not to have children. Many cannot afford homes or are choosing to

Chapter 7

Understanding Consumer Behavior

Terms to Know

behavior	psychological motive
buying behavior	rational buying motive
motive	emotional buying motive
buying motive	product motives
response	patronage motives
physical motive	direct mail

Chapter Objectives

After studying this chapter, you will be able to:

- explain the importance of understanding consumer behavior;
- discuss the stimulus-motive-response buying pattern;
- define and classify buying motives;
- name the internal and external influences on a person's decision to buy or not to buy; and
- explain the difficulty of understanding consumer motives and behaviors and suggest ways to help marketers better understand consumer behavior.

Case Study

Brysec Markets Biodegradable Diapers

Ken Dafoe originally advertised his product as the world's first biodegradable, disposable diaper. Brysec Company (originally known as Dafoe & Dafoe, Inc.), which is headquartered in Brantford, Ontario, targeted environmentally conscious parents. Its marketing activities emphasized the problems that conventional disposable diapers pose in landfills and their higher chemical content. The company placed ads in such upscale magazines as *Child*. The ads urged parents to "change the world one diaper at a time" (at a premium price).

Brysec used different approaches to target two customer segments. It marketed biodegradable diapers in upscale stores at upscale prices under the brand name of TenderCare Biodegradable. The company marketed TenderCare nationally, primarily through specialized mail-order houses. Regionally, TenderCare were marketed through specialty and natural food stores.

Brysec marketed a second, almost identical diaper, called Nappies, to cost-conscious customers. Nappies were distributed on the East Coast, through major grocery chains. They were priced at about $1 per box below brand-name products such as Pampers and Luvs, the diaper industry leaders. Yet, the price allowed retailers an above-average profit through a larger volume of sales.

Initially, the targeted audience responded enthusiastically. The product brought its distributor $500,000 in sales during its first two months on the market.

A third target for Dafoe's diaper products was an industrial segment: day-care centers. One of Dafoe's distributors provided Nappies at a wholesale price to day-care centers. The day-care centers, in turn, sold them to families and other day-care centers.

In 1991, Brysec Co. repositioned its disposable diaper, promoting it as chlorine-free and more earth friendly. This repositioning may have been in response to a possible court challenge which charged that Brysec's claim to having a completely biodegradable diaper could not be proven. According to the Federal Trade Commission's rule, a biodegradable product must "decompose into elements found in nature within a reasonably short period" after disposal. Some speculate that the company could not comply with the FTC's rule.

Other industry analysts conclude that Brysec dropped its biodegradable claim because environmental issues are no longer of utmost importance to diaper customers. According to their studies, today's diaper customers are not spending money on environmentally friendly products for their babies. Brysec was merely responding to its customers' buying motives and perceptions.[1,2,3]

Understanding Consumer Behavior

To market its products effectively, marketers have to understand how people make buying decisions and what motivates them to buy. For example, customers buy diapers for child cleanliness. But all diapers do this.

So, why would one customer segment insist on an upscale, biodegradable, disposable diaper and another segment prefer a similar but relatively inexpensive diaper? Why might another segment agree to purchase only cloth diapers? To answer these questions, marketers need to understand consumer behavior.

Market Information

As you know from Chapters 5 and 6, marketers can gather a great deal of information about the consumer market and market segments. For example, by looking at a particular geographic area, a marketer can learn:

A marketer benefits from trying to identify how much rational and emotional motives influence consumer behavior. It is certainly easier to determine which goods and services to offer customers if you know their buying motives.

Trying to determine these motives is always a challenge for marketers. This is especially true for salespeople who are trying to help customers find just the right products to meet their needs. The fact that not all customers are conscious of their reasons for buying particular goods or services further complicates the challenge of determining appropriate buying motives. What is a rational motive for one person may be considered an emotional motive by others, including salespeople.

Product and Patronage Motives

Product motives are based on the customer's choice of a particular product. They are usually influenced by a specific feature or characteristic of the product and are often based on the customer's experience with it.

Patronage motives are based on the customer's choice of a particular business. They are generally the result of a business's favorable image. Patronage buying motives may also be the result of helpful salespeople, a positive prior experience with the business, reputation for good service, a convenient location, and a reputation for having a good assortment of appropriately priced goods and services. (See "Where Consumers Buy" in Chapter 8.)

Consider a customer who wants to buy a particular brand of computer because two of her friends recommend it. She compares the price of the computer at a local discount store with the price of the same computer at a specialty store. Finding that the discount store sells the computer at the lower price, she buys it there. Hers is a product motive.

Another customer who needs a computer might visit his favorite department store and ask a salesperson to recommend a brand. He likes the store and the service he has received there in the past. He trusts the salesperson's judgment. His is a patronage motive. Many retailers compete on the basis of service and reputation because they cannot match the prices of mass merchandisers or discount outlets.

It is not unusual for a customer to make a buying decision based on both a product motive and a patronage motive. Suppose, for example, that you want to buy a pair of running shoes and you prefer Reebok. You know that a number of local stores carry Reebok, but you prefer shopping at a certain department store. Your motive for selecting Reebok running shoes is a product motive, but your motive for selecting the store is a patronage motive.

Buying Response: Action

When buying needs are realized through a stimulus and buying motives are aroused, action follows. The action starts as a mental process and ends when the purchase is made and the need is satisfied. The response, whether to buy or not to buy, is also influenced by the individual's personality and such group influences as family, friends, co-workers, and other reference groups. (See Figure 7–1.)

Marketers need to understand the mental processes associated with buyer behavior and the internal and external influences on one's decision to buy or not to buy. Once this is understood, marketers can develop and use appropriate marketing strategies to help customers make buying decisions.

The Mental Process of Decision Making

The mental decision-making process that people go through when buying goods and services involves perceiving, remembering, thinking, and judging. For example, Sally Schultz is shopping for a video recorder. She *perceives* the product she wants by looking at various catalogs, magazines, and store displays. She *remembers* the brand names and dealers that have good reputations. She *thinks* about the product features and the dealer services. Finally, she *judges* that one brand and one dealer will best satisfy her needs. She then makes the purchase.

How large a part these mental processes play in a buying decision varies according to the sales situation. When a person buys an expensive or important product, such as a large stock investment, a house, or a computer, he or she will spend considerable time on the mental processes before reaching a final decision. However, when making a

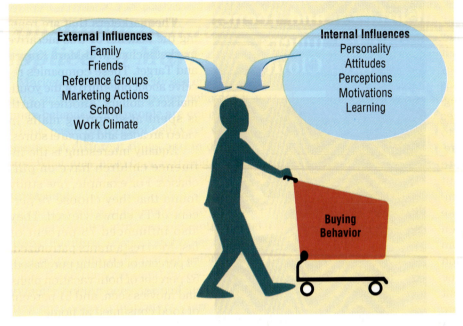

External Influences
Family
Friends
Reference Groups
Marketing Actions
School
Work Climate

Internal Influences
Personality
Attitudes
Perceptions
Motivations
Learning

Buying
Behavior

■ ■ ■   *Figure 7–1 Buying Behavior Influences*
There are many influences on buying behavior. What are the major influences on you? on your friends and family?

routine purchase, such as toothpaste, a person will spend a minimum of time thinking about the product before buying.

Internal Influences on Buyer Behavior

Internal influences affect the amount of time and mental effort people devote to buying decisions. People have different motivations. What is exciting for one person may be boring for another. People also learn differently. Some are slow learners, some are fast. Some remember what they are taught, and some don't.

People's unique personalities also tend to affect their buying decisions. For example, generally happy people tend to wear bright, colorful clothing; more serious people tend to wear grays and blacks. Assertive and aggressive types tend to buy sports cars; more conservative people tend to stick with sedans.

Perception is another factor that influences buyer behavior. Every consumer perceives a marketing strategy differently.

Consider two consumers: Luis is in New York City on a budget vacation. He is from a small town. Sarah is on a business trip in New York City from Los Angeles. She has a company expense account. Sarah and her company do not mind paying $160 a night for a hotel room. Luis thinks $160 a night is too

much. The difference in their price perception may be caused by how much money each has at the time or by each person's prior hotel experiences.

Attitude also influences individual buying behavior. We all have positive or negative feelings toward things. When you respond that you like or dislike a certain firm or product, you reveal your attitude toward these things. Suppose that a local survey showed that people tend to distrust large stores or shopping centers. Small retailers might reinforce this attitude by stressing the homey, personal service in their shops. The large department stores might respond by advertising their employees as neighborly salespeople who can offer great service. Marketers try to reinforce positive attitudes and change negative attitudes by altering their products.

External Influences on Buyer Behavior

A number of external influences affect buying decisions. These include people—family, friends, and acquaintances—and the surroundings in which the potential customer moves.

The effect of a person's family on his or her buying behavior can readily be seen when you look at shoppers in various buying situations. Each family member often plays a part. Studies consistently

The Sweet Scent of Success

A men's cologne called Drakkar Noir is giving Ralph Lauren and Calvin Klein a run for their money. This European import has become one of the top-selling men's department store fragrances.

Drakkar (pronounced DRACK-car) Noir was launched in the United States in 1986 by Cosmair. By 1990, Drakkar ranked third among the top men's department store fragrances, behind Ralph Lauren's Polo and Calvin Klein's Obsession for Men. In some stores, such as Marshall Field's in Chicago, it is the number-one selling men's fragrance. Even such exotic new introductions as Klein's Eternity, Lauren's Safari, and Burberry's for Men have failed to affect Drakkar Noir's sales.

The cologne is targeted at 18- to 24-year-old, sports-conscious men who see themselves as macho. "Its woody fragrance," says fragrance economist William Fitzgerald, "happens to be a combination of smells that men like."

New and related products were developed. Cosmair introduced a one-ounce eau de toilette splash, a deodorant, an aftershave, a shaving foam, and a Conditioning Sport Tonic. Says Laura Lee Miller, vice president of marketing, "…we're dealing with a different man in the Nineties than we were in the Eighties. We're reaching an audience that has a different sensibility."

Retailers originally called it a word-of-nose success. "Men are smelling it in locker rooms and then buying it," says Marshall Field's John Stabenau. And now, with added product and promotion, Cosmair's Miller says, "Drakkar can really entrench itself and fortify its position in the marketplace." [1, 2, 3]

1. Name one buying motive for Drakkar by (a) teenage men, (b) male college athletes, and (c) young women.

2. Discuss the stimulus that Cosmair uses to motivate consumers to buy Drakkar Noir.

3. Describe the target consumer market for Drakkar Noir. Make a general statement about the market segment to whom Cosmair is promoting its Drakkar items.

4. Identify various marketing strategies used by the fragrance company to help influence consumer decision making. Relate these to the five stages in the consumer decision-making process.

5. There is much competition today in the men's fragrance market. Check current periodicals or newspapers. *Women's Wear Daily* is an excellent source for information on men's fragrance. How is Drakkar Noir doing competitively today? What do you see as some factors that have caused it to advance or decline in the marketplace?

Since the introduction of Drakkar, Cosmair has experimented successfully with a number of marketing activities to promote it. During the 1980s, Cosmair's promotions consisted primarily of TV commercials and in-store events. It also ran elaborate promotions and contests offering sports cars, ski trips, and motor scooters as prizes.

In the 1990s, Cosmair switched its marketing strategies in response to a shifting economy and changing target market. It used extensive gift-with-purchase promotions and increased the number of free samples it gave out. It broadened its advertising considerably. TV ads were updated to target its youth market. Mail samples were distributed to retailers. Print ads appeared in *Gentlemen's Quarterly*, *Esquire*, *Rolling Stone*, *Playboy*, *Vanity Fair*, and *Sports Illustrated*. In addition, more than 1 million scented strips were placed in editions of *Gentlemen's Quarterly*.

CASE NOTES

1. "Drakkar Noir's New Tactics," *Women's Wear Daily*, 3 January 1992, p. 10.
2. "Drakkar Noir Updates for a Younger Crowd," *Women's Wear Daily*, 17 April 1992, p. S10.
3. Elizabeth Sporkin, "This Men's Cologne Smells of Success," *USA Today*, 18 April 1989, p. Dl.

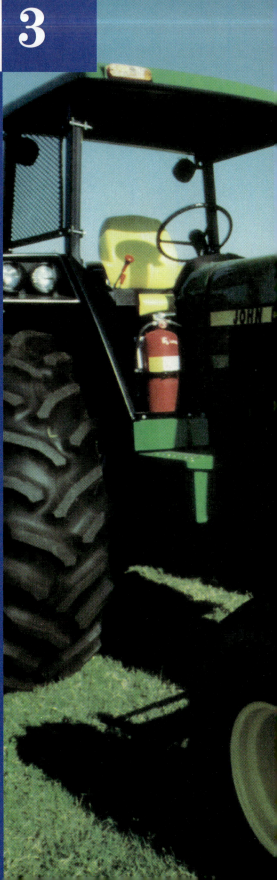

UNIT 3

Special Markets

Chapter 9

Industrial and Agricultural Markets

Terms to Know

industrial market

industrial goods

industrial services

derived demand

intermediaries

raw materials

process materials

component parts

installations

manufacturers' agent

distributor

consumer farm products

industrial farm products

Chapter Objectives

After studying this chapter, you will be able to:

* compare and contrast the marketing of consumer and industrial goods;
* describe the six segments of the industrial market;
* classify and describe industrial goods and services;
* discuss how the marketing of industrial goods differs from the marketing of consumer goods;
* describe the motivations of industrial buyers;
* tell how farm products are marketed to industrial users and final consumers;
* identify the marketing services involved with handling farm products; and
* discuss how cooperatives aid farms.

Case Study

Marketing to the "Y"

Larry Scramlin is proud of the new Limestone Family YMCA, which serves several counties in southern Ohio and northern Kentucky. As its executive director, Scramlin has seen the "Y" grow to more than 4,000 members in less than a year. Young and old alike keep fit and socially active through its many programs.

Larry gladly gives visitors a walking tour of the Limestone Family YMCA facility. As he and the guests go around the jogging track on the second floor, he points to the air conditioning units on the roof. He explains that the Carrier-Bryant units are zoned so that different areas of the building can be cooled at his discretion. This saves energy and, in turn, cuts down the utility expenses.

Downstairs in the workout room, there is equipment galore—for cardiovascular exercise including treadmills and exer-cycles. Patrons build, strengthen, and tone their bodies with Nautilus equipment.

At the swimming pool there are water pumps, vacuum machines, and diving boards. A water cooler and a snack food dispenser provide quick refreshment.

All this equipment installed by the building contractor or by concessionaires is collectively called industrial equipment. They are sold to businesses such as the YMCA to provide services to the public.

The Market for Industrial Products

The customers in our economy can be grouped into two basic markets: the consumer market (which you explored in Unit 2) and the industrial market. The **industrial market** includes all the potential customers for goods and services used in the production of other products, for use by organizations or businesses in daily operations, or for resale.

The customers in the industrial market are businesses such as manufacturers, contractors, farms, and institutions. Businesses buy raw materials, vehicles, equipment, furniture, and stationery, among many other items. These are **industrial goods**—tangible products bought by firms or organizations for business use rather than for personal use.

Many businesses also buy such services as consulting services, mail service, and insurance. These are **industrial services**—services intended to satisfy the needs and wants of businesses or organizations by supporting business activities.

Some industrial goods and services cross over into the consumer market, depending on who buys them. For example, if a company buys a desk for an office, it is being sold to the industrial market. If you buy the same desk for your home, it is being sold to the consumer market.

So the demand for industrial products depends on the demand for consumer products. For example, if consumers are not buying automobiles (consumer goods), the demand for steel (industrial goods) drops. If customers are not buying stoves, refrigerators, and washing machines, the demand for steel slides further. And if customers are not buying new stereos, sporting goods, or clothing, the industrial demand for steel falls still further.

Stereos, sporting goods, and clothing are not all made of steel. However, the machinery and tools used in producing them are. Since the demand for industrial goods is derived (comes) from the demand for consumer goods, this demand is a **derived demand**. Derived demand is an unique feature of the industrial market.

Industrial Market Segments

Six major segments make up the industrial market:

- extractors;
- manufacturers and contractors;
- service organizations;
- institutions and nonprofit organizations;
- federal, state, and local governments; and
- intermediaries, including retailers.

Extractors are companies involved in mining ores, drilling for oil, and taking seafood from the rivers and oceans. Farmers are technically extractors, because they extract food and lumber from the earth. However, farmers form a special market segment that you will explore later in this chapter.

Manufacturers are engaged in processing materials—for example, turning crude oil into gasoline—and in making products for use by the consumer or by businesses. There are more than 358,000 manufacturing firms in the United States. They process such materials as hides, food, rubber, or ores. They make such products as machinery, musical instruments, computers, and transportation equipment. To process materials, they need equipment, supplies, and services.

Service organizations include airlines, banks, insurance companies, beauty salons, restaurants, hotels, and consulting firms. To conduct business, they also need equipment, supplies, and services. A movie theater, for example, buys film projectors, carpeting, and restroom equipment. A hotel buys laundry service, furniture, television sets, and stationery.

Institutions and nonprofit organizations, such as hospitals and schools, also buy equipment and supplies. Like hotels, hospitals need laundry service and furniture. Of course, they also need medicine, food, and surgical supplies. Schools are a significant market for textbooks, desks, and classroom equipment. We will take a more extensive look at these two markets in Chapters 10 and 11.

The federal government is the largest single customer in the industrial market. Its various departments and agencies buy airplanes, automobiles, furniture, computer equipment, uniforms, construction materials, cleaning services, and hundreds of other goods and services. State and local governments buy products such as highway construction materials, computers, park benches, and snowplows. We will look at government markets in Chapter 10.

■■■ *Which of the six major segments of the industrial market does this oil drilling company belong to?*

Intermediaries are business organizations that perform buying and selling services which aid the flow of products from the producer to the customer. Wholesalers and retailers are examples of intermediaries. Intermediaries also need supplies, equipment, and services.

Industrial Goods

Businesses buy industrial products for direct or indirect use in producing other products or in operating a business. Industrial goods are divided into four categories:

- materials;
- installations;
- accessory equipment; and
- operating supplies.

Materials become a permanent part of the finished product. Installations, accessory equipment, and operating supplies are necessary to manufacture the product and to conduct business. Let's take a closer look at each of these.

Materials

Manufacturers construct their finished products from three basic materials. These are raw materials, process materials, and component parts.

Raw materials are goods that are more or less in their original form and that need processing to become useful goods. Examples of raw materials include wheat from the field, sand from the quarry, trees from the forest, iron ore from the mine, and fish from the sea or fish farm.

Raw materials used in manufacturing the finished product are called **process materials**. Examples include cloth that is made into a coat and milk that is turned into cheese.

Component parts are similar to process materials except that they keep their original form throughout the manufacturing process. For instance, component parts such as tires, spark plugs, and batteries are used to make cars. These parts are easily recognizable in the final product—the car.

Installations

Installations include the buildings and major equipment used to produce goods or render services. In manufacturing or processing plants, equipment is the machinery used to produce the finished product. For example, robots are now common equipment in most modern factories. Many robots are machine tools with movable arms which can be programmed to weld, paint, load machines, and rivet.

In a service organization, buildings and equipment are required to produce the service; equipment is also directly involved in that service. For example, beds and televisions are equipment in a motel. Hair dryers are equipment in a hair salon. Gas pumps are equipment in an auto service station.

Type of goods	Examples
Materials	
Raw Materials	iron ore, lumber, oats, corn, soybeans, cotton, and crude oil
Process Materials	lime in cement, stamped auto parts, baking powder in baked goods, tannic acid in leather production, and oil in paint
Component Parts	cummins engines in trucks, Delco batteries in cars, and G.E. fluorescent tubes in light fixtures
Accessory Equipment	computers, forklifts, power saws, and display cases for stores
Installations	cummins engines in trucks, Caterpillar tractors for contractors, Westinghouse generators for power stations, and Jeep trucks for U.S. Postal Service
Operating Supplies	repair parts, dust cloths, lubricants, typing paper, cleaning agents, brooms, and diesel fuel

■■■ *Table 9–1 Industrial Goods*
Industrial goods can be divided into four types. Which type comes from raw materials and is used to manufacture the finished product?

Accessory Equipment

Equipment that is needed to operate a business but which is not used in manufacturing a product or providing a company's main service, is *accessory equipment*. Examples of accessory equipment include forklifts used in warehousing activities, telephones, office computers, and hand tools used to build display cases and displays.

Operating Supplies

Items necessary for the operation of a business are *operating supplies*. Such supplies are usually low in unit cost. Operating supplies in a hotel, for example, include furniture polish, scouring powder, rug cleaner, and floor wax. Examples of operating supplies used by all types of businesses and organizations include stationery, paper towels, computer disks, printer ribbons, and paper clips. (See Table 9–1.)

Industrial Services

A number of services are sold to the industrial market. Among the more common ones are consulting services, protection services, and maintenance services.

Often a business needs expert advice but does not want to pay the cost of adding an expert to its permanent staff. In such a case, the firm can hire a consultant. For a fee, the consultant agrees to do a certain amount of work for the firm.

For example, the firm may want a consulting architect to research the cost and feasibility of adding a new wing to a processing plant. Or a retail store may hire a visual display consultant to help it design holiday windows. In both cases, the consultant does the job, collects the fee, and moves on to the next client.

Many factories, offices, and stores need to provide security. Their security guards may be full-time staff members, or they may work for a security service that supplies trained guards to businesses that request them.

At one time most businesses hired their own maintenance workers. But an increasing number of businesses now contract for maintenance services.

More and more companies are coming to prefer hiring the services of specialists. As a result, industrial service firms are increasing in number and size.

■■■ *Businesses purchase industrial services so they can focus their efforts on what they do best. How does a buyer save money by hiring an industrial service?*

Marketing Industrial Products

Many of the same techniques are used to market both consumer goods and industrial goods. However, the industrial consumer's needs differ from the average consumer's. Buyers of industrial products have a more complex buying process than buyers of consumer products usually do. They buy farther ahead, apply more rigid specifications, and use more formal cost analysis than do most consumers.

The marketing of consumer goods and the marketing of industrial goods differ in two major categories. These include the promotional methods used by industrial sellers (often called suppliers) and the buying motives and procedures of industrial customers. Let's take a look at these two factors.

Promoting and Selling

Promoting and selling to the industrial market differs from promoting and selling to the consumer market in four ways.

1. The number of buyers of industrial products is smaller by far than the number of buyers of consumer products. Therefore, industrial marketers place greater promotional emphasis on personal selling than do marketers of consumer products. Because there are fewer industrial buyers, salespeople are able to establish a more personal relationship with each industrial buyer than is possible with the consumer market.

Global
MARKETPLACE

Would You Ignore 95 Percent of the World's Market?

Some companies want to wait and see if foreign markets are lucrative and secure. Not Loctite. The Connecticut-based industrial adhesives company has taken a "stick your neck out" approach in more than 80 countries. The payoff? Nearly 60 percent of the $561 million in 1991 sales came from overseas. Loctite's philosophy: why ignore 95 percent of the world's market?

2. Industrial purchases are larger and involve more money than most consumer purchases. Therefore, industrial marketers must assure buyers that they are a reliable source for products and can supply the quantity and quality of products desired at the prices specified.

3. The responsibility for industrial buying is often shared by several people. Therefore the industrial marketer must learn who is involved in each buying situation before deciding on how to promote the product. For example, if it is a group of people making the buying decision, a group presentation may be the most effective sales approach.

4. The industrial buyer is often a specialist in technical knowledge—that is, in information about design, operation, or maintenance of the product. Therefore, in order to be effective, industrial marketers must be specialists in their fields. Industrial salespeople must be knowledgeable and well-trained.

Buying Motives

An industrial buyer bases buying decisions on the company's need to make a profit. Emotional appeals may affect a consumer. But they have only a slight influence on the industrial buyer who always needs to get the most suitable materials at the lowest price. Factors that the industrial buyer considers before making a purchase for the company are quality, reputation of the supplier, product efficiency, customer service, and price.

Quality

The industrial buyer does not always buy the best possible grade of product. Instead, he or she chooses a quality suited to the company's use of the product.

For example, a buyer for a manufacturer of men's shirts looks for inexpensive but durable fabric to be turned into moderately priced shirts. The sales representative must be able to describe the fabric in technical terms and tell why it is best suited to the manufacturer's use.

Reputation of the Supplier

Alert industrial buyers are looking for suppliers with integrity who will deliver what they promised. They look for suppliers with reputations for reliability and who delivers on time.

Production Efficiency

One of the best ways for a manufacturer to meet market demand is to increase productivity. This means buying the most efficient installations and accessory equipment available.

Customer Service

Many companies offer a similar product. In this case, an industrial buyer is likely to choose the supplier who offers the most valuable customer services. These might include repair and maintenance work or technical assistance. It may include making adjustments or handling returns.

Price

Two firms may offer products of identical grade, backed up by similar service, delivery guarantees, and reputation. In that case, the buyer's decision will nearly always favor the lower priced product.

As you can see, industrial buyers benefit from the same utilities of marketing we studied in Chapter 4—time utility, place utility, possession utility, and information utility. An industrial buyer tries to secure the right product, raw material, or service at the right time to meet production or service demands. The buyer also seeks the product with the lowest price that meets quality demands.

Buying Sources

Once an industrial buyer decides what to buy, the next step is to find the best sources for materials, equipment, and operating supplies. This often requires a good deal of research. Once the industrial buyer establishes the best sources of supply, materials are purchased in three ways:

- buying directly from manufacturers;
- buying from a manufacturers' agent; and
- buying from distributors.

Buying Directly from Manufacturers

Industrial buyers may place orders with a sales representative in person. They may also place an order by telephone or fax, or order by mail.

Buyers prefer direct buying from the manufacturer when the manufacturer can ensure prompt service. Many manufacturers send their customers industrial catalogs that range from short lists to huge books. They contain illustrations, detailed descriptions of the items offered, price information, and order forms.

Buying from a Manufacturers' Agent

A **manufacturers' agent** is an independent representative who sells part or all of the output of one or more manufacturers within a sales territory. The agent is paid a commission based on sales. The agent does not take title (possession) of the industrial goods and usually does not physically handle them. Agents often give industrial customers useful technical information about the goods and the market.

Buying from Distributors

A **distributor** is an independent intermediary who stocks the products of various manufacturers and sells them to industrial users. Some distributors buy from independent agents who supply technical and market support in specialized fields. There are four advantages to buying from a distributor.

1. A distributor often handles many different manufacturers' lines of goods. For a buyer who purchases goods from several of these lines, the purchasing task is simplified because the buyer only needs to place one order with the distributor.

2. A distributor is usually located closer to the industrial user than to a manufacturer. So, the distributor can offer the buyer quick delivery service.

3. The distributor, a local businessperson, makes a point of knowing the buyer's needs and can offer a variety of products geared to those needs.

4. A distributor will locate hard-to-find equipment and supplies, thus saving the buyer both time and effort.

Marketing Agricultural Products

Bill Mers, a farmer in Mason County, Kentucky, raises Holstein heifers, tobacco, hay, and vegetables. He buys feed and fertilizer from farm cooperatives. He buys petroleum products to keep his truck and tractors running. He depends on stockyards to market his cattle and truckers to deliver them. His efficient operation relies on marketing businesses that distribute his products and make agricultural goods and services available to him.

But marketing associated with producing agriculture is only a part of agricultural marketing. Agribusinesses such as florists, nurseries, farm equipment manufacturers, feed and seed stores, orchards, and many more are also a part of agricultural marketing, too.

Farm products are familiar to everyone. You buy meat, eggs, and milk at your local store. You may buy fresh tomatoes, apples, lettuce, or corn at a roadside stand. Products such as these that reach the consumer without undergoing major changes in form are **consumer farm products**. About 20 percent of all farm products reach the consumer without undergoing a major change in form.

On the other hand, products that reach the consumer having undergone a major change in form are **industrial farm products**. The consumer rarely sees them in their original form. During the manufacturing process, they become a part of another product. For instance, tomatoes become part of spaghetti sauce. The wool from sheep is dyed, spun, and woven into cloth.

■ ■ ■   *This farm produces apples which it sells at a roadside stand. Does this farm market a consumer or an industrial farm product?*

About 80 percent of all farm products are industrial farm products. More than $100 billion in farm products is sold in the United States each year.

Classification of Agricultural Products

Most farmers are producing products for sale rather than for home use. Their products can be classified as crops or livestock.

Some common crops include grain, flowers, vegetables, and cotton. Livestock includes live animals such as calves and cattle, chickens, turkeys, hogs, and sheep. Some typical livestock products are hides, eggs, bacon, and wool.

Marketing Services for Agricultural Products

Farm products are often more expensive to market than other industrial products. For example, the cost of marketing a bus may add up to 30 percent of the selling price. The cost of marketing a head of lettuce may add up to as much as 60 percent of the selling price. The main reason for the difference is that, like many farm products, the lettuce must be packaged to prevent bruising, refrigerated against spoilage during shipment, and displayed in a refrigerated case until purchased.

Marketing functions that are essential in handling farm products are transporting, storing, and grading and standardizing. Each service not only adds to the final cost but also adds to the value of the product. (See Table 9–2.)

Item	1970 (in billions of dollars)	1980 (in billions of dollars)	1989 (in billions of dollars)
Total Consumer Expenditures for Farm Foods	110.6	264.4	423.4
Farm Value	35.5	81.7	103.0
Marketing Bill	75.1	182.7	320.4

Source: *Statistical Abstract of the United States 1991*, p. 658.

■ ■ ■   **Table 9–2 Civilian Consumer Expenditures for Farm Foods**
This table shows the total amount consumers spent on farm food, and how much consumers actually spent for the value of farm products and for marketing costs. What are three marketing services that consumers are paying for?

Principles into Practice

Japanese Go Nuts for Blue Diamond Almonds

How about a bag of dried baby sardines and slivered almonds with your lunch? While that may not sound appealing to American youth, Japanese students cannot get enough of it. In fact, the snack combination, called Calmond, has become so popular in Japan that the entire harvest of sardines was depleted one year to meet the demand.

Blue Diamond Almond Growers, a California-based farm cooperative, developed Calmond. It aimed to meet the need for calcium among schoolchildren in Japan where dairy products are scarce. The cooperative markets the product to the national school lunch program. The program feeds 98 percent of Japan's elementary students.

Thirty years ago almonds were an unknown product in Japan. Today, Japanese food manufacturers develop more than 100 almond-food products each year, including items such as almond tofu, almond rice crackers, and soy-flavored almonds. The products are meant to appeal to Japanese tastes and traditions, and have created a demand for almonds in that country. Japan

has become the second leading export market for California almonds. In one recent year, Japan bought 48 million pounds of almonds valued at more than $60 million.

Blue Diamond Almonds has designed ads and promotions to specifically target this market. The cooperative also employs 60 Japanese nationals in Japan to develop product and marketing strategies. Says Rex Lake, Blue Diamond's sales manager for Asia and the Pacific Rim, it's "a new phenomenon, a marketing opportunity presented by Japanese consumers."[1,2]

1. When might almonds be considered consumer farm products? When might they be considered industrial farm products?

2. What motives might buyers at the Japanese schools have to use the Blue Diamond cooperative as a supplier?

3. Why do you think Blue Diamond employs Japanese product and market analysts?

Transporting

Farm products go through several steps on their way from farmer to the consumer or to the industrial user. Each step involves transportation.

Farmers usually take their crops and livestock to the local market by truck. Here they sell their products to an intermediary who operates the market. The intermediary, in turn, transports products to the central market which may buy the products, store them, and arrange to resell or trade them. Central markets are often located in key cities. Chicago, for example, is a central livestock market.

As you can imagine, different goods require different transportation methods. For example, perishable goods such as dairy products need to arrive quickly at their destination. Thus, they are shipped by a bulk carrier, such as a refrigerated rail car or a trailer truck. Less perishable goods, such as cotton and grain, can be transported on ships and barges. These are the cheapest (and slowest) forms of freight transportation.

Storing

Most farm products are seasonal. Thus, storage is a vital marketing service.

In the days when transportation and storage facilities were poor, perishable, seasonal items such as peaches, strawberries, and grapefruit seldom reached a large market. Today, these products are either frozen and then stored in commercial freezers for use throughout the year, or imported from warmer climates. Less perishable products, such as cotton or wheat, are stored in local or central warehouses until the market price is most favorable for their sale.

Grading and Standardizing

Grading and standardizing are services provided by intermediaries such as grain elevators and produce wholesalers, or by farm cooperatives. *Grading* is the act of sorting goods into categories according to specifications. For example, grain is graded No. 1, No. 2, etc., according to the foreign matter it contains, such as cracked grains, dirt, or weed seeds. The heavier, drier, and cleaner grain is No. 1. Lighter-weight grain with more moisture, dirt, or weed seeds is No. 2.

Certain products are rated according to defined qualities called standards. *Standardizing* is the act of classifying goods and ensuring the presence of these stated qualities.

For example, in the case of purebred cattle such as Hereford, each animal must meet standards ensuring pure blood lines. Records are kept on the cattle's background and breeding. Purebred cattle are sold with papers stating that bloodline standards have been protected.

Grading and standardizing allow a buyer to easily know the quality of a farm product. Consider cotton, for example. There are roughly 1,500 varieties of cotton. Grading makes it possible for the textile company to get the same type and texture of cotton with each purchase.

Farm Cooperatives

Sometimes farmers band together to process and market their products. This type of association is a *farm cooperative*. A cooperative may replace the local market. It may even compete on a larger scale with central markets such as the Chicago or Kansas City livestock markets. Familiar trademarks such as Sunkist, Land-O-Lakes, Ocean Spray, and Welch's appear on products sold through cooperatives.

The primary purpose of the farm cooperative is to improve members' profits. To do so, a cooperative uses five marketing techniques.

1. *Marketing at the Proper Time.* The cooperative may withhold a portion of each season's harvest and wait for the best time to sell the products.

2. *Stimulating Demand.* The cooperative advertises its members' products and may try to develop its own brand name. For example, FS (Farm Supply) is a popular brand name for gasoline, oil, feeds, and small equipment sold through farm cooperatives. Sunkist is a brand name used by fruit producers to identify oranges sold through their cooperative.

3. *Processing the Products.* A cooperative may process farm products for its members. For example, it may process cheese, package it, and then sell it under its own brand.

4. *Using Bargaining Power.* Single farmers have limited bargaining power. Often, they must take the price offered by a single buyer. The cooperative can bargain with many buyers because it has a sales staff. It can also offer buyers greater quantity and variety of products than any single farmer could offer. These give the cooperative more bargaining power.

5. *Improving Grading and Standardization.* People who buy farm products want to be assured of uniform quality. Customers are more likely to buy a certain brand of canned peaches if they know that they will get good peaches with every purchase. A bad experience makes customers switch to another brand. The cooperative helps assure continued customer loyalty of uniform quality through grading and standardization.

CHAPTER NOTES

1. Blue Diamond Growers Press Kit, 1992.
2. Maria L. LaGanga, "Japan Going Nuts Over Co-Op's Snacks," *Los Angeles Times*, 26 February 1990, p. D3.

Chapter Summary

- The industrial market includes all the potential business customers for goods and services used in the production of other products, for use in daily business operations, or for resale.
- Six major segments that make up the industrial market are extractors; manufacturers and contractors; service organizations; institutions and nonprofit organizations; federal, state, and local governments; and intermediaries.
- Industrial goods are divided into four categories: materials, installations, accessory equipment, and operating supplies.
- A number of different types of services are sold to the industrial market, including consulting services, protection services, and maintenance services.
- Many of the same techniques are used to market both consumer goods and industrial goods. However, the industrial buyer has a more complex buying process: buying further ahead, applying more rigid specifications, and using more formal cost analyses than do most customers.
- An industrial buyer's motives for buying include quality, reputation of the supplier, product efficiency, customer service, and price.
- Farm products are often more expensive to market than other industrial products. Marketing services such as transporting, storing, grading, and standardizing add to the final cost and value of the product.
- Sometimes farmers band together in cooperatives to process and market their products.

Building Your Marketing Vocabulary

Use each of the following marketing terms in a sentence that explains its relationship to the industrial or agricultural market.

industrial market
industrial goods
industrial services
derived demand
intermediaries
raw materials
process materials

component parts
installations
manufacturers' agent
distributor
consumer farm products
industrial farm products

Questions for Review

1. Define the industrial market.
2. Explain the concept of derived demand in the industrial market.
3. Name six industrial market segments.
4. Name the four industrial goods categories.
5. What three types of industrial services does the industrial market commonly use?
6. What are intermediaries?
7. Tell two ways in which the marketing of consumer goods differs from the marketing of industrial goods.
8. Name five factors an industrial buyer considers when making a purchase.
9. Name three ways in which industrial buyers can purchase their materials.
10. How do transporting, storing, grading, and standardizing help the industrial users of farm products?
11. How does a farm cooperative use marketing techniques to help farmers?

Critical Thinking

1. How do changes in the consumer market affect the sales of industrial goods?
2. Give an example of a good or service that can be either an industrial good or service or a consumer good or service.
3. Name one example for each of the six major industrial market segments. List the various industrial goods and services needed by each company.

4. Name a business in your area. What industrial services might it employ?

5. Name an agricultural product. Discuss how this product may be classified as a consumer farm product and an industrial farm product.

Discussion Questions

1. Suppose you own a timber company. Discuss the potential industrial market for your product. List each market according to the major industrial segment that it falls into.

2. Selecting several industrial goods, discuss their market potential as raw materials, process materials, and component parts.

3. Given what you know about the industrial, agricultural, and consumer markets, which market would you prefer to sell to? Why?

Marketing Project

Charting the Marketing of Farm Products

Project Goal: Given one leading crop and one leading livestock product produced in your state, chart the path of each product from the farmer to the consumer. Indicate the marketing services performed at each step.

Directions: Identify a crop and a livestock product grown in your state. For each product, look up information in the encyclopedia, or talk with a representative of the business that markets the product.

The business may be a local farmer, central market, wholesaler, or retailer. Find out the steps followed in getting the product from producer to consumer. Then determine the marketing services performed at each step.

Based on the information you have obtained, list each product and chart its path from the producer to the consumer. Using the same information, list the marketing services performed at each step.

Applied Academics

Language Arts

1. Interview a local farmer or an industrial marketer in your community. What product(s) do they produce and/or market? How do they market the product(s)? What techniques do they use that are similar to the techniques mentioned in this chapter? What techniques are different? Write your findings in a 200-word report.

Math

2. Suppose lettuce sells for 80¢ a head and marketing costs make up 60 percent of this cost. How much money is the consumer actually paying for marketing services?

Science

3. In this chapter, you learned that there are at least 1,500 varieties of cotton; and that grading makes it possible for textile companies to obtain the same type and texture of cotton with each purchase. Research how cotton (or some other raw material) is graded. Write a 250-word paper on your findings.

Social Studies

4. Research and compare the differences of farming today and farming 50 years ago. What changes have taken place in farming processes? in farming technology? in farming equipment? In your opinion, have these changes improved the agricultural market?

Marketing and Multiculturalism

Some like it hot! And some like it not quite so hot. That's what Del Monte Mexico is finding out as it begins production of chile salsa products aimed at the U.S. and European markets. The Mexican company believes that adapting its products to meet the tastes of the American and European cultures will create a "hot" new market for Mexican agriculture and human resources.

1. What is Del Monte Mexico's main objective in altering its product for the U.S. and European markets?

2. Are the vegetables in salsa consumer or industrial farm products? Why?

3. What marketing services might add to the final cost of Del Monte's salsa products?

4. How would Mexican farmers that sell their produce to Del Monte benefit from a cooperative?

Chapter *10*

Institutional and Government Markets

Terms to Know

specifications   competitive bidding
standards

Chapter Objectives

After studying this chapter, you will be able to:

- explain marketing to and by government agencies;
- describe marketing to and by health institutions; and
- explain marketing to and by educational institutions.

Case Study

A Healthy Challenge

"We've got a real challenge ahead of us. It's up to every employee to energize our company…to make it more proactive, more customer-driven than ever before," says Steve Bow, president of Blue Cross and Blue Shield of Kentucky.

"I want to see this company move back to its original value system, a system of caring for the customer, and a belief that the customer is important," he continues. "In our rapidly changing, complex, and competitive world of health care, it is even more important for us to get back to personal service and products designed to fulfill customers' needs."[1]

To tackle the changing health care market, Blue Cross and Blue Shield of Kentucky recently merged with Blue Cross and Blue Shield of Indiana. Both insurance organizations are strong and well-managed. The merger combines their resources to make the organization more competitive in the marketplace.

Blue Cross and Blue Shield has let its policyholders know that the merger has strengthened the company, thus enabling it to better serve its policyholders. The company uses television, radio, and newspaper advertising to inform people of the availability of health insurance and long-term health care coverage. Salespeople who are assigned to geographic areas of each state emphasize personal contact with prospective customers to market these products.

Blue Cross and Blue Shield of Kentucky realizes that in today's health care industry, it's more important than ever to be customer oriented. So it works to get back to better personal service. This effort includes better marketing.

Institutional and Government Marketing

As you learned in Chapter 9, the industrial market is made up of six segments. This chapter will cover the institutional and government market segments.

Government markets include local, state, and federal governments. Institutional markets include health, educational, and religious institutions. Let's take a closer look at marketing to and by these institutions.

Government Marketing

Government is the largest market or customer in the world for most goods and services. For example, in 1992, the U.S. government spent $1,096 billion on goods and services (see Table 10–1).

The local, state, and federal governments maintain our roads, bridges, and highways. City governments buy many types of products to repair and clean the streets. For example, they may buy salt and sand to spread on the streets and highways in the winter. They may buy asphalt and concrete for road repair work. They must hire repair services for all the equipment they use. To equip the police force, they must buy police vehicles. Governments also buy computer equipment and furniture for government offices.

Each year, government spending tends to increase because of inflation and new needs of the people. Government purchases go mostly to support the military, international peacekeeping, education, and health.

Marketing to Government Agencies

Government purchases differ from purchases by private businesses in two vital ways. First, the government buys goods mainly for use, not for resale at a profit. For example, the Air Force buys jet fuel to operate its planes, but does not sell

	1990	1991	1992
Government Purchases	$1,042.9	$1,087.5	$1,096.1
Federal	424.9	445.1	441.8
National Defense	313.4	328.5	315.0
Non-defense	111.5	121.6	126.8
State and Local	618.0	642.4	654.3

Source: *The World Almanac and Book of Facts, 1993*, p. 130.

■■■ **Table 10–1 Government Purchases (Billions of Dollars)**
Government spending has increased over the years. What does this mean in terms of viewing the government as a market?

transportation services to the public. The federal government rarely competes with private industry in manufacturing goods or in providing services.

Second, legal and budgetary regulations control government purchasing in order to safeguard the use of public funds. Three basic principles guide government buying:

- all goods and services purchased must meet certain specifications and standards;

- all suppliers are given an equal opportunity to compete for government contracts through bids or negotiations; and

- the government must inspect and approve all items a seller offers before it pays the seller.

Specifications and Standards

Almost all government buying is based on specifications and standards. **Specifications** are an accurate description of the goods or services needed. They also describe the quality that will be acceptable. **Standards** limit the number of qualities, colors, sizes, varieties, and types of materials and commodities purchased. The characteristics of those items that will satisfy most government requirements are adopted as standards. The government uses standards to purchase hundreds of products, ranging from batteries to filing cabinets.

Competitive Bidding

Competitive bidding is a process in which several suppliers offer competitive prices for their products to fulfill a customer's stated specifications. In buying many of the goods and services they use, governments regularly encourage competitive bidding among suppliers.

The government uses newspaper advertisements, direct-mail announcements, or other means of public notice to inform suppliers of government product needs. A deadline is set for bids. Each supplier determines the price it can offer and submits that price in a separate bid. The lowest bidder whose offer meets the government's stated specifications is often awarded the job.

For example, when a city government decides to put asphalt covering on the streets, it advertises the specifications of grade of asphalt, blocks or miles to be covered, thickness and width of covering, and starting and ending dates. Asphalt companies bid on the job. The lowest bidder willing to do the job according to the city government's stated specifications is usually awarded the contract for the work.

Global
MARKETPLACE

Beech Aircraft Takes Off

Beech Aircraft Corporation sells airplanes to corporate and government customers around the world. But the company was having trouble getting airplane sales off the ground during the tight financial climate of the late 1980s. Deciding that its current regional marketing approach wasn't flying, the company reorganized, placing an emphasis on global marketing. Beech divided the world into three geographic territories and assigned sales teams to analyze the aerospace needs of each territory. The company now successfully supplies customized goods and services that more accurately meet the demands of its worldwide customer base.

■ ■ ■   *This F-14 Tomcat fighter jet was produced by Grumman Aviation to fulfill a contract with the U.S. government. How are such contracts awarded?*

Marketing by Government Agencies

The federal government sells electricity generated through power plants. It also sells grain and other stored commodities to other countries. State governments promote recreation in their states and sell admission tickets to state parks and other recreation areas. Local governments operate trash collection services, water plants, sewage plants, gas and electric power plants, industrial parks, and other operations. Governments sell or lease these services or goods to individual consumers or to the industrial market.

The U.S. government buys and sells many goods and services through its agencies. Some examples of government agencies involved in marketing are the Tennessee Valley Authority (TVA), the Agricultural Marketing Service (AMS), and the Federal Trade Commission (FTC).

Tennessee Valley Authority

The TVA is wholly owned by the U.S. government. Its electric power program must support itself financially so that government does not have to subsidize it. To do this the TVA markets the electricity produced.

The TVA's program of activities includes flood control, navigation development, electric power production, fertilizer development, recreation improvement, and forestry and wildlife development. To carry out and to support all of these activities, TVA must go to the market to buy materials and supplies.

Agricultural Marketing Service (AMS)

The AMS helps the private marketing system move food and other farm products from producer to consumer quickly, efficiently, and fairly. It is responsible for programs such as standardizing and grading, marketing agreements, marketing reporting services, and promoting fair-trade practices in marketing agricultural products. It also purchases food for USDA food assistance programs, runs research and promotion programs, checks food safety, and conducts research to find better ways of marketing farm products at the lowest possible cost.

AMS purchases food to be distributed through the Food and Nutrition Service; the School Lunch Program; nutrition programs for the elderly; and the Supplemental Food Program for Women, Infants, and Children.

Federal Trade Commission (FTC)

The Federal Trade Commission Act of 1914 prohibits unfair or deceptive business practices. The Federal Trade Commission is involved in marketing in several ways because it does the following:

- promotes competition;
- safeguards the public from deceptive or false marketing practices;
- seeks to prevent discriminations in price;
- checks for false labeling;
- regulates packaging;
- supervises export activities;
- registers trademarks;
- encourages true credit cost disclosure; and
- reports, gathers, and distributes factual data concerning economic and business conditions.

Health Care Marketing

Health care includes hospital health care, physician services, dental services, drug and medical supplies, nursing home care, physical therapy, psychological health care, and substance abuse services. It includes both for-profit and nonprofit businesses. (You will take a closer look at nonprofit marketing in Chapter 11.) In 1991 a total of $756.3 billion was spent in the United States on health care. (See Figure 10–1.) The market for health care goods and services is tremendous.

The approximately 37 million uninsured people in the United States create a huge financial burden on health centers. The state of health care in America makes marketing to and by health care institutions challenging and necessary.

Marketing to Health Care Institutions

To provide health care services, health care institutions must purchase a sizable amount of goods and services. Marketers supply health care institutions with buildings, machinery, medical equipment, office supplies, office equipment, medical supplies, utilities, and insurance. These needs are filled for the most part by advertising and salespeople who are specialists in their fields.

For example, the pharmaceutical industry relies heavily on marketing efforts to sell medicinal drugs to health care institutions. Marketers in this $75 billion industry may spend more than $200 million on marketing just to introduce a new product to the market.

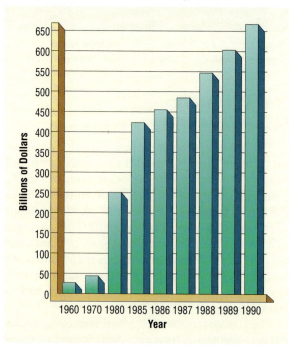

■ ■ ■ *Figure 10–1 National Health Expenditures*
Health care expenditures have increased over the last 30 years. What does this mean in terms of the market for health care goods and services?

Pharmaceutical salespeople make sales calls on doctors to introduce them to new products. They provide physicians with promotional samples to give to their patients.

In addition, pharmaceutical marketers use heavy media advertising such as television and radio commercials, print advertising, and promotional videos and publicationss. For example, Bristol-Myers Squibb Company sends customers a periodic newsletter concerning its product Questran, a treatment for excessive cholesterol. These forms of advertising familiarize consumers as well as physicians about medicinal drugs.[2]

Marketing by Health Care Institutions

Providing health care is a highly competitive endeavor. The number of hospitals has decreased due to consolidations and the need for more cost-efficient facilities. Trauma centers in hospitals and nursing homes are overcrowded and short-staffed.

Health care organizations must compete for patients, doctors, nurses, and financial resources. The number of nursing home facilities has increased during the past two decades. However, more facilities are needed to take care of the growing number of senior citizens.

To meet the challenges of the health care industry, health care institutions must effectively market their services to prospective patients and funding sources. Private and public health care institutions depend on patients' fees, government funds, and contributions to carry out their missions.

Paddy Mullen, Director of Marketing and Communications at Leonard Morse Health Care Corporation in Natick, Massachusetts, says, "from a marketing standpoint, I look at what management wants to accomplish—the objectives they seek to fulfill—and then create and implement plans to achieve these objectives. As in any corporation, most objectives are financial or market driven. But as a health care provider, we always have the mandate to provide quality care and service. Every hospital's mission is one of social responsibility, and all our programs must fall in line with this mission."[3]

Health care organizations use several types of media to market their services. For example, Human

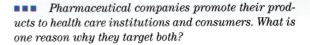

■ ■ ■ *Pharmaceutical companies promote their products to health care institutions and consumers. What is one reason why they target both?*

Health Care advertises and explains its plan through television. Hospice of Hope, a service for terminally ill patients, issues a bulletin soliciting contributions, introducing staff members, and describing its services. CIGNA Insurance Company places ads about its health care programs in magazines. In addition, many doctors and hospitals use newsletters along with newspaper, magazine, radio, and billboard advertising to inform consumers of their services.

Consumer interest in good health has provided new opportunities for marketers. Health products have dominated new product developments in the

Principles into Practice

ACE Markets Its Services to Young Entrepreneurs

More and more young people under the age of 30 are becoming successful and profitable small business owners. In fact, during the 1990s, one-third of all new businesses are being created by people under the age of 30.

However, the climb to the top is often difficult for young entrepreneurs. Lack of management experience, business contacts, and credibility often prevent younger people from starting and running a business.

The Association of Collegiate Entrepreneurs (ACE) helps present and potential business owners overcome common business problems. It markets business resources to young entrepreneurs to help them successfully run a small business.

Founded in 1983 by Wichita State University students, ACE has grown from 60 universities in 24 states to approximately 300 universities nationwide. There are also associations in more than 50 foreign countries, including China and Russia.

Probably the biggest problem faced by young entrepreneurs is acceptance by the business world.

For example, a senior vice-president of a bank may have doubts about lending a 16-year-old money to start a business. To better overcome the problem of inexperience, many ACE programs coordinate the schools' educational programs with real-life job experiences, such as corporate internships. These experiences expose young entrepreneurs to more actual business situations. ACE also sponsors trade shows, campus rep programs, and corporate internships to expose young entrepreneurs to more hands-on, real-world business situations.

To publicize its services, ACE obtains coverage on TV shows, radio, and in major publications such as *Forbes, USA Today, Nation's Business, Changing Times*, and the *Wall Street Journal*. It also publishes its own newspaper, *ACTION*.

1. Describe the goals and purpose of ACE.
2. How does ACE market its services?

---

grocery stores. Figure 10–2 lists predictions of successful health care creations for the 1990s. The necessity of health care will always create marketing opportunities for health care institutions.

Educational Marketing

Educational institutions include preschools; elementary, secondary, and post-secondary schools; colleges; universities; and educational associations. Educational institutions market their services to the millions of people who need education, training, and retraining. These institutions need many goods and services.

Marketing to Educational Institutions

Educational institutions need products such as buildings, utilities, equipment, insurance, maintenance services, books, and supplies in order to operate. The process that schools use to purchase products is similar to that used by the government. When your school system builds a new building, contractors are chosen by competitive bidding. Schools also purchase such products as computers, typewriters, paper, and janitorial supplies the same way.

literacy. Thus, educational institutions throughout the nation obtained computers in order to teach students how to use them.

Marketing by Educational Institutions

Educational institutions market their services in many ways. One effective method is the use of career days for prospective students who are considering attending the school. At these sessions staff members, administrators, and alumni members make presentations on educational matters such as student services, financial aid, courses, and curriculum.

Educational institutions use advertising to promote their services. They sell their courses and programs to prospective students through catalogs, telemarketing, press releases, billboards, radio, and TV.

Alumni associations help to recruit candidates in their geographic areas. They also assist in seeking financial support for school expenses and scholarships to attract enrollment.

Public schools form parent-teacher associations to keep parents informed of their schools' activities and needs. They keep publicity flowing to the media so the public will support their schools and be willing to pay taxes to maintain adequate educational facilities.

Educational associations such as the Association of Collegiate Entrepreneurs (ACE) and DECA market their services to students and teachers. Conventions and special events help them to gain publicity. They also use publications and advertising to create continued awareness of their association.

■■■ *Figure 10–2 Predicted Health Care Product Successes for the 1990s*
Health concerns have influenced many new product developments in the grocery market. Name one current new product that has succeeded for health reasons.

As technology changes, educational institutions must update their facilities and equipment. For example, the use of computers in the home and in business has created the demand for computer

CHAPTER NOTES

1. Customer mailing by Blue Cross/Blue Shield of Kentucky, 1989.
2. John Greenwald, "Ouch! Which Hurts More, the Shot or the Bill? Now Drug Firms Also Feel the Pain as Clinton Blasts Their Prices." *Time*, 8 March 1993, pp. 53–55.
3. Stewart Husted, Dale L. Varble, James R. Lowry, *Principles of Modern Marketing* (Needham Heights, MA: Allyn & Bacon, 1989), p. 140.

Chapter Summary

- The U.S. government is the world's largest customer for goods and services.
- To get better prices, institutions and governments encourage competitive bidding for contracts to supply goods and services.
- The U.S. government sells many goods and services. Some examples of government agencies include the Tennessee Valley Authority, the Agricultural Marketing Service, and the Federal Trade Commission.
- Health care includes hospital health care, physician services, dental services, drugs, and medical supplies.
- Educational institutions market their services in many ways, including career days, advertising through alumni associations, and special events.

Building Your Marketing Vocabulary

On a separate sheet of paper, define each of the following marketing terms. Then use each term in a paragraph describing how government purchases are made.

specifications   competitive bidding
standards

Questions for Review

1. Name two types of products purchased by the government.
2. In what two ways do government purchases differ from private business?
3. What are three basic principles that guide government buying?
4. Name three government agencies.
5. Explain how standards help in the marketing of goods and services.
6. How are specifications used in the process of competitive bidding?

7. How do governments and institutions use competitive bidding when they want to buy certain goods?
8. Name two types of health care organizations.
9. Discuss two marketing tactics educational marketers use to market their products.

Critical Thinking

1. Suppose you are in charge of hiring contractors to build a new wing for your school. How would you go about doing this? What specifications would you include?
2. Suppose you are a buyer for a hospital. What types of products might you purchase regularly?
3. Compare marketing to government agencies with marketing to private business.
4. How is the process used to make educational purchases similar to that used by government?

Discussion Questions

1. Why do you think many marketers avoid selling to the government market?
2. Discuss the types of marketing opportunities that will arise with the growth of the health care industry.
3. As a health care marketer, how might you promote a hospital?
4. Discuss whether you would prefer to sell goods to private businesses or government agencies. Give reasons for your decision.

Marketing Project

Determining Government Expenditures

Project Goal: Given data for annual government purchases for selected years, bring these statistics up to date by referring to the latest material available to you.

Directions: Refer to Table 10–1, page 126. Note that these figures were obtained by referring to *The World Almanac and Book of Facts 1993*. Go to your school library and refer to the latest edition of this book. Look up tables of data showing annual expenditures for goods and services by state, local, and federal governments.

Create a table like the one below showing the most current annual government purchases. You will possibly need to make some calculations yourself. Has there been an increase or decrease in each category? By how many dollars each year?

Year	
Government Purchases	
Federal Purchases	
State and Local Purchases	

Applied Academics

Language Arts

1. Interview a teacher in your school to find out how school purchasing decisions are made. What types of buying motives are the purchases based on? Write a 150-word report on your findings.

Math

2. Obtain three office supply catalogs from your school's front office. Prepare a list of office supplies you think would be necessary in order to run your school's front office for one month. Next, using the three office supply catalogs, determine the best supplier. Finally, prepare an actual order by listing the item, its unit cost, its total cost, and the total cost of the entire order.

Science

3. To market health care products you must be aware of current health problems. Read health and science publications to determine two types of illnesses currently receiving national attention. Write a 250-word paper on the illnesses. Determine types of products you could market to assist patients suffering from these ailments.

Social Studies

4. Governmental agencies have been created to help our society. List and explain the purpose of a governmental agency of your choice. How has it helped our society? Report your findings to the class.

Marketing and Multiculturalism

Research shows that Hispanic physicians see more patients than Caucasian physicians. They also write more prescriptions, especially for brand-name products. In addition, Hispanic physicians and many of their patients are fluent in Spanish. Such information is providing health care marketers with avenues for reaching the Hispanic physician.

1. What types of opportunities may stem from the fact that Hispanic physicians see more patients than Caucasian physicians and write more prescriptions?

2. How might the fact that Hispanic physicians seem to be brand-loyal aid marketers?

3. What can manufacturers of medical products do to promote their products to the Hispanic medical market?

4. What additional information about Hispanic medical care would be useful to health care marketers?

Marketing for Nonprofit Organizations

California Museum of Science and Industry

Howard F. Ahmanson Building

700 STATE DRIVE

Terms to Know

social marketing	place marketing
idea marketing	person marketing
organization marketing	direct marketing

Chapter Objectives

After studying this chapter, you will be able to:

- describe the nature, scope, and characteristics of marketing for nonprofit organizations;
- identify and describe the four types of nonprofit marketing;
- provide examples of nonprofit organizations that have effectively used marketing principles and techniques to achieve their objectives; and
- describe how nonprofit marketers design and use a marketing mix to achieve their goals.

Case Study

Cry of the Wild

As you flip through a magazine, an ad catches your eye. You begin to read.

Snowbound in a remote Minnesota cabin, you hear a thump at the window. You freeze in your tracks as your flashlight picks up the blazing yellow eyes of a wild timber wolf. He is leaning weakly against the window. Is he hurt? Would he attack?

As you cautiously approach, he stares at you, unmoving. You pick him up, carry him inside, lay him by the fire. You wait and watch as the wolf wheezes, gasps, and dies. You learn, later, that the wolf was starved, his hunting impeded by a foot mutilated in a fox trap. That he died of pneumonia...

The National Audubon Society counts on such stories (and on your sympathetic reaction to them) to achieve its goal. But unlike many businesses, the society does not exist to make a profit. Instead, its goal is to make people environmental activists, and, above all, to get them to join the organization.

The National Audubon Society's nonprofit marketing activities are numerous. They include $300,000 in paid advertising and selling environmentally friendly products. They also recruit funds from such nontraditional sources as businesses that sell environmentally safe products. They often cross-promote Audubon's products with such environmentally friendly products as water-based latex paints.

Audubon particularly targets the 35- to 40-year-old adult market. The people in this market, which includes people with more children than other markets, are likely to take family vacations to national parks and do not want to see them destroyed.

You finish reading the ad.

Starving wild animals sometimes do approach people near the end. And, as you share the experience..., you understand why we must save our few remaining wolves—and all of America.

You reach for your checkbook, knowing your support will help this nonprofit organization preserve and protect natural resources, wildlife, and wetlands.[1]

Nature and Scope of Marketing for Nonprofit Organizations

As you know from Chapter 1, nonprofit organizations emphasize goals other than profit making. There are thousands of nonprofit organizations that use marketing strategies and techniques to achieve their objectives.

Generally, the nonprofit organization's major marketing goal is to convince the public to support a particular social cause, idea, political candidate, or better way of life. Sometimes, the organization's goal is to get the public to use its services, such as blood testing at a publicly funded medical facility or psychological counseling at a local mental health association. Often the goal is to get the public to contribute money to a worthy cause.

As you know from Chapter 1, nonprofit marketing consists of marketing activities conducted to achieve some goal other than profit making. Nonprofit marketing applies to intangible goods or services, such as education, health care, culture, or religion. It is also used to promote certain ideas or viewpoints, such as the prevention of forest fires, the advantages of donating blood, and the prevention of cruelty to animals. The National Audubon Society's marketing goal, for example, is to protect our nation's parks and wildlife.

Nonprofit marketing also includes **social marketing**—marketing practices that try to gain acceptance of a social idea, cause, or practice by a targeted group. Three prominent examples of social marketing include the stop smoking campaigns, don't drink while driving campaigns, and the "Just Say No" (to drugs) campaign aimed at young adults.

The specific marketing goals of nonprofit organizations may vary widely. For example, some organizations such as the Democratic and Republican political parties use marketing techniques to try to convince the public to support their ideas or candidates. The March of Dimes and The Multiple Sclerosis Society encourage people to donate money so that these organizations can fund medical research. Greenpeace and the Sierra Club use nonprofit marketing to encourage people to protect the environment.

Most vocational and technical schools, colleges, and universities use marketing strategies to inform potential students about their academic programs and services. High school students see videos or receive catalogs from colleges informing them about available academic programs.

Still, lots of other organizations use nonprofit marketing to encourage us to eat better foods, patronize symphonies and the community theater, wear car seat belts, and hug our kids. Table 11–1 shows examples of recently marketed ideas and social issues.

Characteristics of Nonprofit Marketing

Recall from Chapter 1 that marketing is the process of planning and executing the conception,

pricing, promotion, and distribution of ideas, goods, and services to create exchanges that satisfy individual and organizational objectives. There really are not that many differences between profit-oriented and nonprofit marketing.

Like profit organizations, nonprofit organizations plan and perform marketing campaigns for ideas or services that satisfy their organization's objectives. However, nonprofit organizations do have a special set of characteristics that make marketing their ideas, services, causes, or people unique and often challenging.

Measurement of Performance

The difference between a profit-oriented business and a nonprofit organization is how each measures its performance. For example, a profit-oriented company such as Coca-Cola constantly measures its performance by its profits. Its profits indicate how well the company is satisfying its market and how efficiently it is using its resources.

A nonprofit organization such as the Brookfield Zoo in Chicago does not measure its performance by the profit it makes but by how effectively it achieves set goals. Unfortunately, because its services are intangible, it isn't always easy for a nonprofit organization to set goals or know if it is achieving them. Nevertheless, it must do its best to

911 emergency number	Crime prevention	Free enterprise	Military recruiting	Population control	Suicide hot line
Abortion rights	Drug abuse control	Gay rights	Museums	Prayers in schools	Tax reform
Affirmative action	Energy conservation	Gun control	Nature conservation	Prison reform	Trade associations
AIDS prevention	Environment	Health maintenance	Nuclear energy	Productivity in industry	United Negro Colleges
Alcoholism control	Equal opportunity	High school graduation	Nutrition	Recycling wastes	United Way
Blood donations	Euthanasia	International peace	Obesity prevention	Religion	Urban planning
Cancer research	Fair housing	Literacy	Outdoor living	Right to life	Vegetarianism
Car pooling	Family life	Litter prevention	Peace	Safety	Veterans' rights
Child abuse prevention	Family planning	Mainstreaming	Peace Corps	Save the whales	Voter registration
Child adoption	Fire prevention	Marriage	Pet responsibility	Scouting	Wife abuse prevention
Consumer cooperatives	Fluoridation	Mass transportation	Physical fitness	Seat belt use	Women's rights
Continuing education	Foster parenthood	Mental health	Pollution control	Solar energy	

Source: Richard L. Lynch, Herbert L. Ross, Ralph D. Wray, *Introduction to Marketing* (New York: McGraw-Hill Company, 1984), p. 32.

■■■ **Table 11–1 Current Ideas and Social Issues that Have Been Marketed**
Here are examples of current ideas and social issues that have been marketed by nonprofit organizations. Name an organization that markets a current idea or social issue listed here.

Some pretty colorful
characters wet their whistles
at our watering hole.
They're just part of the
wild crowd that frequents
our new *Habitat Africa!*
exhibit. Stop in.
But be prepared: Even
though *Habitat Africa!*
is close to Chicago, it's far
from tame. For directions,
call 708-485-0263.

BROOKFIELD ZOO
Where Imagination Runs Wild

Illinois®
Don't Miss It!™

■ ■ ■   *This ad was effective in promoting Chicago's
Brookfield Zoo. How might the zoo evaluate the success
of its marketing campaign?*

at least try to set goals in order to effectively evaluate its marketing program. For example, goals against which the zoo might evaluate its marketing campaigns include:

- to increase Sunday's attendance by 500 people;
- to enlarge the petting zoo area by two acres;

- to increase staff to accommodate five more weekly field trips from elementary schools; and
- to raise $250,000 from private donors.

Multiple Publics

Generally, profit-oriented businesses target customers because customer sales provide profit. Nonprofit organizations, however, target at least two different publics: contributors and clients.

The marketing director of a zoo, for example, must constantly direct marketing attention to various contributors who might donate funds to the zoo. He or she must plan fund-raising activities to get contributions from citizen and business groups, charities, and local government officials.

Clients are the consumers of an organization's ideas, money, or services. They are the organization's parishioners, patients, visitors, audience, or students. For example, a zoo's clients are its visitors.

Marketers may also target other publics. For example, the zoo may direct a marketing campaign to a foreign country such as Brazil in order to assure it that the zoo's climate is ideal for exhibiting one of Brazil's rare breeds of animals.

Would you like to name this puppy?

Over the next year, this loving puppy will be patiently trained to be the faithful eyes of a blind person. But she needs your help. Any contribution you can make, $5, $10, $25, will be very much appreciated. Or you, your company, or organization can sponsor the entire cost of schooling ($4,000) and choose its name. It's a wonderful way to be man's second best friend.

**Guide Dog Foundation
For The Blind, Inc.**
Dept. P-89
371 East Jericho Turnpike,
Smithtown, NY 11787.
516 265-2121.

■ ■ ■   *The Guide Dog Foundation for the Blind, Inc., is targeting this ad to donors. Even though this organization is collecting money to provide services, it is still nonprofit. Why?*

Public Scrutiny

Public funds support many nonprofit organizations which, in turn, provide public services. Thus, these organizations are closely watched by the public. For example, an attempt to raise admission prices at the zoo or to make any major changes might attract the attention of local government officials, citizen groups, and school groups who might withdraw their support.

When public funds are involved, public scrutiny has an impact on marketers' considerations. For example, tax monies heavily fund the Brookfield Zoo. Thus, special interest groups, politicians, and heavy users of the zoo's services want to have some influence over the changes made at the zoo. The zoo's marketers will focus their efforts on all of these groups, including taxpayers.

Intangibility

The ideas, causes, performance, and services marketed by nonprofit organizations are intangible. They are different from consumer products in that you cannot touch, see, hold, examine, try on, or test them. For example, people cannot try the zoo's services or the city's symphony performances before they actually pay the price of visiting the zoo or attending a symphony. Thus, nonprofit marketers face similar challenges to those faced by for-profit service marketers. Nonprofit marketers must constantly look for new and creative ways to determine and influence the motives of their multiple publics. They must also bring more tangibility to their ideas and services. By doing so, they help to achieve their organization's goals.

Types of Nonprofit Marketing

As with profit-oriented business marketing, marketers for nonprofit organizations must emphasize benefits in their marketing messages. To help us market benefits and to help us further understand nonprofit marketing, like profit marketing, nonprofit marketing can be classified into four types: idea, organization, place, and person marketing. Let's take a look at each.

Idea Marketing

Idea marketing is best identified with the definition of social marketing you learned on page 135. **Idea marketing** involves marketing activities that try to gain a target market's acceptance of a cause or way of thinking. Effective idea marketing often tries to get us to change our ideas or beliefs, and then to change our behavior.

For example, stop smoking campaigns work to change the idea that smoking is glamorous by pointing out its harmful effects on health. They also try to prohibit smoking in most public places. Thus, marketers of stop smoking campaigns depict smoking as an "uncool" and dangerous habit. They want to discourage people from ever smoking and to change smokers' behavior by encouraging them to quit.

Many companies, groups, organizations, and government agencies sponsor idea marketing campaigns. Popular examples of such campaigns include protecting the environment (Smokey the Bear), public service (Join the Peace Corps), American patriotism (Buy It in the USA), and support of higher education (Give to the College of Your Choice).

Organization Marketing

Organization marketing involves those marketing activities that establish or change a target market's beliefs and/or behavior toward a particular

■■■ *This ad is an example of idea marketing. What idea is being marketed here? How might the ad help to change the public's attitude?*

organization. It tries to get the target market to think positively about a particular nonprofit association, group, or organization. It markets the organization's image.

Churches, police departments, labor unions, and government agencies often use marketing techniques to gain support or build a positive attitude toward their organizations. In fact, the U.S. government is one of the top 25 advertisers in the country. The largest federal advertisers have been the military; the Postal Service; and the Departments of Treasury, Education, Transportation, Energy, and Environmental Protection.

An example of organizational marketing used to gain support for a government agency was the U.S. Army's "Be All That You Can Be" campaign targeted to young people. This excellent campaign did much to create a favorable public opinion toward Army enlistment.

Another example of effective organization marketing is done by DECA, the national organization for high school and postsecondary marketing education students. Each year, DECA develops a marketing campaign to gain members. The campaign targets young people in high school and postsecondary marketing programs.

Marketing teachers are also targeted annually for membership by national organizations. These include such organizations as the Marketing Education Association, American Vocational Association, and the National Education Association.

GET A HANDLE ON DINNER.

■ ■ ■ *What type of nonprofit marketing is being promoted in this beef ad?*

Place Marketing

Place marketing includes those marketing activities that establish or change a target market's beliefs and/or behavior toward particular places. The place being marketed may be a vacation site, a business site, a city, a county, a farm, or even a country. The benefits of the place are usually attractively depicted in illustrations and words.

Nearly every region, state, city, town, or park area interested in attracting tourists or vacation travelers carefully conducts marketing activities to do just that. Two examples of popular place campaigns include "I Love New York" and "Come Home to Virginia."

Countries are increasingly marketing themselves as attractive opportunities for business investment or travel. For example, Canada, Ireland, Greece, Turkey, Sweden, Australia, and Malaysia all run newspaper ads and TV commercials to attract business and tourists.

Person Marketing

Person marketing includes those marketing activities that influence or change a target market's opinion about particular people. All kinds of people and organizations practice person marketing. For example, virtually every celebrity or politician today engages in considerable marketing activity to gain publicity and enhance their careers. We regularly see actors, athletes, authors, and artists appearing on talk shows, endorsing goods or services, or signing autographs at new store openings. During elections, pictures of political candidates appear in all types of advertising.

Principles into Practice

Before 1973, all U.S. males could be drafted into military service. When the draft ended, the Army faced a severe manpower shortage. It soon realized it had to use marketing activities to recruit high school seniors and recent graduates if it was to meet its objectives.

The Army recognizes that it has two major publics to serve. The first is the U.S. taxpayers who provide it with resources. The second is clients—the enlisted personnel, officers, Army National Guard, and members of the Army reserved forces.

The Army has three primary objectives. These are providing the nation with the military strength it needs, increasing the number and quality of recruits, and educating soldiers.

According to Colonel Thomas E. Faley, Jr., the operating strategy of the U.S. Army is to encourage people to find a successful career in the Army. The Army wants to help each individual become a better person. This objective was popularized in the now famous advertising slogan of "Be All That You Can Be."

The Army's demographic market is male high school juniors and seniors and recent graduates between 17 and 21 years of age. Its secondary market is females of the same groups. A third market is those with occupational specialties, such as nurses and computer analysts. The psychographics include leadership qualities, outgoing personality, determination, and career focus.

The Army's research showed that the top reasons for joining the Army included:

- earning money for college;
- getting skills training;
- serving the country;
- improving self-confidence;

Be All that You Can Be

- having a well-paid job; and
- patriotism and pro-military sentiment.

Based on the objectives, research, and segmented information, the Army continues to market its particular brand of military service. Ads frequently appear in newspapers, on TV and radio, and in magazines typically read by high school students. One popular ad was the "Count on Me" theme. This 30-second commercial showed quick shots of soldiers in the field. Its message was that American people can count on confident, competent soldiers.

Army recruiters (salespeople) regularly visit high schools and community colleges to give presentations on the benefits of Army training. Exhibits are set up in shopping malls and at youth conferences. Recruiters give speeches to civic groups. Cash bonuses are offered to all who complete basic training. The Army emphasizes education and skill training in all of its promotional materials. College credit is given for some of the skills people learn in the Army.

What are the results? The quality of Army recruits has improved drastically. More than 60 percent score in the top half of the math and verbal ability sections of the Armed Services Vocational Aptitude Battery.

Data show that there is indeed pride among the Army's soldiers and officers. Many are earning college degrees. Nearly all complete their Army service with marketable skills.[2, 3, 4, 5]

1. Why did the Army decide to begin using marketing activities?
2. To what do you attribute the success of the Army's marketing campaign?

Nonprofit organizations often use person marketing to better achieve their goals. By associating themselves with credible, well-known personalities, they hope to create a favorable image and gain public support. In turn, the people being marketed benefit by being able to enhance their careers, reputations, ideas, elections, causes, and, of course, their income.

For example, Mothers Against Drunk Driving may use Stevie Wonder to promote safe and sober driving. UNICEF (United Nations Childrens Fund) uses Harry Belafonte, Julio Iglesias, and Liv Ullmann to help raise funds for food, clothing, school materials, and health care for children devastated by war in Europe and Asia. Cher, Elizabeth Taylor, and other celebrities work with AIDS organizations. The Beef Industry Council used Cybill Shepherd and James Garner in its "Beef—Real Food for Real People" campaign to get people to eat beef.

■■■ *Faith Ford from TV's "Murphy Brown" supports Citizens and Neighborhood Networks, AIDS Project Los Angeles. Why do marketers use celebrities to endorse products?*

The Marketing Mix in Nonprofit Organizations

Marketing principles and practices are just as important to nonprofit organizations as they are to profit-oriented businesses. Effective nonprofit marketers try to determine the needs, wants, attitudes, and behavior of their targeted groups. They conduct research to try to understand the various market segments and then create a marketing mix to satisfy the needs and wants of the segments. Some conduct opinion surveys. They review and analyze such secondary data as population trends. They interview prospective donors to determine financial situations, emotional needs, or attitudes about certain ideas or causes.

Charities such as the American Cancer Society or the American Heart Association may find that people will donate money for several reasons.

1. They believe in the cause or causes. Perhaps they know someone who is suffering from cancer or heart disease.
2. They feel it is their civic duty to give a certain amount of their income to charity.
3. They always give to any respected group that asks for a donation. They simply cannot say no.
4. They need a tax deduction.
5. It is in their best interest. By giving, they will achieve recognition, status, or a sense of personal satisfaction.

Once an organization has used market research to identify the different market segments and the potential contributions from each segment, it can then design and use a marketing mix to achieve its goals. Just like marketing for a profit-oriented business, nonprofit marketers must pay attention to product, place (distribution), price, and promotion strategies.

Product

A nonprofit organization's product may be the idea, social cause, or organization being marketed. The organization must decide whether to offer a single product or a mix of related products.

Many nonprofit organizations actually sell products to raise funds to support their ideas and causes. Marketers of these products must pay attention to brand, packaging, warranty, and other product identification decisions. Many nonprofit organizations, such as the Girl Scouts, Boy Scouts, and the YMCA, use symbols and trademarks to distinguish their product offerings.

Colleges and universities use nicknames (a form of brand name) to identify themselves. Examples include the Fighting Irish at Notre Dame, the Buckeyes at Ohio State University, and the Rambling Wreck from Georgia Tech.

Understanding customer needs and wants is important in developing product features and benefits. For example, the U.S. Postal Service conducted research to determine what its customers wanted to buy. Based on that research, it developed a series of new products. It introduced Express Mail overnight delivery service with a money-back guarantee if not delivered the next working day, Priority Mail two-day service, Mailgram (a cross between regular mail and a telegram), and presort mail for large mailers willing to sort their outgoing mail by zip code in return for a postage discount.

These new postal products have all been branded—that is, they have been given a name, symbol, and design that sets them apart from other similar products. Several of these products use distinctive labeling and packaging so they can be easily recognized as U.S. Postal Service products. You will look at branding, labeling, and packaging in greater detail in Chapters 17 and 18.

Place or Distribution

Typically, the channel of distribution for most nonprofit organizations is simple and short. The channel goes directly from the organization to its consumers or patrons without intermediaries.

Organizations such as the Salvation Army and the United Fund solicit directly from the public. Some nonprofit organizations, such as performing arts groups, use a ticket agency to market themselves. A few charity groups and nearly all political campaigns employ fund-raising specialists.

A major place decision is location. Obviously, the easier it is for people to locate the nonprofit organization, the easier it is for them to donate money.

■■■   *The U.S. Postal Service introduced Priority Mail. Why?*

The easier it is to hear about the issue or see the well-known person, the more likely it is that the public will accept the idea, cause, place, or person being marketed. If the museum, state college, or zoo is conveniently located, people are more likely to use its services.

Price

Pricing is an important element of the nonprofit organization's marketing mix. Nonprofit marketers can use four pricing strategies to accomplish a variety of organizational goals.

1. *Large Donations.* Marketers may use a single event to raise large amounts of money. For example, political parties may charge $1,000 a plate for dinner and a speech from a candidate.

THE FUTURE IS NOW

A Prescription for Success

Disney World is not the only attraction drawing foreign visitors to Central Florida. Tampa General Hospital has developed a global marketing campaign to promote its state-of-the-art medical services to 23 countries where advanced treatment and technology are not available. In 1991 international patients came to Tampa General for treatments including heart and kidney transplants, burn care, and long-term rehabilitation—and brought in $980,000 of additional revenue.

Promotion

Nonprofit marketers use all types of promotional strategies. The U.S. Postal Service, the Army, and the United Negro College Fund have relied heavily on television ads. Politicians and celebrities typically use radio and TV talk shows. Many organizations use **direct marketing**—that is, marketing by mail, telephone, or electronic marketing (with computers) or television to reach customers directly. The Easter Seal Society and The Multiple Sclerosis Society use telethons. The Special Olympics uses direct mail.

Small, local groups often seek publicity and conduct public relations efforts. Hospice directors and volunteers typically give speeches to local civic clubs and small groups of potential patrons. Many groups use posters.

University recruiters and fund raisers often rely on personal selling, brochures, videos, and direct mail. Some charitable groups, such as the American Legion, the Salvation Army, and door-to-door solicitors, have used paper flowers, badges, "I Gave" stickers, and other specialty advertising items to identify contributors and to promote their particular cause.

Promotion is indeed important in effective marketing for all nonprofit organizations. In the future, it is expected that more nonprofit groups will further develop strong communications programs that blend all aspects of the marketing mix, including promotion to reach their target markets.

2. *Cost Recovery.* Many nonprofit organizations, including government agencies, try to recover operating costs. City transportation systems, publicly supported community colleges, museums, and toll roads often charge just enough to recover their costs of operation. However, many times nonprofit organizations do not take in enough funds to cover their costs. For example, many public colleges and universities typically charge students only about one-third of their operation costs. Taxpayers pay the rest.

3. *Differential Pricing.* Some nonprofit organizations may charge different prices for different segments. For example, performing arts groups charge different prices for different seat locations. Season ticket holders are often given quantity discounts. Sometimes nonprofit organizations charge different types of consumers, such as students and senior citizens, lower fees. For example, admission to a museum may be lower for a senior citizen than it is for an adult. Medical and mental health facilities often base their fees on the user's ability to pay.

4. *Nonmonetary Costs.* Many nonprofit organizations do not charge fees, but they do get other forms of commitment from their consumers. Alcoholics Anonymous, for example, gets a commitment from its clients to stop drinking and to admit their drinking problem to peers.

CHAPTER NOTES

1. Howard Schlossberg, "Ecology Groups Make Emotional Appeals for Members," *Marketing News*, 25 May 1992, p. 7.

2. Steven W. Colford, "Military Launches Ads," *Advertising Age*, 4 March 1991.

3. Colonel Thomas E. Foley, Department of the Army Memorandum, 1 February 1989.

4. Eric Schmitt, "As Military Cuts Back, It Still Needs Recruits," *New York Times*, 12 September 1992.

5. U.S. Army Recruiting Command, "Opportunities and Options: U.S. Army Service as an Edge on Life," (Fort Sheridan, Illinois, 1989), pp. 13–20.

Chapter 11 Review

Chapter Summary

- Nonprofit organizations increasingly use marketing principles and strategies to achieve their objectives. Nonprofit organizations emphasize goals other than returning a profit. Generally, their primary goal is to convince the public to support a particular social cause, idea, political candidate, or way of life.

- Nonprofit organizations differ from profit-oriented businesses in that they have nonprofit objectives; they must direct their marketing activities to multiple publics; the organization's activities are usually accountable to the public; and the ideas or products to be marketed are intangible.

- Four types of nonprofit marketing include idea, organization, place, and person marketing.

- As with profit-oriented businesses, nonprofit marketers must employ the marketing mix.

Building Your Marketing Vocabulary

On a separate sheet of paper, define each of these marketing terms. Then use each word in a 250-word paper on nonprofit marketing.

social marketing   place marketing

idea marketing   person marketing

organization marketing   direct marketing

Questions for Review

1. What generally are nonprofit organizations' major marketing goals?
2. Describe four characteristics of nonprofit marketing that distinguish it from the profit-oriented marketing.
3. Name two publics to which nonprofit organizations must direct their marketing activities.
4. How is the success of a nonprofit organization measured?

5. Why does public scrutiny affect many nonprofit marketers more than profit-oriented marketers?
6. Identify and briefly describe four classifications of nonprofit marketing.
7. What elements of the marketing mix must be considered in planning and executing a marketing campaign?

Critical Thinking

1. Does the definition of marketing on page 136 include marketing of nonprofit organizations? Explain your answer.
2. Name a nonprofit organization that interests you. What segments of the public must this organization market to?
3. What type of marketing is done by the organization you chose in question 2?
4. Effective nonprofit marketers try to determine the needs, wants, attitudes, and behaviors of their targeted groups. What needs, wants, attitudes, and behavior do you think the organization in question 2 tries to appeal to?
5. Design a marketing mix for the organization from question 2.

Discussion Questions

1. Would the efforts of social marketers be hindered if they were to make a profit? Explain your answer.
2. Discuss various promotional marketing activities used to market national political candidates such as those for U.S. President or the Senate.
3. Why must marketers be cautious about the celebrities they choose to endorse their products?
4. Discuss which type of nonprofit marketing— idea, organization, place, or person—you feel would be easiest to market. Give reasons to support your answer.

5. Do you think marketing a nonprofit business is easier or more difficult than marketing a profit-oriented business? Explain.

Marketing Project

Marketing for a Nonprofit Organization

Project Goal: Identify strategies for each element of the marketing mix for a nonprofit organization.

Directions: With your teacher's permission, visit with a marketing specialist for a nonprofit organization in your community. This could be a person at a local community college, at the office of your community's United Fund, the executive director of your area's Chamber of Commerce, etc.

Learn how that organization uses marketing activities to achieve its objectives. Be sure to ask about its market research activities. Obtain information about the various segments (contributors and users) to whom marketing activities are directed. Ask about specific strategies that the nonprofit organization uses for each element of the marketing mix: product, place, price, and promotion. Where possible, obtain such marketing materials as brochures, print ads, market research instruments, and specialty items.

Prepare a ten-minute oral report to present in class describing how the organization uses marketing activities to achieve its objective(s). Be sure to give the name of the nonprofit organization and the person you interviewed at the beginning of your report.

Applied Academics

Language Arts

1. Write a 250-word paper describing the promotional techniques that you would use to promote your school's marketing education program to your community.

Math

2. Count how many students are enrolled in your marketing education class. How many more students would it take to increase the enrollment next year by 10 percent? What strategies could you use to ensure a 10 percent increase?

Social Studies

3. How do nonprofit organizations affect the lives of others? Explain your answer. Use an example to support your answer.

Marketing and Multiculturalism

The Los Angeles County Fire Department serves a population of nearly 3 million people in 50 cities in the Los Angeles metropolitan area. That population is 39.7 percent Caucasian, 37.8 percent Hispanic, 11.2 percent African-American, and 10.8 percent Asian-American. To meet the needs of such an ethnically-diverse populace, the fire department provides fire prevention and earthquake preparedness information on two local Spanish-language television stations. It also places information in newspapers directed specifically toward African-American and Asian-American readers, as well as through general media sources.

1. What is the fire department's marketing goal?

2. Is the fire department marketing to clients or contributors?

3. Which of the four types of nonprofit marketing is the fire department using?

4. Does public scrutiny have an effect on the fire department's marketing? Explain.

5. What other programs might the fire department use to communicate with its ethnic publics?

6. If the fire department wanted to reach the retired Hispanic population in Los Angeles County, what methods might it use?

Chapter 12

The Global Market

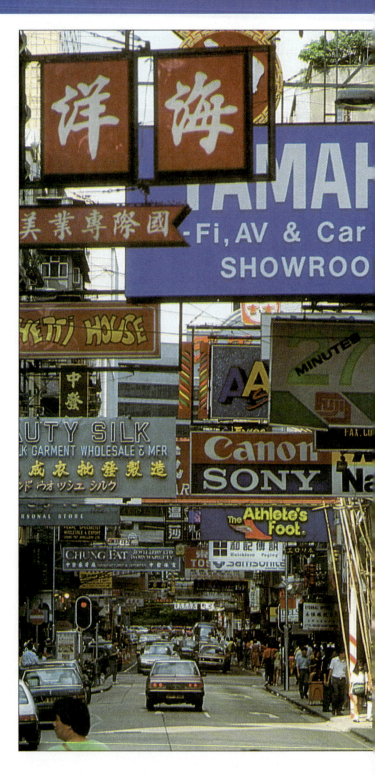

Terms to Know

international trade

international marketing

imports

exports

absolute advantage

comparative advantage

balance of trade

trade barriers

tariff

quotas

embargo

contract manufacturing

common markets

Chapter Objectives

After studying this chapter, you will be able to:

- explain how trading nations develop comparative and absolute advantages and become interdependent;
- discuss the disadvantages and barriers to international trade;
- describe methods of entering global markets;
- give examples of imported products, and report on recent developments in international trade;
- name special factors to consider when entering a foreign market; and
- discuss the efforts taken to promote international trade.

Case Study

Living in the Global Marketplace

Every Saturday morning Andy Lixey awakens to his Timex watch alarm. He rushes to the bathroom, hoping to get there before his sister, Johanna. He brushes his teeth with Pepsodent, rinses with Signal, and showers with Lifebuoy.

Then Andy and his family have a quick breakfast. The family catches the morning news on their Panasonic television. Dr. Lixey serves Nestlé's hot chocolate, Hills Brothers coffee, and Stouffer's frozen waffles (right from his Sharp microwave oven) with Mrs. Butterworth's syrup. Even the family cat, Midnight, gets her can of Friskies. Leftovers are put in the Frigidaire refrigerator.

Soon it's time to leave for swimming practice. The children are driven in the family Honda Accord, fueled with Shell gasoline and rolling on Firestone tires. On the way they enjoy some Sony tapes that Mrs. Lixey recently bought. As Andy and Johanna get out of the car, they ask their parents if they can have lunch at Burger King.

Perhaps your Saturday morning starts like the Lixeys'. You may be surprised to learn that every brand name or company the Lixeys use in this example is made or owned by a foreign-owned business.

Ironically, for decades the United States has led the world in delivering products to international markets. American products from companies such as Coca-Cola, Kodak, Procter & Gamble, and McDonald's are in stores, restaurants, and homes around the world. However, the United States is also a major market for our foreign competitors.

Japan, Germany, Great Britain, and other foreign nations have had a major impact on our economy and on our daily lives. Each of these nations is involved in international marketing, the subject of this chapter.

The Advantages of International Marketing

Every nation buys and/or sells products across international boundaries. This exchange of goods and services among nations is **international trade**. The marketing activities that facilitate this trade are collectively called **international marketing**.

Companies involved in international trade import or export products. **Imports** are those goods and services purchased by companies in one nation from organizations in other nations for domestic use. **Exports**, on the other hand, are goods and services produced in one nation and sold in other nations.

Approximately 39,000 U.S. manufacturers—about one in ten—export their goods. The top 250 U.S. *multinationals*—corporations that operate in several countries and have a substantial part of their assets, sales, or labor force in foreign subsidiaries—account for about 85 percent of our $400 billion in exports.[1] (See Table 12–1 on page 148.)

Advantages to Consumers

International trade brings several advantages to consumers. First, consumers have a much wider selection of goods. We can import wicker furniture and baskets from Taiwan, crystal and linen from Ireland, sophisticated stereo and camera equipment from Japan, and other consumer and industrial products that the United States may not produce. Exporting gives the Chinese Coca-Cola, the Russians wheat, the British IBM computers, and the Nigerians John Deere tractors.

Another advantage to consumers is lower prices. For example, the United States can often import products at prices that are lower than they would be if those same products were manufactured in the United States. Such is the case with many toys from Taiwan, clothing from Indonesia, and shoes from Brazil.

Also, since foreign marketers bring additional goods into a country, supply increases. This naturally tends to lower prices as well. Foreign goods also increase competition which helps maintain the quality of domestic goods. International trade affects the economic interdependence of nations. Each nation relies on other nations for its economic survival.

Company	Foreign Sales As Percent of Total	Best-Selling Product Abroad	Biggest Market Abroad
Boeing	46%	Commercial Airliners	Western Europe
Caterpillar	50%	Earthmoving Equipment	Western Europe
Dow	55%	Industrial Chemicals	Canada
Eastman Kodak	45%	Amateur Film	Britain
Ford Motor	25%	Escort Subcompact	Britain
General Electric	22%	Aircraft Engines	Germany
Hewlett-Packard	52%	Computer Workstations	Germany
Merck	50%	Vasotec (Blood Pressure Medication)	N.A.
Outboard Marine	20%	Outboard Motors	Canada
Scott Paper	38%	Bathroom Tissue	Western Europe
Sun Microsystems	42%	Computer Workstations	Japan
3M	46%	Pressure-Sensitive Tape	Germany

Source: Alex Taylor III, "The U.S. Gets Back in Fighting Shape," *Fortune*, April 24, 1989, p. 45.

■■■ *Table 12–1 Top Global Marketers*
This table shows the percentage of business done by U.S. companies with foreign countries. What is one advantage to international trade?

Advantages to Workers and Producers

International trade has several advantages for workers and producers. For U.S. workers, exporting provides an estimated 7.2 million full-time jobs. For producers such as Coca-Cola, exporting means more customers and thus greater profits. Coca-Cola obtains approximately 46 percent of its sales and 68 percent of its earnings from foreign countries. Foreign companies also invest in the United States, building factories that employ U.S. workers. Similarly, U.S. companies invest abroad. Another advantage is the achievement of economies of scale. As the market grows larger, the producer can manufacture more at a lower cost. This usually results in greater profits for producers and lower prices for consumers.

Advantages to Nations

International trade plays a major role in the world's economies. For example, in the United States today, imports and exports account for about a quarter of our gross national product (GNP).

Many nations will specialize by exporting products for which they have an absolute advantage and importing the products that other countries can produce more efficiently. Nations achieve an **absolute advantage** when they are the only country producing a product or when they can produce the product at a lower cost than any other nation.

An absolute advantage can result from a nation's natural resources, labor, technology, and/or climate. It can also result if the nation has a monopoly on the world market. For example, South Africa enjoys an absolute advantage in diamonds. It is one of the few locations in the world where a large concentration of diamonds is found.

Most nations do not have unique natural resources or specialized production capabilities. Instead, they utilize their comparative advantage. A nation has a **comparative advantage** when it specializes in those products it can supply more efficiently and at a lower cost or with greater benefits than other nations.

The United States has gained comparative advantage in the production of chemicals, airplanes, automobiles, and electrical machinery. By concentrating on what they do best, nations are better able to use their natural resources, technology, labor, and climate to produce more efficiently.

When actively engaging in international trade, every nation must be concerned with its balance of trade. A nation's **balance of trade** is the difference between the value of its imports and exports.

A *positive balance of trade* occurs when a nation exports more than it imports. This results in more jobs and less debt because the nation is producing more than it consumes. A *negative balance of trade* occurs when a nation imports more than it exports. (See Figure 12–1.)

In recent years the United States has experienced a negative balance of trade. Despite being the world's leading exporter, the United States bought more products than it sold. This balance of trade reflects the nature of the U.S. economy. It is changing from an economy based on agriculture and manufacturing to one based on providing services.

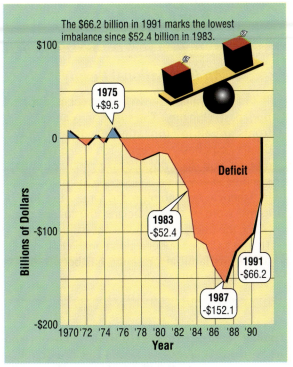

The $66.2 billion in 1991 marks the lowest imbalance since $52.4 billion in 1983.

Billions of Dollars

$100

1975
+$9.5

0

Deficit

1983
-$52.4

-$100

1991
-$66.2

1987
-$152.1

-$200

1970 '72 '74 '76 '78 '80 '82 '84 '86 '88 '90
Year

Source: *News & Daily Advance*, February 14, 1992.

■■■ *Figure 12–1 U.S. Trade Balance*
Shown here is the U.S. trade balance from 1970 through 1991. When does a negative balance of trade occur?

As a result, the United States must import products it once produced but are now produced more efficiently abroad.

Disadvantages and Barriers to International Marketers

Although there are many advantages to international trade and marketing, there are also such drawbacks as legal difficulties, trade barriers, and political risks. Let's look at each of these.

Legal Difficulties

When trading with other nations, a marketer cannot expect the laws to be the same as those in the United States. For example, some nations forbid profits from leaving their territory because they have weak economies. Such is the case in China, which requires joint venture partnerships. International *joint venture partnerships* are arrangements in which the manufacturing or marketing operations are owned in part by a domestic company or by individual domestic citizens and in part by a foreign company or foreign citizens.

One celebrated joint venture partnership exists between Chrysler and the Chinese government. Together they own and operate the Bejing Jeep Corporation. The majority of profits earned stay in China. Like many joint venture partnerships, the Bejing Jeep Corporation has created its share of difficulties for Chrysler.

For example, production once stopped for two months because the Chinese refused to provide the funds needed to buy component parts. Legally, Chrysler could do nothing. Finally, Chrysler (then AMC) agreed to make a new model.[2]

Some countries do not recognize U.S. trademarks or copyrights. Therefore, U.S. movies, records, books, and designer labels can be freely copied. In other words, there is little or no protection offered by the law.

Trade Barriers

As you now know, nations trade for many reasons. Nevertheless, some governments restrict free trade to protect their country's products from foreign competition. They do this by creating **trade barriers**, which are restrictions, such as tariffs, quotas, and embargoes on imports.

The most commonly used trade barrier is the **tariff**—a tax placed on imported goods. Tariffs are flexible, selective, and can provide both revenue and protection.

For example, in the United States, tariffs are placed on such products as autos and televisions from Japan or crystal from Ireland. The amount of the tariff is based on the original cost and the nation of origin.

Quotas are limitations on the amount of goods legally imported into a nation. For example, the Japanese voluntarily placed a $2.3 million quota on the number of autos exported to the United States.

Another type of trade barrier is the embargo. An **embargo** is the total ban of a good from entering or leaving a nation. For instance, before U.S. forces ousted Panamanian leader Manual Noriega for drug trafficking and government corruption, former President Reagan imposed embargoes and other economic sanctions against Panama. The United States lifted all sanctions after Noriega was ousted from power. The United States also embargoed grapes from Chile when a partially poisoned shipment was found. The embargo was lifted after several weeks.

Risks

The political risks of engaging in international marketing seem to increase each year. Marketers should consider these risks when deciding to trade internationally.

First, there is the risk of a nation's possibly nationalizing or taking over the business. This happened to a U.S. business in 1938 in Mexico when the government decreed expropriation (or took possession) of foreign petroleum companies. Other risks include the kidnapping of personnel, other acts of terrorism, and possible war which would halt trade.

Methods of Entering Global Markets

Once a business decides to market a product in a foreign country, it must then determine the best method of entering that market. Choices include exporting, joint ventures, licensing, contract manufacturing, and direct investment. Let's look at each of these.

Exporting

Exporting is the simplest method of entering a foreign market. Companies can use either direct or indirect exporting. The use of international marketing intermediaries to sell a company's products is called *indirect exporting.*

For example, a company could use the services of export trading companies such as Sears or Kmart

Global MARKETPLACE

An International Beauty

Imagine walking down Vaci Street in historic Budapest, Hungary. The street signs and storefronts are all in Hungarian. Then a window display catches your eye—Estée Lauder cosmetics! You do a double-take. You could be standing at any Estée Lauder counter anywhere in America. Everything is the same—the "uniforms" worn by sales associates, the counter displays, the fragrances. You're not hallucinating. Thanks to Estée Lauder's global marketing campaigns, its familiar presence has been established around the world.

Trading Services to export to wholesalers or retailers worldwide. *Trading companies* are organizations authorized by the Export Trading Act of 1982 to expand American exports. Their goal is to help foreign retailers design, build, and manage stores and to supply them with U.S. goods.

If a company handles its own exporting efforts, it engages in *direct exporting.* For example, suppose IBM opens a branch in Paris and uses its own sales force to sell computers to the French. It is then involved in direct exporting.

This method is more risky and expensive than indirect exporting, but the potential rewards are greater. The company also has greater control of its distribution channels. Often a company starts with indirect exporting and switches to direct exporting.

Joint Ventures

As you know, an international joint venture is a partnership between a domestic and a foreign company. This arrangement allows companies to operate production facilities in other countries. Often, in fact, many foreign governments require firms entering their countries to form joint ventures. Joint ventures may include licensing, franchising, and contract manufacturing.

In 1990, McDonald's and the Russian city of Moscow jointly opened the first McDonald's restaurant in that city. PepsiCo and the government of India reached a similar agreement to bottle and sell Pepsi. This joint venture in India created 1,000 new jobs.

Licensing

Licensing is a temporary agreement that allows a company (the licensee) to use a trademark, patent, copyright, or manufacturing process that belongs to another company (the licensor). The domestic company, the licensor, then earns a fee or royalty. For example, Calvin Klein and Jordache have entered licensing agreements with Brazilian manufacturers. The Brazilian manufacturers (the licensees) are allowed to manufacture these products for a fee paid to the U.S. companies (the licensors).

A form of licensing is international franchising. It is very much like franchising in the United States. In an international franchising agreement, however, the foreign licensing partner, the licensee, maintains greater control over the company. Wendy's, Kentucky Fried Chicken, Burger King, and other fast-food restaurants have been very successful with their international franchising operations.

International franchising is also popular with other companies such as Holiday Inn, Merry Maids, Manpower, and Hertz. More than 400 U.S. companies operate international franchises.

Contract Manufacturing

In **contract manufacturing** the domestic company contracts with a foreign manufacturer to produce products to its specifications and with its label. This method is very cost-effective because it avoids investment costs and often takes advantage of inexpensive labor. One disadvantage is that sometimes U.S. jobs are lost to foreign labor forces. For example, Ford makes Escorts in Mexico. Johnson & Johnson makes first-aid products in Argentina.

Direct Investment

Companies that want to own and operate their own manufacturing plants in foreign countries use the direct investment method. This is often a cost-effective way of entering a global market. Some companies, such as Swiss-owned Nestlé, will invest directly by purchasing existing plants in which to

■ ■ ■   *Kentucky Fried Chicken opened the world's largest fast-food restaurant in Beijing, the People's Republic of China. What method did Kentucky Fried Chicken use to enter this global market?*

manufacture their products. (See Figure 12–2 on page 152.) For example, Nestlé purchased Carnation, the evaporated milk and food producer.

Special Concerns for International Marketers

Marketers who export or import goods or services face special marketing concerns. These include communications difficulties, customs and traditions, and differences in buying habits. Let's take a closer look at each of these concerns.

Country	Selected Companies and Products
Anglo-Dutch	Royal Dutch Shell; Shell Oil; Unilever: Wisk, All, Breeze, Rinso, Lux, Dove, Caress, Lifebuoy, Signal, Aim, Close-up, Pepsodent, Imperial, Mrs. Butterworth's Syrup, Lawry's seasonings, Lipton teas and soups, Wish-Bone salad dressings, Knox gelatin, Lucky Whip
Brazil	Copersucar: Hills Brothers coffee
France	Club Mediterraus'e: resorts and youth camps (Copper Mtn., CO). Société Bic: Bic pens and lighters
Japan	Bridgestone Tire: Firestone tires Brother Industries: business machines Honda Accord and Acura cars, lawnmowers, motorcycles and electronic parts Matsushita: Quasar TV sets; Datsun trucks Nissan: trucks Sharp: TV sets and microwave ovens Sony: records, videotapes and audio-disks
Norway	Olsen, Lehmkul Families: Timex watches
Sweden	Electrolux: Eureka vacuum cleaners, Frigidaire, Westinghouse, Kelvinator, and Gibson microwave ovens and air conditioners
Switzerland	Nestlé: Nescafé, Taster's Choice, Carnation Co., Libby's canned food, Stouffers restaurants and frozen foods, Nestea, Nestlé chocolate bars Sandoz: Ovaltine
Allied	B.A.T. Saks Fifth Ave. and Gimbels department stores Beechum Group: McLeans Aquafresh, Sucrets, Cling Free, Brylcreem, Calgon British Petroleum: BP, Sohio, Boron gasoline, Purina animal feeds W. Lyons: Baskin-Robbins Reckirt and Culman: French's mustard Grand Metropolitan: Pearle Vision Centers Pillsbury: Burger King, Green Giant, Jeno's, VandeKamp, Häagen-Däzs
Germany	BASF: Auto paint, chemicals Tengelman Group: A&P Bayer: Alka-Seltzer, One-A-Day Vitamins, SOS Pads; plastics, herbicides, typesetting equipment Bertelsmann: Bantam books Hugo Mann: Fed-mart department stores Continental: General Tires
Canada	Campeau Corp: Federated Department Stores

■■■ *Figure 12–2 Made in the U.S.A. by Foreign Companies*
Foreign companies have increasingly become interested in establishing companies within the United States. Why?

Communications

You don't have to travel abroad to experience communications problems. If you live in upstate New York, you undoubtedly realize what an asset it is to speak French. In the Southwest or in southern Florida, knowing how to communicate in Spanish is helpful. Obviously, if you don't speak the same language as your trading partner, you have a problem. Over the years U.S. businesses involved in international trade have made numerous communications blunders.

Take, for example, Chevrolet, which tried to market its popular Nova model in South America. After a long period of slow sales, the firm finally realized that *No va* in Spanish means "does not go." Another classic was the faulty translation of Pepsi's "Come Alive with Pepsi" slogan. The German translation used in ads was "Come alive out of the grave." [3]

Customs and Traditions

Customs and traditions are part of a nation's culture. Cultural differences are the most significant and troublesome variable for international marketing firms. It is important to understand cultural differences.

For example, when negotiating with an Arab, it is unwise to set deadlines. Arabs feel threatened by deadlines, and they only serve to delay rather than expedite progress.

Even something as simple as gift-giving can cause problems. In many countries, gift-giving by businesspeople can be considered a bribe. However, in some countries such as in the Middle East, gifts are expected to be given publicly. In contrast, gifts are given privately in Asia to avoid embarrassment.

Differences in Buying Habits

Before offering products to foreign consumers, the international marketer must study the market carefully. Research must try to answer these basic questions:

- Is there a need for my product?
- Who are my potential customers?
- What is their level of earnings?
- What are their buying habits?
- What are their buying motives?

Each country has its own culture and customs that influence buying decisions. Therefore, marketers must conduct research in each country in which they are selling products.

Buying motives in foreign markets are not always the same as those in U.S. markets. Each country has its own social patterns. People make buying choices according to their country's value system.

For example, in Britain, General Foods discovered too late that English shoppers look for gelatin in cakes or cookies. Marketers also misread the British market when they first introduced Campbell Soups to Britain. They positioned Campbell Soups in concentrated form on shelves next to British soups which already had the water included. The British felt the larger English cans, which were sold at the same price, were a better bargain.

Colors are also culturally significant. Many colors have special meanings. In Brazil purple is a death color, as is white in Japan. In Africa green is the color of disease. Marketers consider the cultural significance of color especially when deciding on packaging and labeling colors.

Efforts to Promote International Trade

To maintain a favorable balance of trade, governments and multinational corporations must promote their products. Several types of activities have been developed to increase world cooperation and to assist in international marketing.

For example, the U.S. Department of Commerce runs more than 50 promotional programs. These include a worldwide computer network to match prospective U.S. exporters with buyers in key importing nations. Also included are trade missions in major foreign cities. Trade missions are a staff of international trade specialists. They are assigned to embassies and consulates to facilitate trade. Other examples of promotion and international cooperation involve international financial assistance, foreign-trade zones, and common markets.

Principles into Practice

North American Free Trade Agreement (NAFTA) vs. The European Community (EC)

Canada and the United States are the world's two biggest trading partners. In late 1987 the United States and Canada signed an historic free-trade agreement to eliminate all trade barriers. In 1992, the controversial agreement was expanded to include Mexico.

The net effect will be an expansion of markets for all three countries. The expansion will create an estimated 150,000 jobs in Canada, 48,000 in Mexico, and 300,000 in the United States—a total of almost 500,000 new jobs.

In reality the United States, Mexico, and Canada are creating a free-trade area (versus a common market). Increasingly, these three countries will operate as a single $6 trillion continental economy. This will be 13 percent larger than the United States on its own and 18 percent larger than the European Community (EC). Eventually, the NAFTA treaty will mean the following:

- easier border crossings between Mexico, the United States, and Canada for business purposes;

- a lifting of purchase restrictions on U.S., Mexican, or Canadian goods by government agencies; and

- a reduction or removal of tariffs and other barriers on 27,000 goods and services from advertising to car parts to financial services and textiles. Between 1993 and 2008, as many as 20,000 separate tariffs will be rolled back.

Being larger and more powerful than the EC is very important to the United States. In 1992 the 12-nation EC with 325 million consumers lifted most internal trade barriers. The EC seeks total economic integration among member nations. According to EC officials, this move gives a one-time boost to the EC economy and creates 5 million new jobs.

This makes Europe a mass market. It could also give the EC a competitive advantage unless companies in the United States can position themselves to become more involved in the European Community. This can be done through direct investment and joint ventures between U.S. and European companies. Regardless, the NAFTA has the EC worried.

In general, the United States, Mexico, and Canada will see a shift in manufacturing strategies. Production systems must be overhauled and revised to compensate for the changes that a no-tariff system will bring. High-volume production lines are being shifted to the United States and Mexico, and small-volume, specialized lines are being shifted to Canada. Before long "Made-in-the-USA," "Made-in-Mexico," and "Made-in-Canada" will no longer have the same meaning.

Although the trade agreement may not have an immediate impact on you, the effects of the agreement will be felt by businesses worldwide. The end result will be a stronger and more competitive U.S. economy that can better maintain our high standard of living.[4, 5, 6]

1. Why will "Made-in-the-USA," "Made-in-Mexico," and "Made-in-Canada" no longer have the same meaning?
2. Describe how the United States will benefit from NAFTA.

International Financial Assistance

There are several sources of financial assistance available to importers and exporters. One source is the Export-Import Bank (Eximbank), founded as an independent U.S. government agency in 1934. Today the Eximbank finances loans to exporters who cannot find funds through commercial sources and to foreign nations that need funds to purchase U.S. products.

The world's less-developed and poorer nations can obtain international financial assistance from either the World Bank or the International Monetary Fund (IMF). The World Bank was founded in 1946. It has 149 member countries and is associated with the United Nations. In the late 1980s it lent more than $15 billion a year for long-term projects ranging from factories to health care. Its counterpart, the IMF, has 151 member countries. It works to secure international cooperation, stabilize exchange rates, and loan short-term funds to needy nations for private enterprise projects.

Major industrial nations that support the IMF and the World Bank, such as the United States, Japan, the United Kingdom, and Germany, believe that increased trade increases everyone's wealth. Resources provide useful products and more jobs.

Foreign-Trade Zones

Foreign-trade zones promote international marketing cooperation. A *foreign-trade zone* is a designated area set aside to allow businesses to store, process, assemble, and display certain products from abroad without first paying a tariff. A tariff is eventually paid when the product leaves the zone. However, it does not apply to the cost of assembly or to the subsequent profits.

The Foreign Trade Zone Act of 1934 authorized the use of trade zones. The first foreign-trade zone was established in New York City. The use of trade zones grew slowly. In 1970 there were only ten trade zones in the United States. But, challenged by foreign competition, the number grew to more than 250 in the 1990s.

Countries create foreign-trade zones to attract foreign investment and to create jobs at home. For instance, the Berg Steel Pipe Co., a French-German joint venture, employs American workers in Panama City, Florida, to manufacture pipe for the oil industry.

Berg can move raw materials into this foreign-trade zone without paying tariffs. Finished goods in the United States are taxed at a lower rate than raw materials. Berg pays no U.S. tax on goods that it ships outside the United States.

Common Markets

Common markets are groups of geographically associated nations that trade as a block. Presently, there are 12 trading-block groups around the world.

Common market members agree to limit trade barriers among member nations and to apply a common external tariff to products entering their nations. The best-known common market is the 12-member European Community (EC) founded in 1958. The members include France, the United Kingdom, Ireland, Denmark, Germany, Spain, Greece, Italy, Belgium, Portugal, the Netherlands, and Luxembourg. The EC is expected to expand to as many as 20 members during the 1990s.

In 1992 the EC completed the standardization of most existing corporate laws and accounting procedures. It dropped all trade barriers among member nations. As a result, most American companies will find tougher competition along with more opportunity.

The North American Free Trade Agreement (NAFTA) is a free-trade agreement with some similarities to a common market. Its member nations include the United States, Canada, and Mexico. It constitutes the world's largest free-trade zone—363 million people and a combined economy of $6.4 trillion.

CHAPTER NOTES

1. William J. Holstein, "Little Companies, Big Exports," *Business Week*, 13 April 1992, p. 70.
2. Louis Kraar, "The China Bubble Bursts," *Fortune*, 6 July 1987, p. 88.
3. David A. Ricks, *Big Business Blunders* (New York: Dow-Jones, 1983), pp. 7–8.
4. Barbara Rudolph, "MegaMarket," *Time*, August 1992, pp. 43–44.
5. Susan Katz, "Cold Trade Winds from the North," *Insight*, 2 November 1987, pp. 34–35.
6. Stewart W. Husted, "European Community '92: An Impossible Dream?," *Perspective on Marketing*, January 1991.

Chapter Summary

- International marketing benefits consumers, workers and producers, and nations. Some advantages include: greater selection of products, lower prices, more jobs, the achievement of economies of scale, and a higher standard of living.

- Some nations will specialize in and export products which only they can produce or which they can produce at a lower cost than other nations. This is called an absolute advantage. Because most nations do not have an absolute advantage, they will produce products which they can supply more efficiently and at a lower cost than they can other items. This is called a comparative advantage.

- Drawbacks when dealing with international trade include legal difficulties, trade barriers, and political risks.

- Companies have several methods for engaging in international marketing, including exporting, joint ventures, licensing, contract manufacturing, and direct investment.

- Before entering an international market, companies must consider communications, customs and traditions, and differences in buying habits.

- Methods used to promote international trade include financial assistance (Export-Import Bank and the IMF), foreign-trade zones, and common markets. In addition in the United States, the Department of Commerce runs more than 50 programs to assist our businesses in international competition.

Building Your Marketing Vocabulary

On a separate sheet of paper, define each of these marketing terms. Then using each term, write a 250-word paper on international marketing.

international trade	trade barriers
international marketing	tariff
imports	quotas
exports	embargo
absolute advantage	contract manufacturing
comparative advantage	common markets
balance of trade	

Questions for Review

1. Explain why nations engage in international trade.
2. Describe how international trade affects the economic interdependence of nations.
3. How does a country achieve an absolute advantage in trade?
4. When is the balance of trade favorable? Describe the current U.S. balance of trade.
5. Name three disadvantages to international trade.
6. List and describe three types of trade barriers.
7. What are five methods of entering global markets?
8. Besides legal difficulties and trade barriers, what three special types of concerns must international marketers consider?
9. Name three types of activities that have been developed to promote international trade.
10. What is the purpose of the European Community?

Critical Thinking

1. Name a product imported by the United States that has a comparative advantage over a U.S. product.
2. What can a country do to remedy a negative balance of trade?
3. Why would a country place a quota on the number of goods it exports to another country?
4. Suppose you are marketing clothing to Japan. Would you use indirect or direct exporting to market your product? Why?
5. Suppose you are marketing toothpaste internationally. What types of concerns might you have about marketing internationally? What types of specific research information would you want to obtain?

Discussion Questions

1. Give three examples of imported products. Discuss why you might buy these products over comparable U.S. products.

2. Discuss the causes of international economic interdependence.

3. Do you think a comparative advantage can have a positive effect for all nations involved?

4. Discuss what you feel are the pros and cons of NAFTA.

5. Discuss possible disadvantages and barriers to international marketers. Give examples of businesses that have faced these difficulties.

Marketing Project

Analyzing a Foreign Market

Project Goal: Given a specific product, analyze the market for that product in a foreign country.

Directions: Select a product that is exported from the United States. Then select a potential foreign market. After carefully studying the market for your product, design a chart like the one below and state your findings in the appropriate columns. Give your sources of information about the market you studied.

	Example:
Name of Product/ Country	Cosmetics/Japan
Potential Customers	Female teenagers/ young adults
Level of Income	Lower- to middle- income
Buying Habits	Frequent
Buying Motives	Romance, better appearance
Recommended Exports (Yes/No)	Yes

Applied Academics

Language Arts

1. As a marketer for an international business, you have been asked to develop an advertisement promoting stereos in Spain. Research Spanish customs and traditions to determine the best way to approach this audience and how to avoid a cultural communications problem. Write your findings in a 250-word paper.

Math

2. Suppose you are importing 15,000 pounds of goods. The tariff on the goods is 25 cents per pound. How much will the total tariff be?

Marketing and Multiculturalism

Now, as a result of increased use of technology, world consumers are able to sample the cultures of countries firsthand without even leaving their homes. For example, American consumers can lunch on fish flown in directly from Japan. Japanese consumers can obtain American outdoor clothing overnight by placing a fax order with such companies as L. L. Bean. Japanese executives have even been known to experience the flavor of the Wild West by importing log cabins from Montana. This increased exposure to global culture provides endless opportunities for the creative marketer.

1. What multicultural global products have you purchased that may not have been available in the United States 50 years ago?

2. Discuss how the increased exposure to global cultures is providing new opportunities for marketers.

3. Discuss three U.S. products that are popular in other countries. What effect are they having on these countries?

4. What impact will global products have on the cultures of countries?

5. Explain why marketers still may use different advertising campaigns when marketing products in other countries.

Doctors Without Borders

In 1991, millions of people were dying from starvation in Somalia. A severe drought and a civil war had wreaked havoc on their society. Long before American troops arrived, long before world governments took action, Doctors Without Borders was in Somalia fighting famine with more than 100 volunteers. Surgeons, anesthetists, doctors, nurses, and logistics experts worked around the clock running feeding centers and providing emergency medical care.

The goal of Doctors Without Borders is to serve people around the world who need emergency medical care. It is the world's largest private nonprofit emergency medical aid organization. There are millions of people today

suffering the effects of war and disaster who benefit from the services of Doctors Without Borders. In fact, Doctors Without Borders is often the first relief organization to arrive at a crisis scene. "We are, by nature, unable to tolerate indifference, and we believe that it is *possible* and *necessary* to take action," says Dr. Rony Brauman, president of Doctors Without Borders.

Founded in France in 1971, the organization undertakes about 700 worldwide missions a year. During its existence more than 5,000 doctors have voluntarily worked for Doctors Without Borders. Emergency relief missions have taken them to countries such as Bosnia, Croatia, Serbia, Bangladesh, Liberia, Cambodia, Somalia, Ethiopia, and Sudan.

Once Doctors Without Borders receives notice of an area requiring emergency medical care, it sends in a team of experts who determine the medical, nutritional, and sanitary needs. Using the team's information, a coordination center is set up to organize the budget, personnel, and medical equipment needed. Medical teams can then be sent into the traumatized area to provide medical treatment. The average mission lasts about six months.

It takes millions of dollars to fund these missions. Private donors contribute 50 percent of its European funds. The rest of the funds come from governments and international organizations such as the European Community and UNICEF. Doctors Without Borders raises funds and public awareness through such efforts as concerts, exhibitions, book sales, records produced for the organization's benefit, and galas.

In 1992, the Los Angeles office of Doctors Without Borders' annual gala raised more than $100,000 for the organization. The event included a silent auction of items donated by local stores and photographs from a recent mission shown by actress Jamie Lee Curtis, a Doctors Without Borders supporter.

In 1993, Doctors Without Borders was chosen as the official charity of the Los Angeles Marathon. Being affiliated with such high visibility events gives the organization additional positive recognition.

Doctors Without Borders also conducts direct-mail campaigns to recruit donors. The American office sends out approximately 500,000 pieces of mail in a single marketing effort to obtain donations. In addition, to keep its donors abreast of the latest developments and to gain greater recognition, it publishes a semiannual newsletter.

Taking on Doctors Without Borders' immense and noble mission is no easy task. But extensive marketing efforts have allowed this nonprofit organization to forge ahead to meet its goals. [1,2]

1. Into what type of market does Doctors Without Borders fall?

2. Based on this case and what you learned from Chapter 11, describe the nonprofit marketing characteristics of Doctors Without Borders in terms of:
    a. measurement of performance;
    b. multiple publics;
    c. public scrutiny; and
    d. intangibility.

3. What types of nonprofit marketing does Doctors Without Borders undertake?

4. Describe the marketing mix of Doctors Without Borders.

5. As you know from Chapter 12, politics can interfere with international marketing efforts. Discuss the possible political risks that Doctors Without Borders may face.

CASE NOTES

1. *Doctors Without Borders USA Inc., Newsletter,* Vol. 2, No. 2, Winter 1992–1993.
2. Press kit from Doctors Without Borders, March 1993.

UNIT 4

Marketing Research

The Importance of Marketing Research

Terms to Know

marketing research

marketing information
    system (MIS)

market research

sales research

product research

advertising research

preliminary research

formal research

research plan

Chapter Objectives

After studying this chapter, you will be able to:

- define *research* and explain the aims and justifications of marketing research;
- name and explain four kinds of marketing research;
- list the five steps in the problem-solving process and identify preliminary and formal research;
- explain the purpose of the marketing research plan; and
- write a preliminary plan to solve a local marketing problem you have identified.

Case Study

Why the Yellow Pages Began to Talk

"Most of the consumers who use Yellow Pages directories have already made up their minds that they want to buy a product or service," says Kenneth O. Johnson, president of Donnelley Directory. "They're only deciding *where* to buy it. Business-people who advertise in the Yellow Pages know their ads will be targeted not just to likely buyers but to *certain* buyers."[1]

The Yellow Pages are an established marketing tool for businesses. People naturally turn to the telephone book when they want particular information. Research shows that the average household refers to the telephone book 65 times a year.

When marketers at Donnelley Directory were seeking ways to make the Yellow Pages even more valuable to users and advertisers, they conducted marketing research. It showed that consumers wanted a lot more information than the Yellow Pages offered at the time. The information consumers considered most useful dealt with their daily activities—that is, up-to-the-minute life-style information, such as the news, weather, and sports.

Other research showed that Yellow Pages business advertisers would like to offer up-to-the-minute or time-sensitive information and promote new products, special services, or reduced prices. For example, a hardware store might offer a spring sale with special prices on mowers, grass seed, and fertilizers.

Both the consumer life-style information and the desired business ads were time-sensitive. Donnelley Directory needed to figure out how to present such information in a publication printed annually. Was it possible to offer Talking Yellow Pages?

Fortunately, the technology existed in the form of audiotex—voice-response computers programmed with prerecorded messages. By dialing a nine-digit number and a four-digit code, Yellow Pages users can hear the latest life-style information such as traffic conditions, stock market reports, entertainment information, and even book reviews—all at no charge.

As you can see, the Yellow Pages did begin talking. The Talking Yellow Pages are presently in more than 50 major markets. By using marketing research, the company continually measures and monitors its effectiveness.[2]

Marketing Research

What is marketing research, and how does it work? Research is the careful study of a subject. **Marketing research** is the gathering, recording, and analyzing of facts related to marketing goods and services. The Donnelley Directory and other companies find out what their customers want through marketing research.

In today's competitive marketing world, more decisions are based on the results of marketing research than ever before. Although research may not always contain all the answers to marketers' questions, it can provide useful information. It links the consumer, customer, and public to the marketer through information that is used to identify and define marketing problems; to generate, refine, and evaluate marketing actions; to monitor marketing performance; and to improve understanding of marketing as a process.

Marketing research specifies the information required to address these issues and designs the method for collecting information. It manages and implements the data collection process. It analyzes the results and communicates the findings and their implications.[3]

Marketing Research and the Marketing Concept

As you learned in Chapter 1, the objective of the marketing concept is to fulfill the wants and needs of customers at a profit (or other gain for a nonprofit organization). Marketers use marketing research to find out what customers want and need.

■ ■ ■ *Customers can do their own research—for example, determining the best prices per ounce with the help of a calculator on the grocery cart handle. Why is research important?*

Before Donnelley Directory offered the Talking Yellow Pages, for example, the company determined that consumers were interested in calling to hear recorded messages about a good or service. Marketing research helps individual marketing organizations such as Donnelley and its business advertisers to decide what they can best provide customers at a profit.

Research Is Widespread

Every business does some marketing research. Often it is informal. For example, the manager of a small diner may study customer demand to decide whether to add barbecued beef to the menu or stick to hot dogs, hamburgers, and pizza. A shoe store manager may think it would be good for business to give toys to toddlers. He or she then monitors this practice to see if it pays off in more sales and happier customers. These are forms of marketing research.

The larger the business, the more detailed and elaborate are its marketing research activities. Information is stored and analyzed with the help of computers. This sophisticated way of collecting information is known as a **marketing information system** (called an MIS). An MIS is an organized way of continually gathering, sorting, analyzing, evaluating, and distributing information to marketing managers.

General Electric, Chrysler, and Colgate-Palmolive use an MIS system and spend millions of dollars on marketing research each year. They not only have their own large marketing research staffs, but they also hire the services of independent marketing research organizations.

Marketing research information is one of several kinds of information a company includes in its marketing information system. You will explore MISs in greater detail in Chapter 15.

Costs and Benefits

The use of marketing research is growing among marketing businesses. More and more marketers are applying the marketing concept. They may conduct their own research or hire an outside research organization such as A.C. Nielsen Company.

However, any marketing research, whether done informally by a small organization or formally by a large organization, takes time and costs money. It is worth the cost only when marketers use the results of the research in practical ways to help improve a business.

Marketing research helps improve business and makes marketing more efficient and effective by doing the following:

- reducing the costs of marketing;
- generating market demand;
- making competition more keen; and
- improving the quality of life.

This efficiency can result in better products at lower prices and thus bring the business profit.

Kinds of Marketing Research

Marketing research activities can provide vital information about the potential market for a product and about customer likes and dislikes, sales trends, and the effectiveness of advertising. In addition to learning about customers' wants, another goal of marketing research is to improve the marketing mix.

To make this improvement, businesses often use various kinds of marketing research. Four of the most popular forms of marketing research are market research, sales research, product research, and advertising research. Let's take a look at each of these.

Market Research

The study of the nature and characteristics of a market is **market research**. (Note that market research is one kind of marketing research.) Through market research the marketer can determine how well a particular product is likely to sell.

Consider a marketer who is planning to sell a line of outdoor barbecue grills in the Midwest. This marketer wants to know the average temperature and the amount of rain the Midwest gets each month in order to determine those months when people are most likely to cook outdoors. By using market research to get such information, marketers can be more effective in planning their advertising and sales programs, and in coordinating production and shipping activities.

Sales Research

A question marketers often ask is "How does my product sell in comparison to my competitors'?"

■■■ *Why does Walker Research tell potential customers who do not use research to keep a rabbit's foot handy?*

Automobile manufacturers, insurance companies, cosmetics distributors, retail stores, and food processors, among others, all keep careful track of their competitive position through sales research. **Sales research** is the study of sales data.

For example, each Fanny May Candies learns through sales research how many pounds of candy were sold recently, what percentage Fanny May Candies sold, and what percentage competitors sold. With such information Fanny May managers can determine whether they need to take action to improve their market share—that is, their part of the total sales.

Such action might include increasing the amount of candy the store carries at peak periods such as

The World of Marketing Research

People know when they've been "sugged." The phone rings. While they think they're answering some questions for a survey, all of a sudden the caller asks if they want to buy some insurance or have a family portrait taken. This is *sugging* (selling under the guise of research). Sugging and true marketing research do not mix.

Unfortunately, sugging is increasing. According to a recent survey, 22 percent of the consumers surveyed said that in one year they had received at least one telephone call that began as a survey and turned into a sales message. This percentage was up from the previous year's 16 percent.

The Direct Marketing Association, the trade organization of direct marketers (those who sell via telephone, mail, and other direct ways), is trying to stop this practice. Sugging generally hurts the reputation of direct marketers.

Sugging also has made it much more difficult for real marketing research organizations to conduct telephone surveys. Increasingly, those people being called hesitate to cooperate with a marketing research telephone survey in order to avoid sugging.

In an attempt to combat this reluctance, one marketing research organization conducted an experiment. It prepared survey questions.

To one group of respondents, researchers immediately explained that they were not selling anything. To the other group, they went ahead and surveyed without referring to sugging. What were the results? When the phrase "We're not selling anything" was *not* used, cooperation improved immensely. What was the researchers' overall conclusion? Tell people what you *are* doing, not what you are *not* doing.[4,5]

1. What is your opinion of the business ethics of those organizations that try to sell products under the guise of conducting marketing research?
2. In this environment, what difficulties exist for the authentic marketing research organizations?
3. What is the effect of sugging on the consumer who believes he or she is participating in marketing research?

---

during the holidays. Or it could mean offering a wider variety of candies, introducing a new type of candy, or promoting a new way of packaging candy.

Sales research also involves a careful study of a company's own sales figures. Are sales up? And if so, are profits up, too? Or have expenses increased even more rapidly? Are sales in line with the sales estimates? If not, why not?

If a product showed one rate of sales last year and another rate of sales this year, how should future sales be forecast? The answer to each one of these questions can help a marketer improve business operations.

Product Research

U.S. businesses design new products and modify old products every year in their laboratories. Before businesses manufacture these new or changed products in large quantities, they conduct product research to see how consumers are likely to accept them. **Product research** is the study of consumer reactions to a product.

Often, the reactions of consumers toward a product are totally negative. In these cases, the business changes the product drastically or abandons it entirely.

 *Before businesses design new products or modify old ones, they conduct research. What form of marketing research enables marketers to offer customers new and improved things to buy?*

But sometimes the product is successful. For example, whoever thought that juice would be drinkable after being packaged in a paper carton without refrigeration? Yet, these cartons are on supermarket shelves today because packaging technology made the "paper can" possible.

Product research determined that customers would buy products in these new containers. Customers find juices in a carton much easier to pack in school lunches or take on picnics than canned or bottled drinks.

Product research can also lead to increased variety and specialization. In the 1960s there was basically one type of athletic shoe. With the trend toward fitness in the late 1970s and 1980s, product research uncovered demand for more specialized athletic shoes. Today, consumers can choose from athletic shoes specially designed for tennis, basketball, aerobics, jogging, volleyball, walking, and other activities.

Again, business used technology to meet marketing needs. Nike-Air shoes, for instance, cushion the shock of the foot hitting the pavement with a gas-filled sac at the heel. Marketers carefully researched the design of Nike-Air shoes to produce the best result for the customer.[6]

Global MARKETPLACE

Digestive Marketing Research

"I won't sell what I wouldn't eat," says Toshifumi Suzuki of 7-Eleven Japan Co. He and 20 top managers taste noodles, prepackaged sandwiches, snacks, and other vending machine items vendors hope to sell in the 4,809-store chain. Conducting product research through personal experimentation and computer product-tracking allows 7-Eleven Japan to plug into consumer trends. It is so successful that its 42 percent operating margin far outshines that of rivals.

Advertising Research

A study conducted to determine the effectiveness of a company's advertising is **advertising research**. Most companies keep records of their advertising efforts. Some smaller organizations such as retail stores paste their ads in scrapbooks and note next to each ad when it appeared, how much it cost to produce, and the sales just before and immediately after the ad appeared. The scrapbooks serve as treasure houses of ideas for the marketer, and they tell which ads have proved the most successful.

Some advertisements contain coded coupons. When marketers receive the coupons, they can trace the code to the ad and the publication in which it was placed. These codes tell the marketer how effective both the ad and the media were.

Major advertisers rely on research organizations such as A.C. Nielsen to check on the performance of their advertising and other promotions. For example, imagine that Valley Coffee Company typically schedules a coffee promotion in the supermarkets in February. The company sets sales goals and plans advertising. It puts coupon inserts in newspapers and in promotional materials to accompany in-store coffee displays.

After the promotion is over, the company sees that some stores sold more coffee than planned while others sold less. Through Nielsen's advertising research, Valley Coffee learns that those stores selling the most coffee had set up in-store coffee displays and timed them with advertising and coupons in the newspapers. This information helps managers organize future advertising and promotions more effectively.[7]

The Problem-solving Process

When a company conducts marketing research, it usually does so because it faces a problem or wishes to improve some part of its operation. The problem may be a decline in sales or the need to market new products to meet competition. The company uses marketing research to help solve the problem. There is a five-step problem-solving procedure followed in marketing research.

1. Identify the problem and establish the goal of the research.
2. Develop a research plan for achieving the goal.
3. Collect information about the problem.
4. Prepare and analyze the information.
5. Apply the results of the research to the problem.

The first two steps constitute preliminary research. **Preliminary research**, then, is the process of identifying a problem and devising a plan for solving it. You will look at these two steps in this chapter.

Steps three and four constitute formal research. **Formal research** is the process of collecting and analyzing information about a problem.

Step five involves implementing the results of the research. These steps are illustrated in Figure 13–1. You will look at them again in Chapter 14.

Identifying the Problem and Setting the Goal

The general goal of any company's marketing research program is always to increase profits or avoid losses. A specific goal of a total marketing research program is to identify a certain marketing problem and set a goal to solve it.

For example, the purpose of one marketing research project might be to determine how consumers like a new type of shoe that keeps a shine without polishing. Another project might try to find out how customers like frozen meals for children that feature chicken nuggets, pasta, or hot dogs.

The specific goal of each project would be to determine consumer acceptance of a particular product. However, both projects would be undertaken with the ultimate goal of making more sales for the company and thus increasing profits.

Sometimes a company knows that its sales are dropping and it wants to find out why. No research activity would be set up around the goal of finding out why sales are declining; the objective of the research has to be more specific.

Consider Tina Ling, owner of a small boutique that carries accessories, scarves, belts, handbags, and custom jewelry that she makes herself. Tina is faced with one big problem: not enough people are stopping in her store. Thus, sales are declining.

Tina Ling could look at her empty shop all day without getting any closer to a solution. But she has

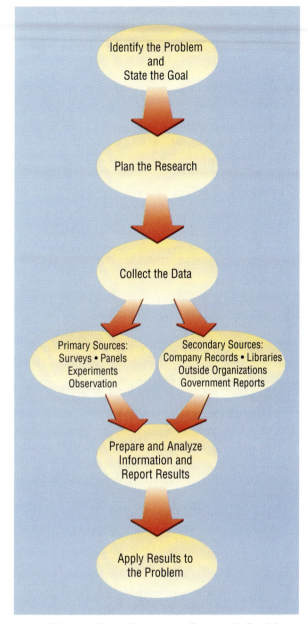

■ ■ ■ *Figure 13–1 Marketing Research Problem-solving Process*
Marketing research is a five-step process. The goal and plan (steps one and two) involve preliminary research. Which steps involve formal research?

a specific goal for a marketing research activity once she has asked herself, "Is my selection the best I can offer my customers?" or "Can they do better at Deborah's Boutique down the street?" Her goal is to find out whether her competition has a better assortment. The answer to this question may help solve Tina's problem or lead to other research questions.

Developing the Research Plan

Once a marketer decides on a specific goal, he or she must then choose the right method to gather information. Small business owners such as Tina Ling usually do their own research. If Tina wanted to compare Deborah's Boutique selection with her own, she could simply visit her competitor and look over the lines of merchandise. She would compare the differences in terms of style, quality, and price.

Research planning for a larger project, however, is not that simple. A **research plan** is a step-by-step outline of everything that is to be done during a research project. It lists the kinds of formal research that are to be done, when they are to be done, and in what order. It specifies the kind of personnel needed to do the work. It states the amount of money that the business must budget for the project and details how it is to be spent.

A good research plan serves as both a guide and a control. The plan shows each person what is to be done and indicates the budget for each phase.

When a marketer identifies a problem and sets up a research plan, the preliminary work is done. The next step is to do the formal research. You will explore formal research in Chapter 14.

CHAPTER NOTES

1. "Dedicated to the Success of Our Customers," The Dun & Bradstreet Corporation 1988 Annual Report, (New York), p. 18.

2. Interview with Bill Zierolf, Director, Business Development, Donnelley Directory, Purchase, NY 10577, 24 April 1990.

3. American Marketing Association, letter to members, 4 May 1987.

4. Harold C. Daume, "Don't Give Answer to 'Sugging' Question that Hasn't Been Asked," *Marketing News*, 2 January 1989, p. 2.

5. "The Persistence of Sugging," *Marketing News*, 28 September 1992, p. 4.

6. Bryan Iwamoto, "Just Do It," *Express Magazine*, Winter 1989, p. 10.

7. *Nielsen Sales Management*, Nielsen Marketing Research, The Dun & Bradstreet Corporation, 1988.

Chapter Summary

- Marketing research is the gathering, recording, and analyzing of facts related to marketing goods and services. Marketing research links the public to the marketer through information that is used to find marketing problems and to generate and evaluate marketing actions.
- There are several kinds of marketing research. These include market research, sales research, product research, and advertising research.
- There are five steps to the problem-solving process in marketing research. The first two steps involve preliminary research—the process of identifying the problem and developing a plan to solve it. The next two steps involve formal research—collecting and analyzing information about the problem. The last step is applying the research results to the problem.
- A marketing research plan is a step-by-step outline of everything that is to be done during a research project.

Building Your Marketing Vocabulary

1. On a separate sheet of paper, explain the difference between each set of terms below.
   - marketing research—market research
   - sales research—product research—advertising research
   - preliminary research—formal research
2. Write a 150-word paragraph that describes how a marketer uses each of the terms below.
   - marketing information system
   - research plan

Questions for Review

1. What does the term *research* mean?
2. How does marketing research relate to the marketing concept?
3. Name four ways in which marketing research makes marketing more efficient and effective.
4. Name four kinds of marketing research and explain the marketing areas that each covers.
5. List the five steps of the marketing research problem-solving process.
6. Identify the two steps involved with preliminary research.
7. What is formal research?
8. What is the purpose of the research plan? Why is it necessary?

Critical Thinking

1. Select three of the following products. For each product, describe a possible problem and a marketing research project to solve that problem: lawn chairs, men's after-shave, athletic socks, cat food, children's watercolor sets, plastic drinking glasses, kite string, step ladders, and tape cassette caddies.
2. Suppose you notice that the clothing catalog you receive every month is smaller this month. What type of research might the company be conducting by testing the catalog size?
3. What type of market research information might you want to obtain if you are considering expanding your tennis racket line into Canada?
4. Suppose sales for your line of cosmetics have dropped dramatically in the last six months. In what areas might you want to conduct research? Why?
5. How might information from market research relate to the advertising of a product?

Discussion Questions

1. Discuss what might happen if you introduce a new product without doing marketing research.
2. Do you think it is necessary for a company to conduct research for a product with a great sales record? Explain.
3. Discuss the possible actions you might take if you find through sales research that your competition is taking away your customers.
4. After choosing a local business in your area, discuss a marketing problem it may face and explain how you would use the five-step procedure to conduct marketing research.

Marketing Project

Initiating Marketing Research

Project Goal: Given a marketing problem of one or more local businesses, determine how marketing research could help solve the problem.

Directions: With the guidance of your teacher, interview a local marketer. Discuss a marketing problem either within the business or within the local business community. Ask the marketer to suggest ways of reaching solutions to the problem and to indicate how marketing research could help achieve each solution. Create a form like the one below and use it to conduct your preliminary research. Then write a preliminary research plan for conducting the marketing research needed.

Type of Business	Problem Faced	Plan for Resolving Problem
Example: Small yogurt shop	Should sugar-free items be added?	• Employees will keep track of requests for sugar-free products. • Create a questionnaire.

Applied Academics

Language Arts

1. Choose a good, service, or idea and develop a market research survey to determine its popularity in your school. Prepare a 250-word report on your findings. Based on your research, discuss the potential for marketing this good, service, or idea in your community.

Math

2. Bravo Jeans Company's planned sales for its annual promotion were set at $400,000. However, after the promotion, actual sales were $375,000. By what percentage were Bravo's actual sales below its planned sales?

Science

3. As a marketer of camping equipment, you are planning to sell your product in several states. Using an almanac, research the geography of a state you are not familiar with. Report in a 250-word paper on whether or not this would be a good state for your product, based on geography. Tell in which months it would be best to sell your products.

Marketing and Multiculturalism

Marketing research indicates that 19 percent of cosmetics and health and beauty aids, and 31 percent of all hair products, are purchased by African-American women. This is a considerable percentage, given the fact that African-American women make up only about 12.4 percent of the population. In addition, African-American and Hispanic women outspend other women on upscale cosmetic products.

1. Of what type of research is this an example?
2. What does this research say about the African-American and Hispanic markets for cosmetics?
3. What decisions might marketers make based on this research?

Chapter 14

Conducting Marketing Research

Terms to Know

primary data
secondary data
survey
mall intercept
focus group

mail questionnaire
experimentation
test marketing
observation
bias

Chapter Objectives

After studying this chapter, you will be able to:

- distinguish between primary and secondary data and describe methods of gathering each;
- explain the problems involved in sample selection and research bias;
- explain the steps involved in preparing and analyzing the data for a research report;
- describe the purposes and contents of marketing research reports; and
- prepare a research report.

Case Study

McKids Clothing Store Just for Kids

"You can go in that door," said five-year-old Linda Beacham to her mother. "I'll take this one."

Her mother agreed, watching Linda swing open the four-foot high door that seemed designed for her. Mrs. Beacham walked upright through the full-size air curtain door. Over those doors stood the Golden Arches that begin a world-famous word starting with the letters *Mc*. But this was no restaurant. McKids was a specialty store designed for children and filled with clothing, toys, and books.

"This store is made for me," cried Linda happily. "It's all my size!" The store—a cooperative effort between McDonald's and Sears, Roebuck & Co.—had six outlets in Illinois and one in Orlando, Florida.

McKids was planned and built to make children like Linda feel invited into the store. The bright interior featured white walls with red, yellow, and blue airplanes. Clothes were hung on easy-to-reach racks a child can handle.

Books, toys, and stuffed animals sat on display shelves where children could touch and hold them. The fitting-room mirrors were held at a child's height by frames in the form of Grimace, a McDonaldland character.

When children tired of shopping, a play area in the back of the store drew them in to sing-along video, painting, playing games, a special magic show, or a story hour. Meanwhile, TV monitors throughout the store let parents continue shopping while their kids play.

The ideas behind the McKids store grew from marketing research. Children were invited to test the height of fixtures and the size of benches. Managers even sat on the floor with children to see things as kids would.

McKids seemed to be a perfectly thought-out concept. However, after only a few months in operation, McDonald's and Sears closed almost all of the free-standing stores and offered the McKids brands only in Sears stores.

Sometimes the research a company does cannot provide all of the answers or predict success. McKids did not produce the sales volume anticipated. On the other hand, marketing research did let McDonald's and Sears know that the venture was not doing well. In the long run, marketing research saved needless expense.[1]

Collecting the Data

Businesspeople must make many important marketing decisions before opening a new business or introducing a new product. They must base their decisions on accurate information about their products and markets.

Gathering this information is the job of marketing researchers. They study markets, consumers' reactions to new products, and selling and advertising methods.

Marketing researchers must carefully collect, summarize, and interpret marketing research data. (Data means facts. Thus, when you use the term *data*, it is always plural.) Data are collected and processed to produce useful information and to help determine business trends, product acceptance, potential markets, and the effectiveness of advertising and selling.

Market researchers classify data as *primary* or *secondary*. Data gathered originally by researchers themselves for current use are **primary data**. Data already collected for another purpose, but which may be of use for the task at hand, are **secondary data**. Primary and secondary data do not refer to the value or usefulness of the data. They simply identify their source.

Primary and secondary data can be further classified as internal or external. Data collected from sources within a firm, such as sales figures, are internal. Data collected from sources outside a firm (from a survey, for example) are external.

Most marketing research involves collecting both primary and secondary data. The nature of the research project determines how much and what type of data are collected. Each type of data has its own characteristics as well as its own advantages and disadvantages.

Primary Data

Tom Tryon, the owner of Main Street Sporting Goods, faces a problem. A chain sporting goods store is opening up in the new shopping mall about a mile from his store.

Tom worries that the increased competition will hurt his business. Since he lacks the money to expand, he feels that providing services that the chain store cannot match may be the best way to compete.

Tom believes he knows his customers better than the chain store does. He is considering expanding his services to keep his current customers and attract new ones. In the winter, he does well with skis and ski apparel. He also offers ski repair. He is considering offering ski rentals, ski lessons, and ski equipment storage. In the spring and summer, he sells hiking and camping gear. He is considering offering hiking and camping trips.

However, Tom operates on a budget. Before making any changes, he wants to be sure that these additional services would be successful and profitable. His goal is to keep his present customers and to attract new ones. Therefore, over the next several weeks, he asks his regular customers various questions and writes their responses in a notebook. Here are his questions:

- Would you like to have a place where you could store your skis out-of-season and have them ready to use in the winter?

- Would you be interested in a ski rental service?

- Would you be interested in ski lessons offered by the store on the nearby ski slopes?

- Would you be interested in regular hiking or camping trips organized by the store?

From the data gathered, Tom Tryon can determine what services customers want. If the customers do not want the services Tom is considering, he will have to find other ways to keep present customers and attract new ones.

Tom served as the researcher in his own marketing research project. He gathered his primary data through a commonly used method of collecting it: the survey. Other common methods of collecting primary data are the panel, experimentation, and observation. Let's take a look at each method.

The Survey

The **survey** is a method of collecting opinions by questioning a limited number of people chosen from a larger group. The survey is one of the most widely used ways of getting primary data.

The people surveyed are chosen to represent a larger group. They are called a *sample*. A sample is used to conduct a survey because it is usually too costly to contact every person who could give information on a research subject. The people included in a survey may be chosen at random or according to such specific characteristics as age, sex, education, or income.

For example, suppose the executives of an automobile insurance company want to know how its 500,000 customers regard the firm's cost, service, and dependability. The company cannot question every customer. Instead, it selects a random sample of about 500 people, assuming that the group's answers will reflect the opinions of the rest of the company's customers. In a true random sample, the results tend to be accurate since everyone has the same chance of being selected for the study.

There are several types of marketing research surveys. Three common types are the personal interview, the telephone interview, and the mail questionnaire.

Probably the most effective type of survey is the personal interview, in which the researcher questions a person face-to-face. Although the personal interview is the most expensive type of survey, it often gives the most information. Besides getting answers to the questions, the interviewer can gather more information by watching the expressions and reactions of the interviewee.

One popular form of personal interview is the **mall intercept**—a survey taken at a shopping mall or center. A researcher stands near the entrance of major stores in the mall and stops (intercepts) shoppers, asking if they would answer a few questions.

The advantage of the mall intercept survey is that it may be done quickly. The disadvantage is that some shoppers may be too hurried or tired to carefully contemplate and answer questions. Also, researchers do not consider a mall intercept a true random sample; that is, not everyone has an equal chance of being interviewed. Therefore, the results may not be truly accurate.

■■■   *Focus groups consist of a small number of consumers who meet with a leader to discuss given goods or services. Why are personal interviews such as this one one of the most effective types of surveys?*

A widely used form of personal interview is the **focus group**. Typically, focus groups consist of six to ten consumers who meet with a leader to talk about how they feel about given products.

The focus group may concentrate on a product's image or its packaging. Focus groups may deal with various topics, such as advertising, customer service, or acceptance. For example, before marketing

	Personal Interview	Telephone Interview	Mail Survey
Immediate Feedback	Can adjust questions based on interviewer's needs and reactions	Can adjust questions but not as flexibly as in person	No immediate feedback
Cost	High	Lower than personal interview	Very low unless the return is poor
Time	Fairly fast	Very fast	May be slow if returns are not prompt
Control Over Who Responds to Questions	Large quantity	Fair quantity	Large quantity
Bias	Questions can be rephrased; interviewer bias possible	Questions can be clarified; close supervision may eliminate interviewer bias	No way to clear up any questions that may be confusing

■■■ *Table 14–1 Three Ways of Collecting Data*
This table compares three ways of collecting survey data. Which is the most expensive type of survey to conduct?

its line of swimsuits to store buyers, Daffy swimwear conducts a series of focus groups among girls and young women ages 15 to 25. These consumers review the various swimsuits in the line and select the ones they like best. The company's sales representatives are then able to tell the store buyers which suits consumers seem to prefer. The ideas brought out in focus groups also may form the basis for additional surveys and other research.

The telephone interview can be conducted more rapidly and less expensively than the personal interview, but often it does not provide as much information. This is because increasingly people do not like to be interrupted at home and do not want to give information freely over the phone to someone they do not know.

The **mail questionnaire** consists of a list of questions mailed to the survey group. The recipients are asked to answer the questions and mail the questionnaire back to the researcher. When a survey group is spread over a wide geographic area or when the marketing researcher wants a cross-section of opinions from the entire country, a mail survey may be the most economical and convenient way to gather data.

Mail surveys, however, require simple and clearly worded questions. Often, people are slow in returning them. Many people do not return them at all. Thus, the response rate to the mail questionnaire is often low. (See Table 14–1.)

The Panel

When researchers need to study the buying habits of people over a period of time, they use a panel. A panel is a selected group of people who serve as subjects of a continuing survey.

Marketing research organizations such as A.C. Nielsen Company and Market Facts, Inc., use continuing panels in their research. Advertising agencies such as Chiat/Day also use them.

Each week, panel families located in various parts of the country record food, drug, or even pet-care purchases in diaries. They also note the prices paid for those products.

Marketing researchers gather this information and report it to their clients. These clients are generally manufacturers of the goods surveyed. They want to know what consumers are buying and how often. Manufacturers use this information to judge the marketability of their products, the effectiveness of their advertising, and the strength of the competition.

Experimentation

A form of research involving a scale model or representation of a real marketing situation is called **experimentation**. All elements of the real marketing situation are present, but each one is scaled down in size. Experimentation allows the researcher to judge the effectiveness of his or her marketing plan on a small scale before attempting a full-scale operation.

For example, a retailer may want to know whether an advertisement is more effective in color than in black and white. Two ads are prepared—one in black and white and the other in color. The color ad is sent to one group of customers, and the black-and-white ad is sent to a similar group of customers.

An order-reply form, coded to identify the ad that the customer received, is included in both mailings. If the response to the color ad is much greater than the response to the black-and-white ad, the retailer can justify the added expense of using a color ad.

Businesses constantly use experimentation. Probably the most important use of experimentation is in test marketing.

Test marketing is the marketing of goods to consumers in several carefully selected areas before the goods are released on a wide scale. Through test marketing a marketer may determine a proposed package design's appeal or consumers' acceptance of a new product.

Observation

The process of collecting information about customer buying behavior, product acceptance, and sales effectiveness by watching the actions of people without actually interviewing them is **observation**. Market researchers may observe customers who are shopping. They may note such things as whether customers compare prices before selecting a brand, read the labels, or hesitate before making selections.

A retail store may hire market researchers to observe how well its sales staff is performing.

Market researchers would then go into the store posing as customers. They would observe the salespeople's selling effectiveness, their knowledge of the merchandise, and the brands they promote most to customers. The researchers would then report their findings to the retailer. Retail management uses these results in a variety of ways—for example, in planning employee training programs.

Research subjects may also be observed by mechanical or electronic means. For example, in a retail store, a hidden camera may be used to record how carefully customers read brand labels or how many customers stop to look, handle, or buy a product.

An electronic device (a People Meter) may be attached to people's televisions in their home to record how often they use their TV sets and what stations they watch. In short, electronic devices may be used to gather data about customers and consumers, such as in Figure 14–1, that would otherwise have to be collected by less convenient or more expensive methods.

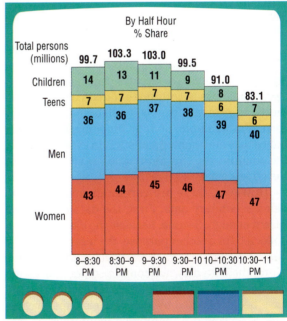

Source: Nielsen Report on TV, 1990. Nielsen Media Research, New York, p. 9.

■ ■ ■ *Figure 14–1 When People View Prime-time Television*
This graph shows the times of the evening—in half-hour periods—when people watch TV. For example, 43 percent of the 99.7 million viewers watching TV from 8:00 to 8:30 P.M. are women. Which half-hour period is the most popular among all viewers?

Secondary Data

When marketing researchers use information already collected by others for a different purpose, they are using secondary data. For example, suppose the Super Cola Company wants to set up four distributorships in Wisconsin. Each distributor should have a territory equal to the others in population and average income.

The company's marketing researchers use secondary data to decide how to divide the state among the distributors. They look at the U.S. Census population reports for the state of Wisconsin. They also look at reports for each county within the state and those for the large cities. They find out that the population is more dense in the southeastern part of the state and along the shores of Lake Michigan.

Because family income is an important sales factor, Super Cola's researchers next consult government publications that list average family income for each county. They also study sales reports of the soft drink industry. They use these to figure out the probable size of the Wisconsin soft drink market. Thus, secondary data give Super Cola researchers all the details needed to do the job.

Using secondary data offers several advantages. Usually, the information is considerably less expensive to collect, and researchers can collect it easily.

In some cases, information that cannot be collected in primary form is available in secondary form. For example, no individual marketer could collect age and income statistics on every person in the country. Yet, this information is available from the government.

However, there are certain disadvantages in using secondary data. First, the data may not be recent enough. Second, because the data have been collected for another purpose, the information may contain some facts that researchers do not need. Third, the data may not contain some information that they do need. Finally, because secondary data have been collected by someone else, researchers cannot be sure how carefully the information was collected and thus how accurate the data are.

Important sources of secondary data include company records, libraries, outside organizations, and the government. To use data effectively, researchers must have identified a problem, established goals, and made a plan for meeting these goals.

Company Records

Usually, the first source that researchers use for data is the company itself. Company records include salespeople's reports, customers' invoices, and complaints and suggestions received from customers. These sources provide information about past sales records, the size of the market, and customer reactions to company goods or services.

Company information should be easy to find. However, this is not always true. Even though everyone in a company ideally works for the success of the company, sometimes one department may not let another department examine its files. Or people may simply lose track of the information they already have. So, today many marketers place all useful information where it is readily available to everyone in the company, typically storing it in their computers.

Libraries

Marketers can solve many market research problems by using material in a library, whether it is in a library maintained by a school, a college or university, a city, or a company. The modern, well-equipped library carries a computer database and a wide assortment of magazines, periodicals, and up-to-date reports that are of value to market researchers.

Trade Associations

Another major source of secondary data is trade associations—organizations made up of the people and businesses in a certain industry whose purpose is to promote that industry. For example, the National Retail Federation (NRF) is the trade association of department stores and other large retailers nationwide. Its merchandising and operating reports (MOR) of member firms are available as secondary data to those organizations subscribing to its MOR service. Information from these reports lets retailers throughout the country compare their sales and costs with those of other similar retailers.

A trade association may collect data on many topics such as new and proposed laws; wages, insurance, and other costs of doing business; and successful marketing practices. Data from trade associations are often available at little or no cost to member businesses and can be useful to marketers. For example, a department store using the NRF's MOR service to examine the cost of sales personnel in the menswear departments' could learn the cost percentages of similar departments of member stores. It could then decide if its costs were typical.

Advertising Media

Advertising agencies, the media they serve, and marketing research firms are also good sources of secondary data. Both advertising agencies and advertising media are likely to have their own research departments. These departments concentrate their research on the customers reached by advertising. The research reports they prepare are usually available to any interested people, such as prospective media users.

Marketing Research Companies

There are two types of marketing research firms: syndicated data firms and consulting firms. Syndicated data firms specialize in collecting certain types of information and then selling that information on a regular basis. They generally collect information about brand recognition, public opinion, and fashion trends. Probably the best-known syndicated data firm is the A.C. Nielsen Company, which surveys television viewing and consumer food and drug purchases.

Consulting firms perform specific jobs for clients, such as obtaining for a manufacturer a national sales forecast for a new product. Two well-known marketing research firms that do consulting are Market Facts, Inc., and Arbitron Ratings Company.

The Government

The largest single source of secondary data is the federal government. Surveys by the Bureau of the Census provide fundamental marketing research information in this country. These surveys are supplemented by research done by other federal government bureaus and agencies, such as the Bureau of Labor Statistics and the Federal Power Commission.

The information collected by the federal government is available at a very low cost to anyone who wants it. Perhaps the greatest bargain in the secondary data field is the *Statistical Abstract of the United States*. This annual publication of the U.S. Department of Commerce consists of some 1,000 pages of summarized statistics about the country.

Preparing the Data

Earlier we discussed Tom Tryon's research. He collected data by asking customers questions at the checkout counter. Even after obtaining the customers' answers, he still was not ready to make his decision.

The information was in the form of raw data—a jumble of facts, opinions, and figures. Tom had to check the data and classify them before they could be analyzed.

Checking for Accuracy

Raw data can be checked for accuracy by a two-step procedure. First, researchers spot-check to see whether the data were collected properly. Second, researchers check several facts or figures to verify that they were recorded correctly. If the data were collected correctly, and if the facts and figures were accurately recorded, it is assumed that the data are accurate enough to be useful.

Classifying

The next job is to organize the data into meaningful categories. Market researchers usually decide on these categories at the time the research plan is made. Some changes may be made, however, after the examination of the data begins.

For example, suppose researchers are to classify the data obtained from people who were questioned about their hair-care product purchases. They might first classify the answers according to the age and hair color of the customers, as they had decided to do when they arranged the survey. However, after looking at some of the answers, the researchers might decide to add one more classification: people who tint or dye their hair.

Once the data have been checked for accuracy and classified, they are no longer considered raw data. They are now ready to be analyzed.

Analyzing the Data

To analyze means to study the various parts of something in order to understand the whole. Marketing research begins with a problem to be solved. That problem is divided into parts, and data

Principles into Practice

TV Ratings

Have you had one of your favorite TV programs go off the air? Did you wonder why this happened?

Poor television ratings were probably responsible. Television ratings are statistical estimates of the number of homes tuned in to a program. Independent research organizations, such as Nielsen Media Research, collect the ratings. These organizations do not measure the quality of a program, only how many people are watching it.

The independent research organizations such as Nielsen have nothing to do with the final programming decisions. The management of the TV network, local station, or cable system decide on the television programs that will be aired.

According to the researchers, more than one low rating is necessary before the television managers remove a program from the air. Some programs continue to be shown despite low ratings. There are several reasons for this:

- Station managers may believe it is their civic duty to air them (such as town and city council meetings).
- They may think that the quality of the audience will attract sponsors (as might be the case with documentaries).
- They might think that the audience is composed of many people who, but for this program (such as an historic event featuring world leaders), would not be watching TV at the time.

Generally, however, ratings affect advertising rates and have a direct impact on a TV station's income. As managers of an entertainment business, TV programmers want as many people as possible to watch their station.

The Nielsen ratings that you may see in the newspapers are obtained by means of an electronic device called the People Meter. A People Meter is connected to every TV set in those households chosen for the statistical sampling (currently about 4,000 households), forming a nationwide panel. Every TV-owning household in the United States has the same chance of being part of this panel. This makes the results statistically accurate.

The People Meter electronically records when the set is turned on and to which channel, when the channel is changed, and when the set is off. This information is then retrieved by Nielsen's computers and processed daily. The viewing is then matched with TV program schedules and released to subscribing businesses requesting the information.

The ratings game is a popularity contest, with each viewer having a potential vote. Program managers have to decide how to interpret the results.

Unfortunately, if few people tune in to your favorite show, it may be voted off the air. Of course, with the trend toward market segmentation and so many channels to choose from, you may find that show back—at a new time and on a new station.[2, 3, 4]

1. As an automobile manufacturer, how would TV ratings be useful to you?
2. As the owner of a small advertising agency, in what ways would you find ratings valuable?

are collected on each part. Next, researchers must examine the data from each part of the problem. Their job is to study data, such as those from the survey in Figure 14–2, and determine a possible solution or several possible solutions to the problem.

While collecting and analyzing data, researchers must take steps to eliminate all forms of bias. In marketing research, **bias** is a prejudice for or against an idea or object. In spite of a researcher's efforts to be fair, bias can easily interfere.

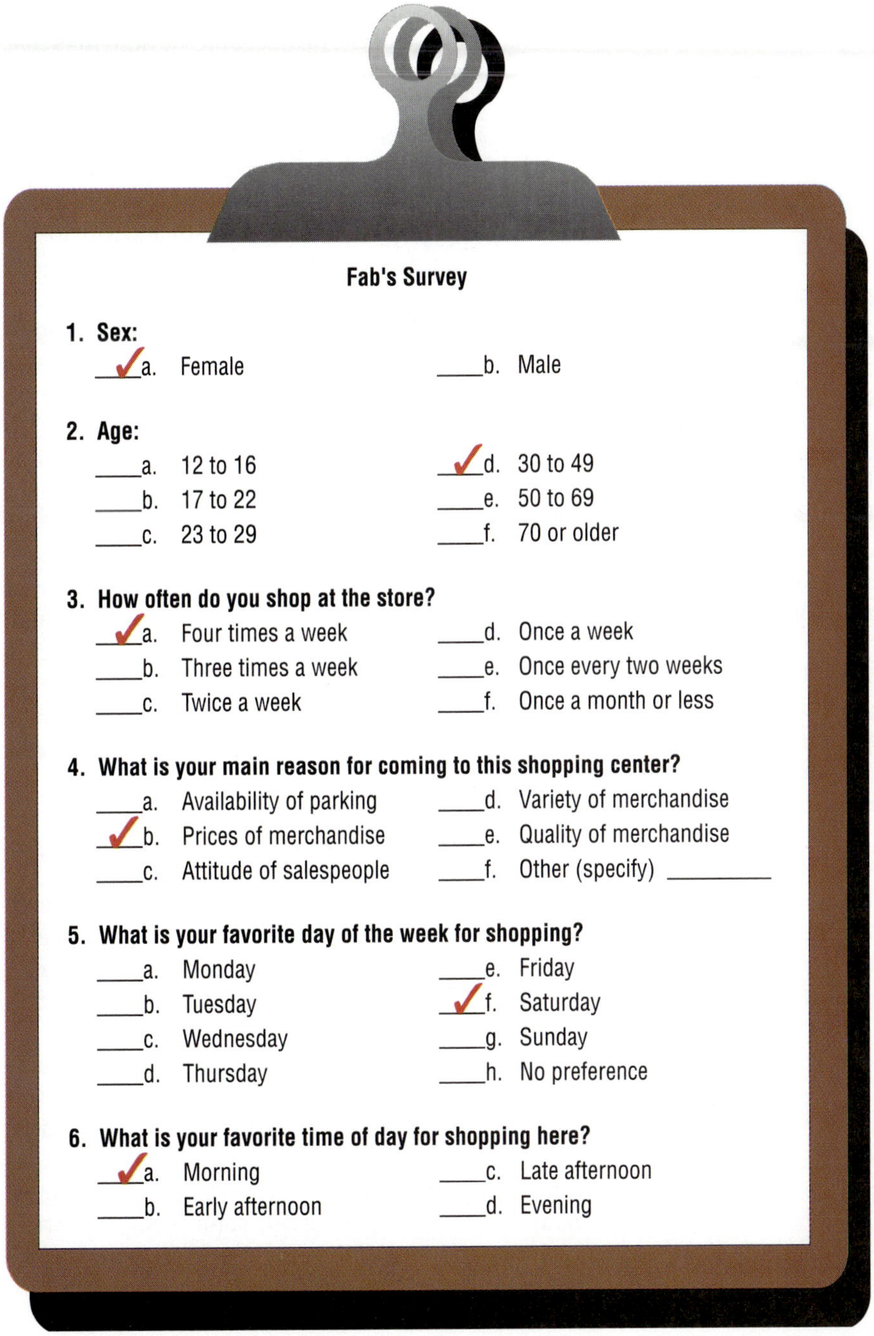

Fab's Survey

1. Sex:
____✓ a. Female   ____ b. Male

2. Age:
____ a. 12 to 16   ____✓ d. 30 to 49
____ b. 17 to 22   ____ e. 50 to 69
____ c. 23 to 29   ____ f. 70 or older

3. How often do you shop at the store?
____✓ a. Four times a week   ____ d. Once a week
____ b. Three times a week   ____ e. Once every two weeks
____ c. Twice a week   ____ f. Once a month or less

4. What is your main reason for coming to this shopping center?
____ a. Availability of parking   ____ d. Variety of merchandise
____✓ b. Prices of merchandise   ____ e. Quality of merchandise
____ c. Attitude of salespeople   ____ f. Other (specify) _____

5. What is your favorite day of the week for shopping?
____ a. Monday   ____ e. Friday
____ b. Tuesday   ____✓ f. Saturday
____ c. Wednesday   ____ g. Sunday
____ d. Thursday   ____ h. No preference

6. What is your favorite time of day for shopping here?
____✓ a. Morning   ____ c. Late afternoon
____ b. Early afternoon   ____ d. Evening

■ ■ ■ *Figure 14–2 Survey for Fab's Shopping Center* *After a survey has been conducted, it must be analyzed. Why?*

For example, a person who is interviewed about a product may prefer a certain brand because he or she has used it for a long time and has never tried competing brands. To minimize bias when interviewing, research organizations often conceal the identity of the product.

Eliminating bias is more difficult when the researchers themselves have preferences about the product or idea being researched. They may deliberately influence answers for or against a product or idea. Researchers should always be wary of their own personal biases.

The job of collecting and analyzing data is not a simple task, nor is it always inexpensive. If marketing researchers gather and study biased or unnecessary data, they waste both time and money. For this reason, researchers must be able to determine without bias what data are appropriate to solve the problem.

Preparing the Research Report

Research can only be put to use after the results are made known. After the data have been collected, prepared, and analyzed, they must be assembled into a final usable form—a research report. This document contains the results of research.

A research report is the basis for action. Only after market researchers prepare the research report can the project be considered complete.

Sometimes researchers report the results of a research study orally to the executives who will act on them. Other times, they prepare a formal written report instead of, or in addition to, the oral presentation.

One of the most important skills researchers can develop is writing a clear, concise, well-organized research report. To do this, they must know what goes into a research report and how to organize it. A complete research report contains these parts:

- title page;
- table of contents;
- introduction (purpose, scope, and goals of the project);
- organization of the project;
- methods;
- results;
- conclusions;
- recommendations;
- appendix (including any tables, charts, graphs, and pictures); and
- bibliography (a list of the secondary sources of information).

The body of the report can be divided into two parts. The first part (introduction, organization, and methods) tells what was done and why. It explains the background of the project and the activities that took place.

To someone unfamiliar with research work, it may seem unnecessary for a research report to go into such detail about the purpose, scope, goals, and organization of the project, as well as the methods used in research. But that information helps the reader judge the usefulness and accuracy of the results.

The second part of the report (results, conclusions, and recommendations) gives details about what was learned. It may also include the conclusions and recommendations of the researchers. (To speed up the decision-making process, sometimes the recommendations are placed after the statement of the problem in the introduction.)

The results of research are given as clearly and precisely as possible. Often findings are presented in tables, charts, or graphs that dramatize the major points of the study.

Acting on Research Results

Marketing research costs money. The marketer considers it worth the cost only when the results of the project can be used to help the company. Thus, the conclusions of the project must be acted on. (See Figure 14–3.)

Here is how the Shop-Rite supermarket organization set up a research project and then used the research results. The project involved the establishment of a supermarket in a small town. The town had a narrow main street with a small downtown shopping area. When supermarkets came along, they were built on the edges of the town because there was no room for them in the downtown shopping area.

The Shop-Rite food chain was considering the town for a possible location for a supermarket. Preliminary research suggested that a supermarket near the town's main shopping center would attract many people who preferred to combine their food shopping with other kinds of shopping. But there was no available land. Part of the area surrounding the downtown shopping center was residential, and part of it was industrial. All the land was in use.

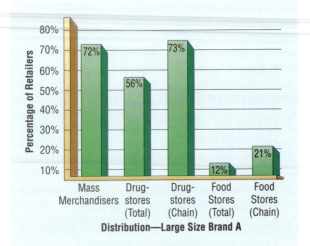

THE FUTURE IS NOW

From "Rags" to Riches

R. H. Macy and Company was losing money. Then along came sales tracking. Now a new computer system tracks buying patterns for each store. It advises store buyers on what to buy and how much inventory to stock. Inventory orders are filled in days; and shoppers are more likely to find the style, color, and size they need. Being able to better anticipate demand means higher sales for Macy's.

■ ■ ■ *Figure 14–3 Applying Research Results to the Problem*
Research should inform marketing decisions. As this graph shows, the large size of Brand A (a beauty product) is carried by 72 percent of mass merchandisers but only in 12 percent of food stores. In general, the larger sizes of health and beauty aid products are more acceptable in chain drugstores and mass merchandise outlets. What decision might be made as a result of this research?

Student Research

Marketing research can be an exciting adventure, not only for professionals but also for students. Some student projects have influenced marketing practices in their communities.

One Iowa chapter of DECA conducted research on consumers' opinions about dairy products which helped the entire dairy product industry. When the DECA members completed the survey and tabulated and summarized the results, they sent a copy of their report to the state's dairy council. The council found the results valuable in increasing sales of dairy products. The DECA chapter received state and nationwide recognition for its marketing research project.

Perhaps you will have the opportunity to participate in one or more marketing research projects in an area of your choice. You will find that taking part in them is an exciting experience.

Shop-Rite's research staff began the formal research. They gathered and analyzed data on many factors, such as the location of competing businesses, convenience to shoppers, available parking space, and available land for sale.

Their research uncovered a good possibility. Just behind the downtown shopping area was a large lumberyard. Its only building was a decrepit wooden shed. The rest of the property was used for open storage. With very little work, this property could be cleared for a building site.

Then came the action. Shop-Rite executives approached the owner of the lumberyard, offering to buy this land and pay the costs of transferring the business to another part of town. When the owner agreed, Shop-Rite began construction.

Today, the area is a huge shopping plaza. As expected, Shop-Rite attracts customers because its central location permits them to combine their supermarket shopping with their downtown shopping. Shop-Rite was able to make a decision that led to outstanding success for the new store only after careful research.

CHAPTER NOTES

1. "McKids: Designed with the Child in Mind," *Stores*, March 1989, pp. 14–15.

2. Nielsen Media Research, "What TV Ratings Really Mean, How They Are Obtained, Why They Are Needed," (Northbrook, IL, 1987).

3. "And Now, a Word with Their Sponsors," *Business Week*, 18 June 1990, pp. 26–28.

4. Susan Duffy, "Why the Networks Can't Change Channels on Nielsen," *Business Week*, 18 June 1990, p. 27.

Advertising Researchers Focus on Life-Styles

Advertising research used to focus on the product. In the past, for example, the advertising agency for Avon's Sun Seekers skin lotion researched who bought the lotion and how they used it. The agency then used the results

to develop commercials stressing the benefits of Avon's Sun Seekers skin lotion.

As more and more similar products crowd the marketplace, however, many advertisers have now switched their focus from product research to market research. Their main goal is to determine how consumers' life-styles tie them to a product rather than to find out how consumers react to a product.

Advertisements that once featured product benefits now emphasize the target market's life-style. For example, in the early 1980s, Kool-Aid advertising emphasized product quality. "I keep a pitcher ready so they can have those fruity flavors and vitamin C anytime," a smiling mom said in one 1982 TV spot.

The research that led to this campaign was "brand-specific," explained Barbara S. Feigin, research director at Grey Advertising, Kraft General Foods' agency for Kool-Aid. According to Feigin, the questions researchers asked consumers were:

- "How do you use it?"
- "When do you serve it?"
- "What do you think about it?"

In 1988, Grey Advertising replaced this campaign with one featuring several young men and women sitting at a kitchen table, without a child in sight. A pitcher of Kool-Aid is on the table in front of them. Their conversation runs from BMX bicycles to the cost of living.

"The new ad was the result of research designed to find out the social and cultural influences on consumers," says Feigin. "Brands have become so similar to one another that the real leverage in the advertising is no longer the content of the product but the placement of the product in the consumer's life."

Other marketers have also realized the need to focus on the consumer. One spring, 500,000 students who rented tuxedos for their junior or senior proms got a gift package containing product samples from a variety of national advertisers. These gift packages were a result of market research that showed teenagers have become more important decision makers and have their own brand loyalties. The purpose of such gift packages was to get teens to try the enclosed products before making purchase decisions.

Market research also revealed marketing opportunities for frozen yogurt manufacturers. After conducting research, marketers found that 18-to 40-year-old women are particularly diet- and health-conscious. By appealing to this market, out-of-home frozen yogurt sales soared to $500 million in one year.

The growing marketplace will continue to affect the impact of advertising. Only constant research will provide marketers with new avenues for reaching consumers.[1,2,3]

---

1. What shift has been occurring in advertising research? Give an example.

2. What is the difference between market research and product research?

3. Name two ways in which market research has benefited the companies discussed in this case study.

4. Tell four ways in which the market researchers involved with marketing the products above could collect primary data.

CASE NOTES

1. Randall Rothenberg, "Ad Research Shifts from Products to People," *The New York Times*, 6 April 1989.

2. Scott Hume, "Prom Night: Free Samples with Tux," *Advertising Age*, 13 March 1989, p. 53.

3. Christy Fisher, "Frozen Yogurt Rejects Subculture," *Advertising Age*, 10 April 1989, p. 26.

UNIT 5

The Product

Chapter 16

Product Development and Management

Terms to Know

product planning	product life cycle
product item	introduction stage
product line	growth stage
product mix	maturity stage
prototype	decline stage
test marketing	product modification

Chapter Objectives

After studying this chapter, you will be able to:

* describe the process of product planning and development;

* define product terms and explain their role in product planning;

* explain how changes in the consumer market, competition, and production capabilities influence product planning;

* list the six stages of product development;

* describe and discuss the characteristics of a product's life cycle; and

* suggest and evaluate new product ideas.

Case Study

Greeting Cards Go High-Tech

Computer-generated greeting cards are emerging as a possible $200 million per year industry. Greeting card companies are now providing consumers with computer-equipped kiosks that generate greeting cards. You can now use the computer's touch screen, keyboard, and a variety of software to edit or design a greeting card of your choice. For an average price of $3.50, you can print a card that includes a personalized message.

Hallmark Cards, Inc., which introduced the first mass-marketed computer greeting cards, now has more than 2,000 kiosks in its stores. Hallmark's "Personalize It!" kiosks also laser-print calligraphy invitations on blank card stock.

Inscribe, another greeting card company, offers a computer printer for in-store use. Stores use the printer to create quality wedding invitations.

American Greetings Corp. offers a different kind of computer-generated greeting card. Instead of printing words on a card that already has a picture on it, the customer uses a plotter pen on a CreateaCard kiosk to write the message and draw one of the 1,000 pictures available. The computer then prints out the customer's line drawing that looks like a doodle. One advantage to the CreateaCard is that it doesn't have to be accompanied by a rack of cards. Thus, they are ideal for airports and small drugstores. American Greetings has placed more than 2,000 kiosks nationwide in such outlets as Wal-Mart and Kmart.

Computer-generated greeting cards are just one example of new product developments. As we near the twenty-first century, we will surely see more advanced product development technology, such as computers that interact with customers to design and develop goods and services.[1,2]

Product Planning

Product planning is the direction and control of all stages in the life of a product—from the time of its creation to the time of its removal from the company's product line. Product planning decisions may be the most important ones marketers make because they commit a company's money or capital.

In addition, it takes a great deal of time and effort to plan new products or to change established ones. The marketing research involved and the designing of a test product may be very expensive. Manufacturing and equipment costs may be high. Inventory development, handling, and storage may become major expenses. Thus, a mistake in product planning can cost millions of dollars.

Changing technology greatly increases the need for effective product planning. Manufacturers can produce more products in less time today than ever before. More new products have been introduced in the past 40 years than in all previous history. Customers are being offered a much wider selection of products. This means that to remain competitive, marketers must develop new and better products or find new uses for old products.

Product planning is also important because markets are always changing. A product that is profitable today may not be profitable tomorrow. Because of this, marketers work by the motto "innovate or perish."

Product Terms Defined

To discuss product planning in detail, you must understand four important terms:

- product;
- product item;
- product line; and
- product mix.

As you know from Chapter 1, a product is all the physical features and psychological satisfactions received by the customer. The term *product* refers to goods or services. Soft drinks are products and so are haircuts.

A **product item** is a specific, physical product. Individual goods are product items. For example, a pocket-sized AM-FM transistor radio with unique styling and design is a product item. A product item often carries a specific name or number designation, such as the Apple Macintosh LC II microcomputer or Levi's 501 jeans.

A **product line** is a group of similar types of product items that are closely related because they satisfy a class of customer needs, are used together, or are sold to the same customer groups. One marketer might sell a product line of sporting goods. This line might include golf clubs, baseball equipment, tennis rackets, and other sporting goods items. Another marketer's product line may consist of numerous brands, models, and sizes of tennis rackets.

A **product mix** is the total of all product items and product lines offered for sale by a company. Some large manufacturing firms, such as 3M Corporatin, have hundreds or even thousands of products in their product mix. Most large companies develop a broad product mix for growth and diversification. They hope that profits in one product will offset losses in another.

■■■ *These and other product lines make up Campbell's product mix. Why is it important for the products in Campbell's product lines to be related?*

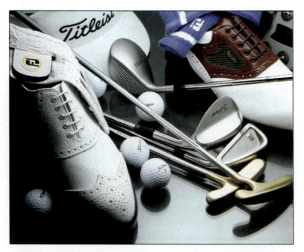

■■■ *The Titleist and Foot-Joy Worldwide group of American Brands, Inc., produces a line of golf balls, clubs, and related accessories. Why do you think they carry a product line rather than concentrating on one product?*

Influences on Product Planning

Product planning involves finding answers to seven questions.

1. What products do our customers need and want?
2. When should we introduce a new product?
3. How broad a product mix should we offer?
4. Should we expand or modify any product line?
5. What product or products should we drop?
6. How can we develop new uses and a new image for our product?
7. How should the product be packaged and branded?

The answers to these questions will be guided by the company's product objectives. These objectives usually involve increasing or maintaining market share, sales, and/or profits. Some objectives focus on cutting costs. Strategies to meet product objectives may include:

- introducing new products;
- improving existing products;
- developing a complete product line; and
- eliminating unprofitable products.

Sales and profit objectives depend on effective product strategies. Product objectives are also influenced by changes in the consumer market, competition, and the company's production capabilities.

Changes in the Consumer Market

The demands of a constantly changing consumer market are a powerful influence on product planning. For example, Franklin, a sporting goods manufacturer, added a new line of street hockey equipment because of the growth of in-line roller skates. In another case, the increased customer demand for more graphic capabilities persuaded Logitech, a computer accessory company, to enter a new market with a line of digital-computer cameras. Changes in life-style, such as increased adult participation in active sports, caused Murray, a bicycle manufacturer, to create a new line of mountain and all-terrain bikes.

Competition

Competition is one of the strongest influences on product development. Some marketers constantly seek to make their products different from those of their competitors.

If two competing products are very similar, one marketer may try to make a better-quality product or offer better service. For example, Prodigy upgraded and expanded its on-line computer services to better compete with CompuServe. Another marketer may attempt to take on the competition by planning products that offer unique advantages. Still other marketers may compete by developing products that copy the features of a competitor's successful product.

Production Capabilities

Although a marketer may feel that a product needs to be changed, production limitations may prevent changes from taking place. For example, the machines used to produce a given product may not be adaptable for adding a new feature. The cost of changing existing machines from production of a metal body for an appliance to production of a more colorful plastic body may be too great.

In many cases, however, the marketer has been able to successfully adapt existing methods of production or to discover new and better ones. With such production changes, the marketer can modify a product so that it is much better than a competing brand.

Developing New Products

New products do not just appear. Once a consumer need is established and product planning objectives are known, the company is ready to begin the actual product development.

The product development process, shown in Figure 16–1 on page 206, is divided into six steps:

1. generating ideas;
2. screening ideas;
3. evaluating ideas;
4. preparing a prototype of the product;
5. testing the product; and
6. introducing the product into the marketplace.

Let's take a closer look at each step.

Generating Ideas

Ideas for new products can come from a company's customers, employees, research staff, competitors, or computer software programs. One computer program called Ideafisher features a database containing more than 700,000 associative connections and more than 5,900 problem-solving questions that help companies generate ideas. Ideas can also come from other organizations that know the market well. Sometimes an idea can even be born from a mistake.

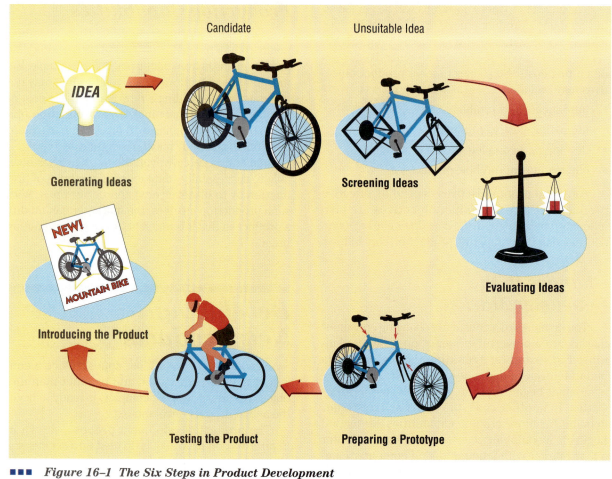

■■■ *Figure 16–1 The Six Steps in Product Development*
*The six steps in product development are generating ideas, screening ideas,
evaluating ideas, preparing a prototype of the product, testing the product, and
marketing the new product. How are ideas generated?*

Customer Ideas

Customers are an important source of new product ideas. Their reactions to a new product help to determine whether it will be a success. Marketers collect new product ideas from customers in a number of ways. They conduct customer surveys, invite product suggestions, and study what customers prefer to buy.

Employee Ideas

Company employees can also be a good source of new product ideas. Company salespeople, for instance, have studied the features of existing products. They also know their customers and maintain an awareness of their wants and needs. Wholesale salespeople regularly talk with dealers and get their ideas for products that will sell. In addition, managers know the strengths of the company. They may know what product ideas the company is best able to fulfill.

Researching Ideas

Many companies find new product ideas through laboratory research. They conduct experiments using new materials and new technologies. Two good product ideas developed in laboratories are clothing products created of synthetic fibers and new electronic products developed from transistors.

Research organizations and trade associations are good sources of new product ideas because of

THE FUTURE IS NOW

Bioengineered Breakfast?

"Lets see…I'll have the cholesterol-free eggs, the bio-engineered potatoes (with the protein of meat, minus the fat), fluoridated chocolate milk, and naturally caffeine-free coffee." Engineered-for-health foods are the wave of the future. Sales of low-calorie food and drinks are expected to reach $49 million in the late 1990s.

their general knowledge of a particular industry and the market it serves. Such organizations suggest new product ideas and often screen and evaluate them.

Unexpected Sources

Some new ideas are discovered long after the technology is developed. For instance, Spencer F. Silver, a young scientist at the 3M Corporation, was experimenting with molecules called monomers. His experiments resulted in a glue that did not stick as well as most other glues.

No product use was immediately found for Silver's glue. Years later, another company scientist, Arthur Fry, used the glue on some paper slips to mark songs in his hymn book. The glue did not damage the pages, and the bookmarks could be peeled off and replaced a number of times. The idea for Post-it Notes, inspired in a church, has developed into one of the top five office products in the United States.[3]

Other popular products have been discovered by mistake. In 1878, a Procter & Gamble workman forgot to turn off his blending machine when he went to lunch. As a result, tiny air bubbles were beaten into a batch of soap, making it buoyant. This floating soap became known as Ivory. Procter & Gamble has been selling Ivory soap ever since.

Recognizing the potential of new products, regardless of their sources, is the mark of an experienced marketer. Nevertheless, most companies consider a range of ideas before investing in product development and promotion.

■■■ *The idea for Post-it self-sticking notepads came from an unexpected source. After generating the idea what step would a company, such as 3M, take next in developing the product.*

Screening Ideas

A company interested in developing a new product usually starts out with a large number of ideas. It then reviews them, saving those that have special merit and eliminating those that seem unfit. One or more people within the company who specialize in product development usually screen the ideas. Ideas that pass the screening test deserve serious attention. Of course, a marketer could thoroughly examine every single idea. But this might use up the entire development budget.

Evaluating Ideas

Companies carefully evaluate the ideas that pass the screening stage. They are subjected to a thorough business analysis. Some of the questions asked about them include:

- Will the product meet a definite customer need?
- Will the product be a logical addition to the company's product mix?
- Can the product be developed, produced, and marketed at a reasonable cost?
- Will the product produce a profit for the company?

This last question is very important. A marketer is in business to make a profit. A company only seriously considers a product idea when it shows strong evidence of being profitable.

This careful evaluation usually eliminates a few more ideas. When a company completes its evaluation, it will have reduced the original large collection of ideas to one, two, or three ideas. These ideas will offer enough promise to make further investment in their development reasonable.

Preparing a Prototype

After a company screens and evaluates a new product idea, work on the actual physical product begins. Up to now, the product has only been an idea on paper. Now the process moves to a stage involving an even larger investment of time and money.

A company must develop a product it can manufacture easily at a competitive price. It must design the product and determine the kind and quality of materials to be used in manufacturing.

When all the specifications for the product have been planned, a company usually makes a model of a new product called a **prototype**. It is the first form of the product that a company makes.

A prototype is often made by hand rather than on the production line because of the unexpected problems that may arise and the time needed to solve them. This handwork makes the prototype very expensive to produce. However, making a prototype is a necessary step in the development of a product. The prototype enables a company to see how the specifications for a proposed new product work and how a finished product will look.

Many companies develop product brand names and package designs during this stage. These should not be afterthoughts, but should be a planned part of the product development.

Testing the Product

Once a prototype has been made, it is tested. It may be tested in a laboratory, by a special group of customers, or under actual market conditions. A company may test a newly developed product under all three of these conditions.

For example, Procter & Gamble might put a new line of Duncan Hines microwave brownies through several tests. First, it may test several different recipes in kitchen laboratories to make sure they are microwaveable and that they taste good.

Next, Procter & Gamble may ask groups of employees and consumers to test the product. They might even be asked to take samples home for the family. Later, they are asked how the family liked the product.

Finally, once Procter & Gamble selects the recipe and perfects it, a market test is arranged. **Test marketing** is the introduction of a product in a small marketing area to check customers' reactions. The test marketing area is chosen as representative of the total market. Thus, the brownies are distributed in grocery stores located in cities that are representative of the typical brownie eater. The sales results and customers' reactions are then carefully studied.

Marketing the New Product

When a new product passes all the tests, it is ready for full-scale introduction to a market. It may be introduced nationwide. Or it may be introduced to a limited market, such as a state, a type of consumer, a geographic region, or a type of marketer. Production, distribution, promotion, and pricing efforts focus on making the product a success in the chosen market.

Introducing a new product is expensive. Seldom do sales immediately repay that expense. However, if a company develops a product carefully—and if the market accepts the new product—then sales will gradually pay off the development costs and begin to yield a profit for the company.

Product Life Cycle

The **product life cycle** (PLC) is an identifiable cycle in a product's life. The life cycle is represented by a product's sales history over a period of time. The product life cycle is usually divided into four stages:

1. introduction;
2. growth;
3. maturity; and
4. decline.

Marketers need to be able to identify a product's stage in the PLC. The stages of PLC are influenced by marketing conditions such as competition, fashion, and consumer behavior. Knowing the PLC stages helps marketers develop strategies to improve the sales volume and profitability of a product, whatever the marketing conditions. (See Figure 16–2.)

Stages of the PLC

The **introduction stage** of a product life cycle is the first appearance of the product on the market. During the introduction stage, a company puts all its effort into marketing and production in order to make the product a marketing success.

This is the same as the final introduction stage in the product development process. It is the least profitable segment of the product's life. It normally takes several years for a company to break even or to recover the cost of introducing a new product.

Immediately after the introduction stage comes the product's **growth stage**—the period when sales

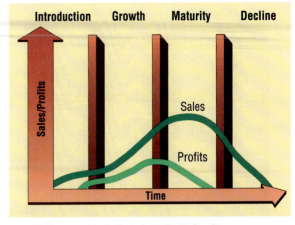

■■■ *Figure 16–2 Product Life Cycle*
A product's life is measured by its sales and profits, which rise until a product is said to be mature. Sales and profits of older products tend to decline. Why?

and profits are rising. The length of the growth stage depends on the product and the marketing techniques used. One product, such as Microsoft's Windows for computers, may catch the market's interest and sales may grow rapidly. Another product, such as CD players, may have a long growth stage during which sales rise steadily but slowly.

In any case, in order for a product to experience growth, it is important that sales increase at this time. If sales do not increase, marketers must change the marketing strategy. A product's profits are highest during the growth period.

The next stage occurs when sales begin to level off. This period, in which sales remain at a fairly even level, is the **maturity stage**. The leveling off of sales and continuing decline of profits can occur for different reasons. For example, the market for the product may be saturated. This may happen because competing products have been introduced and are taking much of the business. The market's interest may be shifting away from the product. For example, this happened when the market for automatic coffeemakers became saturated. The market shifted to specialty coffeemakers such as espresso and cappuccino makers.

A product's maturity stage can last a short time or a long time. For example, Ivory soap's maturity stage, despite some ups and downs, has lasted for decades and is still going strong. When a product matures, it is time for marketing management to consider ways

CALL SOMEONE, SOMETWO, OR EVEN SOMEFOUR.

Introducing a new way of calling that lets you see a face full or a roomful, all in full color.

The all-new AT&T VideoPhone. Just plug it in. You'll never look at phone calls the same way again.

Call 1 800 457-9504 for the location of your nearest AT&T Phone Center or other fine retailer.

AT&T

■■■ *AT&T Videophone is a new product. What stage of the PLC is it in?*

to extend the product's life cycle, gradually phase it out, or replace it with another product.

Unless management acts, the product sales may decrease. The period during which sales slow down is the **decline stage**. At this stage, the end of the product's life cycle is usually in sight. For example, the sale of recording cassettes gradually decreased as CDs entered the market.

Sometimes an increased marketing effort will boost sales again for a while, but the sales gain is usually temporary and sometimes not worth the cost. A company can delay the end of the product's life only if the company can think of interesting new product uses that would make it almost new in customers' eyes.

Influences on the PLC

Managing marketing strategies is difficult because many factors can influence the PLC at the same time. For instance, customer needs can change while a product is being developed. The product may not perform as expected. The product may pose a safety or environmental threat.

Developing and testing innovative ideas costs time and money. Although government restrictions on products such as drugs, toys, cars, and cosmetics have tried to protect the public, they also have slowed the rate of innovation.

Three other major influences on the PLC are competition, the product's features, and consumer reactions and fashion. Let's take a closer look at each of these.

Competition

Throughout the PLC, competition influences the market. Duncan Hines found its soft cookie formula imitated, even while it was being tested. General Electric was battling 52 competitors two years after it introduced the electric toothbrush.

Even long-established products face challenges. Perrier, for example, battled Pepsi's $H_2Oh!$ Given the large number of products competing with each other in the marketplace, product life cycles are getting shorter.

Product Features

The nature of the product influences the PLC. A new product with obvious advantages should reach its PLC growth stage quicker. Hallmark Card's "Personalize It!" kiosks are one good example.

A successful product will also conform with society's values, but those values can vary. During a fuel shortage an economical car has an advantage. In better times people may prefer more luxury or performance.

Consumer Reactions and Fashion

Consumer reactions to new products also influence the PLC. People's desires to try products vary. Some people want to be the first to wear new fashions or to own new appliances. Other people wait to see whether a product is successful before they buy. The marketer may benefit from appealing to the consumers seeking the newest products early in the PLC. A different strategy may appeal to the slow-adopting consumer.

Fashion—the style preferred by the majority of consumers at any given time—is a strong influence on PLC strategies. But the length of time that clothes, cars, and other products remain fashionable varies greatly.

In women's clothing, a certain fashion may peak in one season. On the other hand, fashions in furniture may not change for a number of years. To a large degree, fashions change because people become interested in new and different items.

If a new product becomes fashionable, its growth stage will be strong, and the sales during its maturity stage will be high. However, when consumers decide that the product is no longer fashionable, a marketer can do very little to keep that product from going into its decline stage.

Strategies to Manage Existing Products

How should a marketer manage an existing product? First, a marketer must study the product's performance and potential. Then the marketer can create a strategy to meet customer needs. The product could be modified. Perhaps its life would be extended with a new marketing mix. Sometimes, the best strategy involves eliminating a product entirely.

■ ■ ■   *To increase sales, Frito-Lay introduced the Cheddar and Sour Cream flavor line of Ruffles brand potato chips. What type of marketing management strategy is this an example of?*

Product Elimination

The decision to eliminate a weak product may be difficult. Even though the sales of a product decline, many customers may still depend on it. Dropping it may cause customers to question the marketing ability of the company. The company image may be hurt.

For these reasons, marketers often withdraw a product slowly and give customers time to make other plans and stock replacement parts. Companies such as computer and car manufacturers usually continue service and support for discontinued products. For example, IBM and Compaq Computers still provide parts and service on older 386 model personal computers which are no longer produced.

Dropping an old product also allows the marketer to steer customers to more profitable and newer products. Weak products must be eliminated because they are costly. They take management

time, consume display space, waste promotion dollars, and may delay the introduction of other products.

Product Extension

A marketer may discover that changing a successful product actually would lose customers. The sales and profit position of the product may be strong. Research might predict continued growth without any change. This could be a chance to add a new product to the line, or to gain more customers by changing the marketing mix in other ways.

Promote New Uses and Benefits

Old products can have new uses. For example, Arm & Hammer baking soda, which was originally marketed for baking, is now also promoted as a

Principles into Practice

Building a Better Mousetrap

There is an old saying: "Build a better mousetrap, and the world will beat a path to your door." Well, look no longer. There is a new product called "The Better Mousetrap" by Trap-Ease. Invented by Mel Melton, a retired rancher from Idaho, the Better Mousetrap overcomes the hazards and shortcomings of spring traps and poisons.

Like many new product ideas, Melton's came from an unexpected source. He first thought of the idea while repairing irrigation pipes on his ranch. After retiring to Southern California, he decided to put his idea to work for a neighbor with a pest problem in his garage.

While watching a baseball game, he made a prototype of his trap with some tin from a tennis can, balsa wood, and magnets. He then went to a pet store and bought some mice to test the invention. His success was immediate, and Melton received his patent in 1985. Today he also holds patents in 60 other nations.

The trap is a long plastic tube bent at an angle so the tube is off

the ground. Mice are caught when they enter the tube and upset the balance with their weight. When this occurs a plastic door slams shut, thus capturing the mouse. It is then up to the trapper to dispose of the mouse or give it freedom.

Trap-Ease has lots of competition, and thus sales results have been modest. According to the U.S. Patent Office, more than 2,000 patents for animal traps exist. Its best-known competitor is the popular Victor Mousetrap made by Woodstream. This trap, which has been around for more than 100 years, is found in most grocery and hardware stores. Woodstream has also worked to develop a humane trap. Its version is called Have a Heart.[4]

1. Where did Melton get the idea for his product?
2. Which of the strategies for managing an existing product discussed in the chapter would you suggest Trap-Ease employ?

---

refrigerator freshener and toothpaste. Procter & Gamble, the makers of the household cleaner Top Job, originally promoted the product as a glass cleaner. Then, they promoted its effectiveness for other household cleaning tasks. Similarly, Johnson & Johnson promoted its baby shampoo for adult use, emphasizing its mildness.

Marketers sometimes discover new benefits in old product uses. The mouthwash Listerine claimed to kill the germs that cause bad breath. Its makers

then promoted it as a fighter of dental plaque as well. A high-fiber cereal that was once sold to an older audience might be promoted to a younger market for the product's health benefits.

Change Pricing or Distribution

To answer a competitive challenge, a marketer may raise or lower the price of a successful product. Although the product does not change, its image

■ ■ ■   *Arm & Hammer has been very successful in finding new uses for its baking soda. Why did it do this?*

may. Customers may consider it a new bargain or a new prestige item.

Marketers may also appeal to new customers without changing a product by extending its market area. A local product could be distributed across the country or even worldwide. Remember, the product itself is only one element of the marketing mix.

Product Modification

A marketing analysis may call for a **product modification**—a planned change in a product or its packaging. This may include changes in features, quality, or style. Most products are changed periodically just to hold a competitive position.

Some product modifications involve manufacturing methods and their related costs. Calculators and computers, for instance, have been made smaller and less expensive. Better manufacturing methods allow lower prices.

New packaging can build customer interest. A new car body is a common packaging modification. The model may be almost the same as last year's, but the new look will attract attention.

Packaging can also add convenience. Cardboard packaging for fruit juice, no-drip containers for bleach, and resealable plastic bottles for motor oil all modify the product.

New features also can enhance existing products. For example, a manufacturer may add a safety air bag to an automobile. A computer manufacturer may build a CD-ROM disk drive into a popular model.

Although new features add obvious value to products, they may raise the price or reduce profit. Competitors may also copy them. Furthermore, adding new features too frequently can erode customer confidence. People will expect the new model to be replaced as quickly as the last. Some may think the product was faulty and wonder why the company can't seem to make an adequate model. Despite the costs and risks, marketers continue to consider product modifications when they plan product strategies.

CHAPTER NOTES

1. Joan E. Ridgon, "Old-Fashioned Sentiments Go High-Tech," *The Wall Street Journal*, 9 November 1992, p. B1.

2. Jon Pepper, "A Warm Greeting to Technology," *Information Week*, 9 December 1991.

3. Stewart W. Husted, Dale L. Varble, and James R. Lowry, *Principles of Modern Marketing* (Needham Heights, MA: Allyn & Bacon, 1989), p. 244.

4. Phoebe Hawkins, "A Humane Way to Catch a Mouse," *Insight*, 20 October 1986, p. 46.

Chapter Summary

- Product planning is the direction and control of all stages in the life of a product.

- Marketers must be aware of the changes that influence product planning: changes in the consumer market, competition, and production capabilities.

- The product development process can be divided into six steps: generating ideas, screening ideas, evaluating ideas, preparing a prototype of the product, testing the product, and introducing the product into the marketplace.

- The product life cycle consists of four stages: introduction, growth, maturity, and decline. The marketer needs to know the stage a product is in, in order to develop an appropriate strategy.

- Existing products can be managed with several strategies: eliminating the product, extending the product by changing the marketing mix, promoting new uses and benefits, or modifying the product.

Building Your Marketing Vocabulary

On a separate sheet of paper, define each of the following marketing terms. Then use each term in a sentence about product planning.

product planning	product life cycle
product item	introduction stage
product line	growth stage
product mix	maturity stage
prototype	decline stage
test marketing	product modification

Questions for Review

1. Name two reasons why product planning is important.

2. What are three influences on product objectives?

3. What are the six steps in product development?

4. List three ways marketers can generate ideas for new products.

5. What is a prototype? Why is making a prototype a necessary step in product development?

6. What are three methods that may be used to test a new product?

7. Describe the characteristics of each of the four stages of a typical product life cycle.

8. Name three influences on the product life cycle.

9. List three strategies marketers may use to extend the life of an existing product.

Critical Thinking

1. Explain why marketers work by the motto "innovate or perish."

2. Identify the product item, product line, and product mix of a large company of your choice. Possible companies include Nestlé, Bristol-Myers Squibb, Borden, Campbell Soup, and Procter & Gamble.

3. Suppose you marketed pens that had erasers on them. Explain the marketing strategy you would use at each stage of this product's life cycle.

4. Discuss changes in the consumer market that would influence the product planning of microwave foods.

5. Suggest modifications for each of these goods or services: chewing gum, hair dryer, child care, and lawn mowing.

Discussion Questions

1. Suppose you are a marketer for a barbecue equipment company and an employee of yours came up with the idea to market a barbecue grill with a built-in lamp. Discuss reasons for and against this product idea. Discuss the types of questions you will want to ask to evaluate this product.

2. Name products such as Ivory soap that have had a long life cycle. Discuss factors that may have contributed to the success of this product.

3. Often products are developed to appeal to what is in fashion. However, what is "in" may only last for one season before it is "out." Why do you think marketers spend the money to develop a product that will be so short-lived?

Marketing Project

Analyzing a New Product

Project Goal: Given a new product, describe the marketing techniques used to introduce and promote the product and analyze its position in the market.

Directions: Select a new product that has been introduced to the market recently. Obtain information about the product from sources such as advertising, salespeople, customers using the product, manufacturer's written material, and your own observation about the product. Collect advertisements, booklets, tags, labels, and other materials about the product. Based on the information you gather, answer the following questions.

1. At what market is this product aimed?
2. How was the product introduced and promoted?
3. What is the product's relationship to the competition?
4. Why, in your opinion, will this product be successful or unsuccessful?

Using your answers to the above questions and the material you collected, give an oral or written report, as your teacher directs.

Applied Academics

Language Arts

1. New products start with an idea. Write about an idea you have for a new product. Include the stages of generating ideas, screening ideas, and evaluating ideas.

Math

2. Annual sales from 1990 to 1994 for a battery-operated screwdriver retailing at $15 have been $378,297, $595,276, $633,843, $516,300, and $410,234, respectively. Analyze the sales figures, determining the number of screwdrivers that have been sold annually. Graph the sales data, then determine the screwdrivers' current PLC stage of growth. Make a recommendation for managing the product at this stage.

Social Studies

3. Trace a product through its life cycle. Describe each stage in detail and explain company and consumer reactions when the product reached maturity. Was the product extended? How?

Marketing and Multiculturalism

The introduction of makeup for the ethnic market has given new life to makeup lines experiencing sales slumps. Cosmetic companies have added color shades expressly for ethnic customers. Prescriptives Inc., a subsidiary of Estée Lauder, introduced its All Skins line of cosmetics in 1991. In less than a year, sales increased 15 percent. Maybelline's Shades of You makeup produced sales of $15 million in the first ten months. Other companies that have followed suit include Revlon with its Darker Tones of Almay, and Clinique with its Color Deeps.

1. What type of strategy did these cosmetic marketers use to manage their product lines?
2. Given what you know about the ethnic market and product life cycles, describe the introduction and growth stages of the product life cycle for these new ethnic makeup lines.
3. Why do you think that Prescriptives and Maybelline experienced such successful introductions of their ethnic makeups?
4. What influences may affect the product life cycle of All Skins?
5. When these new products hit their maturity stage, what might marketers do to extend their product life cycles?

Branding Strategy

Chapter Objectives

After studying this chapter, you will be able to:

- discuss the types of brands and the reasons that marketers brand their products;
- define a trademark;
- discuss several marketing actions that help to protect a brand;
- discuss branding strategies and licensing; and
- describe the characteristics of effective brand names.

Case Study

What's in a Name?

Finding a good name for your product is not always an easy task. Toyota recently discovered this when trying to find a name for its new luxury car.

The company turned to the consulting firm of Lippincott & Marguiles. Consultants at Lippincott & Marguiles came up with 219 possibilities, including Alexis. While doodling during a meeting, the product manager dropped the *A*, changed the *i* to *u*, and Lexus was born. Toyota wanted a name that suggested luxury. The letters *l* and *x* are in luxury.

Unfortunately, the term *Lexis* has been used since 1973 by the Mead Corporation's computer database for legal research. Mead claimed the use of Lexus infringed on Mead's use of Lexis.

After trying to negotiate a settlement, the case went to court. In 1989, the U.S. district court ruled that Toyota could no longer use the name *Lexus* in its advertising. U.S. District Judge Davis Edelstein said, "It is more than likely that, even among Mead's customers, the word 'lexis' might first bring to mind Toyota's car." Judge Edelstein gave Toyota the choice of dropping the name or paying damages to Mead.

Toyota then appealed the decision. It claimed that Lexus wouldn't be confused with Lexis because the products and industries were so different. The previous lower court decision was later overturned, and the car was launched on schedule.

Never have good brand names been so valuable. In just one year, more than 10,000 new products hit the shelves with more than 1,500 new brand names. The U.S. Patent and Trademark Office receives more than 70,000 new product names a year. It is becoming increasingly difficult and risky to find a brand name. Once a good one is found, it pays to protect it.[1, 2, 3, 4]

Types of Brands

Branding is one of the best ways to identify a product and improve its appeal. A **brand** is a name, symbol, design, or any combination of these that identifies products and sets them apart from their competitors.

A **brand name** is that part of a brand that can be spoken. It may be a word, a group of words, a letter, a number, or any combination of these. Almost all of the products in the marketplace carry brand names. The U.S. consumer is familiar with such brand names as Kellogg's, Kleenex, Betty Crocker, and 7-Up.

The distinctive symbol that is used along with a brand name on a product is a **brand mark**. Some familiar brand marks are the shell sign of the Shell Oil Company, the pentagon and star of Chrysler Corp., the polo player of Ralph Lauren, and the colonel of KFC.

A **trademark** is a brand name or brand mark that has been legally registered with the U.S. Patent Office. (See Figure 17–1 on page 218.) A trademark cannot be used by anyone else without the permission of the person or company that owns it. Trademarks are usually identified in printed matter by a small encircled R (®, which means registered) placed immediately after the trademark. Sometimes the abbreviation ™ (trademark) or the abbreviation *Reg. U.S. Pat. Off.* (Registered in the U.S. Patent Office) is used. The registration and protection of trademarks are discussed later in this chapter.

Manufacturers and intermediaries may brand their goods and services. Much of their business depends on how well their brands are respected and remembered by consumers. Therefore, they try hard to make their brand names well-known and recognized as symbols of reliability.

Manufacturer's Brand

A manufacturer's branded product is called a **national brand**. National brands are also referred to as name brands, brand-name products, producer's brands, and manufacturer's brands.

The term *national brand* does not refer only to products that are distributed on a national scale. In

fact, several national brands are distributed only on a regional or statewide scale. The term merely indicates that such products carry the labels of their manufacturers and would carry them wherever they were distributed. Examples of national brands are Coca-Cola, Eastman Kodak, Pillsbury, and Mobil.

Intermediary's Brand

A product that carries the label of the intermediary (wholesaler or retailer) who sells it is called a **private brand**. A private brand is also referred to as an intermediary's brand, a retailer's brand, a distributor's brand, and a private-label brand.

Examples of private brands include the Kenmore brand of Sears, Roebuck & Co. and the Avondale brand of the Kroger Food Stores. Although a private brand may be sold on a national scale, it remains a private brand because it carries the label of the intermediary rather than that of the manufacturer.

Most private brands sold through retail stores are made by manufacturers of nationally known brands. For example, Michelin makes the Roadhandler tires sold by Sears. Customers who buy a private brand put their trust in the retailer selling it because they usually do not know the name of the manufacturer. They depend on the retailer to stand behind the merchandise, and retailers generally do.

Retailers use private brands to create customer loyalty and earn more profit. Customer loyalty for private brands ensures repeat sales because the store is the only outlet for these brands. Sometimes an intermediary's brand is unique, since the intermediary has had the manufacturer make certain changes in the standard design. Retailers can make more profit on private brands because they cost less to produce and can be marked up more and still be sold for less than national brands.

Private label merchandise is often in direct competition with national brand merchandise. Intermediaries may push the sale of their private brands by vigorous selling programs and by special advertising campaigns. They may display private brand goods more prominently than national brands.

In building the reputation of their own brands, intermediaries may sometimes advertise the national brand names of the materials used in their products. Allied Stores, for example, point out that their Millay brand of women's stockings uses DuPont nylon. A customer unfamiliar with the retailer's brand is often glad to see that the materials that make up the product line are those of a familiar, nationally known manufacturer.

Sometimes a private label brand becomes so well established in its own right that customers respect it as much as a national brand, or even prefer it. Many professional carpenters and do-it-yourselfers purchase Craftsman tools by Sears and Powr-Kraft tools by Montgomery Ward because these brands have come to stand for quality and dependability.

Why Brand?

All marketers take pride in their products. Marking their products with a brand name is one way of showing it. Also, as mentioned earlier, manufacturers have three other important reasons for using a brand name:

- to create a favorable impression of their products;
- to build a reputation for quality; and
- to encourage repeat sales.

Let's take a closer look at each reason.

Creating a Favorable Impression

A brand name plays a large role in the impression a product makes on prospective customers. If customers are favorably impressed by the brand name of a product, they are likely to buy the product.

For instance, customers may buy certain brands of cosmetics because they convey the image of love, strength, or increased charm. House hunters may be attracted to model homes with names such as "Aristocrat" or "Excelsior" that create the impression of luxury and elegance.

In recent years, several companies changed the brand names of their products to create a more favorable impression in the marketplace. For instance, Nissan made a variety of products including Datsun cars and trucks. Although Datsuns sold well, Nissan changed the Datsun name to Nissan. This created a single marketing identity for all of its products.

Building a Reputation for Quality

Customers learn to depend on and trust a quality brand-name product. Thus, a company working to build and maintain its reputation must provide the customer with consistently high quality brand-name products regardless of where they are purchased.

■■■ *The introduction of king-size Hershey's into test markets reflects Hershey's ability to build upon proven brand successes. Why do you think the company introduced a new size rather than a new brand?*

For example, a customer expects a Cadillac to have the same qualities whether it is purchased from a dealer in Miami, Indianapolis, or Seattle. A company with a reputation for a quality product usually invests much time and effort in improving it. Such improvement is essential for the product to stay ahead of competition. The aim is always to offer a product that maintains a reputation for quality and that continues to satisfy customers' needs and wants.

Encouraging Repeat Sales

If a customer is satisfied with a particular brand, he or she tends to buy it again. Branding encourages repeat sales because the customer has used the brand-name product, knows that it fits his or her needs and wants, and has little reason to take a chance on another brand. Once customers find the brand they like, shopping becomes easier. No longer does the customer have to make a decision about which product to buy on each shopping trip.

In retail stores the products of various manufacturers are often stocked together on the shelves. A customer without a strong brand preference is likely to buy any brand. To prevent this, a manufacturer must build strong customer preference for one brand. Only then will this product be able to withstand the intense competition in the marketplace.

Brand-Name Strategies

A business organization usually follows a certain strategy in choosing a brand name. This strategy has a strong influence on the marketing methods used to promote and sell a product.

An organization may decide to use one brand name for a whole family of products, one brand name for each product line, one brand name for each product, or one brand name for each grade or price line. Or a marketer may license a brand name. (You will look at licensed brands on page 222.)

Family Brands

A brand name that is used for all the products of a company is a **family brand**. Examples of well-known family brands are Campbell's, Heinz, Sunbeam, and Gerber.

Principles into Practice

Trademarks for Our Times

Like people, trademarks must change over time to reflect the differences in our society. This is especially true of trademarks that use people, real or imaginary.

For instance, the Betty Crocker name has adorned more than 200 General Mills products. In her 70 years as the trademark for the company, she has undergone six "facelifts." Regardless of her changes over the years, she still exudes the reliability and common sense that have kept her a popular company trademark.

Betty Crocker's last change in 1986 transformed her from a housewife to a younger dressed-for-success professional. The idea was to make the famous trademark look more like the people she was talking to.

Betty is not the only corporate symbol to be modernized over the years. Campbell's pudgy kids have gotten taller, trimmer, and more athletic. Aunt Jemima has lost weight. These changes reflect a more health-conscious society. Other recent changes in trademarks include Nabisco's Blue Bonnet Sue and Quaker Oats' Mama Celeste.[5, 6]

1. Why did General Mills alter its Betty Crocker trademark?

2. Why do you think General Mills didn't adopt a completely new trademark rather than revise its original trademark?

3. Think of a trademark on a common household product. Has it been updated recently? If so, how? If not, how would you update it?

A major advantage of using a family brand is that any new products introduced by the company will benefit from the established reputation of the existing products. Each marketing effort for any given product in the family tends to promote all the products sold under the family brand.

A family brand is best suited to products in the same category such as Jell-O brand pudding and pie fillings. Including a product outside the category could spoil the image of the other products. Consider what customer response would be if a baby food manufacturer were to extend the line to include floor wax. The dissimilar product could possibly lessen the customers' faith in the baby food line.

The word *family* suggests that all the products in a line have a similar quality, use, or other characteristic. Thus the name *Kodak* on a package immediately tells customers that they have a product related to photography, and *Kellogg's* means breakfast foods. To maintain consumer acceptance of the brand name, all products in the family should be of a similar type and should meet similar standards of quality.

Product-Line Brands

Most distributors have their own private lines of products. They may give each line a brand name. The trend today is to use fewer single-product brand names and to promote the image and reputation of product-line brand names. This strategy has the same major advantage as the family brand name. Any new products introduced into the line will benefit from the established reputation of the existing products.

Some large retailers use separate brand names for their various private lines of sporting goods,

■ ■ ■ *The Kawasaki brand family includes small recreational vehicles and a line of portable generators. What is one advantage of using a family brand?*

appliances, clothing, and automobile accessories. For example, Montgomery Ward has established brand names for a number of its product lines, including Powr-Kraft for tools, Signature for appliances, and Wester Field for outdoor sporting goods.

Individual Product Brands

Many manufacturers develop separate names for each of their products, especially when the products face stiff competition. For example, Procter & Gamble makes the shampoos Prell and Head & Shoulders. Rather than use a common name for both products (such as Procter & Gamble's shampoos), the manufacturer assigned each a brand name. This way, the products can be more heavily promoted individually than if a single family brand were used for both.

Sometimes a company wants to enjoy the advantages of both a family name and a product name. Post's Grape Nuts is a typical example. The Post family name helps the product to gain consumer respect. The brand name *Grape Nuts* helps to individualize the product and publicize it in advertising and sales promotion. The paper products of the Scott Paper Company—Scott Towels, Scotties, and Scotkins—are other examples of products that benefit from using the company name.

Price-Line Brands

Sometimes, within the same line of products, a company will offer different grades of the product. The company assigns a different brand name to each grade because each grade represents a different price line.

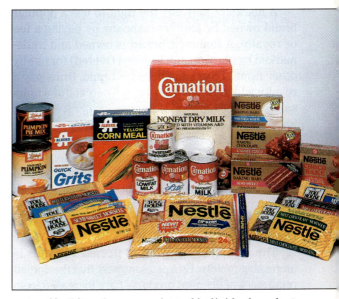

■ ■ ■ *Nestlé produces a variety of individual product brand names. Why does Nestlé give products their own brand name?*

A LOT GOES INTO BEING THE BEST.

THE SAME IS TRUE OF THE PRODUCTS SHE CHOOSES TO PLAY WITH.

Rawlings
A FIGGIE INTERNATIONAL COMPANY

Official Basketball for NCAA® Championships, NJCAA® Championships and the Women's Basketball Coaches Association.®

■■■ *The NCAA licenses its name to Rawlings for use on basketballs. What type of trademark is NCAA?*

Global
MARKETPLACE

Made in the USA—
Used around the World

From Captain Kirk to razor blades to fiber optic cable, American brand names are showing up in the most unlikely places. In Budapest, Prague, and Warsaw, Uncle Ben's rice and Wrigley's gum are now in the marketplace. In Taiwan the hot car is GM's Saturn. Look for movies, TV hits (such as "Murphy Brown"), plus a wealth of other made-in-the-USA exports.

important for the marketer to know what is involved in legally protecting a brand.

In the United States, trademarks are registered with the U.S. Patent Office. Such registration establishes ownership of a trademark and guarantees exclusive rights to its use. Four kinds of trademarks may be registered with the U.S. Patent Office.

1. *Trademarks* used to identify goods and distinguish them from goods manufactured or sold by someone else.

2. *Service marks* used to distinguish the services of one company from those of another (such as the trademark *Martinizing*, which describes a dry-cleaning process).

3. *Collective marks* used by associations of marketing companies (such as the "Grown in Idaho" trademark used by the Idaho Potato and Onion Commission, an association of Idaho farmers).

4. *Certification marks* which indicate that goods or services meet certain standards (such as the seal of approval used by *Good Housekeeping* magazine for products that have met the standards of its testing laboratories).

Legal protection of trademarks dates back to 1870, when the first federal Trademark Act was passed. The Lanham Trademark Act of 1946 gave additional protection to owners of trademarks. These federal laws and some state laws prohibit the use of a company's trademark by another company or an individual.

The laws, however, do not protect trademark owners from another danger: the possibility that the trademark will become a generic term through repeated use. A *generic term* refers to all products of a certain kind, rather than a branded product made by one specific manufacturer. The word *typewriter* is a generic term, but *Brother* is a trademark for a specific manufacturer's typewriters.

A marketing problem arises when the brand is so popular that is becomes legally generic. Aspirin, for example, was once Bayer's trademark for acetylsalicylic acid. But as this pain reliever became more popular, Bayer lost its exclusive right to use the term. Now any manufacturer's acetylsalicylic acid products may be called aspirin. Other generic names that were once brand names include cola, nylon, kerosene, escalator, zipper, shredded wheat, and linoleum.

Marketers today take definite action to prevent their trademarks from becoming generic terms. In their advertising campaigns, they emphasize that the product's brand name is registered by including the encircled R (®) after every use of the brand name. The use of the generic name of a product in connection with the trademark keeps the trademark from being applied to any other company's version of that product. Examples are Kleenex tissues, not Kleenex, and Dacron polyester fiber, not simply Dacron. In addition, many marketers adopt distinctive ways of writing their names, such as in an unusual script or in a special style that customers can recognize and remember.

CHAPTER NOTES

1. John Schwartz, "What's Really in a Name," *Newsweek*, 30 November 1987, p. 55.

2. Robert Johnson, "Naming a New Product Is Tough When the Best Names Are Taken," *The Wall Street Journal*, 19 January 1988, p. 33.

3. Gregory Witcher, "Toyota Loses Court Ruling on Lexus Name," *The Wall Street Journal*, 4 January 1989, p. B1.

4. "Court Says Toyota Can Use 'Lexus' in Its National Ads," *Marketing News*, 24 April 1989, p. 6.

5. "Betty Crocker Lets Her Hair Down," *Terre Haute Tribune-Star*, 23 August 1986, p. C1.

6. Martin Siegel, "Classic Trademarks Put Best Faces Forward," *Marketing News*, 6 July 1992, p. 17.

plastic laminates. Like cardboard boxes, the containers are light and easy to pack; they have no round corners that waste space. Like metal cans, they are durable and airtight. Like glass bottles, they leave no flavor. They are also inexpensive. The one-liter boxes used for Hi-C fruit juices cost the manufacturer about half as much as cans and 30 percent as much as bottles. In addition, since aseptic goods experience a shorter heating period during sterilization than canned goods do, their flavors are truer.

Combination of Materials

Another form of packaging is the **pump dispenser**—a metal, plastic, glass, or combination container that releases its contents in spray or foam when a valve is pressed. Pump dispensers are used for such products as hair sprays, shaving creams, hand lotions, insecticides, and toothpaste.

A **dispensing closure** is a cap, lid, or seal through which the container contents can be dispensed in a controlled manner. Shampoos, deodorants, liquid soaps, medicines, and household cleansers often come in this type of package. The dispensing closure prevents spills. Consumers usually select a product with this feature rather than a similar product without it.

The **multipack** is a special package design that groups two or more packaged products into a unit for easier display, carry-home utility, or user convenience. Many examples of multipacks can be found in food stores, drugstores, and hardware stores. For example, Quaker State Oil is sold to

■ ■ ■ *These "cardboard cans" are also called* aseptic *packages. Why?*

discount stores and warehouse clubs in multipack boxes of 12 one-quart plastic bottles. Golf balls are normally packaged in boxes of 3; multipacks contain 4 boxes of 12 golf balls.

Packaging and Ecological Concerns

This chapter discusses the many functions of packaging, which include protecting the consumer. However, there is another side of packaging that marketers must also consider: protecting the consumer and his/her environment from packaging.

While packaging is very important, it accounts for an estimated 30 percent—about 1,800 pounds—of trash a year for every man, woman, and child. These are astounding statistics. The Environmental Defense Fund reports that every two weeks we throw away enough glass bottles and jars to fill the 1,350-foot twin towers of New York's World Trade Center. We also toss out enough aluminum to rebuild our entire commercial air fleet every three months. We go through 2.5 million plastic bottles every hour.[5]

For most companies, plastic is a popular packaging material. It is convenient, versatile, shatterproof, lightweight, and extremely cost effective. Despite its good points, plastic has become a nightmare to ocean life. A recent Federal Office of Technology Assessment study concluded that tens of thousands of seabirds and about 100,000 marine animals die each year because they mistakenly eat plastic for food.

Foam, a plastic-based packaging product, is harmful to the earth's ozone layer. This makes it dangerous to land life as well. In addition, the material is not biodegradable and uses more space than paper packaging. These problems caused McDonald's Corporation to stop packaging its fast-food in containers made of chlorofluorocarbons (CFCs), compounds used to make foam.[6]

One solution to packaging problems is recycling or reprocessing aluminum paper, plastic, and glass to create new products. For example, many products such as greeting cards and books display the recyclable symbol. According to the Center for Biology of Natural Systems, 84 percent of household waste can be recycled.[7]

New fresh refrigerated product packaging also poses problems. The Food and Drug Administration (FDA) advised restaurants that the products are dangerous because of the risk of botulism (the most serious form of food poisoning).[8] To date, there have been no reported cases of food poisoning or death from fresh refrigerated packaged foods. Still, experts worry that the demands of the marketplace are outpacing regulators' and scientists' ability to oversee marketing practices.[9]

Today, most marketers strive to use **green packaging**—packaging that is neither excessive nor harmful to the environment. Consumers are demanding green packaging. From a cost and space aspect, marketers will also benefit. Normally, green packaging requires less packaging material and is often recyclable. For example, Downey and Tide have refillable pouches that take up less shelf space and cost less to produce. Consumers can buy these to refill their original containers.

Packaging and Labeling Laws

Many packages and their labels must conform to standards established by local, state, and federal governments. These standards prevent sellers from using misleading labels and packaging. Some of the published standards give marketers the opportunity to voluntarily follow them. Marketers must follow other standards or face penalties.

Fair Packaging and Labeling Act

Sometimes package labels can be misleading. Terms such as *giant economy size* or *super half-quart* that are used to describe quantities can confuse consumers.

In 1966, the Government passed the Fair Packaging and Labeling Act to protect people against deceptive labeling. The act states that the information given on a package should tell the consumer exactly what the package contains. Consumers can then compare the product with those of other manufacturers.

The Fair Packaging and Labeling Act covers most supermarket products. It requires that the label state the package's contents and weight, and the name of the manufacturer or distributor. The U.S. Department of Health and Human Services, the Federal Trade Commission (FTC), and the Department of Commerce administer the law. These organizations review complaints about unfair or deceptive methods of packaging or labeling.

Environmental Labeling Standards

Since 1990 several states and the federal government have banned deceptive environmental claims in ads and on product labels. In 1992, the FTC issued "Guides for the Use of Environmental Marketing Claims." These guidelines set common-sense standards for often misused terms such as *recyclable* and *biodegradable*. The new guidelines demand that specific terms are used correctly. The FTC will fine those manufacturers who do not change deceptive or misleading product claims.[10]

■■■ *The Fair Packaging and Labeling Act states that information on a package must tell exactly what the package contains. What does this act prevent?*

Principles into Practice

Music Companies Introduce Green CD Packaging

Since 1982, music lovers have purchased their compact discs (CDs) in a box within a box. The hard plastic inner box is called the "jewel box." The outer cardboard box, twice the jewel box's size, is called the long box. It was adopted for two reasons: to hamper shoplifters and to enable retailers to display CDs in racks formally devoted to record albums.

Now, after years of complaints from artists, consumers, and environmental groups, CD producers are developing stripped-down packaging. However, trying to make a package that does not harm the environment, is helpful to retailers, and is convenient for consumers has not been easy.

Environmental groups feel that selling CDs in just the jewel box is the most acceptable solution. But producers, retailers, and wholesalers have repeatedly spoken out against the idea. For these groups, the reason is simple. It will cost the retail music industry alone $100 million for new display racks. Producers, on the other hand, fear the down-sized packages will cost them valuable shelf space.

In an attempt to satisfy all parties, Ivy Hill, a packaging subsidiary of Warner Music group, introduced the Eco-Pak. This package, mostly cardboard, is designed as a long box for retailing but can be refolded into jewel-box size by the consumer. This design is also popular with marketers because it allows more space for fancy graphics than the plain jewel boxes do.

There are still many people in the music industry who are opposed to the Eco-Pak because Ivy Hill has not committed to recycling the packaging. Officials at the company claim they are testing a process to recycle both the paperboard and the plastic tray on which the CD rests. In the meantime, several independent entrepreneurs have created their own plastic packages which they hope the consumer and the music industry will choose. Only time will tell which green package emerges as the on-the-shelf winner.[11, 12, 13]

1. Why is CD packaging being changed?
2. Discuss why it makes good sense for music producers and retailers to adopt green packaging.

Nutrition-Labeling Standards

In 1975, the Food and Drug Administration established a 12-part set of nutrition-labeling standards. These standards require that all food products that advertise nutritional value must clearly list relevant nutritional facts on their labels.

For example, the label on a can of corn may state the quantity of calories, protein, carbohydrates, fat, and vitamins per one-cup serving. The sodium content, which is high in corn, must also be listed since the label discloses other nutritional information. In other words, the manufacturer must list all the nutritional information not just the benefits.

In 1992, more extensive labeling rules went into effect on virtually all packaged foods. These rules carry out the 1990 Nutrition Labeling and Education Act. Restaurant menus and individual meals served at restaurants are exempt. Most of the standards encourage marketers to voluntarily label products to help consumers make wise decisions.

Other Related Acts

Marketers must be aware of and conform to several other packaging and labeling acts. The Wool Products Labeling Act (1939) requires that clothing containing wool be labeled to explain clearly what

Global MARKETPLACE

Body in a Bottle

Anita Roddick started The Body Shop (products for the skin) in Brighton, England, in 1976. Utilizing an in-store refill counter and minimal packaging, resources are conserved, waste is reduced, and customers save money. Everything possible is recycled and only plentiful natural resources are used to make products and packaging. It must work. The Body Shop now has over 600 branches in 40 countries and trades in 20 languages.

kinds and percentages of wool have been used. The Fur Products Labeling Act (1951) requires that a label for a fur garment state the natural name of the fur and its country of origin.

The Textile Fiber Products Identification Act (1958) requires that the fiber content of textile products be identified. The Food, Drug, and Cosmetic Act (1938) regulates the labeling of drugs, foods, cosmetics, and medical devices. The Consumer Product Warranty Act (1975) attempts to make warranties strong, clear, and understandable. The Consumer Product Safety Act (1972) establishes strong safety standards for almost all consumer products.

Legislation helps to maintain the consumer's right to be informed about products. Marketers must develop packaging and labeling strategies that meet these laws and satisfy consumers.

Packaging and Labeling Trends

Packaging and labeling are dynamic marketing activities. The combination of consumer, government, and marketplace demands creates a constant challenge for marketers. Although packaging and labeling purposes do not change a great deal, the following are important trends.

1. Packages and labels are steadily moving toward the metric system. Labels will indicate volume and length in liters and meters, such as a 2-liter bottle (67.6 ounces) or a car 4.57 meters long (15 feet). Packages will list all weights and measures in metrics by 1997.

2. Labels will clearly warn consumers of potential harmful effects of using the product.

3. Packages will be safer for the consumer.

4. Packages will be easier to use and even more convenient.

5. Packaging materials will be improved for recycling purposes.

6. Packaging will contribute less to the pollution problem.

7. Packaging and labeling will provide more usable information.

8. Packaging and labeling will continue as integral parts of product and marketing programs.

CHAPTER NOTES

1. John Wall, "State-of-the-Mart Product Packages," *Insight*, 19 January 1987, pp. 62–63.

2. "Hot News: Microwave Ice Cream," *Changing Times*, January 1988, p. 8.

3. "S & O Sees Packaging as a Product Repositioning Tool," *Marketing News*, 18 December 1988, p. 9.

4. Diane Schneidman, "Plastic: Progress and Peril," *Marketing News*, 18 December 1987, p. 1.

5. John Elkington, Julia Hailes, and Joel Makower, *The Green Consumer* (New York: Penguin Books, 1990), p. 32.

6. "N.Y. Seeks Changes in McDonald's Packaging," *Marketing News*, 18 December 1987, p. 2.

7. Elkington, Hailes, and Makower, *The Green Consumer*, p. 44.

8. Trish Hall, "New Packaging May Soon Lead to Food that Tastes Better and Is More Convenient," *The Wall Street Journal*, 21 April 1986, p. 21.

9. Alix M. Freedman, "As 'Fresh Refrigerated' Foods Gain Favor, Concerns About Safety Rise," *The Wall Street Journal*, 11 March 1988, p. 19.

10. Marc Silver, "A Big Red Flag for Little Green Claims," *U.S. News & World Report*, 5 October 1992, p. 92.

11. Meg Cox, "Music Firms Try Out 'Green' CD Boxes," *The Wall Street Journal*, 25 July 1991, p. B1.

12. Laura Loro, "More Testing of Less," *Advertising Age*, 8 July 1991, p. 24.

13. Bill Paul, "Package Firms Find It's Hard Being Green," *The Wall Street Journal*, 25 May 1990, p. B1.

■■■ *Many retail businesses offer revolving credit charge accounts. What is one disadvantage of a revolving account?*

issue their own revolving charge accounts, including J. C. Penney, Sears, and Macy's.

The revolving account involves a monthly service charge. One important advantage is it encourages sales without encouraging customers to assume more debt than they can afford.

Budget, or 90-Day, Account

The budget, or 90-day, account is becoming increasingly important among larger retail stores. With the budget account, the customer makes a purchase and agrees to pay one-third of the total amount of the charge every 30 days. Thus, the payment is made in full at the end of a 90-day period. The budget, or 90-day, account does not require the customer to pay a service charge and returns the

retailer's money quickly. Customers frequently use the budget account to buy clothing, accessories, gifts, and household items such as electrical appliances and furniture.

Credit Card Companies

Credit card companies include the American Express Company, Carte Blanche, Discover, and Diners Club. Customers can use the credit supplied by these businesses to purchase anything from lunch to vacation packages.

Most credit card companies charge their customers an annual fee. They require prompt monthly payment and may add a service charge on overdue bills. Some credit card companies do not charge an

Sears Offers SearsCharge Credit Card

"Play the game and win $6,000,000. It's not too late to join the fun! More than 300,000 possible winners each week!"

This sounds like a state lottery. But it is part of Sears' promotion to sign up customers for its store credit card. Customers whose credit card number matches those displayed by Sears each week are winners.

The store credit card is called SearsCharge, and there is no annual fee. Customers who pay their full account balance within 30 days of the billing date pay no finance charge. Those who do not pay the balance within the grace period are charged at an annual rate of 21 percent unless they live in a state where the legal rate is lower. For example, Connecticut limits the finance charge to 15 percent.

Sears offered another credit card called Discover. But in 1993 Sears sold Dean Witter and the Discover credit card. However, Sears still accepts Discover, as well as VISA and MasterCard. Unlike most other major credit cards, Discover does not charge a membership fee. A generous line of credit is offered to those who qualify. With every Discover

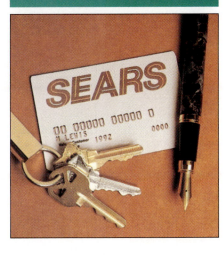

Card purchase, the customer earns a yearly Cashback Bonus of up to 1 percent of the total cash purchases based on the annual level of spending.

Discover Cardmembers can get cash advances instantly at more than 700 full-line Sears stores, at participating Automated Teller Machines (ATMs) nationwide, and by writing Discover Card Checks. Discover Cardmembers also receive Value-Finders coupons that offer discounts on an assortment of brand name goods and services. Finally, they have access to a wealth of protection services: protection for all valuables purchased with the card, credit card registration, term life insurance at group rates from Allstate, and automatic $100,000 travel accidental death insurance.[4]

1. Why would Sears have offered both a store credit card and a universal credit card through its finance company?
2. What advantages do you see to using Sears cards?

annual fee but add a service charge to the cardholder's balance each month.

Users of such credit do not have to carry much cash—an important consideration for anyone who travels often. In addition, the credit card bills provide the customer with a complete record of expenses. For this reason, many people use credit cards when they travel.

A customer using a credit card to make a purchase signs a multipart form that includes a credit card draft. This draft is similar to a check. It is drawn on the credit card company's funds rather than on the customer's personal bank account. That is, the credit card company pays the merchant for the customer's purchase. The merchant can deposit the credit card receipts in the bank and have immediate use of the money. But, the credit card company may have to wait 30 days or longer for payment by the credit card customer, and has the risk of nonpayment by the customer.

Credit card companies do not redeem the drafts at the full sales price. The merchant usually allows the credit card company to take a 3.5 to 5 percent discount when redeeming the drafts as payment for the service provided by the credit card company. For example, suppose the total amount of goods and services sold on the credit card equaled $5,500. If the arrangement allowed a 5 percent discount, the credit card company would pay the merchant $5,225.

Bank Credit Cards

A bank credit card is issued by a bank and may be part of a package of financial services. VISA and MasterCard are examples of bank credit cards.

Bank credit cards have become very popular. In 1965 there were fewer than 5 million bank credit cards in circulation. Today, there are more than 200 million in circulation, with about 1 million more cards being issued each month.

Banks usually charge bank credit card holders a small annual fee. Retailing businesses may deposit signed credit card drafts directly in their bank accounts, along with the currency and personal checks received from customers. Banks accept these credit card drafts for immediate deposit, so the retailer can consider bank credit card sales as cash sales.

In exchange for handling credit card drafts, retailers pay a monthly service charge to the bank. This charge usually runs between 1.25 to 3.5 percent of the total amount of the drafts deposited during the month.

Today, banks even offer young people credit cards. For example, Denver's Young American's Bank, which caters to youths, issues a MasterCard for children. Cardholders must be 12 and have a parent cosign. The card carries a $15 membership fee and 18.8 percent interest on unpaid balances. The cards have a $100 credit limit.

Some banks also offer **debit cards**—cards that withdraw money from a customer's account. Debit cards act like electronic checkbooks. Using the debit card, the purchase amount is transferred from the cardholder's account to the merchant's account. Although debit cards look like credit cards, no credit is involved. Payment is made at the point of sale.

The card a customer puts into a bank's automated teller machine (ATM) is a debit card. It withdraws (debits) money from the customer's account.

Global MARKETPLACE

Credit Goes Round the World

The three major credit card companies, MasterCard, Visa, and American Express, are all accepted at locations worldwide. They are also all competing for a share of the world's customers. For example, in Singapore, these credit card firms compete for customers using contests for cars and condos.

The use of an ATM card by a customer at a retail store, makes the transaction a cash sale and qualifies the customer for any cash discount available with the purchase. Banks may put a VISA or MasterCard logo on the corner of the ATM card. That card will then be accepted in any store or restaurant anywhere in the world that also takes VISA or MasterCard. Think of a debit card as an electronic check.[5]

As you can see in Figure 19–2, the use of consumer credit has risen steadily from 1970 to 1990. Only recently have we seen a slight decrease in the use of consumer credit. Debit cards may reduce the amount of money consumers owe through excess use of credit cards.

Credit Cards for Credit Risks

People with poor credit ratings can still get credit cards. Some banks will help a person establish or reinstate credit within a year by offering MasterCard or VISA cards in exchange for cash deposited as collateral. Banks offer these secured credit cards to first-timers or to people with poor credit records who meet salary requirements and have no outstanding debts.

Those who get credit cards this way should understand that the bank may add on application fees, annual dues, late payment fees, and charges for exceeding the credit limit set, which is sometimes as low as $300. (Finance charges may be as high as 24 percent.) They should check to be sure

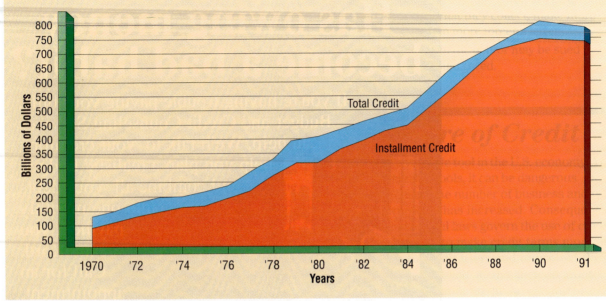

Source: *The World Almanac and Book of Facts*, 1993, p. 144.

■■■   *Figure 19–2 Consumer Credit, 1970 to 1991*
U.S. consumers borrowed more money each year between 1970 and 1991. By approximately how much has consumer credit borrowing increased during this time?

the bank reports to a credit bureau—the means by which customers improve their credit rating.

Trade Credit

The form of credit used by a manufacturer to buy raw materials and operating supplies is **trade credit**. This type of credit is also used by wholesalers and retailers to buy inventory or used goods for resale. Trade credit is often offered by the suppliers of the materials, supplies, and inventory as a marketing service to their customers: manufacturers, wholesalers, and retailers.

Sources of Information About Businesses

Companies check businesses that apply for credit in the same way that credit companies check consumers who apply for credit. They get credit information on businesses in several ways. First, trade organizations furnish information about the businesses within a particular trade. Second, salespeople who visit a firm know the quality and variety of its stock and its reputation for dealing with owners or employees. Third, local attorneys often know the firm personally. Fourth, local banks are a good source of credit information.

The most important credit information on a business may perhaps come from Dun & Bradstreet. Dun & Bradstreet gathers credit and financial information about businesses and makes it available to subscribers. It prepares a report about each company and keeps the information current. Each company is given a rating based on its financial standing. This rating, in turn, reflects the credit status of the company.

Types of Trade Credit

Unlike consumer credit, trade credit does not involve credit cards. In most cases, a letter, draft, or credit memo is the only visible sign of credit. However, the result is the same as with consumer credit: money is loaned, or goods and services are delivered on an agreement to pay later.

UNIT 6

Pricing

UNIT 7

Place

Chapters ▼

Intermediaries	Title to Goods	Functions Performed
Agent	No	Selling, promotion
Wholesaler	No	Storing, packaging, financing, transporting, and selling
Merchant Wholesaler	Yes	Buying, selling, packaging, financing, storing, and transporting
Retailer	May or may not	Buying, selling, advertising, pricing, providing an assortment of goods, and customer service repairs

■ ■ ■ **Table 23–1 Intermediaries and Functions They Perform**
Intermediaries buy, sell, or arrange sales and purchases. How is the agent's role as intermediary different from the role of the wholesaler?

Direct Channels of Distribution

A **direct distribution channel** takes place when a manufacturer sells products directly to the final user. Many manufacturers market industrial and consumer goods this way when little or no services are needed. For example, Lands' End, the clothing manufacturer, sells its clothing direct to customers through its catalog. A dry cleaner sells its services directly to customers.

Indirect Channels of Distribution

An **indirect distribution channel** occurs when the manufacturer uses an intermediary to act as a bridge between the seller and the user. For example, gasoline is marketed through indirect channels.

There are two types of intermediaries that a producer may use to get the goods to market: agent wholesalers and merchant wholesalers. Merchant wholesalers own the goods handled; agent wholesalers do not. Depending on the specific needs, a producer may use either or both of these types of intermediaries.

Reverse Channels of Distribution

When aluminum cans or old newspapers are sent back to producers for reprocessing, a reverse marketing channel is created. (See Figure 23–1.) A **reverse marketing channel** is used when the goods to be reprocessed move from consumer to intermediary to producer. Once the producer has reprocessed or repaired products returned by customers or retailers, the producer sends the products back through the distribution channel to the customer.

This process creates an aftermarket—a market for products used in the repair or enhancement of a product. For example, products such as cans or newspapers are broken down by the producer and processed for use in the manufacture of new cars or newsprint. Damaged and broken products such as auto parts that are returned to a producer are repaired for return to the marketplace.

Linked Channels of Distribution

Throughout its path along a distribution channel, a product is not changed. An intermediary may break down large shipments into smaller quantities for resale, but the basic product remains the same.

The product is consumed or changed in form only at the end of the channel of distribution. *Linked channels of distribution* are used when a product travels through more than one distribution channel.

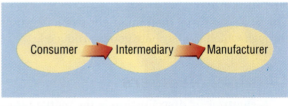

■ ■ ■ **Figure 23–1 Reverse Marketing Channel**
In a reverse marketing channel, the consumer or industrial user starts the distribution channel and the manufacturer ends it. Why are these products returned to the manufacturer?

Federal-Mogul Corporation

The automotive aftermarket supplies replacement parts to the 200 million vehicles on the road today when they need maintenance or repairs. This market represents more than $200 billion in North America alone.

Federal-Mogul Corporation serves both the original automotive equipment (OE) market and the automotive aftermarket. Its aftermarket business supplies approximately 75,000 part numbers to almost 10,000 customers in more than 90 countries around the world. These products are supplied through a network of more than 70 service centers worldwide. Primary customers include retail parts stores, industrial bearing distributors, distributors of heavy duty vehicular parts, and independent warehouse distributors who redistribute products to local parts suppliers called jobbers. Federal-Mogul maintains its strong position in the global automotive aftermarket by offering quality and value through a strong commitment to quality and customer service.

The Maysville, Kentucky, distribution center employs more than 200 people who process, package, and ship some 35,000 different automotive aftermarket parts. The operation consists of two

facilities totaling 258,000 square feet of warehouse space and using state-of-the-art computers to track inventory.

The primary operation is a Pass Thru facility responsible for packaging and distribution of automotive parts such as bearings, pistons, valves, tie rod ends, ball joints, and other many automotive replacement parts. Each year, approximately 55 million parts pass through this facility en route to customers around the world.

The much smaller Returned Goods facility is responsible for inspection and re-boxing automotive parts that have been returned through the dealer channel after having been on the market. Parts that meet extremely high inspection standards are re-boxed and given a new lease on life in the automotive aftermarket. Parts not meeting the company's quality standards are scrapped.

1. What happens to automotive parts returned to the manufacturer through the reverse channel of distribution?

2. How does Federal-Mogul benefit from a reverse channel of distribution?

Many raw materials travel through several linked channels of distribution before they reach the consumer. The marketing of baked goods, for example, requires three linked channels of distribution to convert raw wheat to baked goods.

First Channel

- A wheat farmer begins one distribution channel when the crop is sold to a grain elevator company—an intermediary that stores wheat for future sale.

- The grain elevator company sells the wheat to a central market, another intermediary.

- The central market buys the wheat for flour from many grain elevator companies and sells it to a milling company.

- The milling company processes it into flour. Because the milling company is the last organization to receive the wheat in its natural state, the first channel of distribution ends at the mill.

Second Channel

- The milling company produces flour and sells it to a flour wholesaler.

- From the wholesaler it goes to commercial bakeries. Because the flour will be changed into baked goods at each of these bakeries, the second channel of distribution ends here.

Third Channel

- At one of the bakeries, production is started on rolls and pastries to be sold to a large restaurant chain.

- The third and last distribution channel is begun when the bakery delivers its baked goods to the various restaurants in the chain. This distribution channel ends when the baked goods are sold to consumers.

Channels for Consumer Goods

An intermediary usually specializes in handling either consumer or industrial goods. Thus, a manufacturer of consumer goods usually deals with intermediaries who distribute only consumer products. A manufacturer of industrial goods deals with intermediaries who handle only industrial products.

The channels of distribution for consumer products are separate from those for industrial products. Let's take a look at these different channels. (See Figure 23–2.)

Manufacturer to Consumer

The simplest channel of distribution for consumer products is the direct distribution channel from manufacturer to consumer. No intermediaries are involved.

In selling consumer goods, the manufacturer can use several types of direct channels. Sales can be made at the point of production, at the manufacturer's own retail store, door to door, or by mail. You will look more closely at this channel of distribution in Chapter 25.

Manufacturer to Retailer to Consumer

Some manufacturers or producers do not need the services of agents or wholesalers to market their goods to retailers. They do their own selling, warehousing, delivering, and financing.

Manufacturers use this distribution channel when they deal with large retail stores that can afford to buy and accept delivery in large quantities. Inexpensive cookware, pottery, office equipment, yard goods, and work clothes are examples of products distributed through this channel.

Manufacturer to Wholesaler to Retailer to Consumer

The most frequently used distribution channel is manufacturer to wholesaler to retailer to consumer. Most retailers are too small to buy goods in large quantities directly from manufacturers. In turn, many manufacturers are not able to handle many small shipments to retailers scattered across the country. They prefer to ship their goods to area wholesalers who sell and ship to retailers in their regions.

Goods typically marketed through this channel include supermarket items, shoes, golf balls, light bulbs, lawn mowers, candy, and gasoline. You will take a closer look at wholesalers in Chapter 24.

■ ■ ■   *Fanny May Candies distributes its product directly to the consumer through its retail stores. What other direct channels might a manufacturer use?*

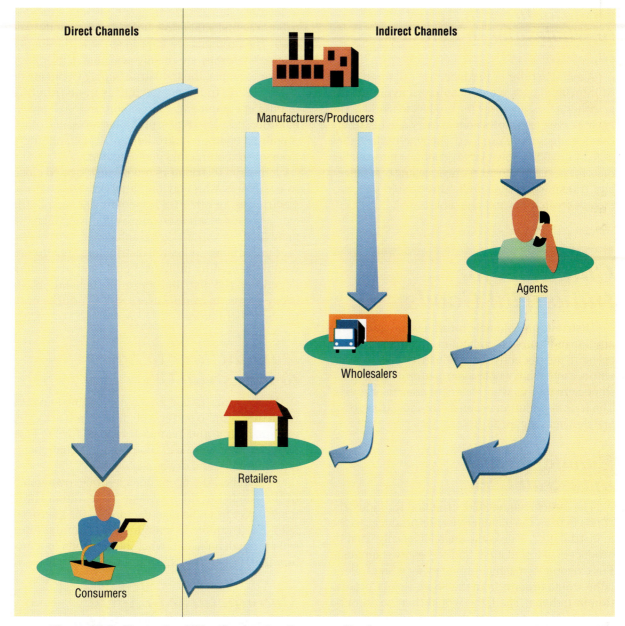

Direct Channels

Indirect Channels

Manufacturers/Producers

Agents

Wholesalers

Retailers

Consumers

■■■ **Figure 23–2 Channels of Distribution for Consumer Products**
Producers use five major distribution channels for consumer goods. Which is the simplest channel?

Manufacturer to Agent to Retailer to Consumer

If a manufacturer can handle storage and transportation but does not want to hire and train a sales force, an agent may handle the selling activities. After the sale is made to the retailer, the manufacturer takes over by storing and transporting the products.

The agent does not take possession or ownership of the goods but merely brings the buyer and seller together. Goods sold this way include expensive cookware, farm fertilizer, meat, hosiery, apparel and accessories, and fresh vegetables.

Manufacturer to Agent to Wholesaler to Retailer to Consumer

A manufacturer or producer uses all three types of intermediaries when wishing to avoid all the activities necessary to get the product to market. The agent persuades wholesalers to carry and distribute the manufacturer's product. The wholesaler takes care of breaking down large quantities into smaller ones for resale purposes, storage, selling to retailers, and transporting the goods. Goods sold this way include fresh fruits and vegetables.

Channels for Industrial Goods

Distribution channels for industrial goods are similar in nature to consumer channels. Agents assist in selling activities. Industrial distributors, who are merchant wholesalers, perform much of the same activities as wholesalers of consumer goods. The four distribution channels for industrial goods are shown in Figure 23–3.

Manufacturer to Industrial User

The direct channel of distribution for industrial goods is from the manufacturer or producer to the industrial user. This is the channel usually used by producers of installations and accessory equipment. For example, a machine shop buying a South Bend lathe would order it from the South Bend Corporation in Indiana. The lathe would then be shipped direct from the factory to the machine shop.

Some manufacturers train a sales force to sell their products directly to industrial users. Since the manufacturer's sales force is part of the company, the channel of distribution—manufacturer to industrial user—is still considered to be direct.

Manufacturer to Industrial Distributor to Industrial User

The **industrial distributor** sells equipment, standardized parts, and operating supplies to industrial users. Unlike an agent, the industrial distributor actually takes ownership of the goods handled. The products are kept in stock in the supply house. Thus, they are readily available to users.

For example, the Industrial Supply Company of Terre Haute, Indiana, specializes in distributing plumbing equipment. Plastic soil drainage pipes, bathtubs, cast-iron pipes, plumbing tools, and other plumbing equipment are kept in stock and made available to contractors and plumbers.

Industrial distributors are usually located close to customers who may be plumbers, contractors, electricians, or other tradespeople. The distributor can generally reach users more effectively than the manufacturer within a geographic area.

Furthermore, industrial distributors are often so well respected by industrial customers that they depend on the distributors to fill their orders. In these cases, manufacturers sell products only through distributors.

Manufacturer to Agent to Industrial User

Manufacturers use an agent's selling services when they want to perform all distribution activities except hiring and training a sales force. This happens frequently with construction equipment, farm products, and dry goods.

Remember, the agent does not take ownership of the goods but does arrange sales. Shipment is made direct from the manufacturer to the industrial user. For example, a machine tool manufacturer sells through an agent, who, in turn, sells to a factory that uses the machine tool in production.

Manufacturer to Agent to Industrial Distributor to Industrial User

Small manufacturers often concentrate on production. They leave the distribution to marketing experts. Such manufacturers use agents to sell products to industrial distributors. The industrial distributor will take over the functions for storage, reselling, and shipping. For example, a small manufacturer of pumps sells to a plumbing supplies agent, who sells to a plumbing and heating distributor, who then sells to a contractor.

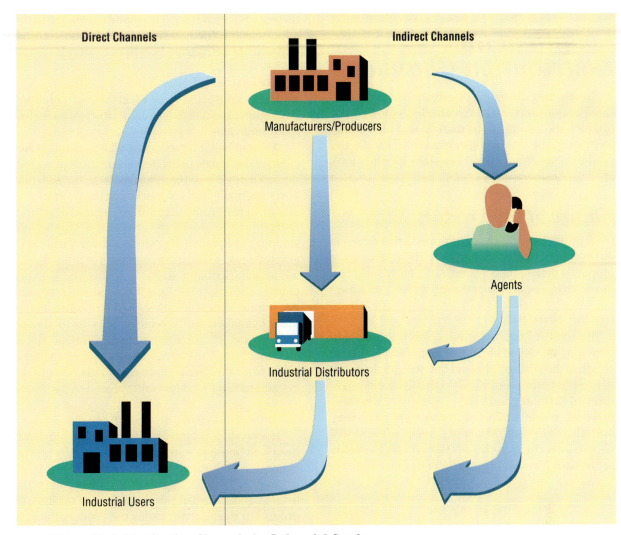

■■■ Figure 23–3 Distribution Channels for Industrial Goods
There are four distribution channels for industrial goods. Name types of manufacturers that are most likely to use the direct channel of distribution.

Selecting a Distribution Channel

No matter how good a product is, it can be a total sales failure if it arrives in the marketplace too late, if distribution costs are too high, or if it is not distributed as widely as a competing product. When deciding how to distribute a product, the manufacturer considers both the length and the width of the distribution channels available.

The length of a channel refers to the number of intermediaries through whom the product will pass on its way to the consumer or industrial user. The width of the distribution channel refers to the number of outlets through which a product will be marketed.

For example, a manufacturer may decide to use the retailer as an intermediary in marketing a product to the consumer. After deciding to market a product through retail stores, the manufacturer next decides how widely to market the product— that is, the number of retail stores that are to carry the product.

Length of the Distribution Channel

In selecting the length of a distribution channel, three major considerations are the nature of the product, the nature of the market, and the characteristics of the intermediary chosen to handle the product. (See Figure 23–4.) Let's take a further look at each consideration.

Nature of the Product

A producer's choice of intermediaries depends on several product characteristics. These include the product's perishability, value, size and weight, and the services required to maintain it after purchase.

Perishability

If a food product will spoil rapidly or if a fashion item may go out of style, the manufacturer must choose a distribution channel that will get the product to the consumer quickly. Usually, a manufacturer of fashion goods sells to retailers who will make the goods available to consumers while they are still in style. A producer of perishable foods will choose a distribution channel that will get the foods to the user fast and protect them from spoiling on

Nature of the Product	Nature of the Market	Characteristics of Intermediaries
Perishability	Competition	Services
Value	Location of Buyers	Reputation
Size and Weight	Volume of Sales	Cost
Service Required		

■■■ **Figure 23–4 Selecting the Length of a Channel of Distribution**
Three major considerations must be made in order to determine the length of a channel of distribution. These are the nature of the product, the nature of the market, and the characteristics of the intermediaries chosen to handle the project. How would perishability influence the length of a channel of distribution?

the way. For example, in transporting lettuce to the supermarket, the marketer would choose transportation by refrigerated carriers.

Value

Unit value is the value of one unit of a product. A computer has a high unit value; a screwdriver has a low unit value.

A steam boiler for a heating plant has a high unit value of thousands of dollars. The manufacturer will market it directly to the industrial user; the high unit cost covers the costs of marketing the product.

On items of low unit value, the manufacturer finds it hard to absorb the cost of selling, packing, shipping, and billing to customers over a wide geographic area. Thus, the manufacturer must use an industrial distributor whose shipping and delivery charges are lower because it operates in a smaller geographic area. The industrial distributor handles many manufacturers' products. Thus, its total sales volume is much greater than that of the individual manufacturer. The increased sales volume makes it possible for the distributor to absorb the cost of marketing products with low unit value.

Size and Weight

If a product is large, heavy, or bulky, moving it from warehouse to warehouse becomes difficult and expensive. Central air conditioning units for large stores or office buildings are examples of such products. To reduce the physical handling of this type of product, a manufacturer sells the product through an agent called a drop shipper.

A **drop shipper** makes arrangements for the direct shipment of goods from the manufacturer to the purchaser. The product stays in the manufacturer's warehouse until the agent has found a buyer. Then it is shipped by the manufacturer direct to the buyer. The agent does not physically handle the product.

Service Required

Manufacturers of highly technical equipment, such as electronic controls, prefer to sell direct to industrial users. Then they can back up their products with service and periodic maintenance checks. Often, the manufacturer does not want to risk using an industrial distributor. If the distributor services the equipment poorly, the manufacturer may lose future sales.

With respect to consumer goods sold through retailers, the manufacturer usually relies on dealers to provide product servicing. Personal computers and automobiles are examples of goods serviced not by the manufacturer but by the dealer.

Nature of the Market

The market is determined by the product itself. Of course, a consumer good is destined for the consumer, just as an industrial good is destined for the industrial user. But beyond that, factors such as competition, location of buyers, and total volume of sales determine the product's distribution channels.

Competition

Every successful manufacturer must know how competitors market their goods. Even a superior product will lose to its competitors if it is not distributed efficiently. By studying a competitor's distribution techniques, a manufacturer may be able to devise even more successful techniques to beat the competition.

Location of Buyers

If the customers for a product are located within a small geographic area, direct marketing is a good way to distribute it. The manufacturer can easily train a sales force and keep in touch with all customers. However, if customers are scattered over a large area, it is more practical for the manufacturer to use wholesalers and retailers as intermediaries, thus using a long channel of distribution.

Global
MARKETPLACE

Something's Fishy

It sounds fishy, but The Resource Trading Company of Portland, Maine, is now importing Russian cod into New England and Canada. Cod fishing off the North American coast has dwindled. Fish processors in Maine and Canada hope that the new import will help them keep markets that might otherwise be lost.

Volume of Sales

If the demand for a product is great, a manufacturer may perform large-scale wholesaling functions. Some large manufacturers of special products even sell directly to the consumer. For example, World Book Encyclopedia and Fuller Brush sell their products door to door. Franklin Mint sells collectibles through mail order. Singer sells its sewing machines through its stores. However, unless the total sales volume is large, a manufacturer must use wholesalers and retailers as intermediaries.

Characteristics of Intermediaries

In selecting the length of the distribution channel, manufacturers must decide which intermediary suits their product best. They should carefully study the characteristics of each intermediary—services provided, reputation, and cost of services.

Services

Manufacturers expect an intermediary to perform the services that they themselves are not equipped to perform. The less manufacturers want to be involved with selling and distributing products, the more they will depend on agents and merchant wholesalers to perform these functions.

If manufacturers want control over distribution but do not want to be involved in selling to the consumer, they will market the product through retailers. If they want control over selling as well as distribution, they will market directly to the consumer. The manufacturer's first consideration in choosing an intermediary, then, is to decide which buying and selling services it needs the intermediary to perform.

Reputation

Manufacturers may want to employ an intermediary who has a good reputation in a geographic area. If such an intermediary is already carrying competitor's products and cannot take on a new line, the manufacturer must find another means of reaching the market. The choice might be to open a sales branch in the area that would act as a wholesaler for the manufacturer's products. The branch salespeople would adopt aggressive selling methods to compete with the established intermediary.

Cost

Cost is a vital consideration in selecting an intermediary. The costs of marketing are reflected in the price of the product. The price affects the consumers' willingness to buy. A channel that offers excellent sales possibilities may also involve high costs.

Channels must be studied carefully to determine the type of services being offered for the cost. A manufacturer might assume that selling the product direct to the consumer would be less expensive than selling it through an intermediary. However, costs of direct selling include hiring and training a sales force, providing storage facilities, risk bearing, and financing. Often, an established intermediary can provide these services at a lower cost than a manufacturer.

Width of the Distribution Channel

The width of the distribution channel will depend chiefly on the nature of the product and the amount of aggressive selling and promotion required to market it. To compete with rival brands, a manufacturer will distribute a convenience item, such as aspirin, to all possible outlets. A manufacturer of a unique product can choose fewer selling outlets.

It might seem that all manufacturers who could afford wide distribution would want it. But there are many reasons why a manufacturer limits the distribution of a product or refuses to allow it to be handled by every available intermediary. How manufacturers figure out the width of product distribution can best be understood by studying the various distribution policies from which they can choose: intensive distribution, exclusive distribution, selective distribution, and integrated distribution.

Intensive Distribution

The form of distribution in which manufacturers distribute their product through any intermediary who wants it is **intensive distribution**. It is used for products that face a lot of competition, such as toothpaste, shampoo, and shaving cream. Most food product manufacturers strive for intensive distribution in supermarkets and smaller food

stores. They know that a customer usually buys a substitute if a particular brand cannot be found. For this same reason, marketers of industrial operating supplies, such as nails and floor wax, try to distribute their goods to all possible outlets.

Exclusive Distribution

Exclusive distribution is the practice of employing a single intermediary in a geographic area. Manufacturers guarantee the intermediary a protected territory; no other intermediary in that area will be able to distribute the product.

In some cases of exclusive distribution, the manufacturer allows the intermediary to handle certain competitors' products. For example, a car dealer might sell both Plymouths and Volvos.

■ ■ ■ *Intensive distribution involves distributing a product to any intermediary who wants it. Why would manufacturers of toothpaste use intensive distribution?*

Sometimes manufacturers will grant a franchise to an intermediary handling their product. As discussed in Chapter 3, a franchise gives a distributor the exclusive right to sell and distribute the manufacturer's product within a certain territory.

Most soda-bottling companies operate under franchise. Each franchised distributor agrees to buy all its syrup, bottles, and other materials from the parent company. In return, the distributor is guaranteed a certain area as its exclusive sales territory.

Exclusive distribution has several advantages for the manufacturer. The cost of marketing is reduced, since the manufacturer does not have to deal with a large number of intermediaries. In addition, exclusive distributors often do a lot of sales promotion in their selling areas. This relieves the manufacturers of the responsibility for all product promotion.

Since high quality is usually associated with a product available only through selected dealers, exclusive distribution lends prestige to a product. It gives manufacturers greater control over prices because they can threaten to withdraw an exclusive distributorship if the intermediary tries to cut prices below the established level. The manufacturer's right to maintain prices is often set down in the original contract between the manufacturer and the exclusive distributor.

Selective Distribution

The form of distribution in which manufacturers carefully choose a number of intermediaries to market their product within a geographic area is **selective distribution**. Selective distribution means choosing those intermediaries who are best equipped to maintain a product's image and to attract suitable customers. Selective distribution allows the producer to cover select areas of the market.

Manufacturers of fine china, for instance, select only fine department stores and jewelry stores as distributors of their product. They would not select variety stores or discount houses for two reasons. First, sales of fine china from these stores might not be very large. Second, the china might lose its reputation as a high-quality product.

Integrated Distribution

The form of distribution in which manufacturers act as their own retailers or wholesalers is **integrated distribution**. Sherwin-Williams paint stores are an example of integrated distribution.

The Sherwin-Williams Company sells its paint at its own stores. In this way, it is assured of an outlet. The company can maintain control over the display and storage of its products. It can also control the selling techniques used by its retail salespeople.

However, integrated distribution has its limitations. Retail stores controlled by manufacturers usually sell at factory set prices. They cannot quickly adjust their prices to meet local competition. Often, the result is lost sales. Also, product selection is limited to one brand. Many customers prefer a store where they can select from several brands.

■ ■ ■ *Sherwin-Williams uses integrated distribution by selling its paint in its own stores. What are two limitations of integrated distribution?*

Chapter Summary

- A channel of distribution is the path taken by a product on its way to the consumer or industrial user. This route is made up of intermediaries who buy, sell, or arrange sales and purchases. An intermediary usually specializes in handling either consumer goods or industrial goods.
- Types of distribution channels include direct channels, indirect channels, reverse channels, and linked channels of distribution.
- Industrial and consumer goods require different channels of distribution.
- The length of the distribution channel is determined by the nature of the product, the nature of the market, and the characteristics of intermediaries.
- In determining the width of the distribution channel, manufacturers can choose from intensive distribution, exclusive distribution, selective distribution, or integrated distribution.

Building Your Marketing Vocabulary

On a separate sheet of paper, define each of the following marketing terms. Then use each term in a sentence on distribution.

channel of distribution
retailer
wholesaler
direct distribution channel
indirect distribution channel
reverse marketing channel

industrial distributor
unit value
drop shipper
intensive distribution
exclusive distribution
selective distribution
integrated distribution

Questions for Review

1. With whom does a channel of distribution begin, and with whom does it end?
2. Are transportation companies and independent warehouses considered members of the channels of distribution? Explain.
3. What is the difference between a direct and an indirect channel of distribution?
4. When does a distribution channel end?
5. Which channel of distribution do manufacturers of consumer goods use most frequently? Why?
6. What are two aspects that a manufacturer should consider when selecting a distribution channel?
7. Explain what is meant by the length of a channel of distribution.
8. When selecting the length of a channel of distribution, what are three aspects manufacturers must consider?
9. What is meant by the width of a distribution channel?
10. When selecting the width of a distribution channel, what are four types of distribution policies manufacturers can choose from?

Critical Thinking

1. Name a consumer product for which you would use a direct channel of distribution. Explain why you would use this distribution channel.
2. Name a product not named in the chapter that is distributed through linked channels. Describe the channels that are involved.
3. Describe channels that you, as a clothing manufacturer, would choose to sell products directly to the consumer. Explain the effectiveness of each channel.
4. How do such factors as a product's perishability, value, size and weight, and servicing requirements affect the manufacturer's selection of a channel of distribution? Give examples.
5. Of the five types of channels used to distribute consumer goods, which would you use to distribute bubble gum? Discuss how the nature of the product and the nature of the market influenced your decision.
6. Based on the various distribution policies, how widely would you distribute bubble gum?

Discussion Questions

1. Discuss cases in which knowing the channel of distribution might affect your consumer buying decisions.
2. Discuss why manufacturers that sell through wholesalers and retailers would not be willing to sell to individual customers who contacted the company directly.
3. Discuss products in which the width of distribution might have a negative effect on sales.
4. Consider the businesses in your area. What channels of distribution are used most often?
5. Do you think a greater emphasis should be placed on reverse marketing channels? How would manufacturers benefit?

Marketing Project

Investigating Distribution Policies

Project Goal: Given the four distribution policies discussed in this chapter, determine how each of them is being used in your community.

Directions: Visit several stores to find products that are marketed by each of these distribution policies: intensive, exclusive, selective, and integrated. For each distribution policy, name a product, the store, and the reason the manufacturer selected that policy for the product.

For intensive distribution, list a convenience product. For exclusive distribution, find one well-known product that is available in only one store in your community. For selective distribution, list one high-quality product. For integrated distribution, list two or three products.

Applied Academics

Language Arts

1. Choose a product you are familiar with and that goes through linked channels of distribution. Illustrate or chart the channels.

Math

2. A semi-trailer load of paper goods carries a list price of $9,250. The manufacturer offers a cash discount of 2 percent if the shipment is paid for in ten days after receipt of goods. What is the price paid if the paper goods are not paid for in ten days? What is the price paid if the paper goods are paid for in ten days? Why might companies not use cash discounts?

Science

3. Research the reverse channeling of aluminum or paper. How are these products recycled? Write a 250-word paper or develop an illustration that describes the process.

Marketing and Multiculturalism

Goya Foods, Inc., is the nation's largest manufacturer and distributer of Hispanic foods, including rice, beans, and frozen foods such as cakes and breads. Founded in 1946, Goya long ago believed there was a tremendous market for Hispanic foods. Its theory paid off. In 1992, sales topped $410 million. Part of Goya's success stems from its aggressive method of distribution. The company employs brokers to meet with supermarket buyers and push its product onto the shelf. From distribution centers, goods are shipped directly to retailers. Goya's goal is to mainstream its product, encouraging the general public to enjoy its 800 different offerings.

1. Is this an example of direct or indirect distribution?
2. Describe the distribution channel used by Goya.
3. How is the length of the distribution channel affected by the nature of Goya's products (nonperishable and frozen food)?
4. Is there an intermediary involved in distribution?

Chapter 24

Wholesaling

Terms to Know

wholesaler's sales representative

warehousing

bulk-breaking

full-service wholesaler

limited-service wholesaler

cash-and-carry wholesaler

rack jobber

truck jobber

broker

selling agent

Chapter Objectives

After studying this chapter, you will be able to:

- describe the functions and roles of wholesaling in the channel of distribution;
- compare and contrast the services provided by different types of wholesalers; and
- identify and classify various kinds of wholesalers according to their ownership of the goods they market.

Case Study

Valerie Pavelle, Manufacturers' Agent

Valerie Pavelle owns her own wholesale business in Dallas. Pavelle is a manufacturers' agent in the apparel field. She specializes in high-fashion women's wear with a Southwestern handmade look. Her firm markets dresses, separates, and suits produced by small design firms that are well known in the fashion industry and among the retail stores who are her customers.

Before opening her own business, Pavelle worked for another manufacturers' agent. There she learned the ropes. She worked in the showroom, traveled to see and show merchandise to retail stores in Texas and nearby states, and learned about the manufacturers whose goods she sold.

When Pavelle started her business in the Dallas Market Center, she knew she would need someone reliable to help her run it. She found Bonnie Denarski, who brought fashion industry knowledge and experience to the job. Denarski had an associate's degree in fashion merchandising. She had also worked in a showroom in the Center, showing sportswear to retail store buyers.

Most people think these women are in a glamorous business. Glamour, indeed, is a part of the fashion industry. It's essential to see the latest in apparel; observe its acceptance in the showroom and at fashion shows; and see who wears it to parties. But an agent's day is made up of much more than fashion shows and parties. Pavelle and Denarski spend most of their time scheduling appointments, showing merchandise, taking orders, and checking on deliveries to their customers.

"Sometimes when a manufacturer is late delivering some suits or dresses a store has counted on, and you're trying to do your best to move them along, you wonder if you've picked the right business," sighs Pavelle. She adds that a manufacturers' agent is only paid a commission (a percentage) on sales volume for the goods that actually reach the stores.

"However," she adds, "when you see that what you've sold to the stores is moving like hotcakes, you're really pleased that you've done well. The business is exciting. There's always something new!"

What Wholesalers Do

As you know from Chapter 23, a wholesaler is a person or firm that sells products from such producers as farms or manufacturers to retail stores, industrial users, and institutions. Wholesalers act as intermediaries between producers and their customers. Wholesalers sell mainly to other businesses, not usually to final customers. They simplify and speed the marketing process by aiding in the flow of goods from manufacturers and producers to customers in several ways.

One way wholesalers simplify the marketing process is by reducing the number of exchanges needed for retailers to obtain goods for their customers. Notice in Figure 24–1 on page 314 that if there were no wholesalers, it would be necessary for the three manufacturers to reach each of the ten retail customers individually, thus resulting in 30 separate exchanges. When the wholesaler serves as an intermediary between producers and marketers, those 30 exchanges can be reduced to 13. This includes a total of three contacts from each of the manufacturers to the wholesaler, and one contact each from the wholesaler to the ten retailers.

Some wholesalers collect the products of a group of manufacturers and maintain an assortment of goods for their retail store customers in the quantities the stores can use. A manufacturer may specialize in one line of products—for example, baseball bats. A sporting goods retailer needs an assortment of products, including bats, baseballs, mitts, and caps. The retailer can purchase a wide assortment of products from a few wholesalers, thus simplifying the retailer's buying task.

Wholesaling functions include the following:

- selling;
- providing marketing information;
- buying;
- warehousing;

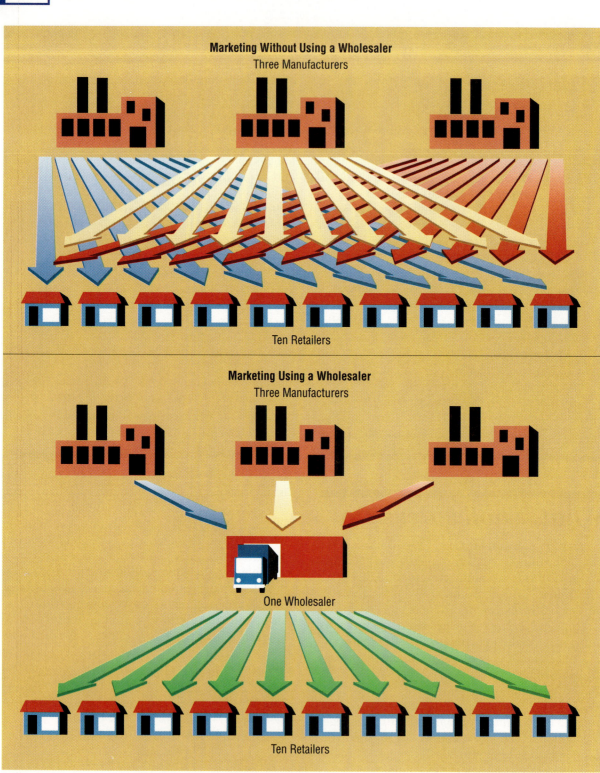

Source: Adapted from Peter D. Bennett, *Marketing,* (New York: McGraw-Hill, 1988), p. 358.

■ ■ ■   *Figure 24–1 Exchanges in the Marketing Process*
Wholesalers simplify and speed the marketing process. How do they do this?

- bulk-breaking;
- transporting;
- extending credit; and
- providing promotional assistance.

Not all wholesalers perform all of these functions. Let's take a look at each.

Selling

The main job of the wholesaler is to speed and smooth the flow of goods through the distribution process. To market goods effectively, most wholesalers maintain a trained sales force.

In many industries, **wholesaler's sales representatives** make regular visits to retail store buyers, industrial firms, and such institutions as schools and hospitals. The sales representatives carry samples, catalogs, and displays that show the wholesaler's complete line of products. The representatives hope to persuade buyers to become regular customers of the wholesaler.

A wholesale representative performs a variety of services in addition to selling. These include:

- checking the stock remaining in the store and preparing order forms for items that need to be restocked;
- advising retailers on advertising new products;
- suggesting retail prices and offering ideas and materials for displays; and
- giving advice on the proper installation and maintenance of technical equipment sold.

Wholesalers often take over manufacturers' complete selling functions. This is the situation in Valerie Pavelle's case on page 313. Valerie represents several manufacturers. She sells their apparel to retail stores in the Southwest. Manufacturers use agents if they do not wish to be involved in sales or are too small to hire and train a sales force. Such manufacturers depend on wholesalers to find customers for their products.

Providing Marketing Information

Wholesalers are in a good position to know exactly what is happening in the market. By telling retailers about new and current products that are gaining or losing popularity, they help retailers increase their own business.

Some of the wholesaler's information may come from local market research. Other information and ideas may come through contacts with retailers. By distributing such information and ideas, the wholesaler can assist retail customers in marketing and other decisions.

Buying

Small retailers would find it impossible to contact all the manufacturers whose products they sell. It would be hard for them to select the products that would sell. They rely on wholesalers to keep in close touch with sources of supply and to offer the most appropriate merchandise.

To have in stock the merchandise that retailers will want to sell, wholesalers study fashion trends, consumer demand, and retail prices. They keep in constant touch with many producers, looking at their new lines, noting their prices, and checking their delivery times. From the lines studied, the wholesalers offer the products that the retailers are most likely to buy. A product's sales history helps wholesalers decide.

Warehousing

Some wholesalers bring the various products they handle to one place. The process of handling and storing goods in one place is **warehousing**. It provides several advantages for the retailer.

First, the wholesaler offers an assortment of goods from various suppliers so that the retailer does not need to buy directly from several manufacturers. Second, the wholesaler's warehouse is usually near the retailer. Thus, delivery from a wholesaler is much faster than from a manufacturer whose plant may be hundreds of miles away.

Third, the retailer need not use limited store space to hold large quantities of goods. The retailer can reorder when stock is almost gone because the warehouse keeps merchandise on hand.

Bulk-Breaking

The wholesaler buys goods in truckloads or railroad carloads. At the warehouse, these large quantities are divided into smaller ones. The process of

■ ■ ■   *Sometimes wholesalers place goods in ware-houses. What services do warehouses perform?*

dividing large quantities into smaller ones for resale purposes is called **bulk-breaking**.

Bulk-breaking provides a service both to manufacturers and to retailers. Many manufacturers will not ship their goods in quantities smaller than truckloads or railroad carloads. Yet, it is impossible for most retailers to buy and store such huge quantities. Bulk-breaking helps manufacturers to dispose of their goods and allows retailers to buy goods in small quantities and in varied assortments.

Transporting

Manufacturers deliver goods in large lots to wholesalers. The cost of transportation is not as great as it would be if the manufacturers shipped in small quantities directly to retailers. Retailers who buy from wholesalers benefit indirectly from this saving. It reduces the total cost they have to pay.

Many wholesalers operate their own transportation services. They are able to maintain tight control over the delivery schedules for all the products they sell. If a retailer were ordering directly from many manufacturers, deliveries might be far less predictable.

Extending Credit

Many wholesalers extend financial assistance to their customers through delayed billing. These wholesalers allow retailers 30 to 90 days to pay for merchandise without extra charge.

For example, wholesalers of lawn and garden supplies may deliver seed to retailers in February but will not require payment until May. This form of credit allows retailers to pay wholesalers with money earned from the sale of the goods. (See Figure 24–2.)

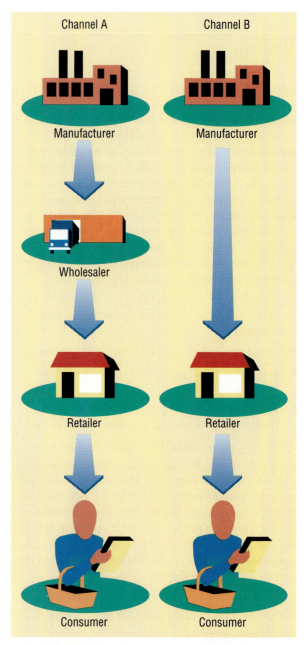

■ ■ ■   *Figure 24–2 Comparison of Two Channels of Distribution*
In Channel B who must perform the functions normally taken care of by the wholesaler?

Providing Promotional Assistance

Some wholesalers provide merchandise display aids to retailers. They may help retailers set up effective window and counter displays. They also may offer retailers help in designing store layout. Often, wholesalers enter into a joint or cooperative advertising effort with retailers; that is, they share the costs of local advertising. (See Figure 24–3.)

Types of Wholesalers

Wholesalers are classified according to whether or not they assume ownership of the goods they offer. As you know from Chapter 23, these two classifications are:

- merchant wholesalers, who assume ownership of the goods; and
- agent wholesalers, who do not assume ownership but assist manufacturers and

retailers in buying and selling. (See Figure 24–4 on page 318.)

Merchant wholesalers own the goods handled, so they must accept a sales loss for unsold goods. Agent wholesalers do not own the goods, but they do earn a fee or commission based on the amount they sell. (As you recall from the opening case, Valerie Pavelle, an agent wholesaler, was paid a commission.) Let's take a closer look at merchant and agent wholesalers.

Merchant Wholesaler

The merchant wholesaler may perform all wholesaling functions or only a limited number. The merchant wholesaler who performs all wholesaling functions is a **full-service wholesaler** or regular wholesaler. One who offers partial service is a **limited-service wholesaler**.

Full-Service Wholesaler

Full-service wholesalers give complete wholesaling service. They carry full lines of merchandise,

What Wholesalers May Do for Their Customers:	What Wholesalers May Do for Their Suppliers:
1. Learn customers' needs — find out what customers want and supply it.	1. Help producers sell goods by seeking out customers.
2. Provide information about prices and product availability and new product development.	2. Provide market information, thus keeping producers informed of customers' needs.
3. Do some of the buying, particularly reordering staple items.	3. Screen potential customers, thus reducing credit risks.
4. Carry an inventory assortment so that their retail store customers do not have to hold on to large quantities.	4. Store inventory, thus enabling producers to cut their storage costs.
5. Deliver merchandise promptly.	5. Locate and secure transportation for producers' products.
6. Grant credit to customers, a particularly vital service to small business customers.	6. Supply capital, thus lowering producer's needs for working capital by buying and carrying inventory.
7. Own and transfer title to products, speeding their distribution.	

■■■ *Figure 24–3 What Wholesalers Do*
Wholesalers perform some if not all of these functions for customers and suppliers. Why do wholesalers do some of the buying?

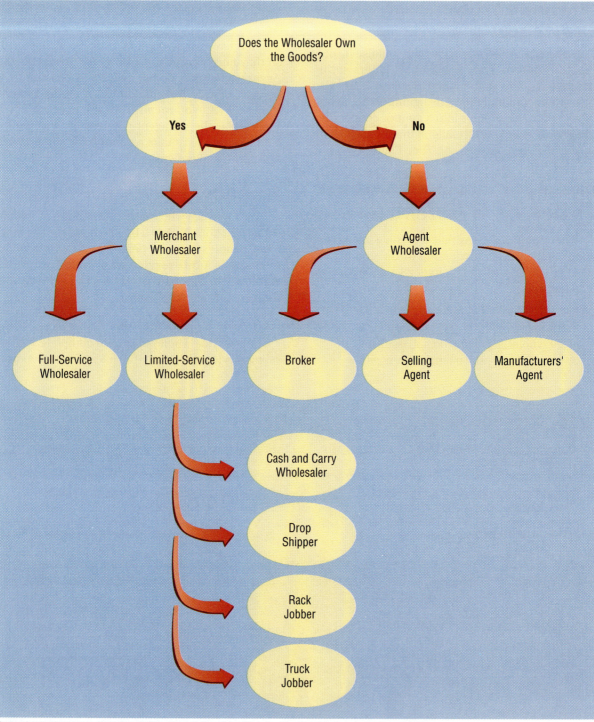

Source: Adapted from Jerome McCarthy and William Perrault, *Essentials of Marketing*, 4th edition, (Illinois: Irwin, 1988), pp. 260–261.

■■■ *Figure 24–4 Classifying Wholesalers According to Whether or Not They Own What They Sell*
More than half of this nation's wholesalers are merchant wholesalers, yet their selling costs are higher than those of agents. Why are merchant wholesalers so popular?

THE FUTURE IS NOW

Automated Replenishment

Wal-Mart Stores, Inc., is among the growing number of retailers using electronic data interchange (EDI). With EDI, manufacturers can track inventory electronically and generate purchase orders electronically for the retailers' approval. The producer moves the goods to the shelf without a merchandise broker, which results in lower costs, higher profits, and faster inventory turnover. The item may even be sold before the store pays the supplier. Now that's marketing!

extend credit, and buy in large quantities to sell in smaller quantities. They provide transportation services, accept risks, and assemble and store goods.

The full-service wholesaler offers a complete assortment of goods in a convenient location. It provides an informal sales force that calls regularly on retailers and extends credit and delivery services.

Full-service wholesalers may carry merchandise in a wide variety of lines—for example, groceries or hardware items. Or they may deal in a specialty such as kitchen appliances or cosmetics.

The full-service wholesaler of a specialty line carries only one or two types of products within a certain field. For example, instead of handling many types of footwear, a specialty-line wholesaler may handle only boots. The specialty wholesaler may be regarded as an expert in his or her area and thus can provide dependable market information to customers.

As you know from Chapter 23, a full-service wholesaler who sells equipment, accessories, standard parts, and supplies to industrial users is usually called an industrial distributor. The services performed for customers in the industrial market are similar to those performed for retailers in the consumer market. In other words, products are centrally available in a wide range of sizes and brands, and prompt delivery is assured.

Limited-Service Wholesaler

In contrast with the full-service wholesaler, the **limited-service wholesaler** performs only certain services. The four main types of limited-service

wholesalers are the *cash-and-carry wholesaler*, the *drop shipper*, the *rack jobber*, and the *truck jobber*.

A **cash-and-carry wholesaler** maintains a warehouse where retailers use their own trucks to pick up such merchandise as produce, canned goods, auto parts, and electronic equipment. Neither transportation service nor credit is provided. Retailers must make immediate cash payment. Because of this lack of services, the cash-and-carry wholesaler offers goods at lower prices than the service wholesaler.

As you recall from Chapter 23, a drop shipper is a wholesaler who takes orders from retailers and arranges for delivery of goods directly from the producer. The drop shipper assumes ownership of the goods before reselling them but does not handle the goods physically. Freight costs are thus reduced to a minimum.

Often, the drop shipper operates with little more than an office, a notepad, and a telephone. Because drop shippers do not maintain a warehouse, break bulk, or offer a delivery service, they can offer lower prices than service wholesalers can offer.

A drop shipper deals almost exclusively with such bulky items as coal, lumber, and building materials, and is located near the customer and at a distance from the shipper or manufacturer. These are products that do not require bulk-breaking; hence, there is no necessity for the drop shipper to handle the product. Customers are willing to accept them in railroad carloads or truckloads.

The **rack jobber** sells specialized lines of merchandise to certain types of retail stores. Most common in the food industry, the rack jobber supplies nonfood items such as health and beauty aids to supermarkets and other food stores. Recently, rack jobbers have begun to display specialized lines of merchandise in drugstores, hardware stores, and variety stores.

Although a wholesaler, the rack jobber performs many of the retailer's functions. The rack jobber usually assumes ownership of the goods, selects the merchandise to be displayed, sets up the display facilities, removes old merchandise, substitutes fresh items, and marks prices. In some cases, the retailer pays the rack jobber in cash for items sold.

A **truck jobber** is a wholesaler who uses trucks for storage, selling, delivery, and collection. Both sales and delivery of merchandise are made during calls on retail stores. For retailers, this means immediate delivery of small quantities of merchandise.

Principles into Practice

Apparel Centers: Wholesaling Clothing Across the Country

Regional wholesale fashion centers across the country serve the retail stores that surround them. They show their lines to buyers from local stores who periodically want new merchandise. The most famous wholesaling district for marketing fashion apparel is New York City's 7th Avenue. Here famous fashion names such as Ralph Lauren, Calvin Klein, Donna Karan, and other designers and manufacturers maintain their showrooms and design centers.

Other popular regional wholesale apparel centers or marts are Los Angeles, Dallas, and Chicago. World-renowned for its California sportswear, the Los Angeles wholesale center attracts buyers from across the country to view 10,000 lines of merchandise in its 2,000 showrooms.

Sportswear with a Southwestern appeal is a major attraction of the Dallas wholesale center, the third largest center in the country. Dallas also boasts a separate mart for menswear.

In Chicago, men's, women's, and children's wear, as well as bridal wear, attract buyers from small and large stores throughout the Midwest. Other centers include Atlanta for men's and boys' wear and women's wear, and Miami for accessories and infants' wear. Miami even attracts store buyers from Central America.

A number of other cities across the nation also contain smaller wholesale apparel centers. Among them are Boston, Denver, Kansas City, San Francisco, and Seattle.

A typical apparel center is a privately owned company with a building that houses the wholesale

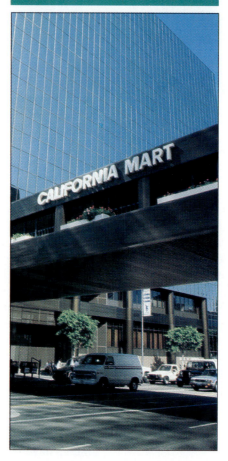

showrooms of many manufacturers and independent agents. The manufacturers and agents show their merchandise to retail store buyers who purchase merchandise for their stores.

The most exciting and busiest times for these showrooms are the "market weeks" held throughout the year to introduce the new season's fashions. Market weeks usually run three to six days and include showings of all the various markets, such as men's wear, women's wear, sportswear, bridal wear, and accessories. A single center might have 14 or so market weeks during the year.

During market weeks an apparel center's marketing strategy is most apparent. In addition to the showrooms featuring new merchandise, the center does everything it can to make the buyers' visits pleasant and stress-free. Apparel centers secure for buyers reduced rates on airline fares and hotel accommodations. Building security is strengthened so that only buyers are permitted in showrooms. And special fashion shows, seminars, and other useful meetings are conducted to keep store buyers informed of important fashion and business trends. This way, wholesalers work to speed and enhance the marketing of much of what we wear.

1. Describe the marketing strategy of the apparel center.
2. What services are provided during market week?

The truck jobber sells for cash and limits stock to nationally advertised specialties and fast-moving items. Most truck jobbers work in the food field. They carry specialties such as mayonnaise, cheese, potato chips, and candy.

The truck jobber's costs are high because of the relatively small orders received from each customer. Consequently, the retailer must charge a higher price for the goods.

Agent Wholesalers

Agent wholesalers do not take title to goods. Their main function is to assist manufacturers and retailers in buying and selling. Three important agent wholesalers are brokers, selling agents, and manufacturers' agents.

Broker

An agent wholesaler who represents either buyers or sellers is a **broker.** A broker does not physically handle the goods or take ownership of them, but rather brings the buyer and seller together. If a sale results, the broker is paid a commission which is a percentage of the total amount of the sale.

A broker usually deals in one type of product, such as food, iron, iron products, wood, dry goods, stock such as Prudential Securities, and real estate. By dealing in only one product, the broker becomes a specialist. He or she can offer clients important information about the market conditions. This might include current prices, the available supply of the product, the current demand for the product, and the best distribution method. Often, a broker may not have a continuing relationship with his or her clients. Each completed transaction may end the client's need for a broker.

Wholesale brokers are important in the food industry. They handle products such as sugar, grain, and produce (fresh, canned, or frozen fruits and vegetables).

Brokers provide service to producers of seasonal goods, such as tomatoes. The canning season for tomatoes is short, and small canneries do not maintain a sales force. As a result, they rely on food brokers to sell the cannery goods. When the entire stock has been sold, the relationship between the broker and the cannery ends. Of course, the relationship may resume the following season.

Selling Agent

An independent product specialist who sells the entire output of a line of goods for one or more manufacturers is a **selling** or **sales agent**. For example, someone who sells gymnasium bleachers to high schools might be a selling agent.

Selling agents usually have full authority in setting prices, terms, and other conditions of sale. They maintain a trained sales force and showrooms in which goods are displayed. There is no warehouse; the goods are usually shipped directly from the manufacturer's plant.

Manufacturers' Agent

As you know from Chapter 9, an independent representative who handles part or all of the output of one or more manufacturers within a sales territory is a manufacturers' agent. The role of the manufacturers' agent is more limited than that of the selling agent. There is little freedom in adjusting prices.

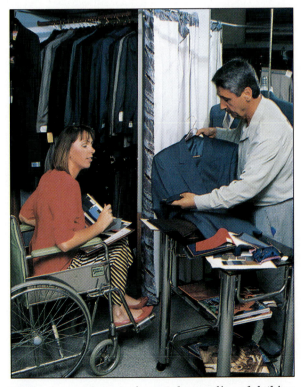

■ ■ ■ *A manufacturers' agent shows a line of clothing to a store buyer. What is the role of a manufacturers' agent?*

Chapter Summary

- A wholesaler sells goods from producers and manufacturers to other businesses, not usually to final consumers. The main job of the wholesaler is to speed and smooth the flow of goods through the distribution process.

- Wholesalers perform certain functions in the marketing process, although not all wholesalers perform all of the functions. These functions include selling, supplying marketing information, buying, warehousing, bulk-breaking, transporting, extending credit, and providing promotional assistance.

- There are two main groups of wholesalers based on whether or not they assume ownership of the goods they market. Merchant wholesalers own the goods they handle. Agent wholesalers do not own the goods but assist sellers and buyers in the marketing process.

- Merchant wholesalers include full-service wholesalers who provide all of the wholesaling functions and limited-service wholesalers who perform only some of those functions.

- Agent wholesalers include brokers, who bring buyer and seller together; selling agents, who may sell the entire output of a manufacturer; and manufacturers' agents, who handle the output of a manufacturer in a certain territory.

Building Your Marketing Vocabulary

On a separate sheet of paper, define each of the following marketing terms. Then use each term in a 150-word paper on wholesaling.

wholesaler's sales representative
warehousing
bulk-breaking
full-service wholesaler
limited-service wholesaler

cash-and-carry wholesaler
rack jobber
truck jobber
broker
selling agent

Questions for Review

1. What functions are included in wholesaling activities?
2. Name four ways in which wholesalers decide what merchandise to have in stock that retailers will want to sell.
3. Explain three benefits that wholesalers' warehousing provides to retailers.
4. Describe how bulk-breaking provides a service both to manufacturers and to retailers.
5. Name the two main types of wholesalers. How do they differ?
6. Name the two types of merchant wholesalers.
7. What is a rack jobber?
8. What wholesaling role does the truck jobber play?
9. Compare the services performed for the manufacturer by the three types of agent wholesalers.

Critical Thinking

1. If you were a manufacturer of paper products, what wholesaler functions would be most important to you? Would you use a full-service or a limited-service wholesaler? Explain your answer.
2. Would a merchant wholesaler or an agent wholesaler be more valuable to a small business that manufactures handmade children's toys? Explain your answer.
3. Do you think the services of a truck jobber would appeal to a small grocery store or a large one? Explain your answer.
4. If you produced oranges in California for sale to supermarket chain stores in the Midwest, what type of wholesaler would you use? Why?
5. How do selling agents differ from brokers? What types of products does each wholesaler specialize in?

Discussion Questions

1. Do you think businesses can function successfully without wholesalers? Explain your answer.

2. Do you think retailers or manufacturers benefit more from the functions of wholesaling? Why?

3. Discuss why only buyers might be permitted in the showrooms of wholesale apparel centers.

4. If you were to become a wholesaler, what type of wholesaler would you become? Discuss why you would make this choice.

Marketing Project

Identifying Types of Wholesalers

Project Goal: Given the five types of wholesalers, locate and classify one type found in your business community or in a nearby city.

Directions: Use the Yellow Pages of your telephone directory to locate the names of wholesale businesses. Look for the names of wholesalers under headings such as brokers, grocers, florists, industrial equipment, office supplies, warehouses, hardware. With your teacher's approval, arrange to talk with one type of wholesaler to find out the kind of products the business sells, whom the business serves, and what services are performed.

Prepare a chart like the one below and record your answers in the appropriate columns.

Name and Address of Wholesaler/ Person Interviewed	Type of Wholesaler and Products Sold	Customers of Wholesaler
Example: Industrial Supply Company, 301 North Ninth St./ Mr. Jim Boggs	Merchant-service wholesaler and industrial distributor. Sells machines, tools, and supplies.	Sells to small factories, and construction firms. Offers credit, delivery, and large inventory.

Applied Academics

Language Arts

1. Talk with a local business owner and determine the kinds of promotional assistance he or she has been given by his or her wholesalers. How has this helped the person's business? Write a 250-word report on your findings.

Math

2. Suppose a manufacturer's cost for shipping its products directly to its retailers is $150,000. By using a wholesaler, the manufacturer can save 20 percent on the cost of shipping. How much money can the manufacturer save?

Science

3. In order to store goods for a long period of time, many warehouses must have their temperatures automatically controlled. Research climate control and write a report of your findings.

Marketing and Multiculturalism

The many cultures in the U.S. marketplace encourage ethnic food wholesalers to expand their offerings. With each new ethnic wave, the wholesaler's list expands. Wholesalers who used to carry Chinese and Japanese food products now offer Vietnamese, Thai, Korean, and other products from a wide variety of Asian countries. Because they can buy in bulk, wholesalers make it possible for a wide variety of products to move onto shelves and into consumers' kitchens.

1. How does bulk-breaking create opportunities for ethnic food wholesalers who want to distribute a variety of lines to each store?

2. What type of marketing information could these wholesalers provide retailers?

3. Is an ethnic food wholesaler an example of a merchant wholesaler or an agent wholesaler?

4. Do retailers save money by using these wholesalers or would it be better for them to contact the manufacturers of these ethnic foods directly?

Retailing Businesses

Terms to Know

retailing	automatic vending
department store	electronic vending
mass merchandiser	telemarketing
variety store	independent store
limited-line retailer	corporate chain
warehouse store	voluntary chain
nonstore retailing	leased dealership

Chapter Objectives

After studying this chapter, you will be able to:

- define the role of retailing in our economy;
- describe the six functions of retailing;
- classify store and nonstore retailers;
- explain and compare the features of department stores, mass merchandisers, and variety stores;
- discuss six types of limited-line stores;
- define and describe direct-to-the-customer retailing and direct marketing; and
- discuss the advantages and disadvantages of six forms of retail ownership.

Case Study

Toys "Я" Us Plays a Smart Retailing Game

The world's largest toy retailer is Toys "Я" Us with nearly 600 U.S. and overseas stores. Toys "Я" Us has prospered because of sound retail planning. Its annual sales amount to around $7.2 billion.[1]

Each 46,000-square-foot self-service Toys "Я" Us store offers some 18,000 items at discount prices. Each store is located near (but not in) a shopping mall. The resulting lower rent means lower store expenses.

Toys "Я" Us is a supermarket of toys. Each store is set up the same way. The wide self-service selection enables customers to find toys easily and buy without sales help. A liberal return policy adds to customer confidence.

The company's communications system lets store managers know what toys to stock. The cash registers in each store send daily sales information to company headquarters in New Rochelle, New York. Managers know how many of each item were sold the day before and how many have been sold year to date. Thus, they can spot trends, reorder popular items, and reduce or omit items declining in sales.

Toys "Я" Us is able to offer lower prices because buying is usually done during slow periods for toy manufacturers who lower prices to keep factories running. By buying early and then storing goods in its own locations, Toys "Я" Us saves money. This, in turn, helps it maintain lower consumer prices.

Toys "Я" Us works with major toy manufacturers to bring new fashions in toys to its customers. The retail planning is working and growing. Kids "Я" Us children's apparel stores, based on a similar store retailing plan, have now appeared as a part of this retail family.[2,3,4]

What Is Retailing?

Retailing includes all forms of selling to the final consumer. Retailing is the last marketing step in a distribution channel. Retailing is a vital part of the U.S. economy for five key reasons.

1. Most of our disposable personal income is spent in retail businesses. Retailing businesses account for $1.5 trillion in sales each year.

2. About 1.5 million retail businesses operate in the United States today. Retailing employs around 19 million (15 percent) of all full-time workers. Many people work part-time in retailing.

3. Retailing adds value to products, creating the utilities of place, time, possession, and information that we explored in Chapter 4.

4. Retailing accounts for a significant portion of the total marketing costs of products.

5. Retailing holds many opportunities for enterprising individuals in all types of retail businesses.

Retailing Terms Defined

Retail stores specialize in marketing to consumers in a specific business setting. They range in size from nationwide organizations such as Wal-Mart, Inc.—the nation's largest retailer—to the local barbershop. They offer a variety of goods and services.

Retailers specialize in selling directly to final consumers, in or out of a store. Your local automobile dealer is a retailer, and so is the hot dog vendor at the ballpark. Retailers sell goods or services in stores, through television programs, by house-to-house canvassing, from vending machines or roadside stands, by phone calls, by mail order, or even by computer.

Sometimes retailers sell to other firms. For instance, a department store may sell office furniture and supplies to businesses. However, if more than half the sales of the store are to final consumers, it is considered a retail business. The word *dealer*, as in automobile dealer, usually means the same thing as *retailer*. A wholesaler is known as a distributor, not a retailer.

Retailing Functions

In providing goods and services to consumers, retailers fulfill six basic functions.

1. Determining the goods and services their customers want and getting them from many buying sources.
2. Providing customers with goods in a range of sizes, colors, types, and brands.
3. Keeping goods in stock.
4. Providing a convenient location for customers to shop at convenient times.
5. Offering customer services to make buying easier, such as credit, delivery service, and parking.
6. Selling goods at the fairest prices consistent with the amount of service and the variety and quality of goods.

Not all retailers fulfill each retail function equally. For example, a retail store with bargain prices does not usually offer a wide variety of services or the highest-quality goods. Neither is it likely to offer a wide assortment of goods or services. It must concentrate on fast-moving items to keep inventory costs down. A higher-priced retail store can afford to carry a greater variety of goods and offer more services such as gift wrapping and delivery.

A retail manager decides which retail functions to emphasize. A decision about one function affects decisions about others. For example, decisions about what products to stock and where to locate the store cannot be made independently. Table 25–1 lists the basic decisions that retail managers have to make and that retail employees should carry out.

Classifying Retailers

Retailers can be classified in many ways. The most popular ways are by the kinds of merchandise they carry and the services they offer, by their location, or by their form of ownership. For our purposes, we will classify businesses according to whether they are store or nonstore retailers. We will also classify them according to forms of ownership.

Target Market Decisions	**Location Decisions**
• Who are our target customers? • Exactly what types of consumers are to be attracted? Age? Income? Gender? Life-style?	• Where should we put our stores? • Should we buy them or lease them? • Should they be near the competition?
Image Decisions	**Pricing Decisions**
• How do we want our customers to see us? As a budget store? A trend-setting store? A traditional store? A middle-of-the-road-store? • How do we get this message to our customers? Newspapers? Magazines? TV? Public relations activities?	• Should we price at, above, or below our competitors' prices? • What average gross margin should we strive to maintain?
Quality and Assortment Decisions	**Service Decisions**
• What brands and types of products should be stocked? • How high should the quality level be? • How wide an assortment should be offered?	• Should we offer credit? If so, what kinds? • Should we offer other services such as delivery, check-cashing, layaway plans, repairs, and/or installations?

■ ■ ■ *Table 25–1 A Retail Store Manager's Decisions*
The welfare of a retail store depends on the manager's decisions. What is one way managers go about making those decisions?

Nordstrom, Inc., Known for Customer Service

Based in Seattle, Washington, a specialty department store called Nordstrom is giving such retailing greats across the country as Macy's, Dillard's, and Saks a run for their money. The business is expanding. Nordstrom has some 50 stores located mostly on the West Coast and in Virginia, New Jersey, Maryland, Illinois, and Minnesota.

John W. Nordstrom originally started the company as a shoe store in 1901. Nordstrom's philosophy was to offer the best service, selection, quality, and value. Later, the company purchased a group of specialty stores and plunged into the apparel business.

Today, members of the Nordstrom family are among the company's managers. The business continues to base its operations on John Nordstrom's philosophy. The stores are known for their luxury, spaciousness, live piano music, and unique merchandise.

They are also known for their keen attention to customers' needs. For example, the company encourages each salesperson to have a list of customers who are called when new merchandise arrives. All customers are treated with courtesy and respect. Salespeople have been known to warm up

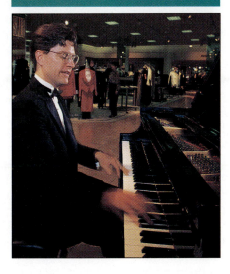

customers' automobiles in wintery weather. Merchandise returned by customers is accepted without an argument.

Attention to the customer does not stop there. Nordstrom also uses a decentralized buying system. Decentralized buying places the buyers for a given store within that store's department. For example, by working in the store's shoe department, the shoe buyers are able to find out what the customers want and then proceed to buy it.

In addition, Nordstrom pays its employees a commission on what they sell and keeps track of each employee's sales per hour. How do the employees feel about this method of payment? Some are loyal to the point of paying their own moving expenses when the opportunity arises to work in a newly opened branch store.

All in all, how is Nordstrom doing? Sales for the early 1990s are estimated in the neighborhood of $2.3 billion and profits at around $123 million.

1. Why are competing stores watching Nordstrom?
2. What could similar stores do to be more competitive?

General Merchandise Stores

A retail establishment that offers a large variety of goods for sale under one roof is a *general merchandise store*. This category of retail business includes department stores, mass merchandisers, and variety stores. Let's take a look at each.

Department Stores

According to the U.S. Bureau of Census, a **department store** is a retail establishment that employs 25 or more people. It offers clothing, home furnishings, gift items, and many other goods and services. In addition to moderately priced goods, many department stores carry high-priced goods such as art objects and designer clothing. Macy's and Marshall Field's are examples of traditional department stores.

According to the National Retail Federation (an association of chain, department, discount, and specialty stores), the definition of department store also includes large fashion-oriented stores that do not carry all merchandise lines.[5] For example, Saks Fifth Avenue and Nordstrom do not have furniture departments. Sometimes they are considered specialty department stores by retailers but not by the federal government.

The largest department store organization in the nation is the J. C. Penney Company. Its 1,300 stores bring in $16 billion in sales annually. Originally, J. C. Penney was a chain of soft goods and home furnishings stores. It repositioned itself so that by 1991, it offered a wide assortment of department store merchandise at affordable prices.[6]

Department stores are organized into individual departments according to the type of merchandise sold. Each department carries a specific merchandise assortment such as boys' wear, coats and suits, housewares, and home furnishings.

Department stores work to make shopping pleasant. They are usually furnished attractively and have colorful merchandise displays. Salespeople are trained to provide customer assistance. Customers often have a choice of payment plans. They can also have merchandise delivered.

Department stores frequently place branch stores in the suburbs. A branch store carries many of the merchandise lines available in the parent store. Usually located in large shopping centers, branch stores are often huge, offer ample parking space, and often provide the same customer services available in the parent store such as restaurants and hair salons.

Mass Merchandisers

Mass merchandisers sell a large number of consumer items at reasonable prices. These stores are often large, plain, and offer fewer services than department stores. They tend to be chain stores able to buy in quantity at low prices. The merchandise tends to be conservative. Many mass merchandisers, such as Target and Montgomery Ward, also offer low-priced, fashionable goods.

All mass merchandisers strive for both high quality and low prices. Some, such as Sears, are better known for high quality. Others, such as Wal-Mart, are better known for low prices. Let's compare quality and discount-image mass retailers.

Quality Mass Retailers

Two major quality mass merchandisers, Sears and Montgomery Ward, got their start serving small towns in the rural United States. They both started out in the mail-order, or catalog, retailing business.

One way mass retailers such as Sears have managed to offer quality goods at low prices has been with private brands. Much of the merchandise in a Sears store carries a Sears label or an in-house brand such as Kenmore and Craftsman.

Private brands help quality mass retailers to save money. For example, if Sears buys mattresses with the Beauty-Rest or Sealy PosturePedic name, it pays the wholesale market rate. But if Sears buys large quantities of mattresses from the same company with the "Sears" private brand attached, it can get a better price for the same quality mattress. Sears can then sell the mattress in its stores for less than the national brand and still earn a good profit. Customers today want to compare national brands with private brands. So, Sears and other stores often carry both.

Discount Retailers

A mass merchandiser or other retail store that makes a policy of selling merchandise at reduced prices is a discount store. Wal-Mart is a discount operation with approximately $55 billion in annual sales.[7]

■■■ *Mass merchandisers sell a large number of items at a reasonable price. How do mass merchandisers differ from department stores?*

In early discount stores, goods were sold strictly for cash, and stock was limited. Customers would often choose their goods from a floor sample or a catalog. In other cases, merchandise was displayed on large tables for easy examination. Few salespeople were needed.

Sometimes, discount stores increase their customer services, improve their decor, and acquire expensive buildings in better areas. This means a compromise of their low-price goal, but may result in a more fashion-oriented image. Developing such an image has been the goal of some discounters, such as Dayton Hudson Corporation's Target stores.

To continue to offer low-priced goods, many discount stores are now marketing their own private brands. Kmart Corporation operates more than 2,400 discount and specialty stores in the United States, Canada, Australia, and Czechoslovakia.[8] Kmart offers well-known brands such as Gitano alongside its own private label, Basic Editions.

Off-Price Stores

Another development is the rapid growth of the off-price store. An *off-price store* sells brand-name and designer fashion goods at discount prices that may be 20 to 70 percent below regular retail prices.

Off-price stores mainly carry well-known brand names and designer labels. They often deal in fashion goods (particularly apparel), home furnishings, and gift items in upper and middle price ranges. Discount stores carry their own brands along with some well-known brands in lower price ranges. They also carry a wide assortment of merchandise. Off-price stores offer:

- manufacturers' overruns (when more goods are produced than ordered);
- stocks left over from canceled orders;
- closeouts or discontinued styles;
- seconds and irregulars (imperfect merchandise);
- goods manufactured off-season to keep the factory open and employees working; and
- importers' unsold merchandise.

To keep costs down, off-price stores locate in less expensive shopping areas with lower rents. Newer shopping malls, such as Gurnee Mills, west of Waukegan, Illinois, are made up of off-price stores.

Marshall's is a well-known national off-price retail chain carrying men's and women's apparel,

■■■ *Off-price stores sell products at a discount. How are they able to do this?*

home furnishings, and gifts. Other off-price stores include T.J. Maxx, Hit or Miss, Burlington Coat Factory, and Loehmann's (the original off-price specialty shop).

Outlet Stores

The *outlet store* is usually operated by a manufacturer and carries only that manufacturer's products. Originally, outlet stores were close to the factory. Today they are often found in outlet malls, that is, shopping centers featuring outlet stores. Outlets offer manufacturers' overruns, seconds, and discontinued items at lower prices. By simplifying channels of distribution, manufacturers with outlet stores lower their marketing costs. Calvin Klein, Carter's Infant's wear, Magnavox, and Nike are among the many manufacturers maintaining outlet stores.

Some retailers also consolidate unsold goods from their various branches into their own retail outlet stores. Among these retail outlets are Sears, Lord & Taylor, and Saks.

Variety Stores

The **variety store** carries a wide assortment of goods in a low-price range. Frank W. Woolworth started the first variety store in 1879. His idea came from an experience he had while working as a clerk in a dry goods store in Watertown, New York.

He set up a counter of small items and placed a sign over it that read "anything on this table, 5 cents." The counter was almost sold out on the first day. Woolworth decided to start a store that sold 5-cent items only.

He opened his first store in Lancaster, Pennsylvania, selling merchandise he had bought with his own savings and with borrowed funds. The store was so successful that he opened other branches. Today, the Woolworth empire consists of nearly 9,000 stores doing $10 billion in sales each year. Woolworth also owns an expanding group of specialty stores, including World Foot Locker and Kinney Shoe Stores.[9]

The Woolworth variety store idea was copied for a time, resulting in other similar stores, including McCrory's, S. H. Kress, S. S. Kresge, H. L. Green, and G. C. Murphy. The variety store appears to be on the way to obsolescence because the expanding discount stores such as Kmart and Wal-Mart carry wider assortments of goods at similar low prices.

Limited-Line Retailers

A retailer that sells only one kind of merchandise, or several closely related lines of merchandise, is a **limited-line retailer**. Limited-line retailers include apparel and accessories stores, home-furnishings stores, automotive dealers, food stores, service stations, and hardware and building material dealers.

A limited-line store that handles a narrow assortment of goods with a unique image is called a *specialty shop*. Specialty shops offer products with a special market appeal, such as top-quality sporting goods, higher-priced apparel, and gourmet food and cookware. Brooks Brothers is a specialty shop that offers apparel and accessories for conservative business professionals. Hammacher Schlemmer is a specialty shop with a catalog business also, offering pricey games, electronic gadgets, and gifts.

Apparel and Accessories Stores

A retail store that sells dresses, suits, children's wear, shoes, millinery, lingerie, handbags, neckties, and other items of clothing is an *apparel and accessories store*. There are almost 142,000 apparel and accessories stores in the United States.

Well-known examples include The Limited, Ann Taylor, Foot Locker, Eddie Bauer, and Kids "Я" Us. In addition to these large chain stores, many communities have their own locally owned apparel and accessories stores.

The typical apparel and accessories store employs fewer than 20 people. The store owner must be especially aware of fashion trends. The owner will suffer a financial loss if he or she overstocks an item that does not sell. If popular fashions are not stocked, customers may begin shopping at department stores, many of which are particularly strong in fashion apparel.

Automotive Dealers

A retail establishment that sells motor vehicles or accessories that go with them is an *automotive dealer*. There are more than 200,000 automotive dealers and automobile service stations in the United States. About 26,000 of these are new and used automobile dealerships.

One recent trend in automobile dealerships is the auto mall—a variety of domestic and imported automobile showrooms combined into one dealership. Auto malls enable dealers to offer a wider selection of automobiles in one location, thus lowering expenses and making auto shopping easier for customers.

Automotive dealers are fortunate in that they have little competition from other retail stores. (See Figure 25–1.) This is not true, however, of auto accessory dealers. They are confronted with the fact that many mass merchandise chains and discount stores are now selling auto accessories.

Hardware and Building Materials Stores

The smaller hardware and building materials stores traditionally carry such items as tools, garden hoses, and locks. Larger stores of this type include

Radios, television sets, and major appliances are often presold by the national advertising done by their manufacturers. Thus, competition is often based on price. For this reason, chain stores such as Circuit City and Silo have an advantage over small independent stores in selling this type of merchandise. The chains can buy from wholesalers in quantity and at a discount. The small independent store can compete by offering such custom services as built-in television sets, specially designed kitchens, and more personalized customer service.

Food Stores

There are now about 236,000 food stores in the United States. They range from the traditional corner grocery stores to the supermarket. Butcher shops, candy stores, and bakeries are included in the food store classification.

As we all know, a large departmentalized self-service food store is a *supermarket*. Well-known supermarkets include Safeway, Kroger, and A&P. Many supermarkets now offer so much in the way of housewares, books, toiletries, and even apparel that they are almost combinations of food and variety stores. Each department within a supermarket may be owned by the store itself or leased by private owners such as bakers or florists.

Price appeal is the strong point of the supermarket. The store depends on a large volume of sales to get a satisfactory profit. The convenience of self-service and one-stop marketing also make the supermarket attractive to the customer.

Specialty and Convenience Stores

Specialty food stores are often sole proprietorships that feature ethnic or gourmet foods. Convito Italiano in Wilmette, Illinois, for example, offers imported Italian foods and freshly prepared bread, pasta, and entrées. Customers may dine at tables in the store or carry delicacies home.

A *convenience store* is a small grocery store carrying a limited selection of staple groceries, carry-out foods, and nonfood items. Convenience stores are open long hours, sometimes around the clock. Some sell gasoline.

Convenience stores average around 2,400 square feet in size, a tenth of the size of conventional supermarkets. Southland Corporation's 7-Eleven stores are an example of convenience stores.

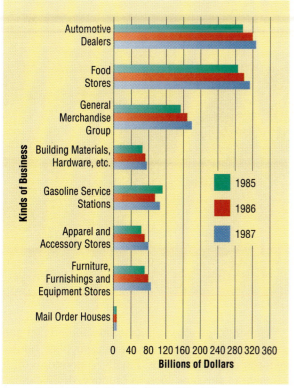

Source: *Statistical Abstract of the United States, 1989*, p. 750.

■ ■ ■ *Figure 25–1 Retail Sales by Kinds of Businesses in Billions of Dollars*
In the late 1980s, retail sales increased in a variety of businesses. Where was the most money spent? What is one possible reason why sales increased for this type of business?

products such as wallpaper, paneling, lumber, housewares, and a host of home improvement items. Examples include True Value, Ace Hardware Stores, and Home Depot.

During recent years, hardware and building materials stores have met much competition from discount department stores. They have tried to respond to this challenge by increasing the selection of items they offer.

Home Furnishings Stores

A retail business that sells furniture and such home appliances as radios, television sets, and refrigerators is a home furnishings store. There are more than 100,000 home furnishings stores in the United States. Examples include Ikea, Wickes Furniture Showrooms, Silo, and Pier 1 Imports, Inc.

■■■ *Supermarkets are a mainstay of retailing in the United States, yet they must compete to succeed. Who are the major competitors of supermarkets today?*

Convenience stores are a response to our fast-paced life-styles. They are particularly popular among single-person households.

Specialty and convenience food stores compete with supermarkets by responding quickly to customer needs. Store managers keep track of demographics, changing tastes, and prices. They offer services, such as food preparation, that larger chains find hard to do.

Combination Stores and Superstores

Larger supermarkets called *combination stores* combine drugstores and supermarkets. Combo stores are bigger than traditional supermarkets and have a higher sales volume. The combination of merchandise offered allows the combo store to compete with mass merchandisers such as Kmart.

Larger still are the superstores. They are similar to supermarkets in that they are low-cost, high-volume, limited-service operations. However, the superstore strives to fill more customer needs than the supermarket or the combo store. It aims to be an authentic one-stop shopping center.

Although supermarkets have been expanding more and more into nonfood items, their basic emphasis is still on food and home-cleaning products. The superstore sells these items as well as personal care products, some apparel, and low-priced housewares and hardware.

Superstores also sell gasoline, some lawn and garden products, stationery, sewing supplies, books, records, and hobby items. Finally, superstores offer household services such as laundry, dry cleaning, and shoe repair. Some newer superstores such as Safeway also rent meeting rooms and provide restaurant service. Superstores such as Kroger average about 30,000 square feet of space and usually generate at least $8 million in annual sales.

Super warehouse stores offer a full variety of merchandise, including quality perishables at low prices. An example is Super Valu's Cub Foods in Minnesota, Wisconsin, Illinois, and Indiana.

Hypermarkets

Hypermarkets, even larger than superstores, carry groceries and general merchandise in stores of 200,000 square feet or more. They carry a wider product mix than superstores, including heavy appliances and furniture. Combining supermarkets with general merchandise discount stores, hypermarkets offer consumer apparel and home furnishings.

Two major discounters, Wal-Mart and Kmart, operate hypermarkets in strategic locations around the country. At this point, however, these corporate chains are opening more new superstores than hypermarkets. The latter's sheer size appears not to be offering the convenience retailers had envisioned.[10]

Warehouse Stores

Imagine a store as big as a football field with a vast collection of food and nonfood items stacked as high as you can see. Cases of detergent, wheels of cheese, designer shirts, video recorders, and other items fill the building. This is a **warehouse store**, a self-service store featuring mainly convenience goods in bulk quantities at low prices.

Totaling more than $26 billion in sales, warehouse stores rank fifth among merchandising businesses, just after supermarkets, discount stores, department stores, and drugstores. The leading warehouse store organization in the United States is Wal-Mart's Sam's Wholesale Clubs. Second is Price/Costco. The third largest is the Kmart Pace warehouse stores.[11]

Warehouse stores are organized on a membership basis, with customers showing some business identification and paying a small fee to join. For this they buy at lower prices than they would in supermarkets and discount stores. However, products are offered in bulk and warehouse assortments are not always complete. These stores market what is available at the moment.

Nonstore Retailing

The selling of goods and services direct to the consumer without the use of stores is **nonstore retailing**. An increasing volume of retail sales takes place through nonstore retailing. In nonstore retailing, products can be sold through:

- direct-to-the-consumer retailing—that is, on-the-street, house-to-house, party-plan selling, and vending machines; and
- direct marketing, such as direct mail, telemarketing, and electronically with computers and TV.

Direct-to-the-Consumer Retailing

Direct-to-the-consumer retailing involves marketing to the consumer at home. In the United States, peddlers have used this method of retailing to sell their goods locally since the 1700s.

■■■   *Warehouse stores offer few services and are often in hard-to-reach locations. What is their big appeal?*

In 1741, two young Irish immigrants, William and Edward Pattison, set up shop in their home making plates, pans, and teapots from sheet tin. They sold these door to door. Eventually, other merchants began peddling their wares. These merchants became known as the Yankee tin peddlers.

On-the-Street Selling

Descendant from the Yankee peddlers are the salespeople who travel residential streets in trucks from which they sell their goods. Some street salespeople display their merchandise on sidewalk stands, selling such items as toys, belts, and fashion jewelry.

Many cities require street salespeople to have permits for their stands. Recent versions of on-the-street selling are the carts or kiosks retailers set up in shopping malls to sell items such as glass figurines, sweatshirts, or men's ties.

Door-to-Door Selling

As you learned in Chapter 23, door-to-door selling involves trying to sell a product in the customer's home. The simplest method of door-to-door selling is cold canvassing. The salesperson goes door to door in a particular neighborhood, without making any previous contact with the customer.

The Fuller Brush Company and Avon do their own retailing this way. Fuller Brush sends its consumers brochures describing the company's products. A few days after sending the brochure, a Fuller Brush salesperson calls on the consumer.

Retailers use the cold canvass method to seek new customers and to introduce consumers to new products. It is used to sell such products as vacuum cleaners, books, magazine subscriptions, cosmetics, and household items.

Another form of door-to-door selling is the appointment method. Companies that use this method provide their salespeople with "leads"—customers they think may buy. Insurance companies and encyclopedia publishers use the appointment method.

Some companies use the route-selling method in which they sell and deliver their products on a regular basis to customers who purchase the service. Many dairies, bakeries, and beverage retailers distribute their products this way. Their delivery trucks cover regular routes, servicing each customer on a scheduled basis.

Party-Plan Selling

In party-plan selling, a company's representative persuades a customer to gather a number of friends at home. There, the representative demonstrates the company's products, takes orders, and seeks hosts for similar parties with other groups of friends.

Hosts are offered substantial gifts as rewards for hosting a party. Hosts also receive additional awards if party sales reach a certain amount. Tupperware (makers of plastic kitchenware), Stanley Products (makers of housewares), and Mary Kay Cosmetics (makers of a variety of skin care products and cosmetics) are examples of companies that use party-plan selling.

Vending Machines

Marketing goods through a customer-operated machine is **automatic vending**. The use of automatic vending is increasing. Many factories, schools, and offices have installed food and drink vending machines. By depositing coins in the machine, the customer can buy lunch, a newspaper, or a cup of coffee.

Today, vending machines sell hot, refrigerated, and frozen foods. Some advanced vending machines can talk, accept credit cards, and dispense goods such as jeans, sweatshirts, jewelry, and even compact discs.

The Florsheim Shoe Company has an interactive video kiosk that lets a customer view a pair of shoes on the screen, order them on the spot, and receive them at home a few days later. The use of computers in these interactive vending machines is called **electronic vending**.

Vending machines offer three important advantages to marketers.

1. By eliminating the salesperson, marketers can sell many convenience goods more profitably.
2. Even in stores with salespeople, such as the Florsheim shoe stores, vending can provide assistance during busy periods or when the store is closed.
3. Vending machines encourage impulse buying. Customers are likely to buy from a machine what they might not buy if they had to wait for assistance.

■ ■ ■ *Direct-to-the-consumer retailing includes vending machines. What is one advantage vending machines offer marketers?*

■ ■ ■   *Direct mail is a form of direct marketing. What is one advantage of direct mail?*

Direct Marketing

People are busier than ever. They pursue careers, family responsibilities, and recreation. Many have little time to shop.

As a result, the average U.S. consumer is buying more merchandise via mail, over the telephone, and by television. Today, a growing number of people also have access to computers that enable them to buy goods and services from their computer terminals. Instead of using a salesperson to market their goods and services face-to-face, some companies use direct marketing—that is, marketing by mail, telephone, or with computer and/or television—to reach customers directly. Let's take a look at each of these methods.

Direct Mail

As you know from Chapter 7, direct mail involves marketing goods and services directly through the mail by means of catalogs and other mailing pieces.

The world's largest direct-mail order company is Otto Versand (known as Otto—*Versand* is the German word for *mailing* or *catalog*) of Hamburg, Germany. It has some 50 million customers in Europe, the United States, and Asia. The Otto family also owns a good portion of Spiegel, Inc., a well-known U.S. mail-order company headquartered in Oak Brook, Illinois.

Spiegel, in turn, owns Eddie Bauer, a sportswear and sporting goods retailer with stores and a catalog business. These stores and most other mail-order businesses have toll-free telephone numbers that enable customers to phone in their orders for rapid delivery.

In one year Spiegel sent out a total of 150 million copies of its 22 different catalogs. They included *Together*, clothing for young women; *Together for Men*; *In Home*, furniture and household goods for young families; and *For You From Spiegel* for larger-sized women. Total sales for Spiegel that year—including catalogs and its ten outlet stores—amounted to more than $1 billion.[12, 13]

Direct-mail catalog selling has advantages and disadvantages. On the positive side, merchandise can be kept in an inexpensive warehouse rather than in an expensive store. No salespeople are required, and delivery costs are usually paid by the customer.

On the negative side, producing and mailing catalogs can be expensive. Clerical tasks are increased, such as computing shipping costs and processing orders. Furthermore, customers often return merchandise because they cannot examine it before delivery.

Two types of establishments deal in catalog retailing: mail-order houses and retail stores. General mail-order houses handle a complete assortment of goods similar to those found in discount department stores. Specialty mail-order houses are like limited-line stores that specialize in one type of merchandise. For example, L.L. Bean of Freeport, Maine, specializes in outdoor and sportswear. Some well-known retailers such as J. C. Penney are also well-known general mail-order houses.

Some specialty mail-order houses have expanded to capitalize on consumer trends. The Sharper Image markets upscale gifts and gadgets. Horchow, owned by Neiman Marcus, carries pricey home furnishings. Lillian Vernon, the originator of small catalog marketing, sells a variety of household items.

Some retail stores issue seasonal catalogs. Neiman Marcus has one of the most famous Christmas catalogs. Over the years, it has featured items such as his-and-her matching automobiles, western riding horses with ornate saddles, submarines, and hot air balloons.

Telemarketing

Telemarketing involves organized telephone marketing efforts. Today the high cost of personal selling has contributed to the widespread growth of telemarketing as an alternative, less expensive means of marketing. The telephone lets retailers personally contact targeted customers. It also makes retailers easily accessible to the customer.

There are two kinds of telemarketing: outbound and inbound. A business using *outbound telemarketing* seeks to contact prospective customers over the telephone in order to negotiate a sale. Magazine sales agents, contractors, and interior decorators are among those who use this method. A business using *inbound telemarketing* maintains a switchboard to receive customer calls, often in response to an advertisement or catalog.

Mail-order houses and most large department stores cultivate inbound telephone business. Some department stores offer telephone-order service and toll-free calls seven days a week, often 24 hours a day. Businesses from J. Crew (Lynchburg, Virginia) to Marshall Field's (Chicago, Illinois) are among those retailers providing inbound telemarketing service.

Of course, small independent stores can also offer telephone-order service. However, they may lack the ready facilities to ship goods in quantity over long distances. Also, they may not have the

funds to advertise extensively. Without the help of advertising, the customer would have to shop in person in order to know what the store offers. However, small independent stores that deal in staple goods, such as groceries, can serve their customers effectively by telephone.

Increasingly popular, especially among small independent businesses, is the fax machine. Fax machines allow a written message to be transmitted to the receiver over telephone lines in the form of an exact duplication on paper. Retailers have many uses for fax machines. For example, real estate agents use fax machines to transmit photographs and descriptions of property to clients. Catalog retailers and even some restaurants use them to receive orders.

Electronic Marketing with Computers and/or TV

Personal computer owners can subscribe to electronic shopping services and order products from their homes. As you learned in Chapter 15, Prodigy is such a computer service. For example, using a computer with an electronic shopping program a customer may select the week's groceries and have them delivered.

The most rapidly expanding form of electronic marketing is marketing via the television, particularly cable television. The Home Shopping Network is one popular channel that appears in many parts of the country, reaching 50 million households. In the early 1990s Home Shopping Network accounted for $1 billion in sales.[14] After viewing a variety of items on screen, such as jewelry, kitchen gadgets, apparel, and art objects, customers have an opportunity to order over the telephone. Stores such as Macy's, Saks, and Nordstrom are among those offering goods on cable television.

Forms of Retail Ownership

Retail stores may be classified not only according to the type of merchandise they offer but also by their form of ownership. Forms of ownership include:

- independently owned and operated stores;
- corporate chains;
- voluntary chains;
- franchise chains;
- leased dealerships; and
- manufacturer-owned stores.

Let's look at each of these forms of ownership.

Independent Stores

Stores that are controlled and owned by one person or a family are **independent stores**. The owner usually manages them. The Mayhaw Tree store in the Unit 7 Case on page 368 is an example of an independent store. Some larger stores offering a wide assortment of merchandise are independent. But the typical independent store usually employs only a few people and offers only one type of merchandise such as groceries, children's wear, hardware, or home furnishings.

Small independent stores generally have less money to spend than large retail chains that operate nationwide. The small stores, therefore, cannot buy large selections of merchandise or promote their products as effectively as, say, chain stores. However, small stores can offer their customers convenience of location, personal attention, and service. The small store may also cater to a niche or special-interest market. For example, a small store may sell only tropical fish.

Corporate Chains

A **corporate chain** is a group of similar stores owned by stockholders and managed through a central organization. Wal-Mart, The Kroger Company, J. C. Penney, and The Limited, are examples of corporate chains.

A corporate chain may sell general merchandise or specialize in one type of merchandise. The central headquarters sets standards for methods of operation, services, and store layout. It also sets standards for merchandise arrangement and equipment. Usually, the headquarters buys the merchandise to be carried in the stores and develops the advertising.

■ ■ ■ *Can a national corporate chain such as the Gap meet the needs of customers all across the country as well as independent stores? Explain your answer.*

Corporate chains enjoy certain competitive advantages. Their costs can be lowered by buying large quantities from wholesalers, although such discounts are to some extent limited by law. They can enjoy large-scale advertising and sales promotion benefits such as hefty color catalogs and newspaper inserts featuring sale merchandise.

On the other hand, corporate chains have certain disadvantages. Because most merchandise and services are standardized, an individual corporate chain store cannot freely adjust selling policies or practices to suit the local community. As a result, the chain store is not always able to quickly take advantage of local market conditions. For example, a small independent store may be able to stock fad items faster than a corporate chain store, which may have to get permission from its headquarters to offer them.

There are national, regional, and local corporate chains. A *national chain* has outlets throughout the United States. Some national chains also have stores in foreign countries. Examples of national chains are Sears, F.W. Woolworth, and Kmart.

A *regional chain* has outlets in a geographic area covering a few states. Examples of regional chains that offer general merchandise are Rhodes Western of Oakland, California, which operates stores in five western states, and P. A. Bergner & Company of Milwaukee, which operates stores in the Midwest.

A *local chain* has outlets within a very small area, usually a city. Local general-merchandise chains include Columbia in Long Beach, California; R.H. Stearn's of Boston, Massachusetts; and Yielding's, Incorporated, in Birmingham, Alabama.

Voluntary Chains

A group of independently owned stores that share some or all their buying is a **voluntary chain**. Each store retains its independence of ownership. But the owner generally adds the name of the chain to that of the individual store.

One advantage of belonging to a voluntary chain is that an individual retains ownership. At the same time, by combining buying power with other retailers, the owner is able to buy merchandise at prices competitive with those paid by corporate chain stores. An example of a voluntary chain in the food field is IGA (Independent Grocers Alliance).

■ ■ ■ *Franchisees give up their individual identities. What do they gain?*

Manufacturer-Owned Stores

Stores that are owned by the manufacturer of a particular product are *manufacturer-owned stores*. By owning retail outlets, a manufacturer controls the entire manufacturing and distribution process. The wholesale step in the distribution channel is bypassed.

In other words, instead of selling to a retailer, the manufacturer sells directly to the consumer. This means the manufacturer has the added responsibility of being involved in retailing as well as production. Many manufacturers prefer to concentrate on their products and leave the selling to retailers. Manufacturer-owned stores include Fanny May Candies and Sherwin-Williams paint stores.

Franchise Chains

As you know from Chapter 3, a franchise is an agreement between a well-known corporation and an independent individual or group who wishes to operate the business locally. A *franchise chain* is a group of independently owned local businesses that are run under an agreement with a sponsoring corporation. Subway, Dairy Queen, and Long John Silver's all have some franchise chains among their retail stores.

Leased Dealerships

A business owned by a particular company but leased to someone else to operate is called a **leased dealership**. The company owns and maintains the land, building, and major equipment. The operator owns the stock, small equipment, and tools. The most common form of leased dealerships are gasoline service stations such as UNOCAL or Shell.

An advantage of a leased dealership is that the operator benefits from the company's national advertising. Also, the operator's initial investment is likely to be less than that of the independent retailer. The disadvantages are that the operator is responsible to the owner company for any material leased. In addition, the operator must deal exclusively in the products manufactured by the leasing company.

CHAPTER NOTES

1. Zachary Schiller, "Clout! More and More, Retail Giants Rule the Marketplace," *Business Week*, 21 December 1992, p. 68.

2. Robert J. Cole, "Toys 'Я' Us to Open Stores in Japan Within Two Years," *New York Times*, 29 September 1989, pp. D1 and D6.

3. Subrata N. Chakravarty, "Will Toys 'B' Great?" *Forbes*, 2 February 1988, pp. 37–39.

4. Amy Duncan et al., "How Toys 'Я' Us Controls the Game Board," *Business Week*, 19 December 1988, pp. 58–60.

5. *Stores*, July 1987, pp. 12 ff.

6. Penny Gill, "NRF Honors William R. Howell," *Stores*, January 1992, pp. 36-73.

7. Schiller, "Clout! More and More, Retail Giants Rule the Marketplace," p. 68.

8. Penny Gill, "Renewal Report Card," Interview with Joseph E. Antonini, *Stores*, December 1992, p. 22.

9. Isadore Barmash, "Chain by Chain, Woolworth Reinvents Itself," *New York Times*, 13 December 1992, F5.

10. Laurie M. Grossman, "Hypermarkets: A Sure-Fire Hit Bombs," *Wall Street Journal*, 25 June 1992, p. B1.

11. "2 Big Warehouse Club Companies to Merge," *Chicago Tribune*, 17 June 1993, Section 3, p. 3.

12. Alice Siegart, "Parental Match Made in Catalog Heaven," Business Section, *Chicago Tribune*, 22 May 1988, pp. 1 and 2.

13. Spiegel Annual Reports, 1987, 1988.

14. Johnnie L. Roberts and Mark Rubichaux, "Home Shopping Channel: From Dazzle of Success to Glare of Scrutiny," *Wall Street Journal*, 14 May 1993, pp. 1 and A4.

Chapter 25 Review

Chapter Summary

- Retailing includes all forms of selling directly to the consumer.
- Retail businesses may be classified by the type, quality, and assortment of merchandise they offer. They may also be classified as store retailers or nonstore retailers and by their form of ownership.
- General merchandise stores offer a wide assortment of merchandise. They include department stores; mass merchandisers such as discount, off-price, and outlet stores; and variety stores.
- Limited-line retailers carry a narrow assortment of merchandise. They include apparel and accessories stores; automotive dealers; hardware and building materials stores; home furnishings stores; food stores (both supermarkets and convenience stores); and warehouse stores.
- Nonstore retailing includes direct-to-the-consumer retailing and direct-response retailing.
- Retail organizations may also be classified according to their form of ownership. Six forms of retail ownership include independent stores, corporate chains, voluntary chains, franchise chains, leased dealerships, and manufacturer-owned stores.

Building Your Marketing Vocabulary

On a separate sheet of paper, define each of the following marketing terms. Then use each term in a 250-word paper on retailing.

retailing	automatic vending
department store	electronic vending
mass merchandiser	telemarketing
variety store	independent store
limited-line retailer	corporate chain
warehouse store	voluntary chain
nonstore retailing	leased dealership

Questions for Review

1. What is retailing?
2. Describe the six functions of retailing.
3. How does a mass merchandiser differ from a department store?
4. What is a limited-line store? How does it differ from a general merchandise store?
5. Name and give examples of four different kinds of direct-to-the-consumer retailing.
6. Explain the three methods of distribution that compose direct marketing.
7. What are two disadvantages of a corporate chain?
8. What is one advantage of voluntary chains?
9. What is one advantage of a leased dealership?

Critical Thinking

1. Cite three decisions that retail store managers must make and employees must carry out concerning customers, merchandise, and store image.
2. Why would you classify hot dog vendors at the ballpark as retailers?
3. What disadvantages are there to on-the-street selling compared to in-store retailing?
4. Name a retail store in your area. How would you classify this store? Give reasons for your decision.
5. Choose one business from Figure 25-1 and decide what form of ownership would work best for this type of store. Explain your answer.

Discussion Questions

1. Do you prefer shopping in a discount, off-price, or outlet store? Why?
2. What type of food store do you patronize? Are there other types of stores available to you? Why do you choose to shop where you do?
3. Do you think mass merchandisers or department stores will be more popular in the future? Explain your answer.
4. As a clothing retailer, would you choose to market your clothing by direct mail or in a department store? Explain your answer.
5. What type of ownership do you think is most efficient? Explain your answer.

Marketing Project

Comparing Types of Retail Stores

Project Goal: Given the types of retail stores, compare the characteristics of two competitive types.

Directions: Select two competitive types of retail stores in your community, such as a department store and a discount store or a supermarket and a small convenience food store. Visit one store of each type that you are comparing. During your visit, observe the characteristics of each type of store and make notes on your findings.

Prepare a form like the one below. In the left column, list the following characteristics of a retail store: (a) merchandise, (b) selling prices, (c) layout and appearance, and (d) customer service. In the center and right columns, list what you observed about each of those characteristics in each store. Your completed form will therefore compare the similarities and differences between the two types of stores.

Characteristics of Store	Store A	Store B
Customer services	Department store has many services and customer conveniences, such as credit, delivery, several salespeople, play area for children, restaurants, and lounges.	Discount store is generally self-service and has limited customer services. There are few salespeople, no delivery, and one snack bar and lounge area.

Applied Academics

Language Arts

1. Interview the owner of a new business in your community. Find out why the store owner opened it where he or she did in your community. Write a 250-word report on your findings. Include the type of retail business you chose and the type of goods it sells.

Math

2. Visit a general merchandise store and a limited-line store in your area. List prices of five products that you find in both stores. Determine which store offers the better prices. Tell how much you would save on the five items if you shopped at that store.

Social Studies

3. Go to your community library to research what your town's business district was like 50 years ago. Compare your findings to what your business district is like now. What changes have occurred. Why?

Marketing and Multiculturalism

Major retailers and boutiques are opening African-American departments offering Afrocentric merchandise that will appeal to the African-American market. The merchandise is meant to reflect the culture and history of African-Americans and has been met by enthusiasm by the market. African Eye, a retail store located near Washington D.C., has found its niche offering women's designer clothes from Africa. The clothes are priced between $50 and $600. They attract African-American customers between 30 and 65 with income levels of $30,000 plus.

1. What type of retail store is African Eye?
2. When deciding on the marketing mix, why would decisions on place be important for African Eye?

Retail Practices

Terms to Know

planned shopping
center

neighborhood shopping
center

community shopping
center

regional shopping
center

cost-profit squeeze

shoplifting

pilferage

Chapter Objectives

After studying this chapter, you will be able to:

- explain the retailing practices used to target
customers;

- create a retail marketing mix;

- cite three retailing challenges; and

- describe some of the ways retailers are meeting
retailing challenges.

Case Study

The Money Is in the Mail

"Look at all these clothing catalogs that came in the mail today!" exclaimed 15-year-old Shawn Peterson to his older sister, Sarah.

"That's because it's the time of year when people think about new clothes," she responded.

"Look at this one called an *Owner's Manual*. It's full of bizarre clothing," remarked Shawn.

Sarah flipped through the pages of *Owner's Manual*. The illustrations showed clothing from different eras. They included a chambray shirt with wooden buttons, a style favored by Thomas Jefferson. Also shown was a long canvas coat called a "duster." It was a style worn for protection by 19th-century cowboys while riding their horses in the rain and dust.

In 1987 the J. Peterman Company of Lexington, Kentucky, advertised this duster three times in the *New Yorker* magazine before orders began to flow in from customers. Now, the company does more than $30 million in business by selling such items in its *Owner's Manual* catalogs.

J. Peterman Company is just one of some 7,200 catalog retailers in the United States. Catalogs featuring various products from apparel to food to office supplies appear in the mail regularly. Some are from store retailers such as J. C. Penney and Eddie Bauer. Others are from strictly catalog businesses, such as Lillian Vernon Corporation which sells gifts and household items and Quill which sells office supplies.

Most aim for a target market. J. Peterman, for example, targets customers seeking historical and romance nostalgia: a cape like Franklin Roosevelt's or a cloak similar to the one worn by the French lieutenant's woman.

An average customer order at the Wisconsin-based sportswear merchant, Lands' End, is $80. At Lillian Vernon, orders average $38. Mail-order catalogs are just one of the ways retailers reach their customers today. They are a vital retail marketing practice that retailers develop to succeed. [1,2]

Retail Marketing Practices

Like all marketers, retailers develop marketing practices that reflect their company's goals. One retailing practice is customer targeting—defining and reaching those customers the business is designed to serve. The next significant practice is creating an appropriate retail marketing mix to target customers. Let's take a look at each of these practices.

Customer Targeting

Retailers must constantly monitor their customers' needs and examine the influences on customer buying behavior. Some of the strongest influences on consumers' retail buying behavior are income; education; occupation; life-styles; and attitudes toward family, work, and leisure time. Furthermore, people's values change over time which, in turn, influence what they buy. Retailers are alert to what concerns their customers, since people spend money on what is important to them.

Research helps retailers segment consumers according to their backgrounds and habits. Diverse organizations such as SRI International, Du Pont, and *The Wall Street Journal* conduct research which retailers use to target customers.

PRIZM, a research method that targets by zip code, has been used by such major retailers as J. C. Penney and Marshall Field's. After customer characteristics are defined, retailers can then focus on meeting customer needs with an appropriate marketing mix of the right product, price, place, and promotion.

Offering the Right Product

For retailers, finding the right products to meet the target customers' needs is a challenge because customers' needs constantly change. Retailers must anticipate those changes and respond accordingly or face losing business.

For example, supermarkets expanded their delicatessens and salad bars and offered more ready-to-eat foods to accommodate the growing number of working people who have less time to shop and cook. Hardware retailers responded to the boom in do-it-yourself home improvements by stocking home building and remodeling supplies. Not long ago, The Limited, an apparel retailer, noticed that more of its customers were career women looking for work clothes. The Limited transformed itself from a casual sportswear store for fun-loving teenagers to a sophisticated apparel retailer. Successful retailers believe that understanding target customers and their life-styles is essential to offering the right product mix.

Matching Price and Service

Retailers must determine whether price or customer service is more important to their target customers. Discount stores such as Target, off-price stores such as T.J. Maxx, and warehouse stores such as Kmart's Pace division are among those offering goods at low prices. These stores tend not to emphasize low prices more than customer service.

At the other end of the scale are the stores whose extensive customer service matches their high prices. These stores include Neiman Marcus, Saks Fifth Avenue, and Nordstrom. Nordstrom particularly is known for its attention to customers. (See page 327 in Chapter 25.) At stores such as these, customers expect and are given such services as free alterations and the ability to return merchandise without question. Of course, they ultimately pay for these services in higher prices!

Today, many people prefer to forego customer services in favor of lower prices. For that reason, retailers need to determine early on just who their target customers will be. The choices that retailers make as to whether they emphasize low prices or customer service are shown in Table 26–1.

Providing the Right Place

Being in the right place is key to a retailer's success. The right place for a retailer today may mean a desirable store location, a well-targeted catalog, or a home shopping show on the right TV channel.

Providing the right place for customers to buy goods and services is tied into the other elements of

Source: Peter Bennett, *Marketing*, (New York: McGraw-Hill), p. 367.

■ ■ ■ *Table 26–1 Retailer's Service and Price Levels*
Retailers know that some customers will forego service for lower prices, while others want more service and are willing to pay for it. How are customer service and merchandise prices linked?

the marketing mix; product, price, and promotion. For example, retailers offering convenience goods—staple, emergency, or impulse items such as paper towels, batteries, and candy—want easy access to such locations as planned shopping centers with convenient parking.

A **planned shopping center** is one that has been especially constructed for shopping, in contrast to a downtown or local business district that has grown over the years without centralized planning. A **neighborhood shopping center** contains an assortment of stores such as a grocery store, drugstore, dry cleaners, and barber, and is accessible to several thousand people within five minutes' travel.

Another choice for these retailers, especially those offering apparel and home furnishings, is a community shopping center. The **community shopping center** is a planned shopping center which typically contains a department store or mass merchandiser, a supermarket, a variety store, and several smaller shops. It is within ten minutes' driving distance for up to 100,000 people. Community shopping centers offer some opportunity for customers to shop around to compare goods and prices.

Retailers offering exclusive specialty items such as jewelry, art objects, or antiques seek locations that appeal to their customers and add prestige to their retail businesses. Sometimes, they locate their businesses on pricey downtown avenues. Sometimes they place their stores in a planned regional shopping center where they are joined by retailers offering shopping and convenience goods. A **regional shopping center** includes one or more department stores, a mass merchandiser, and many specialty shops. It draws more than 100,000 people from a radius of ten miles or more.

Often regional shopping centers are destinations in themselves; many people spend their leisure time there. Newer forms of the regional shopping centers are discount and outlet malls—entire shopping centers containing discount or outlet stores. It is estimated that almost half of the retail sales in the United States occur in shopping malls.

One key way to make shopping attractive is to develop the shopping center as a destination point for visitors. Cities such as Boston, San Antonio, and San Diego have developed shopping centers based on historical or maritime themes. Even more elaborate is Mall of America in Bloomington, Minnesota.

This enclosed mall contains hundreds of stores and restaurants, an aquarium, a miniature golf course, and 14 movie theaters. At the mall's center is Camp Snoopy, a theme park with rides and entertainment.[3] The stores in this 78-acre mall include Bloomingdale's, Sears, Macy's, and Nordstrom.

Malls account for more than $6.25 billion dollars in annual sales. Is it any wonder that retailers are seeking more entertaining and exciting ways to reach customers, and providing more than traditional store settings as avenues to them?[4, 5, 6]

The right place for retail selling does not have to be a store. It can also be a newspaper or magazine ad, a catalog, a TV program, a telemarketing system, or a computer system such as Prodigy. Of course, being in the right place only works if the products offered are timely, have the target customers in mind, if the customers are informed about them, and if they are marketed at the right price.

Creating Effective Promotions

Retail promotion is informing and persuading customers to buy. It includes:

- advertising in such media as newspapers, magazines, and TV;
- sales promotion, such as running a well-maintained store with adequate, fresh, well-lighted merchandise assortments; and offering demonstrations, free samples, and fashion shows;

Global
MARKETPLACE

Mailed from America

The newest craze among overseas consumers is the ease of international shopping offered by U.S. mail-order companies such as L.L. Bean, the Sharper Image, and Lands' End. The advent of fax machines, toll-free calling, and speedier air courier delivery has reduced, if not removed, the geographic limits of international marketing. American products are now just a phone call or fax order away from wherever you are!

■ ■ ■ *Bloomington, Minnesota's Mall of America contains a theme park and a miniature golf course. Why would such an elaborate setting be necessary?*

- public relations and publicity, including free mention of the store's newsworthy events on radio, TV, in magazines, or in the newspapers; and

- personal selling—the face-to-face contact between the customer and the salesperson that can result in a sale.

Like the other elements, promotion is related to the rest of the retail marketing mix. For example, mass-produced and widely distributed convenience goods such as breakfast cereal, detergent, and shampoo are best sold in quantity using self-service. Advertising on TV and in newspapers and magazines is the best way to reach the many potential customers of these products because personal selling would be too costly.

Higher-priced shopping and specialty goods, such as men's suits or a Porsche, invite comparison or explanation. A salesperson is essential to sell such products. The major retail promotion effort goes into personal selling where the salesperson can provide the information necessary to create an exchange.

Promotion can help a retail business change its image to meet the changing needs of its target customers. For example, when Kmart noticed that its customers were becoming more affluent and interested in fashion merchandise, it created life-style departments and hired celebrities to promote its

The "Power Retailers" Are Here!

The largest retailers in the country are quickly becoming the most powerful. The heaviest hitters are the discounters. Wal-Mart, with around $55 billion in annual sales and an aim toward topping $100 billion by the year 2000, is followed by Kmart with an estimated $40 billion. In 1991, these discount stores, along with Target, earned 20 cents of every dollar U.S. families spent for apparel.

In addition to these general merchandise discounters, this group of "power retailers" includes specialty stores such as Toys "Я" Us, Home Depot, and Circuit City; department stores such as Dillard's; and warehouse clubs such as Costco.

Many of these retailers have become what is known as "category killers," that is, businesses capturing a significant portion of the total consumer market. For example, Toys "Я" Us, the world's largest toy retailer, has manufacturers design toys exclusively for its stores. Dillard's Department Stores offers a brand of men's slacks by Haggar made just for its stores. Quick's Candies automatically restocks Kmart's 12 distribution centers nationwide when supplies of its gourmet lollipops are low.

Who has created these power retailers? Certainly, the businesses have grown by offering what customers want in convenient locations at closely watched costs. However, smart merchandising is only part of the answer.

Research on consumer income, age, and location shows that new and more diverse consumer groups are shopping at the power retailers. One survey reports that 27 percent of total discount store shoppers come from households with incomes under $15,000, but 51 percent come from households with incomes between $15,000 and $50,000. And

22 percent come from households of $50,000 or more.

Heavy shoppers at power retailers tend to be younger than other shoppers. Their average age is 42 compared to the average age of 45 for other shoppers. Although more than half of the power retail shoppers live outside the major metropolitan areas, three out of four of all customers have shopped a power retailer within the last six months.

What are the secrets to these retail giants' success? First, they continually keep tabs on what customers want and set out to get it. Target Stores, for example, maintains a group of buyers that travels the globe to find new products.

Second, these giant retailers carefully pick their suppliers. Wal-Mart, for instance, buys whenever possible from domestic manufacturers and displays a sign declaring it has saved some 60,000 U.S. jobs through its "Buy American" policy.

A third reason is the use of electronics. For example, Kmart maintains a satellite hookup among its stores, headquarters, and distribution centers to keep supplies coming regularly and help lower costs.

Will these power retailers kill small business? Not those small retailers and suppliers who are able to give customers what the power merchants cannot: unique goods and specialized service, all based on their ability to interpret and implement the marketing concept.[7, 8, 9]

1. Describe the marketing mix used by these power retailers.
2. How has information on consumer age, income, and location helped power retailers to succeed?

products. For example, Jaclyn Smith promotes Kmart's affordable apparel. Her name is put on handbags, sunglasses, shoes, and other accessories. You will take a more detailed look at promotion in Chapter 28.

Retailing Challenges

Retailing innovations such as those described in the previous section will probably play an even more important role in future marketing efforts. Among the gravest challenges facing retailers are the tightening cost-profit squeeze, increased shoplifting, and tough competition. Let's explore each challenge.

Tightening Cost-Profit Squeeze

Although retail sales are increasing, costs are going up even more rapidly, resulting in less profit for the average retailer. A condition in which costs rise more rapidly than sales and thereby decrease profits is called a **cost-profit squeeze**.

Most goods for resale now cost the retailer more because the goods cost the supplier more to

■ ■ ■ *Jaclyn Smith promotes Kmart products. Why would Kmart use a celebrity to promote its products?*

produce. Moreover, rent, building maintenance, transportation, utilities, labor, and all the other operating expenses of the retailer keep going up. At the same time, retailers face increasing competition and must keep their prices down to stay in business.

Thus, for the retailer, more of every dollar earned must be used for day-to-day expenses. It also means that at the end of each year, less profit is available for future investment in the business. And because much of the economy is in the same situation—facing a cost-profit squeeze—it is not easy for the retailer to get investment money from other sources.

One solution is to cut costs. This means doing the same job for less money, increasing operating efficiency, and doing a better job for the same money.

Shoplifting and Pilferage

The theft of merchandise from a store by a customer is **shoplifting**. Retailers used to consider shoplifting a minor problem. But as the lost merchandise figure has crept higher, many retailers have come to consider it a major threat to their business.

One large New York department store estimated its losses in one recent year at 4 percent of sales. Two factors are probably responsible for the increase in shoplifting: opportunity and motivation.

The use of self-service selling in stores increases the opportunity for theft. To cut costs and speed up the selling process, many stores have brought their stock out into the open and put it on self-service racks, fixtures, and displays. These efforts, in turn, have decreased the need for the number of salespeople on a selling floor.

Customers or just browsers wander about, picking up goods and carrying them from one counter to the other. They are expected to pay for what they decide to take, dealing with either a salesperson or a cashier. But not all customers pay for what they take.

Who steals? Some stealing is done by disturbed people who have a mental illness called kleptomania that compels them to steal. A larger amount of stealing is done by people who steal "just for the fun of it." A third group is made up of professional shoplifters who are habitual criminals. Professional shoplifters probably account for the largest losses of all. Whatever the motivation for shoplifting, it hurts the retailer. It also eventually hurts the customer, who must pay higher prices to cover the store's losses.

■ ■ ■   *Retailers use security devices such as this plastic tag to cut down on shoplifting. What is one other thing retailers can do to prevent shoplifting?*

Shoplifting losses sustained by mass merchandisers alone are more than $1 billion a year. However, the losses caused by employee **pilferage,** or theft, are also large.

Retailers have not yet found an ideal solution to the problems of shoplifting and pilferage. Certainly, store guards, television monitors, and security devices on merchandise itself help tighten store security and protect against theft. Marketers also consult psychologists to explore the reasons for nonprofessional shoplifting in order to determine what can be done to prevent the growth of theft.

Tougher Competition

Risk is a natural part of retailing. Retailers make no profit unless their decisions about what people want to buy are correct. The difficulty of predetermining customer wants is compounded by the fact that desired goods must be ordered weeks or months before delivery. This means the retailer must predict what customers will buy in the future. Charging a high price protects retailers against disaster if some predictions prove faulty. However, it is difficult for retailers to sustain a high markup in today's economic environment. Another factor that makes it difficult for retailers to keep their prices high is tough competition.

One reason retailing is competitive is that it is easy to get into. No one must pass an examination to operate a retail store, and business licenses are easy to obtain.

The fierce competition that results means added value for the consumer. It also means that it is hard for a retailer to establish a monopoly in any part of the retailing field. Even the giant chain stores that control a large part of the business in a given locale are in fierce competition with each other.

Unfortunately, the rate of failure among retail businesses is higher than that for any other kind of business or industry. It is all too easy for underfinanced and poorly qualified individuals to open small stores. Their frequent failure results in economic waste and poor use of human resources.

It is not only small retailers who fail. Even large retailers such as W.T. Grant, B. Altman, and Bonwit Teller have closed their doors. In the retail atmosphere of tough competition, tightening cost-profit squeeze, and increased shoplifting and pilferage, the innovations that create customers and become trends are more important than ever before.

CHAPTER NOTES

1. Diana B. Henriques, "A Tax Catalog Giants Might Like," *The New York Times,* 2 February 1992, p. F15.

2. Ray Schultz, "J. Peterman Is Taking Yet Another Imaginative Leap with New Catalog," *DM News,* 4 November 1991, pp. 2 and 102.

3. Wilma Randle, "Mighty Mall," *Chicago Tribune,* 2 August 1992, p. N1.

4. Joan Bergmann, *Stores,* April 1989, pp. 10 and 72.

5. Forest Fair: Super Mall, "The Minnesota Mallers," *U.S. News and World Report,* 25 June 1989, pp. 38–39.

6. Telephone conversation with Rick Pender of Tepe, Hensler & Westerkamp, Inc., Cincinnati, OH, 20 July 1990.

7. Zachary Schiller, "Clout! More and More, Retail Giants Rule the Marketplace," *Business Week,* 21 December 1992, pp. 66–73.

8. *The Power Retailers,* Mass Market Special Report, *Women's Wear Daily,* 16-page supplement, August 1992.

9. Wendy Zellner, "O.K., So He's Not Sam Walton," *Business Week,* 16 March 1992, pp. 56–58.

Chapter 26 Review

Chapter Summary

- Businesses develop retailing practices that reflect their marketing goals.
- Retailing changes in response to customer demands.
- A retailing trend develops when a number of retailers react to challenges with similar practices. A major retailing trend is customer targeting, that is, the retailer's seeking out potential customers.
- Practices among successful retailers (those using the marketing concept) include creating an appropriate retail marketing mix for the target customers—that is, offering the right product, matching price and service, providing the right place, and creating effective promotion.
- Several challenges face retailers today. These include tightening the cost-profit squeeze, controlling shoplifting and pilferage, and facing tougher competition.

Building Your Marketing Vocabulary

On a separate sheet of paper, define each of the following marketing terms. Then use each term in a 150-word paper describing the challenges facing retailers today.

planned shopping center

neighborhood shopping center

community shopping center

regional shopping center

cost-profit squeeze

shoplifting

pilferage

Questions for Review

1. What is a retailing trend?
2. Name two retailing trends.
3. Why is customer targeting important to retailers today?
4. What is one way retailers determine who their customers are and what the needs of those customers are?
5. Why is determining the right products for target customers such a challenge for retailers?
6. Explain the importance to retailers of quickly determining the relationship of price to service in their businesses.
7. Distinguish between a planned shopping center and a downtown business district. Describe three types of planned shopping centers.
8. Name five elements of retail promotion.
9. What are three challenges that retailers face today?
10. Name three things that retailers have done to prevent theft.

Critical Thinking

1. Why must retailers determine who their customers are before creating a marketing mix?
2. How does a customer's life-style influence his or her retail buying? Give an example to support your answer.
3. Name a new retail product that is not discussed in the chapter that was developed to meet a new customer habit or buying need.
4. How do fast-food restaurants match their prices with their service? Why do they use this match?
5. What can retailers do to counteract their losses incurred by shoplifting?

Discussion Questions

1. As a retailer of stereo equipment, what type of information would you want to know about your customers?
2. Discuss the goals of Kmart in enlisting celebrities such as Jaclyn Smith in its promotional efforts.
3. As a retail employee, what can you do about shoplifting and pilferage?
4. As a retail store owner, what steps can you take to reduce the cost-profit squeeze in your own store?
5. Given the high rate of failure among retailers, do you feel it should be harder for people to obtain a business license? Explain your answer.

Marketing Project

Identifying Retailing Problems and Opportunities

Project Goal: Given a retail business, identify the problems and opportunities facing the retailer because of changes in the market, competition, and technology.

Directions: Select a retail business in your community and ask the manager for an interview. With your teacher's guidance, plan your interview with other members of your class so that each of you visits a different business.

Prepare a form like the one below. In the left column, list the following topics to be discussed with your retailer: (a) store location and layout, (b) shopping hours, (c) customer services, (d) effect of off-price competition, (e) cost-profit squeeze, (f) pilferage, (g) shoplifting. In the center column, write a question to ask about each topic.

When you interview your retailer, ask each question. Write a summary of answers and comments in the right column.

Prepare a ten-minute oral report to present in class on the overall reaction of the retailer to the problems and opportunities being faced. Be sure to give the name and address of the business and the name of the business manager at the beginning of your report.

Topic	Question	Businessperson's Response
Shoplifting	What techniques do you use to prevent shoplifting?	We have an anti-shoplifting training program for all personnel. We also employ detectives disguised as customers.

Applied Academics

Language Arts

1. Working with classmates, develop a direct-mail catalog for either your school store or a store in your local community. Assume your customers are other classmates. Choose at least five products to sell in the catalog. For each product, write a short paragraph clearly describing the product's features. Include price and an illustration, if available.

Math

2. Your wholesaler charges you $2,500 for an order of 10,000 superballs. To cut costs, she will give you a 10 percent discount on your total order if you order an extra 5,000 superballs. How much will you save by increasing your order? How much will each superball cost you?

Social Studies

3. Using your school or public library, research the growth of shoplifting in retailing. Write a 250-word paper on your findings.

Marketing and Multiculturalism

Ten years ago the Tran family came from Vietnam. Today, they own two supermarkets in California. Their business employs 65 people and earns $10 million a year. What is the secret to their success? They specialize in Asian foods and products not easily found in other markets. Some customers drive four hours to reach the Tran market!

1. What retail challenges will the Trans face?

2. Could direct mail be a good way to extend the business? Explain your answer.

3. Do you think that price as reflected in costs of goods is a big issue to the Trans' customers? Why or why not?

Chapter 27

Distribution

Terms to Know

physical distribution
common carrier
contract carrier
private carrier
ton-mile

freight forwarders
distribution center
materials handling
containerization
in-transit storage

Chapter Objectives

After studying this chapter, you will be able to:

- describe the role of transportation and storage in the physical distribution chain;
- name, describe, and compare the services provided by train, motor, ship, pipeline, and air transportation;
- describe the special services offered by express parcel shippers, bus package services, U.S. postal services, and freight forwarders;
- explain why storage is needed;
- identify the different types of warehouses; and
- explain the functions that take place within the warehouse.

Case Study

Distribution Brings GE to Life

Most people probably recognize General Electric (GE) for its lamps and other electrical appliances. But it makes a variety of other products, including satellites, locomotives, jet engines, electric motors, power generation equipment, automation systems, medical equipment, and plastics.

GE operates more than 215 manufacturing plants in the United States and more than 115 plants in 24 other countries. In 1992, it had sales totaling $57.03 billion, assets valued at $192.87 billion, and 230,000 employees.[1]

A corporation producing a wide variety of products depends on an efficient distribution system to move raw materials, parts, and components to manufacturing facilities. The physical distribution process begins with the customer order. General Electric uses a computer-based system to speed up the order-shipping-billing cycle. Upon receiving a customer's order, the computer is used to check the customer's credit standing and determine whether and where the items are in stock. The computer then issues an order to ship, bills the customer, updates the inventory records, and sends a production order for new stock. Once this is completed the computer sends the salesperson a message that the customer's order is on the way. These computer operations all take place in less than 15 seconds.

To move the finished products out to industrial users and to consumers, GE uses a variety of transportation services. For example, GE's Electromotive Division in La Grange, Illinois, must receive a constant stream of parts and supplies in order to produce the locomotives that pull trains carrying passengers and freight across the country. Warehouses and distribution centers must be located where there is only a minimum delay in delivering parts and supplies. Trucks and trains are used to deliver these parts to GE.

Transportation and storage allow GE to move, handle, and store goods so that they may be made available when and where customers want them. They contribute to the value of goods companies such as GE buy and sell to their customers.

Physical Distribution

Throughout the United States, trucks, planes, ships, pipelines, trains, and machinery constantly distribute goods to various destinations. A trailer truck carries a cargo of fresh asparagus to the wholesale vegetable market. A jet cargo plane flies a load of high-fashion suits to an airport to be picked up and delivered by truck to a department store. A freight train delivers a shipment of new automobiles to a site where they are removed for delivery by truck to a dealer. A forklift in a giant warehouse carries a load of books from a loading platform to a storage space.

Each of these activities is a link in the physical distribution chain. **Physical distribution** is the total process of moving, handling, and storing goods on the way from the producer to the user. It includes both transportation and storage.

Transportation Deregulation

Until 1977 the transportation industry was under strict federal government regulation. Rates charged and transportation routes used were controlled. In 1977 regulations for cargo air carriers not engaged in passenger transportation were removed. The 1978 Airline Deregulation Act provided considerable freedom in establishing fares and choosing new routes.

The Motor Carrier Act and the Staggers Rail Act passed in 1980 allowed carriers to negotiate rates and services. Transportation companies are now more competitive as they try to win customers by meeting their needs. Deregulation also has made the distribution manager's job more important, since the flexibility in negotiating with various carriers makes the job more complicated and necessary. It takes a lot of effort to compare the rates and services of many carriers to determine which one will provide the services to fill a specific need at the best rate.

Carriers and Their Owners

A company that transports goods between the producer and the consumer or industrial users is a carrier. There are three types of carriers: common, contract, and private.

A **common carrier** is a transportation company that provides equipment and services to any shipper for a fee. Its rates and services are regulated by the federal government. It usually operates on a set schedule and it cannot operate without the appropriate regulating agency's permission.

Common carriers exist for all types of transportation. Examples of common carriers are United Air Lines, Burlington Northern Railroad, and United Parcel Service (UPS). The company takes full responsibility for the safe arrival of the goods. Some common carriers, such as the Yellow Freight truck line, haul all kinds of goods. Other common carriers specialize in a single kind of good or a related group of goods such as fresh vegetables, grain, or liquid petroleum products. Some cross state lines; others do not.

A **contract carrier** is a company that rents transportation equipment to other companies for specified lengths of time. It does not offer its services to the general public. Independent truckers and chartered planes are an example of contract carriers. A contract carrier is often responsible for servicing and maintaining the equipment it provides. However, the company that rents equipment is responsible for the goods being transported.

Some contract carriers rent on a short-term, one-time basis. Others work so closely and for so long with a company renting their equipment that they almost become part of that company. Contract carriers are regulated by the federal government less than common carriers.

A **private carrier** is a transportation facility owned and used by a firm to transport its products. Its services are not for hire. A baking company that delivers bread in company trucks is using a private carrier. A mining company that ships ore in its own barges is using a private carrier.

The type of carrier companies use depends on their needs. For example, a large company that frequently transports a lot of freight may prefer to buy and operate its own transportation equipment. A smaller company shipping a special kind of product may regularly rent special transportation equipment from a contract carrier. Still another company may find it most economical to ship its goods via a common carrier.

Many marketers use a combination of transportation methods. They may own and use a small fleet of trucks for local shipments and rent trailer trucks from contract carriers for long hauls. They may also use common carriers to send some shipments by rail and some by air or water.

Freight traffic is measured by the ton-mile. A **ton-mile** is the movement of one ton (2,000 lbs.) of freight for the distance of one mile. (See Figure 27–1.)

Railroad Transportation

The most frequently used freight transportation in the United States is the railroad. Before the spread of highways and the growth of airports, the railroads carried more freight than all other forms of transportation combined. Although the overall percentage has dropped, the railroads still carry more freight longer distances than any other single form of transportation.

Railroads have the advantage of furnishing specialized equipment for various kinds of freight. They can also distribute large quantities long distances for rates that are lower than most other forms of transportation.

Railroads do not, however, have the flexibility of truck transportation. They are confined to railroad lines. Door-to-door service is not part of regular service and costs extra.

Railroad Equipment and Services

Railroads will carry almost any kind of good, in almost any amount, size, and weight. Most types of freight are carried in boxcars. However, more

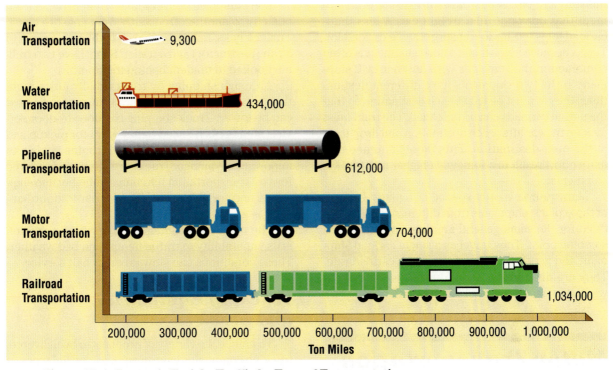

■■■ Figure 27–1 Domestic Freight Traffic by Type of Transportation
Transportation is a critical link in the physical distribution chain. The most frequently used freight transportation is the railroad. What is one reason why railroad transportation is so popular?

specialized cars are being bought by the railroads to meet particular marketers' transportation needs.

Gondolas and hoppers carry gravel, coal, and other kinds of loose material. Covered hopper cars carry grain and malt. Multilevel auto racks carry new cars. Tank cars haul liquids. Refrigerator cars carry perishable foods. Flatcars transport bulk goods that cannot be hurt by bad weather. Two-thirds of domestic coal and 70 percent of grain are transported by rail.

Piggyback and Fishyback

Piggyback or TOFC (trailer on flatcar) service gives freight cars more uses to meet the growing competition from trucks. In the piggyback system, loaded trailer trucks are driven or swung onto railroad flatcars and carried to freight terminals by rail. This gives a shipper the advantages of both rail and truck travel, without the need to unload and reload for each form of transportation.

A citrus grower in Florida might use TOFC (pronounced *tof-see*). When the fruit is ready, it must be shipped north quickly and safely at a cost low enough to make a profit.

The fruit is crated and loaded carefully onto a trailer truck. The truck is driven to the nearest railroad terminal and loaded onto a flatcar. A freight train speeds the flatcar to a northern railroad terminal. There, the trailer truck is taken off the flatcar and driven the final few miles to its destination. Because of TOFC, the shipper (the company sending the goods) receives both the door-to-door advantage of truck transportation and the lower-cost rates of long-distance rail transportation. Moreover, the grower avoids possible damage to the fruit during unloading and reloading.

Fishyback adds water transportation to the piggyback pattern. Trailer trucks are carried piggyback to a port and then loaded onto ships or barges.

Carload and Less-Than-Carload Lots

The two basic classifications in rail freight service are carload lots (CL) and less-than-carload lots (LCL). A *carload lot* is a shipment that completely fills a freight car. A *less-than-carload lot* is a shipment that does not fill a freight car. A less-than-carload lot is harder to transport than a carload lot. This is because a less-than-carload shipment is often combined in the same car with another LCL shipment. If the two shipments have different destinations, the car must be left at each destination so that the partial carloads can be unloaded. The train must pick up the car after each destination and drop it off at the next destination. This inconvenience and extra effort result in a somewhat higher rate for LCL shipments.

Many railroads offer special LCL plans. In most of these plans, shipments from different senders destined for the same general area are combined at a shipping point. They travel as a single carload shipment and get the benefit of the lower carload rate. They are divided into individual shipments again when they reach their rail destination.

Motor Transportation

The railroad's biggest competitor is the truck because of its flexibility. Trucks can go directly from the shipper's door to the customer's. The use of trucks has increased rapidly in recent years, particularly for shorter distance freight shipments. Truck owners are taxed for the use of highways.

■■■ *Motor transportation is one of the most popular means of transporting goods. Why is it considered the most flexible of all goods-transporting modes?*

Long-distance delivery takes trailer trucks from one city to another, frequently from coast to coast. Trailer trucks, regularly seen on highways, consist of a cab (the tractor) and a trailer. Some have two trailers hooked in tandem behind the tractor.

Although shipping by truck usually costs more than shipping by rail, the total transportation cost can be lower. Truck shipping is a door-to-door service, so there is no need to pay extra for pickup and delivery. The flexibility of truck routes is also an important advantage. Trucks are often the preferred form of transportation for compact, high-value shipments and for shipments where door-to-door handling is important.

The main disadvantage of truck transportation is its vunerability to traffic tie-ups and bad weather. These conditions can slow down or halt service.

Trucking Equipment and Services

To handle the variety of products to be delivered, trucking companies have developed special types of equipment. Van trucks carry items such as household furniture, machinery parts, and dry goods. Refrigerator trucks carry such perishables as lettuce, ice cream, and meat. Platform trucks haul products such as bars of steel and bales of cotton. Tank trucks carry fluids, such as oil, milk, and gasoline. Dump trucks transport gravel, sand, and crushed rock. Pole trucks carry goods such as logs, large pipes, and telephone poles. Armored cars, garbage trucks, and cement trucks are other examples of specialized trucking equipment.

Although many shipments fill a truck completely, less-than-truckload (LTL) shipments are the backbone of the trucking business. Trucking companies offer a variety of special route services to meet the needs of LTL shippers, and they give these shippers special rates.

Water Transportation

Ships and barges are among the oldest forms of transportation. They were used on waterways long before railroads and trucks were even dreamed of.

Of course, the ships and barges of today bear little resemblance to their crude ancestors. Some modern vessels have been developed to haul railroad cars and truck trailers. Others have been designed especially for dry cargo such as grain, sugar, and coal. Double-hulled tankers carry liquids such as crude oil. Insulated barges haul goods requiring a constant temperature.

The size of some modern ships, particularly those engaged in foreign trade, is startling. Some oil tankers, for example, are among the largest ships afloat. Their importance has increased because of the vast movement of oil around the world.

Intracoastal and Internal Waterways

In this country, a considerable amount of freight is carried from one place to another on intracoastal and internal waterways. Intracoastal shipping is conducted from one port to another along the coasts or from ports of one coast to ports of another coast. For example, intracoastal shipping is used to move goods from the Atlantic coast, through the Panama Canal, to the Pacific coast. Internal shipping is from one port to the other on waterways such as the Mississippi River and the Great Lakes.

Intracoastal and internal water transportation are most useful to shippers moving large quantities of low-value products such as gravel. Although such transportation is slow and routes are limited, extremely large loads can be carried at low rates.

Overseas Shipping

With the growth of international trade, overseas water transportation is increasing. This shipping is mainly of two types: liner service and tramp service.

Liner service provides freight transportation on regular, scheduled routes. Tramp service is mostly contract business. For example, oil companies use tramp service when they contract with shipping companies to deliver crude oil and gasoline to various destinations not on a regular route and not on a scheduled basis.

The ship route is determined by the type of goods being shipped. Almost all overseas freight is transported by ship and barge.

Pipeline Transportation

Pipelines rank third in volume among freight carriers. Pipelines principally transport oil and gas, but they also transport such goods as wood pulp and finely ground ores. These solids are mixed with liquid called "slurry" and flushed along the pipeline. Pipelines can move these products faster and less expensively than other forms of transportation. Their main disadvantage is that they are limited to carrying only a few types of products.

■ ■ ■ *Pipelines are used to transport products such as oil, gas, and wood pulp. What is one advantage of using pipelines over trucks?*

Most pipelines are owned by the companies using them and are usually considered private carriers. The Alaskan pipeline was financed and built by a group of oil companies working together.

Air Transportation

Airlines are the newest form of freight carrier. They carry the smallest volume of freight, but their share of the transportation business is growing fast. Air shipment is usually the most expensive form of transportation, but it offers a speed unmatched by other forms. Shipments sent by air, therefore, are often light in weight, small in size, high in value, and perishable. Fresh flowers are an example of goods shipped by air.

The advantages of air transportation include speed, frequency of flights, and access to overseas areas that cannot be reached by trains or trucks. The disadvantages include high cost and delay caused by bad weather.

Airlines have increased their appeal to shippers by developing larger aircraft that can carry more freight. They may also reduce the price for air freight shipped at certain times or on certain flights.

Special Services

To transport small shipments and packages, marketers may use a number of special services. United Parcel Service, Federal Express, Emery, and Airborne Express are all private common carriers that specialize in speed and door-to-door delivery. They compete with the U.S. Postal Service, private bus companies, and freight forwarding companies. These companies often combine different types of shipping to transport packages to and from remote destinations. Freight forwarding companies in particular collect small or odd-sized shipments of various businesses and combine them into one truck or railcar load. They then charge LCL rates.

Express Parcel Services

United Parcel Service and Federal Express are among those companies offering express parcel services. A closer look at these two companies will give you a good idea of how express parcel services operate.

United Parcel Service transports small packages weighing no more than 50 pounds and not exceeding 108 inches in length and girth combined. The shipper may send packages C.O.D. (cash on delivery).

United Parcel carries parcels nationwide. Packages are insured for a fee. Deliveries are attempted three times without extra charge. Packages are collected, sorted, and distributed to local and long-distance delivery trucks at modern terminals.

UPS is a giant in the transportation industry. It is the biggest single private shipper on most railroads and also owns a large fleet of airplanes. Basically, however, it is a highway carrier with a fleet of more than 62,000 vehicles. Its drivers call on some 600,000 factories, offices, and stores each day.

Like its competitors, UPS combines shipping methods. A package may be collected by a van driver, transferred to a trailer truck or airplane, and finally delivered by another van driver. Express parcel services control and coordinate the shipping network among the vans, trucks, and airplanes.

Federal Express operates much the same way UPS does. It delivers more than 2.95 million parcels daily, in 400 airplanes and 30,000 vehicles, to 127 countries worldwide. You will read more about Federal Express in the Unit 9 Case Study.

Bus Package Service

Major bus lines, such as Greyhound, provide delivery for small packages. The frequent trips to major cities and the stops at many small towns between cities make the service attractive to marketing businesses. Packages can move hundreds of miles in one day or overnight, at reasonable rates.

U.S. Postal Services

Sometimes the simplest way to ship a small package is through the postal service. Parcel post is the fourth class of mail accepted by the postal service.

Although parcel post is noted for its low cost, it may be slow because of its low priority. (First class letters are sent before parcel post.) For shippers who want quicker service, the postal service offers

You won't see our drivers making deliveries in anything like this. However, you will notice the speed at which our delivery service works.

With 70,000 vehicles on the road and as many as 400 planes overhead servicing over five million customers worldwide daily, it's no wonder every business day we're responsible for doing what no other company can: making more on-time deliveries than anyone in the world.

Which is why, to so many people, our service is already considered up to speed. **We run the tightest ship in the shipping business.**

■ ■ ■   What services do express parcel services such as UPS offer to compete with other types of transportation services?

express mail, air parcel post, and special delivery service—all at higher costs.

Freight Forwarders

Some shippers simplify the transportation of their products by using freight forwarders. **Freight forwarders** are independent companies that collect the small shipments of various businesses, combine them into truckload or carload lots, and ship them by truck or rail. Although they mainly work with railroads and trucking companies, freight forwarders also work with some air and water transportation companies.

Why Storage Is Needed

Businesses try to coordinate product manufacturing and sales through inventory management. Products are stored because they are not needed for

Global
MARKETPLACE

A Better Way to Ship an Elephant

When Ringling Bros. and Barnum & Bailey Combined Shows wants to air-freight an elephant like King Tusk, it gets a *carnet* (no, not a *carrot*). A carnet is a customs document for the duty-free, temporary export of goods for exhibition and professional activities. The Small Business Foundation of America encourages the use of carnets when goods are crossing borders. After all, you do not want to pay for an elephant by the pound.

immediate industrial or consumer use. Firms produce goods to meet current demand. They build inventories of goods and store them for future orders when business expands. The facility that helps businesses manage inventories is the warehouse.

Warehouse Functions

A *warehouse* is a storage and handling facility. It is the heart of the physical distribution system. Nearly every cargo shipment either comes from or goes to a warehouse. Nearly every product marketed travels through or is stored in at least one, and often several, warehouses.

Warehousing serves many purposes. It protects goods, increases their value, helps stabilize prices, and eases financial burdens.

Product Protection

The warehouse protects products against theft and natural risks such as fire, flood, heat, and cold. It also protects against insects and animals. It keeps goods in good condition.

Added Value

Storing goods in warehouses adds time utility to them and thus increases their value. The production of goods and the demand for them are rarely identical.

When the rate of production is higher than the rate of demand—that is, when there are more goods available than there are buyers—the excess goods are stored in warehouses until demand for them arises. At that time, the goods are released from the warehouses to the market.

The condition of some products improves during their stay in the warehouse. This also increases their value. For example, lumber is seasoned in the warehouse; certain meats and cheeses are aged. These products need time to reach their peak condition, and their stay in the warehouse gives them that time.

Stabilized Prices

By keeping excess supply off the market until it is needed, warehouse storage helps to stabilize the selling prices of many products. Without storage, the price of potatoes, for example, would be low during the harvest season when they are plentiful, and high the rest of the year. During the harvest season, low prices would hurt the potato growers, who have put considerable time and money into their crops. During the rest of the year, prices might be so high that many consumers could not afford to buy potatoes. Because potatoes are stored while they are plentiful and are therefore made available throughout the year, extreme price variations are avoided.

Easing Financial Burdens

Products sitting idle in a warehouse represent frozen capital. Marketers cannot turn the frozen capital into cash until these products are sold. Sometimes, however, the marketer may need to borrow money to cover business expenses before the goods are sold. This can be done by obtaining a warehouse receipt.

A *warehouse receipt* is a statement given by the warehouse management indicating the value of the warehoused goods. The marketer can use these warehouse receipts as security to borrow money needed to meet business expenses.

Types of Warehouses

Warehouses are usually found near transportation facilities in manufacturing and marketing centers. There are two basic types of warehouses:

■ ■ ■ *Warehousing serves to protect products, increase their value, help stabilize prices, and ease financial burdens. How does storing add value to the goods?*

public and private. Both public and private warehouses may be bonded—that is, a federal tax must be paid before the product can be removed from the warehouse.

Public Warehouses

An independent business that stores and handles goods for other businesses is a *public warehouse.* The public warehouse owns its building and equipment but does not own the goods it handles. However, it is responsible for protecting these goods. Fees charged by the public warehouse are based on the amount of space the customer uses, the length of time the goods are stored, and the kind of handling or processing required.

The most common type of public warehouse is the general merchandise warehouse. This type of warehouse stores any kind of product that only needs protection from the weather. A public warehouse used for agricultural products that need special care, such as grain and cotton, is called a *special commodity warehouse.* Perishables that need constant cold temperature to keep them from spoiling, such as peaches and melons, are stored in cold storage warehouses.

Special commodity warehouses are often located near inexpensive railroad or water transportation. Cold storage warehouses are located where there is quick access by rail or truck to retailers.

Private Warehouses

Most warehouses are privately owned by manufacturers, wholesalers, or retailers. A *private warehouse* is a storage and handling facility owned by the company that uses it. There are many types of private warehouses. Each company designs its warehouses to suit its own products.

Companies that own their own warehouses try to locate them close to where the goods will be needed. As goods come off the production line at the factory, they are shipped to regional warehouses owned by the company. When the company receives orders for these goods, the factory notifies a regional warehouse to ship the product to the customer. Thus goods do not pile up at the factory.

Wholesalers and retailers also locate their warehouses close to where the goods will be needed for the same reasons. In the food industry, for example, a wholesaler may locate a private warehouse near the supermarkets it serves.

■■■ *The J. C. Penney Distribution Center orders efficiently from many suppliers and fulfills the needs of individual J. C. Penney stores in the region. How does a distribution center differ from a typical warehouse?*

Private warehouses sometimes function as distribution centers. A **distribution center** is the link between the supplier and the customer. It is the place where products are received, stored, processed, and shipped. The goal is to move and assemble products, not to store them.

The distribution center receives customer orders. Order-filling departments check orders for accuracy and make sure the inventory is in the warehouse. They then prepare the invoice and arrange for the ordered items to be withdrawn from storage and transported to the customers. Customers receive bills from the center and respond by sending payments there. Distribution center operations can increase the efficiency of physical distribution systems and benefit both the marketer and the customer. Recently, in some industries, the *retail support center* has taken the place of the distribution center and the warehouse. The retail support center provides an immediate source of supply, expediting the flow of goods through computerized ordering.

Bonded Warehouses

A warehouse used to store products requiring a federal tax is a *bonded warehouse.* Sometimes the federal tax agents place their own seal on the warehouse or sections of the warehouse containing bonded products. A *bonded product* is any domestic or imported product that cannot be removed from a warehouse and sold until taxes are paid. Bonded warehouses are either public or private.

The advantage of using a bonded warehouse is that the required federal tax is not paid until the goods are removed from storage. Thus, money is not tied up while the products are in storage.

Inside the Warehouse

Inside a warehouse products are neatly stored and easy to find because of a planned arrangement of items or containers. One objective is to move products in and out of the warehouse as quickly as possible.

How efficiently the warehouse does its job helps to determine the cost of distributing a product. A good warehouse system can mean lower costs and better service to customers. A poor warehouse system can hurt the sales of a good product.

Warehouse efficiency has been greatly improved by new materials-handling methods. **Materials handling** is the process of assembling, packing, weighing, and moving products from a producer to a warehouse, from a warehouse to a carrier, or from one carrier to another. A rule of thumb for moving consumer goods is that if an item is picked up and put down more than three times, money is lost.

At one time, warehouses were primarily storage centers. Today, goods are stored for as short a period of time as possible. The modern concept of warehousing emphasizes order fulfillment as exemplified by the retail support center. Storage means inventory dollars sitting idle; order fulfillment means inventory dollars making money. (See Figure 27–2.)

Receiving

The first job at the warehouse is to see that shipments are received safely and intact. Shipments are safely unloaded and carefully inspected to ensure that they are in the condition claimed by the shipper. Any discrepancies or damage discovered at the warehouse are noted and reported to the shipper.

Unloading in a modern warehouse may involve automatic conveyor belts or carts that travel to preset destinations. Or it may involve pallets that travel along the floor with a friction-free cushion of air between the pallets and the floor. Other tools operated by unloaders and movers include the driverless forklift truck and the driverless tractor. These tools and systems are designed to make the unloading job efficient.

The shipment received by the warehouse may be containerized. **Containerization** is using specially built shipping containers in transporting goods. The shipper loads the containers at the warehouse. Their contents are not unloaded until the containers reach their destination.

These containers are large and can hold much more than a normal shipping crate. They protect the shipment and enable it to be moved easily from one type of carrier to another. They also eliminate the separate loading and unloading of numerous shipping crates each time the shipment is transferred to a new carrier. Containerization thus reduces transportation time and expense as well as damage and theft.

Shipments also may be *unitized*. This means that as many packages as possible are combined into one load, preferably on a pallet. Steel bands hold the packages together. Shrink wrapping can accomplish the same thing for certain items.

Storing

Once goods are accepted by the warehouse, they are placed in a storage location. The location must be accessible for inspection.

One advanced type of storage equipment for small items is a bank of shelves that swing like pages in a book. These shelves require less space than ordinary shelving while remaining accessible. Warehouse storage equipment also includes bins used for small items, island stacks used for larger products, and overhead racks used for hanging products in spaces that would otherwise be unusable.

Retailers store goods at their own sites, too. Although marketers do not consider these warehouses, they do consider the costs and benefits of keeping quantities of goods in stock. Sales shelf space is the most expensive and most convenient place to store goods. Storeroom space costs less, and goods can be readily moved to the sales floor.

Some bulk items, such as lumber, steel, or automobiles, can be stored and sold from inexpensive outdoor locations. Some products are stored in unusual and inexpensive warehouses. For example, gases, farm goods, or oil may be stored in tanks, caves, or underground vaults.

Processing

The amount of processing a shipment receives in a warehouse depends on the number of services available and the shipper's needs. Many marketers find the warehouse a convenient and inexpensive place for some processing. Shipments may be split up and stored by units. Units may be price-marked and repackaged. An assessment of various products may be put together for an outgoing shipment. Transportation may be arranged and paperwork is handled.

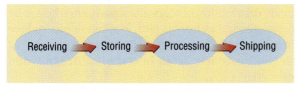

■■■ **Figure 27–2 The Role of Warehouses**
The job of the warehouse includes receiving, storing, processing, and shipping. Why is the objective of warehouses to move products in and out of the warehouse as quickly as possible?

Principles into Practice

Perform: Just in Time for Pets

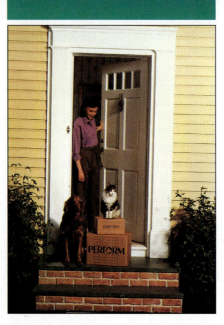

Princess the cat is well fed with fresh cat food. Thanks to Perform's just-in-time marketing system, there is no need for Princess's owners to keep a large supply of cat food on hand. Under a just-in-time marketing system, a firm can buy in small quantities just in time for production. The firm can then produce goods just in time for sale. Perform's just-in-time system allows the firm to deliver fresh food to Princess's home within 3 to 5 days after an order is placed. Or an Automatic Replenishment Program sends a new supply of food every 28 days without word from the cat's owners.

Perform is a division of Nutripet, Inc., Carnation Company and a new entry into the domestic pet food market. After a careful product development research program, the division now sells both canned and dry food for kittens, nursing cats, full-grown cats, dogs, and puppies.

Perform's Just-in-Time Automatic Replenishment Program advertises that it's like getting the newspaper delivered at home, only better. The system provides regular, systematic delivery of pet food. Perform is able to distribute its product efficiently through the use of computerization.

Perform uses a new state-of-the-art distribution center to ship pet food quickly and cost effectively. This results in better service and may mean lower shipping and handling costs for the customer. The Dallas, Texas distribution center is centrally located in the United States. Delivery firms such as UPS or Federal Express pick up orders of Perform from the distribution center and deliver them to the customers' residences or businesses without delay.

Perform's distribution system seems to work. The convenience of receiving fresh, nutritious food for their cats without a trip to the store or veterinarian motivates new customers to sign up for Perform each weekday.

1. Describe the type of distribution system needed to make Perform successful.
2. What types of distribution would *not* be appropriate for Perform? Explain your answer.
3. What is one advantage the distribution center provides?

Warehouses near garment manufacturing centers, for example, bring in shipments from various manufacturers and sort them according to the orders placed by stores. The garments are then put on hangers. Fabric and price tags are attached. Each store's shipment, still on hangers, is loaded onto a truck for express delivery.

In-Transit Storage

In-transit storage is the process of storing manufacturers' goods in storage facilities provided by the railroad between their plants and the consumer until orders are received. Railroads have made distribution centers attractive to marketers by promoting an in-transit rate. Marketers can reduce inventories through in-transit storage and shipping to the customer from in-transit storage when needed.

To make use of in-transit storage, shippers forward carload lots directly to a centralized storage facility from their manufacturing plants. Goods are then stored until orders are received from customer outlets.

■■■   *Storage is provided in a variety of forms. Grain is stored in silos until needed to grind into livestock feed. Where else are goods stored?*

In some cases the goods may be repackaged or even assembled. A carload of mixed goods then can be sent to the final destination. The manufacturer thus provides maximum flexibility and still pays only the standard transcontinental through rate, plus a charge for in-transit storage.

Shipping

The final job of the warehouse is to move shipments out of storage safely and start them on their way to their next destination. The orders to ship goods may come from the owner of the goods. They may also be part of a routine order fulfillment service provided by the warehouse. Public warehouses usually ship in response to direct orders from the merchandise owners. Marketers must decide on the most efficient way to ship goods to their final destination.

To move goods in and out of the warehouse quickly, marketers must view the whole physical distribution process. By coordinating their decisions regarding how goods are received, stored, processed, and shipped, marketers can achieve an effective distribution system that helps fulfill the marketing concept.

CHAPTER NOTE

1. General Electric Company 1993 Annual Report.

The Mayhaw Tree, Inc.: Home of that Wild and Wonderful Jelly!

When four mothers find themselves together at a party, what do you suppose they talk about—their families? their community? Well, when four mothers met a while back in the small town of Colquitt, Georgia (population 2,000), their conversation turned to ways to improve the local economy.

Colquitt is the county seat for Miller County, a rather depressed area in southwest Georgia that the sunbelt boom seemed to have forgotten. Except for the peanut plant, the ladies' underwear factory, and the meat processor (none of which employs more than 50 people), the town depends on local farming for its income. The four mothers, Joy Jinks, Dot Wainwright, Pat Bush, and Betty Jo Toole, wanted to provide more job opportunities in Colquitt by opening a business. They came up with ideas such as making cushions stuffed with pine needles and sewing draperies for mobile homes. And then came another idea: mayhaw jelly.

For years, people in Miller county had been making delicious mayhaw jelly from their own treasured recipes. Few people besides these Georgia residents and their relatives had tasted the coral-colored delicacy because the mayhaw grows wild and the harvest depends on the weather. A member of the rose family, like apples and pears, the mayhaw is bright red in color, small like a cranberry, and tart when eaten raw. It tastes best cooked with sugar and turned into jelly or syrup, or used as an ingredient for other sauces. The women began to think about a business that they could develop using these unique berries.

They found a vacant home for storage. They put ads in the paper offering five dollars a gallon for the berries which grew on just about everyone's land. They paid for the berries with two dollar bills obtained from the local bank, enabling everyone in town to know how the mayhaw harvest contributes to the local economy. When people received a two dollar bill, they identified it with the mayhaw tree business.

The women bought jars and shipping labels. They then rented the delicatessen in the local IGA grocery store to produce their jelly.

While all of the women also held outside jobs—a secretary, a bookkeeper, a representative for a nonprofit organization, and a social worker—none had experience running a business. They worked closely together sharing ideas. All four women did everything from boiling berries, creating the product, setting up sales booths at county fairs, and selling the jelly.

The Mayhaw Tree, Inc., began to grow. The women found their own location for producing the jelly, purchased a pressure cooker, and hired an experienced cook. They also sought out free marketing advice from Georgia Tech University and assistance in product development from the University of Georgia's extension service. They added other products, such as mayhaw syrup, cucumber jelly, Vidalia onion jelly, mustard, salad dressing, and meat marinades. Wearing green and white outfits, the company colors, they marketed their products at local fairs and city gift shows.

The company instigated a Mayhaw Festival, which is now an annual event the second Saturday in May. Some 10,000 visitors crowd the streets during the festival.

The Mayhaw Tree, Inc., is meeting its goals. The business has eight full-time and eight part-time employees. It ships retail mail orders to customers in all 50 states and sells wholesale in 42 states. In fact, the wholesale business is larger than the retail business. Today a wholesale representative markets Mayhaw Tree products to delicatessens and specialty-food stores. You just can't tell what may happen when four mothers talk about the local economy![1, 2, 3, 4]

1. Why did the originators decide on mayhaw jelly as a business?

2. Cite an example of another local business that could be built on a unique product.

3. Discuss three or four ways the company places its product conveniently for its various customers.

4. Since mayhaw jelly is so good to eat, why do you think the company added other products to its line? Do you think it would be a good idea to add more food products? non-food items? What would you suggest?

5. What goals would you suggest now for The Mayhaw Tree, Inc.?

CASE NOTES

1. Susan Ramey Wright, "They Make the Best Jelly in the World," *Progressive Farmer*, February 1988. p. 93.

2. Henry Leifermann, "Squeezing Profits Out of Berries," *New Choices*, December 1988, pp. 32-38.

3. Liza Nelson, "Colquitt, Ga.," *Living Arts*, New York Times, 18 May 1989.

4. Local press clippings provided by Joy Jinks, company publications and a letter from Joy Jinks, President, to Dr. Mason, 27 June 1989.

UNIT 8

Promotion

Chapters ▼

Chapter 28

Promotion at Work

Terms to Know

sponsor

advertising media

sales promotion

visual merchandising

public relations

publicity

personal selling

promotional goals

push strategy

pull strategy

promotional mix

Chapter Objectives

After studying this chapter, you will be able to:

- describe the many forms of promotion;
- define the promotional elements;
- tell the importance of developing promotional goals;
- explain the promotional mix;
- describe and analyze promotional activities and a promotional campaign; and
- suggest plans for promotional activities to satisfy different business situations.

Case Study

Mark Twain Promotes Advertising

Mark Twain was once the editor of a small-town newspaper. He received a letter from an old subscriber who had found a spider in his paper. The subscriber wanted to know whether the spider was a sign of good or bad luck.

Mark Twain replied, "Dear Old Subscriber: Finding a spider in your paper was neither good luck nor bad luck for you. The spider was merely looking over our paper to see which merchant is not advertising. He then can go to that store, spin his web across the door, and lead a life of undisturbed peace ever afterward."[1]

Mark Twain was right about the need for businesses to advertise. Advertising is a form of promotion. In our highly competitive business environment, every business must keep prospective customers continually aware of its goods or services.

Promotion Takes Many Forms

As you know from Chapter 1, promotion includes all the activities designed to bring a company's products to the favorable attention of customers. Promotion takes many forms. People may buy a new product because they have seen it in newspaper or television advertisements. Or they may have been given a free sample. They may have been attracted by a colorful travel exhibit in a hotel, a demonstration in a department store, an advertisement on a bus, or a radio commercial delivered by a well-known personality. Here are some other promotional activities:

- The local shopping center sponsors a weekend antique auto show.
- *Forbes* business magazine flies its customers' advertising directors from Los Angeles to New York via private jet for a dinner cruise and tour of the famous Forbes art collection.
- A real estate agent serves a buffet for other agents at an open house in a home recently put up for sale.
- A local video rental store sends out a card offering a free video rental when customers rent one video.
- A manufacturer provides free samples and a cosmetic case when customers buy a favorite fragrance.

- PepsiCo, Inc., holds a meeting for its bottlers to introduce new products and ends it with a gigantic display of fireworks over San Francisco Bay.
- A sales agency offers customers a TV if they attend a film on buying a vacation condominium.

Marketers are always developing new promotional activities to bring their goods or services to the attention of the public. The alert marketer knows how to make use of the various elements of promotion.

Promotional Elements Defined

The elements of promotion are advertising, sales promotion, public relations, and personal selling. Each plays an important role in marketing.

As you know from Chapter 4, advertising is a sales message paid for by a sponsor that appears in media (carriers) such as television and newspapers. It promotes the company's goods, services, or image and is directed toward a mass audience.

The company that pays for the advertising is the **sponsor**. For example, a television commercial advertising the Blazer automobile is sponsored—paid for—by Chevrolet. The nonpersonal approach of advertising distinguishes it from personal selling.

Advertising media are the channels of communication advertisers use (and pay for) to send their messages to potential customers. Advertising media include radio, television, newspapers, magazines, direct mail, billboards, and other outdoor advertising such as car cards on buses and trains.

Sales promotion is any sales activity that supplements or coordinates advertising and personal selling. Sales promotion includes free samples, coupons, contests, visual merchandising, and other special incentives intended to stimulate sales. **Visual merchandising** is the display of a product at a place of business or near the point of purchase. Visual merchandising includes attractive window and interior displays and eye-catching signs.

Public relations is the total process of building goodwill toward a business organization. It is intended to influence various groups including customers and others. For example, employees, stockholders, suppliers, and the general public are often the target of a firm's public relations efforts. **Publicity** is the unpaid promotion for a company or its products. It is similar to advertising, but the fact that publicity is not paid for and therefore cannot be controlled by a sponsor distinguishes it from advertising. Publicity is often the outcome of public relations activities and of certain sales promotion efforts, such as the introduction of a new product.

Personal selling is the direct effort made by a salesperson to convince a customer to make a purchase. Figure 28–1 shows the elements of promotion.

Promotion Begins with Goals

Promotional efforts for large companies can mean spending millions of dollars. Even smaller organizations devote substantial amounts of money from their total budgets for promotion. Therefore, sponsors want to be certain they are spending wisely. To do this they first develop promotional goals. **Promotional goals** state what the company wants to achieve through a particular promotion.

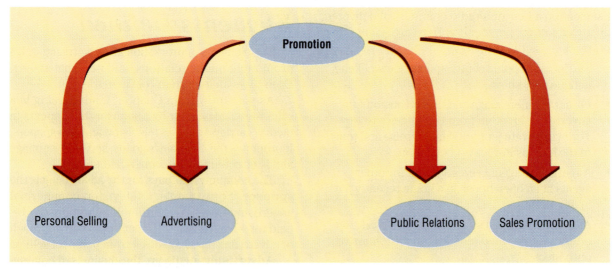

■■■ *Figure 28–1 The Elements of Promotion*
The four elements of promotion include advertising, sales promotion, public relations, and personal selling. How does advertising differ from public relations?

They are based on the organization's main goals and its marketing goals.

For example, suppose an organization's goal is to increase profit by 5 percent for the year. The marketing goal would support this organizational goal and include an increase in sales. To accomplish these goals, the promotional goal might call for an increase in customer contacts through personal selling and an increase in customer awareness of the product through advertising and sales promotion.

Promotional Strategies

Promotional strategies are long-range plans needed to reach promotional goals. The two main approaches are the push strategy and the pull strategy. At times, these strategies are combined. (See Figure 28–2.)

Push Strategy

When a manufacturer aims promotional efforts directly at wholesalers and retailers in order to encourage them to carry a certain product, this effort is known as **push strategy**. The goal is to push the product through the distribution channel toward the consumer.

Often, manufacturers of consumer goods use a push strategy. Their sales staffs call on wholesalers and retailers to introduce new products and offer store banners, displays, coupons, and other sales promotions for a certain product. These manufacturers may also advertise the product in trade publications read by wholesalers and retailers.

Pull Strategy

Using a **pull strategy**, a manufacturer promotes directly to consumers to encourage them to ask retailers and wholesalers to carry the product. Retailers, in turn, ask their wholesalers, who contact the manufacturer.

To implement a pull strategy, the manufacturer may rely heavily on advertising to generate requests. For example, a manufacturer of fine polish for antique furniture may place ads in *Antiques* and other magazines read by antique collectors in the hope that they will ask hardware stores for the polish.

Some marketers combine both push and pull strategies to obtain wide recognition of their products and many outlets for them. For example, a new cereal may be heavily promoted to wholesalers and

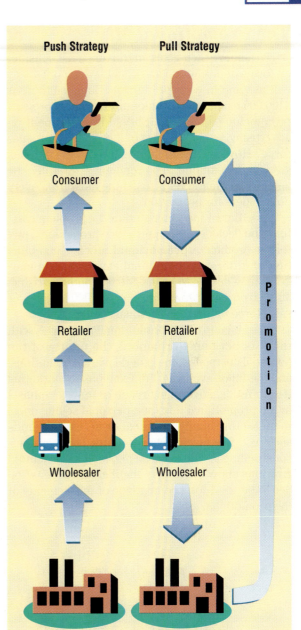

■■■ *Figure 28–2 Promotional Strategies*
A push strategy aims promotional efforts directly at wholesalers and retailers. A pull strategy aims promotional efforts at consumers. When would a marketer use push and pull strategies together?

retailers with store signs and coupons, and also promoted to consumers. Mueslix cereal was introduced with signs and coupons, as well as TV ads and a contest with trips to Europe as the largest of many prizes.

The Promotional Mix

To achieve their goals, marketers must consider all forms of promotion and decide which ones they will use and in what proportion. Suppose there is $100,000 to spend on promoting an existing product or launching a new one. Should it all be spent on advertising, or should most of it be spent for a sales force? How much should be invested in contests, give-aways, exhibits, and premiums? Naturally, the aim of every marketer is to get the most from every dollar spent for promotion.

An efficient marketer studies the problem carefully and decides on an appropriate promotional mix for the product. A **promotional mix** is a combination of different promotional elements. The marketer may decide to spend $40,000 on advertising, $22,000 on sales promotion, and $38,000 for a larger sales force to increase personal selling.

The makeup of the promotional mix varies with the product being promoted, the nature of the potential customers, the general market conditions, and the funds available. For example, in marketing frozen foods, advertising receives more emphasis in the promotional mix than personal selling does. In marketing highly technical or industrial goods such as office machines or forklifts, however, personal selling is vital because personal sales demonstrations show customers the machines' benefits. See Table 28–1 for a comparison of the elements of the promotional mix.

Coca-Cola Classic— One Summer's Promotion

To develop a better understanding of the elements that go into a promotional mix, let's follow one of the most successful products in history—Coca-Cola classic—through a summer promotion campaign. It was the second summer for Coca-Cola classic to be named by the company as the "Official Soft Drink of Summer."

At that time more than 5 million servings of the soft drink were consumed throughout the world every day. In addition, Coca-Cola classic was the only major sugar soft drink to increase its growth in food stores by more than 7 percent each year for the last three years. In fact, Coca-Cola classic led the soft drink industry in sales with a 20.1 percent market share. (Twenty percent of all cola consumers chose Coca-Cola classic.)

Additional marketing research showed that Coca-Cola classic was even more popular among teenagers, with a 25.6 percent market share. At soda fountains its market share was still larger—at 30.9 percent it was almost twice as much as its nearest competitor.

The company's main promotional goal for the summer campaign was to help Coca-Cola classic

Element	Audience	Cost	Advantages	Disadvantages
Advertising	Mass	Inexpensive per contract	Sponsor controls message; reaches many people	Hard to measure results; may not close sales
Sales Promotion	Mass or individual	Can be expensive	Gains attention immediately; easy to measure	Easy for others to copy
Publicity	Mass	Inexpensive	People tend to believe; can create a positive message	Business cannot control what is said
Personal Selling	Individual	Expensive per contract	Permits flexible message and immediate response; can measure effectiveness	Most expensive; relies mainly on salesperson

Source: Adapted from Louis E. Boone and David L. Kurtz, *Contemporary Marketing*, 7 ed., 1992, p. 534.

■■■ *Table 28–1 Comparing the Elements of the Promotional Mix*
The promotional mix is made up of a combination of promotional elements. What factors determine the type of promotional mix that is used?

extend its lead even further in the market. The product's promotional mix was established to take advantage of its number-one position and high sales volume. The company decided that the promotional mix would emphasize two main categories: national advertising and sales promotion.

National Advertising

The McCann-Erickson advertising agency of New York developed the national advertising that promoted Coca-Cola classic as the "Official Soft Drink of Summer." Here are some of the 30-second TV commercials produced.

- *Sunrise/Sunset.* This ad shows views of beach scenes and other reminders of summer. The ad tells consumers that "wherever you go and whatever you do, Coca-Cola classic is there."

- *Jam Session.* This ad is geared to all audiences. The scene is a local Latin jazz club with Tito Puente at the drums. He invites Bill Cosby to join the band, which he does to a spirited Latin rhythm. A Coca-Cola classic is not far away. Tito Puente had appeared on "The Cosby Show" in an earlier season, and the commercial brings them together again.

- *Mask.* Aimed particularly at preteens, this commercial shows three young boys watching a TV monster movie while a mysterious being actually nears their room. The boys cry out when they see the real-life creature. They give it a bottle of Coca-Cola classic as a goodwill gesture.

- *Classic Favorite.* Geared to teens and young adults, this ad shows a young woman beating the heat by bringing Coca-Cola classic to her friends. The background music is a new version of the "Can't Beat the Feeling" Coca-Cola theme song.

- *Porch.* This ad is aimed particularly at parents. It shows a young runaway, hiding under his own porch. He has a change of heart when finding a bottle of Coca-Cola classic that his parents "accidentally" left on the steps.

Sales Promotion

The company developed three national consumer sales promotions to encourage the consumers to buy Coca-Cola products. Coca-Cola classic is featured prominently in each of the promotions.

These sales promotions focused on baseball, movies, and summer beaches.

Baseball

The first promotion was linked to baseball. In March, The Coca-Cola Company announced an agreement that made its products "the official soft drinks of major league baseball." The promotion, announced in May, was a rub-off card game called "Double Play." It featured a grand prize of $1 million and five first prizes of new Chevrolet cars. There were 20 second prizes of $2,000 each. Additional prizes included Official Soft Drink of Summer jackets, T-shirts, and Domino's pizzas. Other Double Play prizes included travel certificates, $100 dollars in cash, pins, posters, and 12-pack cans of Coca-Cola.

Double Play game cards came with the purchase of specially marked cans of Coca-Cola products. Every one of the some 58 million cards contained six rub-off spots, including two that matched. Consumers won by rubbing off only two spots and seeing if they matched. The odds of winning prizes were listed; for example, 1 in 2 for a poster; 1 in 18 for a pizza; and 1 in 577 for a T-shirt.

Special Promotions

Along with Double Play, other promotions were targeted to African-American and Hispanic consumers. The "Jamming at the Apollo" sweepstakes featured 25 weekend trips for two to the Apollo Theater in New York. The sweepstakes "Cinco de Mayo" and "16 de septiembre," both associated with Mexican holidays, offered five trips to U.S. cities and new automobiles as prizes.

Movies

In June, to celebrate the opening of the film *Ghostbusters II*, starring Bill Murray and Dan Aykroyd, The Coca-Cola Company offered a chance to become an honorary Ghostbuster. Contestants could win an authentic ECTO 1A, the 1958 Cadillac hearse used by the ghost busters. Other prizes included *Ghostbusters II* T-shirts and videotapes of the original *Ghostbusters* film. Print ads and cable TV commercials carried much of the advertising for the promotion, which lasted into the next year.

Here are some local businesses that participated in the "Back in Business and Looking for You" *Ghostbusters II* and Coca-Cola classic promotion.

Principles into Practice

Kathleen Demitros: Marketing V. P. for Harley-Davidson

Kathleen Lawler Demitros is the marketing vice president for Harley-Davidson, the world's leading manufacturer of heavy-duty motorcycles. Demitros is no stranger to the world of motorcycles. She is a motorcycle owner whose acquaintance with Harley-Davidson stems from her childhood when her father, a Milwaukee advertising executive, handled the account.

Demitros gained experience elsewhere before joining Harley. Upon graduating from college, she went to work for a Tampa, Florida, advertising agency. She then returned to Milwaukee to work in the advertising department of Harley-Davidson. From there she went on to public relations and marketing. Promoted to director of marketing at a time when the company faced increasing competition from Honda, Yamaha, and Suzuki, she turned to brightening the company's image.

At the time, the image of a typical Harley rider was of a person in a black leather jacket, as seen in such films as *Easy Rider* starring Peter Fonda and Dennis Hopper. Harley-Davidson decided to turn to young professionals, a target market segment with needs for recreation and money to spend. Responding to the needs of these customers who wanted a daring image and comfort, Harley-Davidson engineered a more reliable and smoother operating vehicle with a variety of options.

The marketing department encouraged dealers to brighten up their showrooms. Demitros sought to maintain buyer interest in organizing Harley Owner Groups, known as HOG groups, to meet for local rides, charity benefits, and rallies. Later, Demitros was sent to Great Britain to help build the market share there for Harley-Davidson. The result of these promotion activities, along with an expanding export market in the 1990s, is a near 60 percent share of the heavy motorcycle market for Harley-Davidson. [2, 3, 4, 5]

How does Kathleen Demitros' creation of the Harley Owner's Group focus on the needs of the new target market and serve as a form of promotion?

- *Local bottlers.* Coca-Cola bottlers offered consumers chances to win theme-related T-shirts, videotapes, jackets, caps, theater tickets for the film, and soft drink discounts.

- *Local retailers.* Many local retailers featured coloring contests for children that were sponsored by Coca-Cola. Prizes were *Ghostbuster II* movie tickets.

- *Hardee's.* This official *Ghostbusters II* headquarters offered movie posters, a 32-ounce *Ghostbusters* soft drink cup, and a series of four "Ghostblasters" sound devices to ward off unwanted ghosts. Many of the Hardee's restaurants also featured *Ghostbusters* theme food along with Cola-Cola classic.

- *Circle K.* These convenience stores lowered their prices for some of their Coca-Cola fountain drinks.

- *AMC Theaters.* Many local American Multi-Cinema (AMC) theaters sold Coca-Cola soft drinks in glow-in-the-dark plastic cups. This promotion crossed the border into Canada where viewers of the Much Music television network had chances to win a trip to the June premiere of the film in Los Angeles. Viewers in many Canadian cities were awarded tickets to local showings of *Ghostbusters II*, and Circle K stores offered a rub-off card game with prizes.

Beaches

Movie theaters, TV, and radio promoted Coca-Cola's beach theme. One of the largest multimedia promotions to date resulted from a marketing partnership between The Coca-Cola Company and the Fox Broadcasting Company. It included the Cineplex Odeon theaters and the Westwood One radio networks.

The highlight of this promotion was the Coca-Cola classic "Isle of Dreams Treasure Hunt." Winners of a 7-day "Fun Ship" Carnival Caribbean cruise would take home the grand prize of $1 million. Television, radio, and print ads in *TV Guide* and *Star* magazines, tens of thousands of displays in retail food stores, sign-up programs in movie theaters, and a radio promotion offered the opportunity to win the grand prize as well as other prizes.

In August, a 45-second trailer announcement of the "Isle of Dreams" promotion appeared in 1,200 Cineplex Odeon theaters. Movie fans throughout the United States could register in theater lobbies to win the Carnival cruise.

Labor Day weekend listeners of one of Westwood One's 200 radio stations heard a radio concert featuring the Moody Blues, Huey Lewis and the News, R.E.M., Pat Benatar, and others. During the program these listeners had a final chance to win the Caribbean cruise. By the end of September, 500 cruise winners were found for the cruise scheduled in November. The last day of the cruise, they landed at the "Isle of Dreams" and hunted for Coca-Cola bottle caps. All bottle caps earned a prize; one bottle cap earned a prize of $1 million.

What Happened Next?

At the conclusion of the promotion, The Coca-Cola Company evaluated its effectiveness in terms of its goals and the goals of the company. Did these promotional programs meet the promotional goals of pushing Coca-Cola classic still further ahead of its competition and maintaining sales momentum? Did the promotional mix and these activities meet company goals for the other Coca-Cola products? These questions and others are the ones that the

people in promotion face as they evaluate each promotional effort. According to one executive, the summer promotion was quite successful for The Coca-Cola Company. It increased the sales of Coca-Cola for bottlers throughout the country and conveyed a good feeling about the product. An unexpected outcome of the promotion was that the winner chose to use the money to continue her efforts in helping the children of her community.[6,7]

Promotion— a Broad Field

This brief account of Coca-Cola classic, "The Official Soft Drink of Summer," illustrates how broad the term *promotion* is and how the elements of promotion may be mixed. Exciting stories could also be told about the launching of other products— from breakfast cereals to motion pictures.

The promotional mix always varies with the product and the market. The owner of a roadside fruit stand has one promotional mix—modest though it may be—which is as unique as, but far different from, the right promotional mix of a large airline.

The mix is rarely the same for any two businesses or for different time periods in the same business. Creating a promotional mix is important not only to the successful launching of a new product but also to extending the life of established products.

CHAPTER NOTES

1. Ralph L. Woods, ed., *The Modern Handbook of Humor* (New York: McGraw-Hill, 1967), p. 62.
2. Robert L. Rose, "Vrooming Back," *The Wall Street Journal*, 31 August 1990, pp. 1, A6.
3. John Holusha, "How Harley Outfoxed Japan with Exports," *The New York Times*, 12 August 1990, p. F5.
4. Kate Fitzgerald, "Kathleen Demitros," *Advertising Age*, 8 January 1990, p. 8.
5. Conversations with Harley-Davidson, August 1990 and December 1992.
6. The Coca-Cola Company, press releases from December 1988 through July 1989, and 23 August 1990.
7. The Coca-Cola Company 1988 Annual Report.

Chapter Summary

- The elements of promotion are advertising, sales promotion (including visual merchandising), public relations, and personal selling.

- Promotional activities stem from the goals of promotion which are based on the organization's marketing goals and the company's overall goals.

- To reach its promotional goals, a company develops its promotional strategies. Push strategy is promoting the product to wholesalers and retailers to push it through the channel of distribution. Pull strategy is promoting the product directly to ultimate consumers causing them to ask intermediaries for it, thus pulling it through the channel.

- To reach their goals for each product, marketers develop a promotional mix: the combination of advertising, sales promotion, public relations, and personal selling.

- As one example of promotion at work, The Coca-Cola Company developed a combination of national advertising and sales promotion with the promotional goal of increasing the sales of Coca-Cola classic as well as the company's other products. The national summer advertising consisted of a series of commercials. The sales promotion effort consisted of three contests based on America's favorite summer activities.

- After a promotion is completed, it must be evaluated by the company to determine how well the goals were met. While most promotion is not as gigantic as that conducted by The Coca-Cola Company, every organization creates its own promotional program in order to launch new products and maintain the sales of established ones.

Building Your Marketing Vocabulary

Explain the difference between the following sets of terms.

sponsor—advertising media

sales promotion—publicity—visual merchandising

public relations—personal selling

push strategy—pull strategy

promotional goals—promotional mix

Questions for Review

1. Name four major elements in a promotional mix.
2. How does advertising differ from publicity?
3. Give an example of sales promotion.
4. What are promotional goals based on?
5. What are promotional strategies?
6. What is a promotional mix? Why is it important?
7. What was the promotional goal of The Coca-Cola Company for the summer?
8. Describe Coca-Cola's national advertising campaign with McCann-Erickson.
9. Around what three summer activities were the promotions built, and why did the company choose these activities?
10. Describe Coca-Cola's three sales promotion programs.

Critical Thinking

1. Why does a business use a promotional mix rather than rely on one form of promotion?
2. Would the owner of a card and gift shop use the same promotional mix as the manager of the music store across the street? Explain your answer using examples of promotional activities.
3. Explain how the promotional mix used to market chewing gum would differ from the promotional mix used to market a personal computer.
4. Describe a promotional event you would develop to promote a new line of swimwear.
5. As a marketer of silverware, how might you implement a pull strategy?

Discussion Questions

1. Discuss a promotional activity being conducted in your school or community right now.

2. What is the theme of Coca-Cola classic's current promotion? Suggest a different theme that could be used, and offer two new promotional activities.

3. You have a small business marketing T-shirts on which you imprint letters and designs. Explain the promotional mix you would use to market your product.

4. Discuss examples of sales promotions you have observed used in the marketplace.

5. Discuss why marketers must be careful about the type of publicity they seek. Give examples of how publicity may backfire.

Marketing Project

Identifying Promotional Activities

Project Goal: Given a new product, identify the activities that a marketer uses to promote it.

Directions: Choose a new product sold in your community. Visit a particular business that sells this product and note the advertising and display materials used to promote it. Also, read newspapers and billboards, watch TV, and listen to the radio to determine the promotional techniques used by the manufacturer.

On a form like the one below, list the name of the product you have chosen. Then describe the techniques used to promote it.

Product	Promotional Activities
Example: Crystal Pepsi	TV spots; Magazine ads

Applied Academics

Language Arts

1. Develop a sales promotion for your school store or a business in your community. For example, you may choose to design a coupon, develop a contest, or create a type of visual merchandising. Describe the promotional goals you plan to achieve through your sales promotion.

Math

2. Suppose a business has $150,000 to spend on promoting a new product. The business decides to spend 40 percent on advertising, 25 percent on sales promotion, and 35 percent on personal selling. How much money will it spend on each type of promotion?

Science

3. In order to develop a newspaper ad, you should understand how the printing process works. Research the technology used in printing advertisements. Write a 250-word paper on your findings.

Marketing and Multiculturalism

To promote sales in the African-American community, McDonald's engages in "community marketing." According to Sylvia Dabney, director of ethnic marketing, the company's goal is "to put something back into the communities where we do business." McDonald's offers scholarships to African-American students in underprivileged areas. Another program, Black History Makers of the Future, honors 30 African-American children by including them in national television ads.

1. Why do successful companies such as McDonald's engage in promotional activities?

2. What is the company's goal in offering scholarships and featuring African-American children in these commercials?

3. How did McDonald's tie sales promotion and advertising in this example?

4. How are McDonald's efforts an example of public relations?

Chapter 29

The World of Advertising

Terms to Know

product advertising	cooperative advertising
institutional advertising	industrial advertiser
national advertiser	advertising agency
retail advertiser	commission

Chapter Objectives

After studying this chapter, you will be able to:

- identify types of advertising with which consumers come in contact frequently;
- cite three types of advertisers;
- explain how a company's advertising department functions;
- discuss the organization of an advertising agency, including the services it provides and its sources of income;
- state how advertisers select advertising media; and
- describe the differences among advertising media, including their costs.

Case Study

BBDO Focuses on Breaking Out of the Media Jungle

People almost everywhere are receiving an overwhelming amount of advertising. This poses a challenge for manufacturers and advertising agencies alike. In a recent promotional message, BBDO, one of the largest ad agencies, put it this way.

Today, it doesn't really matter where your company does business. Or what you're selling.

You're likely to encounter a problem of increasing seriousness. And it can occur at any level: local, regional, or global.

We call it perceived product parity.

In reality, it's a headache. An expensive one.

What it comes down to is this. Consumers everywhere are being barraged by a flood of products, promises, and by too much predictable, look-alike advertising.

So even when your firm comes up with something truly different, the overloaded consumer may fail to appreciate the difference.

Whether you're in Kenya. Kyoto. Or Kuala Lumpur.

Fortunately, when it comes to this key international marketing problem, BBDO doesn't offer you the same old solutions.

We see a major opportunity hidden in the global problem of perceived product parity.

Everyone, including your toughest competitor, is trapped in it.

So, once we can separate you from the crowd, you'll have room to move.

That's why we focus first on your product's or service's performance imagery. What does it do?

Second, and usually far more important, its people imagery. How does it make people feel? When they say of your advertising "I get it," will they also think "I like it"?

This discipline gives us a one-of-a-kind creative strategy.[1]

BBDO focuses on performance imagery (how customers perceive a product's ability to do a given task) and people imagery (how customers feel about using the product). The goal of BBDO's promotional strategy and its advertising is to effectively project the kind of imagery that best suits the situation. Advertising is important to all types of companies, especially to companies like BBDO who create and market advertising for others.

Types of Advertising

Businesses use advertising to keep consumers aware of specific goods and services. The type of advertising which stresses goods or services is **product advertising**.

Advertising may also publicize a firm's name. This type of advertising, which builds an image for an organization without mentioning a specific product, is **institutional advertising**.

can be adapted to fit many types of promotional activities. For example, it can be used to:

- support personal selling;
- create consumer interest in a company's goods or services;
- keep the consumer aware of the goods and services of an established company;
- introduce a product to a new market or age group; or
- introduce a new business to a community.

Product Advertising

The primary aim of product advertising is to encourage consumers to buy a specific product. It

Institutional Advertising

Institutional advertising is geared toward establishing and maintaining a company's image, prestige, and public acceptance. Usually, little or no mention is made of a company's product in this form of advertising. At times, the only reference made to the company sponsoring the message is the company name at the end of the ad. Institutional advertising is often concerned with:

- demonstrating the company's role in community affairs;
- presenting information and viewpoints on public questions;
- presenting general or health information of interest to the consumer; and
- keeping the company's name before the public;

Types of Advertisers

Business organizations can be divided into three advertising groups: *national, retail,* and *industrial.* National and retail advertisers promote consumer products. Industrial advertisers promote industrial goods.

National Advertisers

A manufacturer of consumer goods who advertises a product by its brand name, such as Levi Strauss or PepsiCo, is a **national advertiser**. The advertising itself need not be directed at the entire country to be classified as national.

For example, some brand-name products are sold only in certain sections of the country. Advertising for these products is placed in media that reaches people only in those areas. Such advertising, however, is still referred to as national advertising.

Retail Advertisers

A store or service organization whose advertising message encourages consumers to deal with its business is a **retail advertiser**. A retail advertiser may advertise a huge assortment of products or only one product, but the ad's emphasis is on the place of purchase. Retail advertising differs from national advertising in that the emphasis is on the place of purchase rather than on the brand name.

■ ■ ■   *This ad announced the coming of World Cup Soccer to America and lists the World Cup sponsors. Why would these companies sponsor World Cup Soccer?*

The retail advertiser's goal is to persuade consumers to shop at the store. Retail advertising is also called local advertising. This is because ads are limited primarily to newspapers and radio and television stations that reach a consumer market located within shopping distance of the advertising store.

Manufacturers of brand-name products frequently join with retailers in cooperative advertising programs. **Cooperative advertising** is the practice of manufacturers providing money and resources to promote their products in retail advertisements. Both the manufacturer's and retailer's names appear in the ad.

Cooperative advertising is similar to advertising allowances, which are discussed in Chapter 22. Manufacturers often provide retailers with complete advertising material for cooperative advertising. Retailers merely add the store's name and address and buy space for the ad in a local newspaper. The retailer and manufacturer share the cost of cooperative advertising.

Cooperative advertising is a combination of push and pull promotional strategy. The manufacturer encourages the retailer to advertise, while the ad is aimed at final consumers.

Industrial Advertisers

Industrial advertisers promote goods, services, and ideas to the industrial market. Industrial advertising promotes products used by industries in the manufacture of goods or in the operation of their business. Four basic types of industrial advertising are trade, business-directed, professional, and farm advertising. Let's take a look at each type.

Trade Advertising

To encourage retailers to carry their products, manufacturers place ads in the many industry trade

■ ■ ■ *In cooperative advertising manufacturers provide money and resources to promote their products in retail advertisements. How can you tell that this ad is an example of cooperative advertising? Why is it a combination of push and pull promotional strategies?*

magazines that circulate among retailers. Wholesalers and distributors also advertise in trade magazines to stimulate sales to retailers. For example, *Musical Merchandise Review* is intended for owners and managers of stores that stock and sell musical instruments. Manufacturers and wholesalers of such instruments place full-page ads in this magazine to tell retailers why they should stock their brands.

Business-Directed Advertising

Business-directed advertising appears in publications meant for manufacturers of consumer or industrial goods. For example, ads in *American Machinist* explain how the use of certain machines will reduce production costs in machine shops. Ads in *Textile World* describe the merits of various yarns, fabric dyes, and cones for holding thread on cloth-weaving machines. Ads in *Home Builder News* urge home-building contractors to use certain building materials, kitchen equipment, or flooring material in the houses they construct.

Professional Advertising

Professional advertising is addressed to professional people such as lawyers, educators, doctors, dentists, and hospital administrators. Most buy or recommend products such as equipment, books, and supplies.

To inform professionals of the merits of their products, manufacturers advertise in such professional journals as *The Marketing Educator's Journal* and *Hospital Purchasing News*. In addition, they may send out product samples or letters telling professionals how they or their associates or clients can benefit from the use of their products.

Farm Advertising

Several magazines such as *The Progressive Farmer, Farm Journal,* and *Prairie Farmer* are directed toward families living on farms. The ads for consumer products in these magazines are basically the same as those that appear in general consumer magazines. The difference is that farm magazines also carry ads for products appealing mainly to farmers, such as tractors and other farm vehicles, milking and other farm equipment, animal feed, and fertilizer.

The Advertising Business

The typical large business organization manages its advertising through many resources. These include the company's own advertising department and advertising agencies.

The Advertising Department

Many medium-size and most large companies maintain their own advertising departments that are usually directed by an advertising manager. Companies that sell a variety of products may appoint an advertising manager for each product line. For example, the Scott Paper Company manufactures paper products for both industrial and consumer use. It has a manager in charge of advertising its industrial products and another manager in charge of advertising its consumer products.

The advertising manager and that department work closely with the marketing director, the promotion manager, and others who have the responsibility for promoting and selling the product. Together they determine policies and prepare advertising budgets. If the company also uses an advertising agency, the advertising manager works with the agency in preparing advertisements. He or she also selects the types of media—the channels of communications—in which to place the advertising.

The advertising manager is usually assisted by several people, including the copywriter, the art director, and various other personnel. The copywriter writes the message or copy that is to appear in the ad. The art director designs the ads and supervises the artists who prepare the cartoons, drawings, and other illustrations.

The advertising department may also include photographers, editors, writers, and various office personnel. Very large advertising departments may also have a media director and a research director. The media director studies the effectiveness of each type of media and the size and kind of audience represented by each type. The research director specializes in testing the appeal of the ads (often before they are used) and measures their effectiveness.

Advertising Agencies

Most companies that use a wide variety of advertising media seek the help of advertising agencies. An **advertising agency** is an organization that specializes in creating, planning, and placing ads for other businesses and organizations. Nonprofit groups and political parties and candidates also use advertising agencies to reach their markets. The individuals and companies that use these advertising agencies are referred to as clients or advertisers.

Growth of Advertising Agencies

Advertising agencies started more than 100 years ago when a group of people bought "white space" in newspapers and then sold it to various advertisers. In return for getting this business, the newspaper paid a commission to the group.

In time, these groups or agencies realized that they had something to offer the advertiser besides white space. They could offer copywriting, artwork, layouts, and assistance in selecting media. The agency became a specialist, working with the advertiser not only in advertising but also in other promotional activities. Today, a typical advertising agency offering full service to its clients has four departments.

1. The *creative department* creates ads.
2. The *research department* conducts studies of target audiences and their preferences.
3. The *media department* selects media and places ads.
4. The *business department* conducts the agency's business such as client billing.

Today, there are thousands of advertising agencies in the country. The large agencies, like those in Table 29–1, employ artists, designers, copywriters, layout artists, TV scriptwriters, and media buyers. They also employ account executives, who are responsible for managing the advertising activities of clients. There are also smaller limited-service agencies that specialize in one aspect of advertising, such as producing commercials or print ads, copy writing, or media buying.

Methods of Paying Agencies

Advertising agencies receive some of their income from the commissions they receive for placing clients' advertising. A **commission** is a percentage of sales received. The typical commission is 15 percent of the price charged by the medium for space or time.

For example, suppose an advertising agency places a full-page ad in a magazine for one of its clients. The magazine space costs $100,000, but the magazine bills the agency for only $85,000 ($100,000 – $15,000 or 15 percent).

If the client placed the ad directly with the magazine, the bill would have been $100,000. Although the agency pays only $85,000, it bills the client for the full $100,000.

The difference of $15,000 ($100,000 – $85,000) is the agency's commission. From this commission, the advertising agency pays its costs for creating and placing the ad as well as its other business costs.

Use of the commission system is declining. Many advertisers and agencies are not satisfied with it. Large advertisers think that they are paying more for service because they place more advertising. The agencies feel that sometimes they are providing added services without being paid for them. As a result, many advertising agencies now charge expenses plus a markup on outside services and a fee for agency time in creating or placing advertising.

Most advertising is placed with the media by commercial agencies. The remainder is placed by large companies and by media buying services. Large companies may place advertising through their own advertising agencies, known as "house agencies." House agencies are usually granted the same kind of discount given independent advertising agencies.

Rank	Agency
1	Young & Rubicam
2	Saatchi & Saatchi Advertising Worldwide
3	McCann-Erickson Worldwide
4	Ogilvy & Mather Worldwide
5	BBDO Worldwide
6	Lintas: Worldwide
7	J. Walter Thompson Co.
8	DDB Needham Worldwide
9	Backer Spielvogel Bates Worldwide
10	Foote, Cone & Belding Communications

Source: "U.S.-based Consolidated Agencies," *Advertising Age,* April 13, 1992.

■■■ *Table 29–1 Top Ten U.S. Advertising Agencies*
The larger agencies conduct business throughout the world. What can a full-service agency offer its clients?

Media buying services specialize in buying large quantities of media time and space at a discount. They, in turn, sell this time and space to advertisers who have had their ads prepared elsewhere and need only broadcast time or newspaper space.

THE FUTURE IS NOW

Hey, Man, What's Happening?

Hey, Daddy-o, like wow! Beatniks are becoming hip (again). Goatees, sunglasses, sandals, black clothing, and poetry readings in bookstores and coffeehouses are in. So when Kraft Foods wanted to advertise its new iced cappuccino drink, Cappio, it chose Ferdinand, a goateed, bongo-playing beatnik. It's another example of the cross-pollination of advertising and popular culture. If you want to market "cool," use a beatnik. Dig it!

Selecting Advertising Media

The chief advertising media are newspapers, magazines, radio, television, direct mail, and outdoor posters and billboards. Nationally, the number of media choices is staggering—more than a quarter of a million. There are more than 1,800 commercial and cable television stations, nearly 9,000 radio stations, about 900 weekly magazines, thousands of outdoor poster sites, and more than 9,000 daily and weekly newspapers.

From all these choices, advertisers look for the best media in which to promote their products. They read reports published by the media, study

Principles into Practice

Chiat/Day: Advertising Agency of the Year

Every year, *Advertising Age*, a major publication of the advertising industry, selects the nation's most creative advertising agency and names it Agency of the Year. While Chiat/Day of Venice, California, was twenty-sixth in size of all U.S. agencies, with about $500 million in client billings, it was named Agency of the Year twice. By 1992 billings had climbed to $1 billion.[2]

What makes the nation's most creative advertising agency? What kind of advertising did it do that year? Here are a few examples of its ads. You may recall them.

- The U.B.U. Reebok shoe print and TV commercials showing carefree people acting in happy-go-lucky ways since "Reebok lets U.B.U."

- Nissan's TV commercials in serial form of an adventuresome drive through Central and South America in a Nissan Pathfinder.

- Home Savings of America true-life stories of the customers helped by the savings bank.

- Arrow shirt television commercials of a male chorus singing while their shirts and ties change to colorful T-shirts as the music gets livelier.

- Gaines dog food TV commercial "The Woof Train," where barking dogs chug like a steam train.

Although others have criticized some of the agency's work because of its offbeat creative approach, Lee Clow, Chiat/Day's president and executive creative director, responds, "The point in time when no one wants to talk about or criticize your work is the point when you should really worry. As long as they're still talking about us, we're OK." [3, 4]

---

1. How would you classify each type of advertisement mentioned in this case study?
2. What elements do these advertisements have in common that makes them creative?

---

government documents, and keep up to date with advertising trends by subscribing to trade magazines.

To select the best advertising media, John Pavasars, formerly of the Leo Burnett advertising agency, studies the consumer. He says, "I must examine the life-styles and trends of yesterday and today and attempt to project what they will be tomorrow. In a turbulent economy…Americans are forced to make trade-offs. Instead of spending an extra 20 cents on premium grocery products, consumers now scrimp so they can splurge on more expensive items. Advertisers must communicate price/value relationships, because consumers are spending their income more cautiously."

Media experts also conduct their own research. "I must also discover what kind of people buy a certain product and why," Pavasars continues. "This is accomplished by conducting thousands of interviews each year … questionnaires that allow consumers to express attitudes, interests, and opinions about products they buy and media they watch, read, and hear. Once we can identify what type of people buy which products, creative groups can develop a message that is personalized for specific types of people."[5] Research helps advertisers identify and understand consumers. They can then select the most effective media.

Reaching the Customer

The audience an advertiser hopes to reach usually determines the medium the advertiser selects and the kind of advertisement prepared. For instance, if the product is hair conditioner and the

■ ■ ■   *Cineplex Odeon ran this ad to entice advertising agencies to advertise on movie screens. What are two advantages of this type of media?*

audience is women, the advertiser may place the advertising in magazines such as *Mademoiselle*.

Often an advertiser finds that a specific audience can best be reached through television. For example, if the product is a tennis racquet, the advertising may be placed on TV during a tennis match. If the product is a camera, the advertising may be placed on a family TV show. Besides manufacturers of such products, nationwide retailers also reach customers through television. For example, T.J. Maxx off-price stores let TV viewers know each time they visit the store that "it's never ever the same place twice."

Sometimes an advertiser wants to reach an audience located in a specific geographic area. If this is so, then media are chosen to reach only that area. For example, local or regional retailers do not advertise on network TV. A great portion of the network audience is not within shopping distance of local and regional stores. These stores prefer to advertise in local newspapers and on local TV and radio stations.

Some local retail stores, however, will advertise in national magazines if they want to reach a certain geographic market. Retailers of fine furniture and apparel advertise in magazines such as the *New Yorker* or *Southern Living*.

Considering Cost in Choosing Media

The cost of advertising is based largely on the types of media used, the number of people reached, and the amount of space or time purchased. For example, advertising on a national television network costs more than advertising on a local station.

The cost of television advertising is also affected by the day of the week and the hour of the day the advertising is scheduled, because this has a bearing on the size of the audience. For example, advertising for a program scheduled for 8 P.M. costs more than comparable advertising scheduled for an afternoon program, since the evening program is likely to attract a larger audience. Similarly, a full-page ad in a Sunday newspaper costs more than an identical one in a weekday newspaper, because the Sunday newspaper has more readers.

While the cost of advertising is very important in choosing media, cost is relative. That is, money for advertising should be spent on the media that will reach the largest number of possible customers at the lowest cost per person.

A national advertiser may spend more than $121,000 for a full-color ad in *Reader's Digest*. The advertiser considers the cost low because millions of people will see the ad. However, an advertiser spending $120 for space in the classified ad section of a local newspaper might regard the cost as high in terms of the small number of potential buyers who would read the ad. Thus, advertisers must always determine whether the amount of coverage is worth the cost.

CHAPTER NOTES

1. "Creating a World of Difference," BBDO promotional publication (New York, New York).
2. "Chiat/Day's Global Pullback," *Advertising Age*, 23 November 1992, pp. 1, 36.
3. Cleveland Horton, "Creative 'Stretch' Wins Top Honors for Chiat/Day," *Advertising Age*, 23 March 1989, p. 4.
4. "Top 100 in 45th Agency Report," *Advertising Age*, 23 March 1989, p. 48.
5. John Pavasars, "The Elusive Consumers," *Advertising Chicago Style*, Supplement to *Chicago Tribune and Sun-Times*, 26 October 1980, p. 13.

Chapter Summary

- Businesses use advertising to keep customers aware of the goods and services available.

- Two types of advertising are product advertising and institutional advertising.

- Business organizations can be divided into three advertising groups: national advertisers—those manufacturers who advertise consumer goods by brand name; retail advertisers—those retail businesses whose local advertising encourages customers to come in and shop; and industrial advertisers—those who promote goods to the industrial market.

- A typical large organization uses several resources to handle its advertising department and advertising agencies. Key people in a company's advertising department are the advertising manager, the copywriter, and the art director.

- Advertising agencies are outside organizations that specialize in planning and conducting advertising for client advertisers. For their services, agencies may be paid a 15 percent commission on the ads they place in the media, or they may be paid various fees for their services.

- There are a variety of media from which to choose. The challenge is to select the media that are most likely to be seen by prospective customers but at a cost that the advertiser considers reasonable.

Building Your Marketing Vocabulary

On a separate sheet of paper, define each of the following marketing terms. Then, in a 150-word paper tell how each of the terms relates to advertising.

product advertising	cooperative advertising
institutional advertising	industrial advertiser
national advertiser	advertising agency
retail advertiser	commission

Questions for Review

1. Name two major types of advertising and explain how they differ.
2. Name four services that product advertising provides.
3. List three types of advertisers.
4. Name four basic types of industrial advertising.
5. Explain how a company's own advertising department may work, and discuss the staff it may have.
6. Describe the organization of an advertising agency offering full service to its clients.
7. From what source does the agency receive most of its income?
8. How do advertisers seek to find the best media in which to advertise their products?
9. Why are limited-service agencies becoming popular? How do they differ from advertising agencies offering full service?
10. Is the most costly form of advertising always the most expensive? Explain your answer.

Critical Thinking

1. What, in your opinion, are the qualities of a "good" advertisement? Give examples.
2. Why would a company use *both* promotional and institutional advertising?
3. Give an example of a national and a retail advertisement. Compare the purposes of these ads.
4. As a media planner, where might you place an ad for diapers?
5. Why do advertisers look at the past to determine where to advertise in the future?

Discussion Questions

1. Would an advertiser use the same kind of advertising for a new product as for a well-established product? Illustrate your answer with an example from your experience.

2. Some critics say advertising is unnecessary and serves no useful purpose. Why do marketers disagree?

3. Give an example of institutional advertising. Discuss the intent of the advertisement. Do you feel the ad is effective? Why or why not?

4. Discuss reasons why some advertising, despite its creativity, is ineffective. Give examples of ads you feel are not effective.

5. According to BBDO advertising agency, consumers are being hit by an increasing flood of advertising. Do you think this has any effect on the impact advertising has on consumers? Explain your answer. What can advertisers do to make their ads stand out?

Marketing Project

Determining How an Advertisement Is Produced

Project Goal: Given a company's advertising department, determine how an advertisement is produced.

Directions: With your teacher's permission, visit the advertising department of a retail store, manufacturing plant, or newspaper. Learn about the work of the department and which employees are responsible for what tasks. Write a 250-word report showing step by step how an advertisement is created. Illustrate your report with a sample advertisement if possible.

Applied Academics

Language Arts

1. Obtain copies of your local newspaper and consumer and trade magazines. Next, cut out examples depicting national advertisers, retail advertisers, and industrial advertisers. Finally prepare a chart identifying each of your examples.

Math

2. Suppose the cost of an ad is $125,000. How much will an advertising agency receive if it is paid a 15 percent commission?

Social Studies

3. In your opinion how does advertising benefit the consumer? Ask three friends, two relatives, and at least one businessperson the same question. Write down their responses. Present your findings to the class.

Marketing and Multiculturalism

Asian-Americans are the nation's fastest-growing minority group. In the 1980s this population grew 108 percent from 3.5 million to 7.3 million. In contrast the Hispanic population grew 53 percent.

In an attempt to capture a market share of this growing group of consumers, companies are experimenting with the use of Asian models in media advertising. Recent studies compared ads using Asian models to sell high-tech electronic products with the same ads using Caucasian models. Results indicated a more positive response from Asian-American consumers when advertisers employed the Asian models. By integrating Asian models into advertising, a company can communicate recognition and value to the Asian-American consumer. It can also position itself to win the loyalty of this rapidly expanding consumer market.

1. In which of the two major types of advertising were Asian models used?

2. What type of market information would advertisers want to know before using retail advertising to sell electronic equipment to the Asian-American market?

3. As the manager of advertising for a company interested in targeting the Asian-American consumer, what qualifications or characteristics would you look for in an advertising agency?

Chapter 30

Advertising Media

Terms to Know

display advertisements

classified
    advertisements

network advertising

local advertising

outdoor advertising

transit advertising

specialty advertising

program advertising

Chapter Objectives

After studying this chapter, you will be able to:

- describe and explain the advantages of different types of media;
- discuss the steps in selecting advertising media for a given product; and
- describe the importance of the marketing concept in selecting media.

Case Study

One Year's Best Radio Commercial: Mid-Atlantic Milk Marketing Association

This mid-Atlantic Milk Marketing Association 60-second radio commercial by W.B. Doner & Co., Baltimore, won *Advertising Age's* Best Radio Commercial.

OK, I'm here to tell you that drinking milk, whether you choose whole, low-fat, or skim, doesn't matter. It's the most important thing you can do to stay fit.

Today I offer as evidence—The Olympics. Yes. Which countries produce the most milk? Which have the most cows? The U.S. and Russia. Which countries win the most medals? Same countries. Milk-medals. Medals-milk. Rumania? Small country—but a lot of cows—high milk consumption—that translates into medals. Remember Nadia Comaneci? Comaneci means milk, I believe. In Rumanian. And if I'm not mistaken, Nadia means fitness.

How about Australia? Big country—lots of kangaroos—few cows—not much medal activity there.

How about Albania? No cows, no milk...they don't even bother to enter!

Mongolia? Never a contender...recently brought in cows, started drinking milk...I'd keep an eye on 'em.

So...there it is...drink your milk and you'll win at the Olympics. It's up to you, whole, low-fat, or skim. Milk is fitness you can drink. Just ask the Greeks. Where have they been lately?[1]

Radio is just one of many forms of advertising media advertisers have to choose from. Using media wisely ensures that advertisers reach their target audience.

Types of Media

Advertising media, such as radio and television, are the communications channels advertisers use to inform customers about products and encourage potential customers to buy them. Sometimes media are used individually, as when a local store advertises in the newspaper. Other times they are used together and may reinforce each other. Advertisers spend over $126 billion each year with the various media (see Figure 30–1).[2] In this chapter, you will explore the following types of advertising media:

- newspapers;
- magazines;
- radio;
- television;
- direct-mail advertising;
- outdoor advertising;
- transit advertising;
- specialty advertising;
- directories; and
- program advertising.

Newspaper Advertising

In the United States, people depend on some 1,600 newspapers for detailed coverage of national, international, and local events. In addition, weekly newspapers serve specific areas and special interests. Radio and television present the news more frequently, but the reporting is brief and often superficial.

Newspapers not only give in-depth news coverage but also offer something for everyone—world news, editorials, society news, sports news, fashion trends, and comics. Of course, tucked into these same pages are numerous ads.

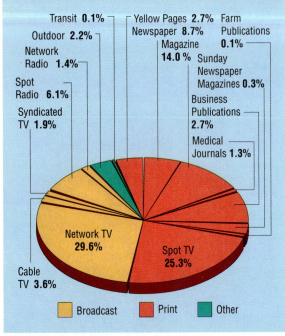

Transit **0.1%**
Outdoor **2.2%**
Network Radio **1.4%**
Spot Radio **6.1%**
Syndicated TV **1.9%**
Yellow Pages **2.7%**
Newspaper **8.7%**
Magazine **14.0%**
Farm Publications **0.1%**
Sunday Newspaper Magazines **0.3%**
Business Publications **2.7%**
Medical Journals **1.3%**
Network TV **29.6%**
Spot TV **25.3%**
Cable TV **3.6%**

Broadcast   Print   Other

Source: *Advertising Age*, April 13, 1992, p. S41.

■■■ *Figure 30–1 Percentage Breakdown of Media Spending in 1991*
Advertisers place advertising in a wide variety of media. Why do you think advertisers spend the most money on network TV?

Many people are as interested in the ads as they are in the news. They study the ads to learn what is new in fashions, home furnishings, and cars, and they compare prices on foods and other necessities. The Wednesday and Thursday supermarket ads and Friday weekend bargains offered by discount houses, department stores, appliance stores, and other retailers are of special interest to many readers.

The most popular newspapers among advertisers are Sunday editions because people have time to read them. That is why there are inserts and other advertisements from such businesses as department stores and travel agencies. It also explains why the Sunday papers are thicker than weekday editions.

Newspapers offer six key benefits to the advertiser.

1. Newspapers saturate the local market. The newspaper is often read by the whole family, because of the wide variety of coverage offered. In the United States, about 80 percent of all families read one or more daily newspapers.

2. Newspapers give information about local businesses. This information often includes products and prices. Even in the 20 or so largest markets throughout the country, newspapers are able to target geographical sections, providing local news and giving local advertisers specific market saturation. For example, the *Chicago Tribune* has developed six *Suburban Trib* sections enabling advertisers in, for instance, Du Page County—directly west of Chicago—to specifically reach readers and prospective customers in that county.

3. Newspapers are timely and flexible. Ads can be prepared and inserted just a few hours before publication. For example, after a heavy snowfall, newspaper ads can quickly be changed to feature snow tires, skis, and cold weather clothing. Magazines do not have this flexibility.

4. Newspaper ads can be cut out and used as shopping guides.

5. Newspaper ads can include coupons. The shopper can clip the coupons and use them toward the purchase of a product.

6. Newspapers are read consistently. There is little significant fall-off in readership—only an estimated 2 percent—during the summer months. This is not the case with television viewing, which declines significantly in the summertime.

There are two types of newspaper advertisements. **Display advertisements** appear throughout a newspaper and use pictures, art, or different type or print styles to attract attention. Businesses are their primary users. The average cost for a manufacturer of a full-page black-and-white ad depends on the paper's readership. A full-page advertisement in the Sunday *Chicago Tribune*, for example, is just under $61,000. This advertisement would reach a total of 1.3 million people.[3]

Classified advertisements are grouped in special pages of newspapers or magazines according to the kind of product advertised. They generally contain only copy. The type style and format of most classified ads follow the pattern set by the newspaper. Classified ads are used to sell such things as household furnishings and pets and to advertise such services as house painting. They are also used by real estate agencies, employment agencies, and car dealers to advertise goods or services.

Magazine Advertising

Magazines (also called periodicals) are a favorite medium of the national advertiser. With more than 11,000 magazines to choose from, marketers concentrate on about 400 general-interest magazines to advertise their consumer goods. More than 80 percent of all national advertisers spend at least $25,000 a year on magazine advertising. Magazines offer three key benefits to advertisers.

1. They permit the advertiser to determine an audience. For example, *Seventeen* magazine appeals to teenage girls. *Better Homes & Gardens*, known as *BHG*, appeals to homemakers. Car buffs, sports enthusiasts, and businesspeople are attracted to magazines such as *Hot Rod Magazine*, *Sports Illustrated*, and *Business Week*. Magazines such as *Yankee* concentrate on a certain area of the country.

2. Magazines can present superior color reproduction, whereas newspapers generally cannot. Thus, magazine ads generally stimulate the desire for goods more effectively than do newspaper ads. Magazine ads can also show greater product detail by illustrating such features as fabric texture.

3. People usually dispose of newspapers soon after they read them, but they often save magazines for future reference. This gives the advertiser more exposure. Studies have shown that each issue of some key magazines is passed along to as many as eight or nine readers.

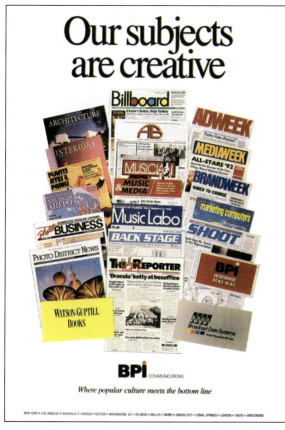

■ ■ ■   *Magazines allow advertisers to determine the audience they target. What type of advertisers is BPI Communications trying to attract?*

Radio Advertising

Ninety-nine percent of the households in the United States have radios; most have five or more. The radio is a source of entertainment for listeners wherever they happen to be: in the car, at home, or at work. During the summer months, more people can be reached with radio advertising than with television advertising.

Radio provides advertisers with more outlets than any other major advertising medium. There are some 1,600 daily newspapers in the United States, but there are about 4,500 commercial AM radio stations and nearly the same number of FM stations.

National advertisers can select the areas that are major markets for their goods or services and advertise on stations serving those areas. Local businesspeople can confine their advertising to the stations within their trading area.

Today, most radio advertising consists of spot announcements ranging from ten seconds to one minute in length. The cost of radio advertising spots ranges from $750 or more in major markets to less than a dollar in small towns. However, a few programs are sponsored. This means that a company pays for a program from 5 to 30 minutes in length and has exclusive advertising rights on the program. For example, a local restaurant may sponsor one radio station's afternoon weather and traffic report. The restaurant is advertised during the commercial breaks.

Television Advertising

From its very modest beginnings in the 1940s, television broadcasting has grown into a powerful advertising medium. It has done so by taking business from other media, especially from radio and newspapers.

Television is now the prime family entertainment medium. More than 89 million homes—98 percent of all homes in the United States—contain at least one television set. More than half of these own more than one set.

The average television set is on 7.1 hours each day. In addition, many households have VCRs. More than 50 percent of all households receive cable TV (subscriber-paid television).

Television offers some real advantages to advertisers. It brings their messages to viewers with the dramatic impact of sight, sound, motion, and color. Moreover, television commands the viewer's close attention. Finally, family members are often likely to watch TV together. They make comments and suggestions to each other about advertised products. All of these factors make television a powerful medium for advertising many goods and services.

Programming

Although many local businesses advertise on local TV channels, television is primarily a national advertising medium. Three major television networks are American Broadcasting Company (ABC), Columbia Broadcasting Company (CBS), and National Broadcasting Company (NBC). These networks face growing competition from other sources such as cable television and the FOX network.

Many television stations are owned by one of the networks. Others are locally owned but are affiliated with a network. These affiliates broadcast many network programs and get a share of network advertising revenues.

Television advertising rates go up as the number of viewers increases. Television stations, therefore, compete to attract vast audiences, offering similar popular programs like sporting events, dramas, and situation comedies.

The publicly sponsored Public Broadcasting System (PBS) offers an alternative. Viewers enjoy a wide range of topics rarely seen on commercial television. Because of increasing expenses, however, PBS does accept some advertising.

Types of Television Advertising

There are two basic types of television advertising: network and local. **Network advertising** is carried across the country by the local stations owned and affiliated with one of the networks. It is very expensive. **Local advertising** is placed on local channels and aimed to an audience in a given geographic area. It is not nearly as costly as network advertising.

Formerly, large organizations such as automobile manufacturers could afford to sponsor entire television programs each week at costs of up to $5 million or more a year. However, because of rising costs, only a few organizations still sponsor entire programs. These are likely to be such specials as popular sports events (for example, a pre-game "dugout" interview). More typically, two to five noncompeting companies will co-sponsor part or all of a program, such as a baseball game.

Advertisers today usually prefer to buy commercials that are 30 seconds in length, although 10-second and 60-second commercials are also available. Typically, advertisers buy commercial air time in a series or a package plan which gives them exposure on a variety of television programs, sometimes on different networks. Total costs vary according to the amount of air time and the time of day.

THE FUTURE IS NOW

Translating Sound into Sight

A new federal law requires that TVs sold in the United States with screens 13 inches or bigger have built-in decoders. These decoders can read and display closed captions for the hearing impaired. The increase in decoders will provide marketers who sponsor closed-captioned TV with the opportunity to reach 28 million hearing impaired Americans. It will also create good public relations for these marketers.

Prime time, the evening hours when television audiences are the largest, is most expensive. Prime time is from 8 to 11 P.M. on the East and West Coast, and 7 to 10 P.M. in the central states. The cost for each 30-second network commercial on prime-time TV programs averages about $123,000.[4] Popular programs may command more. The Super Bowl telecast, which attracts more than 100 million viewers, has charged up to $1.3 million a minute for advertising.

In general, network advertising is done by manufacturers and retailers of goods and services marketed nationwide, such as General Electric, MasterCard, and Sears. Local retailers often choose local stations for advertising. They reach the people near their businesses, and they pay less, too. Thirty-second commercials on local TV stations vary from $25 to $15,000, depending on market size.

Cable Advertising

Cable TV represents a growing segment for advertisers, with markets and advertising methods all its own. (See Figure 30–2.) There are some 8,500 operating cable systems in the United States, reaching about 50 million subscribers.

About half the cable systems accept advertising, and their lower rates reflect their smaller audiences. For example, a typical 30-second commercial spot on the USA Network's reruns of "Murder, She Wrote" would cost $5,200. That same 30-second spot when the program ran on the network could have cost more than twice as much.

A few advertisements are actually 30-minute commercials (known as "infomercials" or "documercials"). They promote new products such as exercise equipment, makeup, and cookware. Organizations such as AT&T, Avon, and Eastman-Kodak are among those exploring the "infomercial" format.[5]

The variety of cable television programs is increasing. Already there are channels that feature one subject such as sporting events, news and business features, arts and entertainment, education, and even channels targeting ethnic groups such as BET (Black Entertainment Television) and Galavision/ECO in Spanish.

Each of these channels carries advertising, thus enabling marketers to target specific audiences. Manufacturers of athletic equipment and shoes

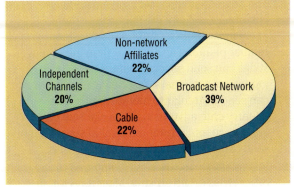

Source: Cable TV Facts, 1989, Cablevision Advertising Bureau, Inc.

■■■ *Figure 30–2 Television Viewing Time Among Households with Both Cable and Broadcast TV*
This chart shows that in homes with network and cable television, 39 percent of all viewing time is spent with network and 22 percent with cable. What would this information tell you as an advertiser?

naturally would be interested in advertising on channels such as ESPN, the Total Sports Network, or Home Sports Entertainment, which serves the Southwest.

One of the areas that is expanding rapidly is shopping at home. For example, the cable channel QVC features goods offered by Saks Fifth Avenue and others. Viewers may order the featured merchandise over the telephone.

Direct-Mail Advertising

Another form of advertising is direct-mail advertising—that is, advertising sent to prospective buyers through the mail. Because of its personal effect, direct-mail advertising is popular among both large and small businesses. For small businesses, it is also an economical way to deliver an advertising message.

Types of direct mail include letters, postcards, circulars, folders, price lists, brochures, catalogs, and house organs (newspapers or magazines prepared by the advertiser). The type of mailer an advertiser selects depends on the impact desired and on the size of the promotional budget. Direct mail offers six key advantages.

1. The advertiser can select the most likely customers and aim the message to them exclusively. For example, a local fashion retailer planning an advance showing of new styles can send special invitations to its important customers. A sporting goods store can send a circular to members of a local country club advertising a special sale on golf clubs. A manufacturer of hospital supplies can send promotional materials to hospitals.

2. It is relatively inexpensive compared to other types of advertising. Most direct-mail advertising is sent third-class bulk rate. Bulk rate, which is available to businesses and organizations sending out large quantities of mail, offers considerable savings over first-class mail.

3. The direct-mail advertiser does not compete with other advertisers; it occupies the reader's attention by itself.

4. Direct mail can be highly creative. It is not limited to any size, color, or shape beyond observing certain postal regulations.

5. Direct mail can make the sale because readers of direct-mail advertising are often asked to place their orders on an enclosed order form or coupon.

6. Finally, the results of direct-mail advertising are easier to measure than those of other advertising media.

Many businesses use direct mail extensively. National firms such as magazine and book publishers, record clubs, and mail-order firms also use the medium.

The greatest enemy of direct-mail advertising is the trash can. An estimated 44 percent of mailings are discarded unopened. The keys to a successful direct-mail campaign are (a) mailing to the right people, and (b) delivering direct mail that begs to be opened.

Using Direct Mail

In small businesses, direct mail is often handled by the owner or manager with the assistance of a word processor. Large businesses that use direct mail have staffs of experts, including copywriters, artists, and layout specialists. Some large businesses hire organizations that specialize in direct mail to conduct their campaigns. Two leading organizations of this type are the Reuben H. Donnelley Corporation and R. L. Polk and Company.

Using Mailing Lists

The key to any successful direct mail campaign is a good mailing list—a list of the names and addresses of potential buyers for the goods or services of a firm. One excellent type of mailing list is made up of the names of the firm's present customers. Some businesses use this list exclusively.

Mailing lists may be compiled from telephone directories, newspapers, and business and professional directories. They may also be bought or rented from businesses specializing in developing lists. Some businesses may exchange mailing lists.

Mailing lists require constant updating. Some customers may have moved, some may have died, and others may have changed their names. A company's advertising dollars are wasted on mailing lists that are out of date.

Outdoor Advertising

Outdoor advertising started in the days when radio and television did not exist and traveling circuses and vaudeville acts were popular forms of entertainment. Several days before one of these troupes was to appear in a community, an "advance" person plastered huge signs on fences, trees, posts, barns, and buildings to announce the big event.

Today **outdoor advertising** includes signs and posters displayed on billboards, building walls, and other rented outdoor spaces. It also includes more exotic forms such as inflatables like the Goodyear Blimp, airplane banners, and skywriting.

Outdoor advertising offers three major advantages to the advertiser.

1. It can be highly localized. For example, in a Spanish-speaking community, the advertiser can use ads written in Spanish. Political candidates can restrict their advertising to districts where their voters live.

2. The message stays where it is for a long time, and passersby can see it again and again.

■ ■ ■   *Why did this advertiser choose an outdoor ad rather than a national magazine?*

3. The message can be made very large, with dramatic use of color, art, and even movement. Messages are most effective when they are brief and the illustration is clear.

Both national and local advertisers use outdoor advertising. National advertisers who make extensive use of billboards—spending over $1 billion a year—usually have their messages printed on posters and pasted to the structures. Local advertisers usually have their signs painted. The cost of billboards depends on the size of the sign, the location in which the sign will be posted, and the length of time the space will be used.

Advertising used in buses, subways, commuter railroad cars, and in railroad, bus, and airline terminals is called **transit advertising**. It is estimated that commuters and other passengers make more than 10 billion trips in public vehicles each year; transit advertising is aimed at this group. Three basic types of transit advertising are car cards, traveling displays, and station posters.

Car cards are advertising signs found in the interiors of buses, subways, and commuter trains. Most of them are 11 x 28 inches. They are used by banks, chewing-gum manufacturers (Wrigley is the largest user of car cards), private schools, many types of businesses, and various nonprofit organizations.

Exterior displays are ads placed on the outside of moving vehicles, mostly buses. As the bus travels its route, the message is exposed to those waiting to ride the bus as well as to pedestrians and motorists.

Both car cards and exterior displays are purchased in what is called a *showing*. A *full-run showing* is one card in or on every vehicle owned by the transportation company. Rates are quoted by the month. A full-run showing in one large-city subway system costs about $26,000 a month.

Station posters are ads located in subway and railroad stations and in bus and airline terminals. Like exterior displays, station posters are purchased by showings. The cost depends on the number of displays used and the length of time they are shown.

Transit advertising offers two primary appeals to advertisers.

1. It reaches people who are likely to be in or near the business area.

2. It is economical, considering the number of people it reaches.

Principles into Practice

One way for several media to participate in a promotion is through *event marketing*. The event is a special promotional activity. The participating media then become *event media*, adding value to the total promotion through their participation.

An example of event marketing was the restoration and furnishing of a 19th-century house by Martha Stewart, a best-selling author, contributing editor to *Family Circle* magazine, and lifestyle consultant to Kmart Corporation. The progress of the home restructuring was highlighted by an editorial featured in *Family Circle*. It was supplemented by advertorial inserts featuring products sold at Kmart stores. Totaling some 60 pages, the advertising sections featured products available at Kmart stores that were useful for the home.

Event Marketing: Kmart Promotes Products with Events

Kmart's promotion also included 42 TV infomercials. They featured Martha Stewart using product's available at Kmart stores relating to the home. Both home magazine readers and Kmart customers were interested in what Martha Stewart created and how she transformed the home. Marketing the event with cross-media references not only allowed the information to reach a wider audience but also gave the participating media added visibility.[6]

1. What are the advantages to event marketing using event media?

2. What are the disadvantages of event marketing using event media?

Specialty Advertising

Advertisers sometimes give potential customers useful items that carry an advertising message. This technique is **specialty advertising**. For instance, banks print calendars to encourage repeat business. The range of specialty advertising products is limited only by one's imagination. Other examples of specialty advertising include address books, license plate frames, buttons, calendars, rulers, shopping bags, and T-shirts.

Specialties have certain characteristics that make them popular as an advertising medium.

1. They are useful items. The recipient actually receives a gift for looking at the advertising message.

2. They provide repeat advertising. Every time people pick up a pencil or a memo pad advertising an insurance company, for example, they see the company's advertising message.

3. Specialties do not require high-priced advertising campaigns, and the cost per item is very low.

4. Specialties can be planned specifically for potential customers. For example, a building supply store can give measuring tapes with the store's name and address printed on it to potential customers.

Directories and Program Advertising

Many trade and business directories accept advertising. These include city, medical, educational, building, and professional directories.

■ ■ ■ *These items are an example of specialty advertising. What is one reason why advertisers would give away such items to customers?*

The most important directory for advertisers is the classified section, or Yellow Pages, of the telephone directory. All businesses that have telephone numbers are automatically listed by classification in the Yellow Pages, which may be bound as a separate volume. While all businesses are automatically listed, the telephone company encourages them to buy display ads in addition to the listing.

People moving into a new neighborhood rely on the Yellow Pages to locate and establish regular buying sources. Established residents and businesses also use the Yellow Pages to find suppliers of goods and services.

Program advertising refers to advertising that appears in such publications as church bulletins, school-play and athletic programs, and school yearbooks. Most businesspeople look upon this type of advertising as a donation, since they expect to receive little benefit from it. For this reason, many do not try to sell their products in the ad but take advantage of the public relations value by including a statement such as "Compliments of Dillard Department Stores, Inc."

New ideas for advertising media are constantly appearing. A recent form of advertising appears on the supermarket grocery cart handle. Cards advertising food items and fastened to grocery cart handles put customers face-to-face with the advertised products as they wheel their carts through the store.

The next step for grocery cart handles may be attached video screens that light up, emphasizing bargains when customers pass certain shelves in the store. Or, recorded advertisements may play as customers walk by the shelves of the advertised products. New forms of advertising are always being tested, sometimes using new media. What new advertising media have you seen recently?

CHAPTER NOTES

1. "Best of '88," *Advertising Age*, 1 May 1988, pp. 34–39.

2. Robert J. Coen, "How Bad a Year for Ads Was '91? Almost the Worst," *Advertising Age*, 4 May 1992, p. 3.

3. Patricia M. Rath telephone interview with *The Chicago Tribune* Display Advertising Department, 22 December 1992.

4. Joe Mandese, "Home Improvement Wins Dollar Race," *Advertising Age*, 6 September 1993, p. 3.

5. John Schmeitzer, "Field's Hopes to Wake Up TV Watchers with Infomercial," *Chicago Tribune*, 1 July 1993, Sec. B, pp. 1, 4.

6. Patrick Reilly, "High Flying Acts Show Some Wear," *Advertising Age*, 24 May 1989, pp. 5, 8.

Chapter Summary

- Advertising media are the communications channels advertisers use to inform customers about products and encourage them to buy.
- Major advertising media include newspapers, magazines, radio, television, direct-mail advertising, outdoor advertising, transit advertising, specialty advertising, directories, and program advertising.
- The most widely used advertising media in terms of advertising dollars spent are newspapers.
- Magazine advertising is popular with national advertisers.
- Radio advertising reaches audiences wherever they happen to be, and nearly everyone has a radio.
- Television is the major family entertainment medium. Ninety-eight percent of the homes in the United States have television.
- Direct-mail advertising is a rapidly growing form of advertising and is used by large and small businesses alike.
- Outdoor advertising, transit advertising, specialty advertising, directories, and programs are all advertising media that are successfully employed by marketers either alone or in conjunction with other media.

Building Your Marketing Vocabulary

On a separate sheet of paper, define each of the following marketing terms. Then use each term in a sentence on advertising media.

display advertisements
classified advertisements
network advertising
local advertising
outdoor advertising
transit advertising
specialty advertising
program advertising

Questions for Review

1. Explain four major benefits that newspapers offer to advertisers.
2. Name three advantages that magazines have as an advertising medium.
3. What are two advantages of radio to advertisers?
4. In what ways can cable television advertising differ from traditional television advertising?
5. What are three advantages of direct mail as an advertising medium?
6. What is the key to a successful direct-mail campaign?
7. When is outdoor advertising likely to be most successful?
8. Name three forms of transit advertising.
9. Give four reasons why specialty advertising is a popular advertising medium.
10. What is program advertising?

Critical Thinking

1. Describe how the people in charge of media selection use the marketing concept in arriving at their media choices.
2. What type of media would you use to advertise a sale at a clothing store?
3. If you were selling billboard advertising, what types of companies would you target?
4. What types of specialty advertising not named in this chapter might you use to promote a family shoe store?
5. Name two products that could effectively be sold through direct mail.

Discussion Questions

1. Which businesses in your community regularly use program advertising? Why?
2. Describe a recent advertisement you have seen or heard. Why did it make an impression on you? How did the advertising media contribute to the ad's effectiveness?
3. Discuss possible new ideas for advertising media.

4. Discuss the types of advertising media you think are most effective. Give examples of advertising of this media that have persuaded you to buy, and explain what factors made this advertisement effective.

5. How do you feel about the amount of space and time magazines and television have devoted to advertising? Discuss the effects that excess advertising may have on these types of media.

Marketing Project

Studying Advertisements

Project Goal: Given a number of ads in your local newspaper, explain the placement and pattern of the ads during a one-week period.

Directions: Study the display ads in a daily newspaper for one week to find answers to the following questions.

1. Which types of businesses run the largest ads most often?

2. What is the approximate ratio of local to national ads?

3. Which types of businesses usually seek the most prominent placements? Which ads consistently appear in the same place?

4. Do certain types of businesses advertise on certain days of the week?

5. Is there a relationship between the location of news articles and the ads?

Write the results of your findings, and prepare to discuss them in class.

Applied Academics

Language Arts

1. Over the period of one week, track the amount of direct-mail advertising your household receives. Also track the amount that is opened, unopened, and thrown away. Write a report explaining which pieces were opened, which pieces were thrown away, and why.

Math

2. Suppose, as a direct marketer, you send out 50,000 pieces of mail in one mailing. It costs you $80 per 1,000 names for your mailing list. It costs $100 per 1,000 to produce the actual mailing piece. It costs $290 per 1,000 for postage. How much does the entire mailing cost you? If your products sell for $125 each, how many products do you need to sell in order to cover the cost of the mailer?

Social Studies

3. Businesses may subscribe to mailing lists in order to obtain consumer names. They, in turn, mail promotional materials to these consumers. Some consumers have asked for guidelines regulating the use of mailing lists. In your opinion how should mailing lists be regulated?

Marketing and Multiculturalism

"Let's Party!" at the great L.A. Zoo. Or, "¡Te esperamos!" ("We're waiting for you!") if you're one of the 40 percent of the visitors to the Los Angeles Zoo who are Hispanic.

After discovering, through a marketing survey, that nearly one-half of the Zoo's visitors are Hispanic-Americans, Zoo marketing officials responded by producing five of its 12 "Let's Party" theme billboards in Spanish. Response to the billboards was so positive that the Zoo has produced a second Spanish-language ad for both billboard and transit media.

1. Discuss the advantages of choosing outdoor advertising media for this ad.

2. What other advertising media might the L.A. Zoo select for its Spanish-language ad?

3. Discuss why Hispanics might be influenced to visit the Zoo as a result of the Spanish-language ads.

4. What advantages might be gained by placing this ad in a Spanish-language newspaper rather than on a billboard?

Chapter *31*

Sales Promotion

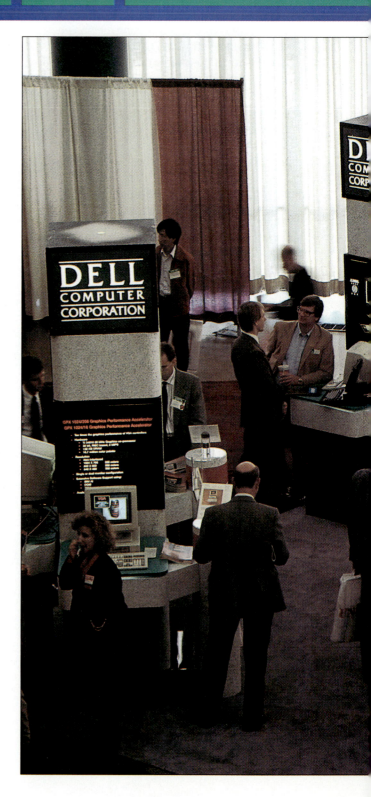

Terms to Know

sales promotion agency
premium
product sample
trade show
price-oriented
   promotion

open display
closed display
model displays
point-of-purchase
   promotion

Chapter Objectives

After studying this chapter, you will be able to:

- explain the term *sales promotion* and name its eight most important forms;
- give examples of the different types of sales promotion;
- apply visual merchandising practices to business situations; and
- explain point-of-purchase promotion and its advantages.

Case Study

The Mileage Plus Promotion

Sales promotion needs pizzazz to succeed. To capture the imagination, sales promotion may promise adventure and glamour, as you can tell from this United Airlines promotion.

From August 1 through December 31, you can enjoy a special discount when you vacation in Australia's oldest and most dynamic city—Sydney. Plus, we're offering you an exciting opportunity to combine your Sydney Holiday with an exotic tropical adventure in the Great Barrier Reef.

Select either one of our exclusive packages, or combine the two. Either way, you'll enjoy special Mileage Plus rates and an unforgettable vacation experience.

Sydney. Shop at the Darling Harbor Complex or enjoy a cruise on the breathtaking harbor. At night, visit Sydney's renowned Opera House, take in a show or dance until dawn.

The Great Barrier Reef. These are among the world's most enchanting islands. Along with a wealth of astonishing beauty, the islands of the Reef offer you a wide variety of popular holiday resorts.[1]

What looks like a regular travel promotion is more than that; it is a sales promotion to encourage air travel. Here, United Airlines is offering special incentives to its Mileage Plus members (frequent air travelers who collect bonus points for the miles they fly).

Travelers may turn in these bonus points for plane tickets, hotel reservations, and rental cars. Additional benefits are given for using certain credit cards. Most major airlines have similar sales promotions, and they have proven highly successful.

The Range of Sales Promotion

Sales promotion consists of all activities in the promotion process except advertising, public relations, and personal selling. Among the most important forms of sales promotion are contests, sweepstakes, premiums, product samples, container promotion, exhibits, price-oriented promotion, and visual merchandising. These techniques stimulate sales and increase dealer effectiveness.

Marketers use sales promotions to achieve short-term results quickly, since they provide additional reasons for consumers to buy right away. For example, when a cereal manufacturer offers a popular toy or game in exchange for sending in a couple of box tops, the sales of that brand usually climb during the promotion.

Increasingly, however, sales promotion programs are seeking more long-term results. This goal is important to marketers, who spend more on sales promotion each year than they spend on advertising.[2]

Sales Promotion to Channel Members

Most major manufacturers have a marketing department that handles sales promotion. Most sales promotion is geared to ultimate consumers. But marketers may also aim it toward retailers and wholesalers.

Sales promotion is also used within a company to build a product's image and create enthusiasm for it, particularly among the company's own sales force. For example, to launch the marketing of a new computer, the manufacturer may hold a series of company-wide meetings. These will explain the computer's features and benefits and thus build interest among members of the sales force. One of these meetings might take the form of a motivational talk or even a musical show. A contest may offer vacations to the winning salespeople. Both the meeting and the contest are forms of sales promotion. In this case, the manufacturer is promoting its product to its own sales staff. Next, the manufacturer is ready to promote the improved model to dealers and customers.

Sales Promotion Agencies

A **sales promotion agency** is an independent organization that specializes in creating sales promotion activities for other businesses. The number of sales promotion agencies has risen as sales promotion has become increasingly important.

Some sales promotion agencies are full-service agencies. They offer many sales promotion services such as long-range planning, point-of-purchase promotions, direct marketing, sweepstakes, games, contests, event marketing, premiums, and even advertising. A list of the major full-service sales promotion agencies in the United States is shown in Table 31–1.

Other sales promotion agencies specialize in certain forms of sales promotion, such as sweepstakes or premiums. Some advertising agencies such as the Ross Roy Group of Bloomfield Hills, Michigan, or Marketing Resources of Overland Park, Kansas, also conduct significant sales promotions for clients.

Sales promotion agencies are working hard to prove that successful sales promotions are essential long-range as well as short-range marketing activities. In the various airlines' frequent flyer sales promotion programs, for example, customers receive points for miles flown. They can turn in their accumulated points for reductions in airfare. Such programs have been in effect since the early 1980s.

Contests and Sweepstakes

Both contests and sweepstakes are popular forms of sales promotion. A contest calls for some degree of skill on the part of the entrant. It may mean writing a slogan or creating a recipe using the sponsor's product. The entrant may be asked for a proof of purchase with each entry submitted.

A sweepstakes, however, does not require skill on the part of the entrant. Sweepstakes winners may be selected at random from all entries, or they may hold winning numbers or matching portions of a trademark, symbol, or design.

Premiums

An item given without substantial charge with the purchase of a product is a **premium**. A premium attracts customers who would not otherwise buy a product or would not buy it as often if the premium were not given.

Premiums used to promote consumer buying come in many forms. Five of the most common premiums are coupons, factory packs, self-liquidating premiums, direct-sales premiums, and sales-lead premiums. Let's take a look at each of them.

Coupons

The use of coupons began about 100 years ago when C. W. Post gave out penny tokens promoting his new breakfast food called Grape Nuts. The tokens could be used toward the purchase of the cereal.[3]

Today, marketers of many goods and services—from cereal to flying lessons—issue discount coupons. Coupons encourage shoppers to try a new product or to continue buying an old one. A typical

Rank 1991	Agency, headquarters
1	**Alcone Sims O'Brien**, Irvine, Calif.
2	**D.L. Blair**, Garden City, N.Y.
3	**Marketing Corp. of America**, Westport, Conn.
4	**Clarion Marketing & Communications**, Greenwich, Conn.
5	**Ross Roy Group**, Bloomfield Hills, Mich.
6	**Cato Johnson Worldwide**, New York
7	**Frankel & Co.**, Chicago
8	**Comart**, New York
9	**Flair Communications**, Chicago
10	**Ryan Partnership**, Westport, Conn.

Source: *Advertising Age*, May 4, 1992, p. 29.

■■■ *Table 31–1 Leading Full-service Sales Promotion Agencies*
What services are provided by full-service promotion agencies?

coupon might offer a free sample or a significant price discount stating, for example, "Save 40¢ on Finesse shampoo."

Coupons are big business. Shoppers cash an estimated $2 billion worth of coupons each year. This breaks down to between $7 and $8 for every American consumer.

People receive coupons by mail, by door-to-door delivery, or in newspaper or magazine ads. Some coupons come with the product and offer a discount on the next purchase. The manufacturer usually offers these coupons.

Although coupons increase store traffic, some retailers criticize their use. Stores are paid 8 cents for handling each coupon, but they claim that their costs are closer to 10 cents each. Also, many consumers and retailers have suggested a standard coupon size—the size of a dollar bill—to make them easier to handle.

Retailers also offer coupons. For example, a restaurant may put an advertisement in the newspaper and include a coupon for a second free pizza when one is purchased.

Factory Packs

Manufacturers of cereals that appeal to children often place a free gift in the package such as a toy or comic book. Manufacturers of laundry detergent have been known to include a dish towel or washcloth in each box. Such gifts, which are designed to encourage consumers to keep buying a product, are called factory packs.

The toy prize in a box of Cracker Jack is perhaps the most famous example of a factory pack. Some of these factory packs have even become collectors' items.

Self-Liquidating Premiums

Sometimes manufacturers offer items bearing their logos. T-shirts, backpacks, and other items are offered at a price that just covers their cost. These items are known as self-liquidating premiums because the price customers pay covers the manufacturer's cost of producing the product. Proof of purchase, such as a package seal, is usually required when ordering a self-liquidating premium. So, for customers, the premiums offer an added incentive to buy the product. For manufacturers, self-liquidating

premiums carry their advertising message wherever they go. What's more, they pay for themselves!

Direct-Sales Premiums

Door-to-door salespeople often use premiums to build sales. For example, Fuller Brush salespeople usually give a small brush or other article to each person they call on, whether or not they make a sale. A gift is sometimes offered to those who watch a demonstration of a higher-priced item, such as a major appliance or an automobile. Sometimes, savings and loan associations offer premiums (or discounts on the purchase of premiums) such as stuffed animals, clock radios, or luggage to customers who open or add to their savings accounts. At one time, *U.S. News & World Report* gave a small AM/FM stereo radio to new subscribers.

Sales-Lead Premiums

The sales-lead premium is a reward offered in return for the names of prospective customers. For instance, salespeople for both Tupperware and Mary Kay Cosmetics offer gifts to people who give them sales leads. These premiums also are used widely with higher-priced items sold door to door. Often, the salesperson must pay for the premium. The person furnishing the lead receives a gift or a price discount from the salesperson only if the referral results in a sale.

Product Samples and Container Promotions

A small sample of an advertiser's product that is given away free is a **product sample**. Often, product samples are used to introduce a new product such as shampoo. Advertisers send some product samples through the mail, deliver some door to door, and give away others at stores.

Food processors offer samples of their cheeses to shoppers in supermarkets. Food processors also use "container promotion," packaging a product in an appealing reusable container. Examples of container promotion are jelly and cheese spreads packaged in useful tumblers.

the person, place, product, firm, or activity being publicized.

For example, a press kit for Calvin Klein contains articles and photographs describing the current season's styles and their special theme. Included are articles on the designer himself and the evolution of his line over the past several seasons.

Copies of the press kit go to newspapers, magazines, and radio and television stations a week or so before the new line is introduced. The media are then able to use the publicity stories from the press kit in conjunction with news coverage of a local Neiman Marcus or Saks fashion show.

News Releases

News releases, which are articles about special events, are also prepared and sent to the media. The releases begin well in advance of the event and build up to it. A portion of the news release for San Diego Zoo's Tiger River is shown in Figure 32–1.

Local newspapers may choose to run any or all of a release, write their own articles based on the release, or write nothing at all about the release.

For these reasons, organizations try to make their news releases as interesting and appealing as possible.

Special Events

Businesses and other organizations plan publicity events aimed at the media. For example, before the opening of a new play or musical production, theater producers will hold preview performances and issue special invitations to entertainment editors for newspapers, magazines, and television. Special seating is set aside for the media. Often, a party is held for them after the show in hopes of creating favorable publicity.

Radio and Television Interviews

When an individual or an organization has a new product to present, radio and television talk show hosts and even news reporters may want to inform their audiences about it. A financial reporter will interview a stockbroker on the radio about new investment opportunities. Or, an author may talk about his or her newest book on a TV talk show.

■ ■ ■ *The San Diego Zoo publicity department wrote this news release for the Tiger River attraction. How does the zoo benefit from publicity?*

FOR IMMEDIATE RELEASE
MARCH 11, 1988
CONTACT: JEFF JOUETT OR
          GEORGEANNE IRVINE
          (619) 231-1515

NEWS RELEASE

The San Diego Zoo
P.O. Box 551
San Diego, California 92112-0551
(619) 231-1515

THE SAN DIEGO ZOO'S NEW TIGER RIVER IS READIED FOR RAIN FOREST EXPLORERS

Zookeepers, construction workers and graphic artists are scurrying to put the finishing touches on a man-made three-acre rain forest replica that marks a dramatic departure from the traditional display of animals and plants at the San Diego Zoo.

Set to open Saturday, March 26, "Tiger River: Kroc Family Tropical Rain Forest" will mix mammals, birds, reptiles and plants from the same bioclimatic zone. The $6 million Tiger River project even attempts to do something about the typically balmy San Diego weather, using a high-tech fog-creating system and a computerized irrigation set-up to substitute for the 100-plus inches of rainfall common to rain forest ecosystems.

Interviews bring the product to the attention of a large audience.

Special Promotions

Special promotions encourage participation and generate publicity. For example, one recent summer, the San Diego Wild Animal Park celebrated its fifteenth anniversary. As part of a summer theme called "Passport to Adventure," the park held evening programs titled "Around the World in 80 Days." Featured were special entertainment and exotic food. In addition, guests took exciting monorail trips to view the park's some 2,500 wild animals.

The special programs, a form of sales promotion, were developed to draw attention and visitors to the park. Press releases describing the programs caught the attention of the media whose anniversary feature stories then became publicity for the celebration.

Publicity and Public Relations at Work

Let's look at an example of how publicity and public relations work together. Suppose that a nationwide retail chain store decides to open a branch store in a small city. How might management publicize the event and get support for the new outlet?

Long before the decision to establish a branch store is made, the company makes many surveys to determine the demand for the store in the community, traffic problems, probable location, and sources of labor. This involves research and discussions with leaders in local government, business, and the community.

Once the decision to establish a store is made, the firm begins to plan its publicity and public relations campaign. One of the first things it does is to arrange for a company executive to speak at a chamber of commerce luncheon. This speech will announce the company's decision to enter the community and is likely to be reported in the local paper.

As soon as construction is ready to begin, a ground-breaking ceremony is held, with key executives, the mayor, and local civic leaders present. Photographs are taken, and the story appears on the front page of the local newspaper. It is also presented on local radio and television.

As construction progresses, the firm sends out a series of news stories. Some describe the company—its major executives, its national growth, and its merchandising policies. Other stores in the retail chain announce the appointment of local people to important jobs in the store, the opening of an employment office, and the training program planned for new employees. One point continually emphasized in the news releases is the importance of the new store to the growth and prosperity of the community. As the opening date approaches, the news releases become more frequent.

About a week before the opening, management holds a preview for the press. Newspaper, magazine, radio, and television reporters and photographers are taken on a tour of the new store and given photographs and news releases. The day before the opening, another preview is held for the leading citizens. Executives greet guests and answer questions.

The formal opening is usually a brief but impressive public ceremony to open the business officially. The store manager and other key executives greet the people, and the mayor welcomes the store to the community. The ribbon-cutting ceremony is held, officially opening the store.

After months of combining public relations and publicity to inform the public about the new store, business is finally begun. The store is off to a good start. Now the job of keeping the goodwill of the community begins.

CHAPTER NOTES

1. "The San Diego Zoo's New Tiger River Is Readied for Rain Forest Explorers," News Release, 11 March 1988, The San Diego Zoo, CA.
2. Douglas G. Myers, "Executive Director's Report," Annual Report, Zoological Society of San Diego, 1987, p. 7.
3. Robert McClure, "General Manager's Report," General Manager, Wild Animal Park, Annual Report, Zoological Society of San Diego, 1987, p. 11.
4. Benny Evangelista, "Convenience on Campus," *Oakland California Tribune*, 3 March 1989.
5. Sharon McCormick, "7-Eleven in a High School," *San Francisco Chronicle*, 3 March 1989.
6. Nancy Solomon, "Logan Opens First Campus 7-Eleven," Fremont, CA, *Argus*, 2 March 1989, pp. 1, 7.
7. "7-Eleven Opens on High School Campus," Davis, *CA Enterprise*.

Chapter Summary

- Most organizations are concerned with public relations—building goodwill toward a business organization. They are also concerned with unpaid promotion for their company—known as publicity.

- Public relations involves all aspects of a company, including the appearance of its buildings and the activities of its personnel. An organization's public relations efforts are aimed at four groups: customers, the community, stockholders or donors, and employees.

- Public relations efforts aimed at customers include consumer advisory boards, consultants, and special events. Community relations includes activities to maintain the respect of the community including the wider community of government. Maintaining good employee relations is important to an organization because the employees are the company to customers and other outsiders.

- The job of the public relations department is to get the company's name and products mentioned favorably whenever possible.

- The publicity people work with the media and others interested in publicizing news about the company and its products. Publicity may be handled within a company or by an agency.

- Publicity activities often include developing a press kit, news releases, special events, radio and television interviews, and special promotions.

Building Your Marketing Vocabulary

On a separate sheet of paper, define each of the following marketing terms. Then in a sentence or two explain how each term is related to public relations and publicity.

public relations agencies

consumer advisory board

community relations

press kit

news releases

Questions for Review

1. What is public relations?
2. Give an example of a public relations activity.
3. What four groups make up the "public" factor of public relations?
4. Name three public relations efforts that companies can use to improve customer relations.
5. What is one way companies can build good community relations?
6. What is publicity?
7. Give an example of publicity as discussed in the text.
8. How does publicity differ from advertising?
9. Explain the work of the publicity department.
10. Describe the publicity and public relations activities that can take place when a new business opens.

Critical Thinking

1. When would a company be likely to call in an outside organization for help in its publicity and public relations activities? When would it tend to rely on its own staff to do these jobs?
2. How does publicity differ from public relations?
3. Why is a press kit one of the best ways to seek publicity?
4. Why might a credit card company send tickets to an opening of an art exhibit to non-card members?
5. Imagine you own a large chain of retail stores. You are planning to open your latest store in a community that has some reservations about having any more new stores in the area. What can you do to create goodwill in the community?

Discussion Questions

1. Describe a recent example of favorable publicity for your school or the business where you work.
2. In what ways might a marketing organization work toward establishing good public relations with its customers?

3. Name two or three public relations activities that your school's student organizations such as DECA or the student council could undertake to advance their cause.

4. Are publicity and public relations "frosting on the cake," or do they perform an essential role in promotion? Explain your answer.

5. Publicity and public relations do not directly increase sales. Why, then, do companies spend money on these areas of promotion?

6. Discuss how you would use publicity and public relations to publicize and get support for a new sunscreen.

Marketing Project

Planning Publicity and Public Relations

Project Goal: Given a particular marketing business, write a plan that contains two ideas for publicity and two ideas for public relations activities to promote that business.

Directions: Select a marketing business such as a retail store, a professional sports team, or an amusement theme park. Assume that your goal is a 5 percent increase in sales. Plan two publicity activities and two public relations activities that you believe will help increase sales. Write your plan for each activity in four short paragraphs. For background information, look through newspapers and magazines and tune in to radio and TV news broadcasts. These media can give you helpful examples of successful publicity and public relations activities.

Applied Academics

Language Arts

1. Write a 250-word news release for the opening of a new store.

Math

2. Determine how much it will cost you to produce 2,000 press kits for your company. Each kit contains ten pages of articles and a photo. The paper for the articles costs $15 per 500 sheets. There are four pages of articles in each kit. The photocopying costs 3¢ a page. Folders cost $26.25 for packages of 25. The photos cost 25¢ each.

Social Studies

3. Interview a businessperson in your community about the types of public relations activities used by his or her business. Ask why these types of activities are used. Report your findings to the class.

Marketing and Multiculturalism

Parlez-vous français... or Arabic, Amharic, Czech, Chinese, Farsi, Filipino, German, Hindu, Italian, Japanese, Korean, Persian, Russian, Spanish, Thai, Urdu, or Vietnamese? Washington State's Puget Sound Power & Light Company does. Between 1980 and 1990 the utility's Asian-American customer base grew 127 percent and its Hispanic-American base by 83 percent. The company responded by developing a language bank to provide translation services for its non-English-speaking customers.

The new 18-language service connects customers simultaneously, through a conference call, with a customer service representative—and with an employee that speaks the customer's language. The company considers the language bank an opportunity to provide the same quality of personal and proficient service to all of its customers, not just those who speak English.

1. How is the language bank an example of public relations?

2. Which of the four "public" groups is targeted in this public relations effort?

3. As a public relations executive for Puget Power, what activities would you aim at the media to seek publicity for this program?

4. What other services might the company implement to respond to the needs of its ethnic customer base?

5. What is Puget Power's main purpose in providing the language bank?

Selling for Retailers

The most familiar form of personal selling is in retailing. Retail salespeople perform the final step in the process of moving goods and services to the consumer. The box office ticket seller, the clothing salesperson, the real estate agent, and the salesperson for door-to-door household products are all retail salespeople who sell directly to the consumer.

Three types of retail salespeople are: in-store salespeople, specialty salespeople, and route drivers. Let's take a look at each.

In-Store Salespeople

Those who sell inside a store are **in-store salespeople**. Their main duties include serving customers, writing up the sale or processing it on the cash register, wrapping merchandise, making change, arranging and replenishing stock, keeping stock clean, and handling customer problems.

Several factors help the retail salesperson's performance. The merchandise is usually available for demonstration. Also, the salespeople concentrate on serving the customers who come to them. For this reason, most retail salespeople are "order getters." Opportunity for creative retail selling does exist, however, particularly for those who sell apparel, shoes, jewelry, and home furnishings.

Some in-store salespeople spend part of their time calling on prospects in their homes or places of business. Appliance stores, furniture stores, and automobile dealers often work in this manner.

People who work at airline ticket counters, in travel agencies, in restaurants, and in similar service establishments are not usually called salespeople yet they are engaged in selling. The way these employees greet and serve customers definitely affects the sales volume of the business employing them.

Specialty Salespeople

People who sell a particular product or line of products to customers at their home or business are called **specialty salespeople**. Many specialty salespeople sell such products as cosmetics, brushes, and storm windows door to door. People who sell insurance and real estate are also specialty salespeople.

Route Drivers

Salespeople who travel an established route, selling products, are **route drivers**. Products commonly sold by route drivers include baked goods, milk, and newspapers.

Many salespeople find route driving challenging and interesting. They enjoy the open air and the immediate contact with people.

Selling for Wholesalers

The wholesaler is the link between the manufacturer and the retail store or industrial user. Some manufacturers sell directly to retailers and to industrial users. However, many use wholesalers to

■ ■ ■ *People who sell real estate are specialty salespeople. Why?*

distribute their products. In some cases, manufacturers use wholesalers in addition to their own sales force.

Wholesalers are distributors. They employ **wholesale salespeople** who sell the products of one or more manufacturers to retailers, businesses, schools, hospitals, and other institutions.

Wholesale salespeople may represent several manufacturers and carry a number of noncompetitive products. The typical wholesale salesperson periodically calls on a regular group of customers. Products often handled by wholesale salespeople include pharmaceuticals, food products, automotive equipment, farm and garden supplies, and apparel.

A wholesale salesperson often deals in hundreds, perhaps even thousands, of items. A salesperson for a wholesale grocer may have as many as 3,000 items to sell.

Often, the wholesale salesperson is required to be a specialist and consultant. He or she must be able to advise customers on what to buy, how much to buy, and when to buy. Some wholesale salespeople serve their customers so efficiently that they are trusted to determine and order the merchandise customers need without actually consulting them.

The wholesale salesperson also informs the retailer about the latest trends in the field. He or she also gives the retailer important information about which products are selling and why.

Selling for Manufacturers

Manufacturers sell to a wide variety of customers: other manufacturers, wholesalers, retailers, government agencies, hospitals, educational institutions, and sometimes to individual consumers. The salespeople who represent the manufacturers in selling to these customers are **manufacturers' representatives**. Often, they are employed directly by a manufacturer.

Other representatives of manufacturers are self-employed, like the Kims in our opening case study. They are called manufacturers' agents. They carry the lines of one or, usually, several manufacturers.

Some independent salespeople are called selling agents. They represent the entire output of a manufacturer. (See Chapter 24.)

Manufacturers' salespeople may handle consumer goods for personal use, such as apparel, cosmetics, or furniture. They may also handle industrial goods for business use, such as grain, lumber, cotton, or office stationery.

Manufacturers of consumer goods employ sales representatives to market their products to retail stores and some wholesalers. A consumer goods sales representative calls on 10 to 15 retail stores a day to maintain displays, check and rotate stock, and take orders. Experience in consumer goods sales may lead to promotion within the company or to specialized work with wholesalers or chain stores.

Technical Competency

Most manufacturers of industrial goods hire salespeople who are technically trained in (or willing to learn about) specialized fields. A well-known type of industrial salesperson is the service salesperson. This person sells, installs, and services such products as air conditioning equipment, personal computers, printing presses, or small motors. The service salesperson needs to have good mechanical aptitude as well as a thorough knowledge of the product and how it works.

Salespeople trained in engineering or other skills serve the industrial user. They sell goods such as metal parts to such clients as airplane manufacturers. Other goods sold by these salespeople include plastics for radio and television sets, desks for schools, and tableware for restaurants. They must thoroughly understand their customers' problems and know how to help solve them.

Sales and Research

The information from salespeople is essential to retailers and their suppliers in shaping the kinds and assortments of products offered. Salespeople know firsthand what customers are buying and what they want that is not available. This information allows marketers to supply precisely what their customers want.

You recall from the chapter opening case study that the Kims' store buyers had mentioned an emerging customer interest in African-American and Hispanic gift items. From their experience, the Kims know how to locate the suppliers of these items. The problem is to find the exact products and the selections that will be profitable to everyone. By determining if there are enough customers among the stores, what kind of goods these customers would like, and when the suppliers could deliver orders,

Principles into Practice

Barbara Proctor's Creative Selling Results in Her Own Advertising Agency

Barbara Gardner Proctor is the chief executive officer, president and creative director of Proctor & Gardner Advertising, Inc. She founded the business some 20 years ago and has built it on her determination, courage, and creative selling ability.

Proctor earned a teaching degree from Talladega College in Alabama and a teaching certificate in North Carolina. After a summer job as a camp counselor in Kalamazoo, Michigan, she headed back to North Carolina, stopping off in Chicago to buy her teaching wardrobe. "I wound up spending all of my money," she says, "and didn't have bus fare to get home."

Instead, she stayed in Chicago and went to work for the Urban League. Then she became a music critic for *Down Beat* magazine and was later employed by a record company. One of her accomplishments there was arranging for the Beatles' songs to be marketed in the United States under the Vee Jay label.

She then turned to advertising. After working for three agencies she realized she could more effectively create what her clients wanted in her own business rather than by working for someone else.

However, she only had $1,000 to invest and needed nearly 100 times that amount to start her own business. She went to the Small Business Administration for a loan. When asked what she would use for collateral, she answered, "Me." She then asked them to call three advertising agencies and ask each agency what annual salary it would pay to employ her as creative director. She said that she would ask the SBA for the same amount to start her company. When the SBA learned the agencies would pay Proctor an average $80,000 annually, it granted Proctor's request and gave the first service loan in SBA history.

Barbara Proctor's personal creative selling ability made it possible for her to begin her own business. She turned it into a $25 million agency with clients such as Kraft and Sears.

In addition, she is a member of the Board of Directors of many organizations, including Illinois Bell Telephone Company, Northwestern Hospital, and the DuSable Museum of Black History. She has received honors from the president of the United States and from many groups.[1,2,3]

What made Barbara Proctor's loan request to the Small Business Administration an example of creative personal selling?

---

the Kims could predict whether their expanded business might succeed.

Thus, by conducting marketing research, manufacturers' salespeople are able to help customers (the stores), suppliers (manufacturers of gifts and decorative accessories), and themselves. In this situation, the Kims are applying the marketing concept—thinking in terms of the customer's needs—to reach a solution.

The typical manufacturers' salesperson has an assigned territory and a list of customers to call on regularly. The salesperson learns the customers' problems and needs, and looks for ways of serving them better.

What It Takes to Sell

To sell effectively, a salesperson must be enthusiastic about selling. Effective selling means getting along well with people, knowing the product, and

■■■ *Why is a business-like appearance important in personal selling?*

managing time wisely. A lack of any one of these abilities can seriously impair a salesperson's performance.

Personal appearance is also important in selling. It's essential to be professionally dressed and well groomed for work. Customers prefer to deal with salespeople whose appearance is businesslike.

Working Well with People

A salesperson must have a genuine interest in people. Successful salespeople enjoy being with others; they learn to see their customers' point of view.

As you recall, thinking in terms of customers' needs is the first part of the marketing concept. After learning a customer's needs, a salesperson can then offer a solution to a problem. Meeting a customer's needs at a profit fulfills the marketing concept and is the basis of successful personal selling.

Outstanding salespeople work hard to develop pleasing personalities. They also develop good communications skills to get their messages across.

Knowing the Product

A salesperson must know and believe in a product to have confidence in his or her ability to sell it. In gaining product knowledge, a salesperson also learns how the product benefits customers.

The result is a magic ingredient called "selling enthusiasm." A salesperson cannot simply turn on enthusiasm. It is acquired through experience, knowledge, and confidence in the product.

A number of excellent sources of product knowledge are available to salespeople. Most companies provide brochures, descriptive booklets, advertising pieces, and merchandise manuals. A *merchandise manual* is a notebook that describes a product. The manufacturer prepares the manual for salespeople as well as for customers.

In addition, manufacturers often attach tags or labels to their products that carry important information. They also hold sales conferences where salespeople acquire product knowledge along with training in sales techniques.

Managing Time and Territory

Professional salespeople call on customers regularly and manage their time and territory well. They must also be self-starters. They must find the courage to make the tough calls along with the easier ones. They must resist the temptation to quit early, particularly after a disappointing day. They know that those late-in-the-day calls sometimes can be the best ones.

They must be willing to devote their evenings to organizing plans for the following day. They must telephone ahead for appointments and prepare schedules to avoid unnecessary travel. They must make sure they have the proper samples. At the end of each day, they must prepare reports on the day's activities.

In brief, the salesperson must be able to operate effectively with little or no supervision. This takes the willingness and know-how to organize a work plan and the determination to stick to it.

Personal selling is a very important job in marketing. The best salespeople never stop training to do the job better.

CHAPTER NOTES

1. "Barbara Gardner Proctor, Role Model," Interview with *Entrepreneurial Woman*, March/April 1990, p. 58.

2. Norma Libman, "Making the Bus Fare—and Then Some—on a 30-year Stopover," interview with Barbara Proctor, *The Chicago Tribune*, 15 July 1990.

3. Biography of Barbara Gardner Proctor and other sources supplied by Proctor & Gardner Advertising, Inc., August 1990.

Chapter 33 Review

Chapter Summary

- Personal selling is the direct effort made by a salesperson to convince a customer to make a purchase. It is often needed to close a sale.

- Salespeople are needed throughout the marketing process. They are expected to carry the major part of the selling effort in situations when the number of customers is limited, the product requires demonstration or explanation, a trade-in is part of the sale, and the dollar amount of the sale is high.

- Selling consists of three tasks: creative selling, order taking, and sales support.

- Personal selling may occur face-to-face or through telemarketing.

- Face-to-face selling includes selling for retailers, wholesalers, or manufacturers.

- There are three types of retail salespeople: in-store salespeople, specialty salespeople, and route drivers. In-store salespeople sell inside retail businesses. Specialty salespeople include those who sell to customers at home or businesses.

- Wholesale salespeople sell manufacturers' products to retailers, businesses, and institutions. Salespeople who represent manufacturers may sell to other manufacturers, wholesalers, retailers, government agencies, and, on occasion, to individual consumers.

- To sell effectively, a salesperson must have enthusiasm, be able to work well with people, and manage time and territory effectively.

Building Your Marketing Vocabulary

On a separate sheet of paper, define each of the following marketing terms. Then use each term in a sentence on personal selling.

creative selling

order taking

sales support

in-store salespeople

specialty salespeople

route drivers

wholesale salespeople

manufacturers' representative

Questions for Review

1. Explain the difference between personal and nonpersonal selling.
2. Name four situations in which the salesperson usually carries the major part of the selling effort.
3. Name three kinds of selling tasks.
4. What is creative selling?
5. What two tasks are a part of sales support?
6. Name four types of selling jobs.
7. How do manufacturers' representatives differ from manufacturers' agents?
8. Name three skills needed to sell effectively.
9. Of what use is product knowledge to a salesperson?
10. What are three good sources of product knowledge for salespeople?

Critical Thinking

1. What do you think of the idea that good personal selling is just a matter of being pleasant and friendly? To sell effectively, what abilities must a salesperson have?
2. Compare and contrast the work of a specialty salesperson with that of a wholesale salesperson.
3. Someone has said that nothing happens until a sale is made. Why is selling vital to our economy?
4. In this chapter you learned about four situations in which the salesperson usually carries the major part of the selling effort. Name a product that would involve each of these selling situations.
5. Compare telemarketing with face-to-face selling. What advantages does each offer? What disadvantages?

Discussion Questions

1. Some companies budget five times as much money for their salespeople's salaries and selling expenses than they do for all other advertising and promotional activities. Discuss

why personal selling is often the most costly element of promotion.

2. Some say that in business today it is all right for a salesperson to dress comfortably for work in casual clothes. What is your opinion?

3. In what ways is the work of a retail salesperson similar to that of a manufacturers' representative? In what ways does it differ?

4. Discuss the statement "A successful salesperson thinks in terms of other people's needs." How does this idea relate to the marketing concept?

5. What qualities make an effective salesperson? Explain your answer. What qualities do you have that would make you an effective salesperson?

Marketing Project

Studying Characteristics of Salespeople

Project Goal: Identify the personal characteristics and abilities needed to become an effective salesperson in a business of your choice.

Directions: Select a business that employs salespeople and arrange an interview with its owner or manager. Ask the following questions:

1. What characteristics do you like in the salespeople who work for you?

2. What characteristics of salespeople do you dislike?

3. What kinds of training do you expect your salespeople to have when you hire them? Then, what kind of training do you give them?

4. In what specific ways do your salespeople help their customers?

5. How important are these salespeople to you and your business?

Prepare a form like the one that follows. Write the name of the person you interviewed and the name of the business at the top of the form. Then, write each of the questions above in the left column. In the right column, write the key points of the businessperson's answers to each question. Use this project as the basis for an oral presentation to your class.

Interview Questions	Businessperson's Answer
Example: What characteristics of salespeople do you dislike?	Dislikes salespeople who do not know the facts about their products, who waste time, who try to pressure customers into buying, and who do not seem to care about the company's business problems.

Applied Academics

Language Arts

1. Interview a salesperson to find out about his or her responsibilities, duties, and training necessary for the job. Write a 250-word report on your findings.

Math

2. You have just taken an order from a customer for 1 blender at $34.99, 2 mixers at $21.49 each, and 1 bowl set at $25.00 a set. Total the order, and be sure to include a 6-percent sales tax.

Marketing and Multiculturalism

A study conducted by Strategy Research Corp. (SRC) showed that 69 percent of Hispanics preferred to be assisted by Spanish-speaking retail salespeople. J. C. Penney, in an effort to serve its Hispanic customers, added bilingual salespeople in Hispanic neighborhoods. It also provides Spanish-language circulars, credit applications, and catalog shopping brochures.

1. Why would Spanish-speaking customers be likely to shop at J. C. Penney's?

2. What can a good retail salesperson do when confronted by a customer whose language he or she does not speak? What personal selling skills may help create a sale in this situation?

Chapter 34

Principles of Effective Selling

Terms to Know

prospecting

endless chain method

cold canvass approach

preapproach

approach

greeting

service approach

merchandise approach

sales presentation

product features

customer benefits

objection

close

suggestion selling

Chapter Objectives

After studying this chapter, you will be able to:

- explain the steps of a sale and the goal that each step accomplishes;

- distinguish between product features and customer benefits in preparing a sales presentation;

- show how an effective salesperson considers the customer's needs and applies the marketing concept; and

- suggest means of handling customer objections.

Case Study

An Artful Approach

A young life insurance salesperson walked into the office of an executive and said to her, "I am selling life insurance, but I don't suppose you'd be interested." The executive, a sales manager for a thriving corporation, looked at the insurance salesperson and curtly said that she did not want any more life insurance.

"In that case," said the salesperson, "I'll try somebody else." He started to leave.

"Wait a minute," said the sales manager. "I employ and train salespeople. I've seen some poor examples of salesmanship, but yours is the worst ever. You'll starve to death if you can't do a better job than that in presenting your product."

At that point, the sales manager gave the young man a brief course in the techniques of selling insurance. She explained to him the seven steps to follow in order to complete a sale. She got so interested in the whole problem that she ended up signing for a $5,000 life insurance policy for herself.

"Let that be a lesson to you," said the sales manager. "Work out a sales presentation for each situation you encounter and use it. Remember, preparation prevents poor performance."

"That's what I've been doing," smiled the young salesperson. "You see, I had you figured out before I came in here. You have just been through my specially prepared presentation for managers who are experts in sales training!"[1]

The Selling Process

Most sales presentations follow a sequence of steps. Each step in the sequence presents its own challenges to the salesperson and requires specific selling techniques. The salesperson may go through the entire sequence in a few minutes. Or, it may take weeks, months, or even years to complete the sale. The salesperson may spend more time on one step than another, depending on the product and the customer. Nevertheless, an accomplished salesperson will cover each step in order to complete the sale. The seven steps of a sale are:

- prospecting;
- the preapproach;
- the approach;
- the sales presentation;
- handling objections;
- the close; and
- the departure and follow-up.

Let's take a closer look at each of these selling techniques.

Prospecting

The word *prospecting* may bring to mind the California gold rush, when miners searched for the gold that would make them rich. Gold prospectors used various means of finding likely places to dig for gold. They listened to stories of other prospectors. They followed their own hunches. And they watched carefully to see where successful prospectors found their gold. In marketing, of course, the gold is the sale. Sales **prospecting** is the process of finding potential customers who could benefit from and buy a good or service. Potential customers are prospects.

Salespeople use several basic methods to find prospects. One is called the **endless chain method,** in which the salesperson gets the names of prospects from customers who have already made purchases. Another method is the **cold canvass approach**, in which salespeople make as many calls as possible without checking them out beforehand. For instance, an encyclopedia salesperson might go from door to door in a neighborhood, hoping to find a satisfactory number of good prospects for the product.

In addition to these methods, there are a great number of sources that a salesperson can use in prospecting for customers. These include telephone directories, trade and professional directories, commercial lists, and local newspapers. The sources for prospecting vary with the type of product being sold. Salespeople cannot afford to ignore a single source in locating prospects for the product.

The Preapproach

Gathering and analyzing information about the prospect and using it to construct the sales presentation is the **preapproach**. The salesperson trying to sell a consumer product will want to gather information about the prospect's buying needs, earlier buying habits, and price expectations. Most prospective customers like the fact that a salesperson has taken the time to learn these facts. This tells the prospect that the salesperson cares.

Getting the Facts

A salesperson who is marketing goods to an industrial buyer needs to know specific information about the prospective buyer's company and how it does business. A salesperson must ask these questions:

- What does the company produce or sell?
- Who is the company's target for its product?
- How well is the product accepted by the market?
- How could the product be improved?
- How would buying the salesperson's product benefit the company?
- Where has the company been buying products similar to those of the salesperson?
- How and when does the buyer for the company normally place sales orders?
- Are there many sources of supply?
- Why does the company buy from the salesperson's competitor?

A salesperson who can answer these questions is well on the road to understanding the buying characteristics of a prospect.

Determining the Customer's Needs

In selling to a consumer or to an industrial buyer, the salesperson must determine the prospect's product needs. Few people buy simply for the sake of buying. Most people buy because they are convinced they will benefit from their purchase. Experienced salespeople who listen to their customers' needs and who know their product can find various ways to fit a prospect's needs with the product and produce real benefits.

Consider Margaret Coe, a salesperson planning to discuss the merits of a new computer with an office manager. After speaking to the office manager on the telephone, she knows he is mildly interested in the computer's memory, graphics, desktop publishing options, and reasonable service contract. The manager is also pleased that this computer can communicate with other computers.

However, the manager's interest will really perk up when Margaret relates these features to customer benefits. The new computer will help keep a competent secretary. It will speed the transmittal of vital product and sales information throughout the company and to customers. The service contract means that the office manager will not have to worry about expensive repairs.

The salesperson collects all the necessary information about the prospect and analyzes it to determine the prospect's needs. After doing this, the salesperson is ready to make the approach.

The Approach

The way the salesperson enlists the prospect's willingness to hear more about a product is the **approach**. The approach, then, is made to gain an interview and make the sales presentation. Salespeople use a number of methods to gain interviews.

Approaching Wholesale and Industrial Customers

Outside of retailing, most sales are made by calling on prospects at their place of business. Timing is important in deciding when to approach the prospect. The salesperson should determine whether the prospect is prepared to buy at this time and what time of the day, week, or month is best to make the call.

In general, salespeople need to make appointments with prospects. This gives the prospect time to think about buying needs in relation to the salesperson's product.

When approaching a prospect, most salespeople find it helpful to use a business card. This identifies the salesperson and his or her company. It also keeps the prospects from feeling uneasy about dealing with an unknown salesperson and company.

The first few sentences a salesperson speaks to a prospect are also considered part of the approach. They should be phrased to capture the prospect's interest.

Some salespeople begin the interview by encouraging the prospect to talk. They may begin with a general opening question such as, "What is your biggest problem in the service station business, Ms. Greene?"

Other salespeople begin their interviews by asking several questions or talking about some recent happenings in the field. The salesperson always hopes to involve the prospect and draw out his or her buying needs in the course of their discussion.

An approach is successful if it gains the interview and gets the prospect interested in listening to the salesperson. The success of an approach is often determined the moment the salesperson steps into the prospect's office. For example, a neatly dressed salesperson who greets the prospect with a smile and firm handshake will make a good first impression. Moreover, prospects are apt to favorably regard salespeople who look them directly in the eye. Salespeople who show confidence in themselves, their product, and their ability to sell are more likely to put prospects at ease and in a listening mood.

Retail Approaches

The steps in the selling process are used in all sales. However, although outside salespeople usually make their customer approach away from their own sales headquarters, most retail salespeople work in stores where their customers come to them. Thus, the retail salesperson adapts some steps of the selling process.

A salesperson in a store usually has little opportunity to prospect for customers. There is also little chance to prepare a preapproach. For the retail salesperson, the approach is the real beginning of the selling process. The retail salesperson must accomplish through the approach alone what the outside salesperson can accomplish through prospecting, the preapproach, and the approach.

Professional retail salespeople use three approaches: the greeting, the service approach, and the merchandise approach. The **greeting** is a cheerful type of retail sales approach, such as "Hello" or "Good morning." It is used when customers enter the store or the department. It acknowledges customers and tells them that the salesperson is ready to help.

The **service approach** includes such questions as "How may I assist you?" or "Would you like some help?" It replaces the lifeless cliché, "May I help you?" It offers the customer more direct help than the greeting approach. In a retail store, it takes the place of the preapproach, may come anytime during a discussion of the product, and can help the salesperson tailor the presentation to the customer's needs.

With the service approach, it is best to use openended questions such as "How may I help you?" or "What are you looking for today?" because the customer must respond with more than yes or no. Thus, it is easier for the salesperson to strike up a conversation and continue the selling process. With

■ ■ ■   *When a customer enters a store, a salesperson may use a greeting as a sales approach. What is the importance of the greeting?*

Global
M A R K E T P L A C E

Hands-on Selling

Tokyu Hands is a high-volume chain store in Japan. Salespeople are the key to Tokyu's success. They are responsible for knowledge of what is selling in their departments and how the merchandise is presented to the customer. They then buy, price, and display the merchandise, and on request will even make products from store materials to meet customers' specific needs.

"closed" questions such as "Would you like some help?" the customer's response is often "No, I'm just looking."

If a prospect says that he or she is "just looking," the professional salesperson follows up with a welcoming comment and invites the customer to ask for help later. For example, the salesperson might say, "Please take as long as you want. If you have a question or don't see what you need, just ask."

Retail salespeople should also try to get more information about customer needs. He or she might ask the customer how he or she will use the product.

The **merchandise approach** is used when customers are already focusing on the merchandise. For example, to a customer examining a rack of clothing the salesperson might say, "These silk shirts are part of our new collection. Aren't they handsome?"

The merchandise approach deals directly with what interests the customer. It gives the customer information about the product, leading right into the sales presentation.

The Sales Presentation

At the heart of the selling process is the sales presentation. During the **sales presentation**, the salesperson demonstrates or explains the product and attempts to build a desire for ownership within the prospect. This is the selling effort for which the salesperson has planned so carefully in the preapproach.

An effective sales presentation often follows this pattern. The salesperson organizes a visual and verbal sales story. Then, the salesperson involves the prospect in the presentation and, finally, concludes the presentation.

Organizing the Story

The unique characteristics of a product that make it different from other products of its type are called **product features**. Product features describe an item objectively. For example, your shoes may be made of leather. The leather is a product feature. Other features include the kind of construction, color, and type of heel.

Customers, however, are more interested in how a product will serve their needs. **Customer benefits** are the desirable effects of product features.

The salesperson must explain customer benefits because they are not always self-evident. For example, the leather in your shoes makes them long-wearing and attractive. The construction gives support, and the heel adds comfort. The color blends with many of your outfits. These benefits are the positive effects of the shoes' physical features that helped you decide to buy the product.

Explaining customer benefits is essential in marketing industrial goods as well as consumer goods. Consider the industrial salesperson selling desks to a school. The salesperson translates the desks' features into benefits for the school. Notice how the following five characteristics describe five product features and then are translated into customer benefits.

1. There are no sharp edges on the desks to cause injury or damage clothing.
2. The desks are made of the best grade of Southern pine and should last for years.
3. The desk tops have a vinyl coating to protect them against stains and scratches.
4. Each desk has a large, book-storage compartment so that the desk top need not be cluttered with books that are not in use.
5. All desks can be washed with soap and water, making upkeep easy and inexpensive.

Each of these points can be fully developed as a part of the complete sales presentation. Salespeople

New!
The medium-weight, weather-fighting SQUALL. Now the jacket for all seasons is for kids of ALL sizes.

Handy locker loop

Polarplus® lining is warmer than wool, wicks away moisture

Raglan sleeves for room to move, or to wear a sweater underneath

Thinsulate® lining adds extra warmth in the sleeves

Rugged Supplex® nylon shell resists wind and rain feels soft as cotton

Storm flap underneath zipper locks out wind

Rib-knit waistband and cuffs keep out cold air, won't "pill"

CALL US TOLL-FREE
1-800-356-4444
CHARGE YOUR ORDER

Turquoise Hot Pink Green Royal Red

Made every bit as rugged as our popular Adult Squall™ jacket. The durable 100% Supplex® nylon shell feels soft like cotton, is wind-and water-resistant. The cozy Polarplus® lining provides a surprising amount of insulation for such a lightweight fabric, feels nice against kids' skin. For added warmth, you'll find a zip-through tunnel collar to block the wind, Thinsulate® lining in the sleeves, a storm flap under the zipper. We also add all the other convenient features detailed above. Machine wash. Made in USA.

Zippered handwarmer pockets and inside pocket keep small items secure

F892

Toddler *Turquoise, Hot Pink, Royal, Red* in S 2T, M 3T, L 4T.   10036122   39.50
Little Girl *Turquoise, Hot Pink, Red* in S 4, M 5-6, L 6X.   10037128   44.50
Little Boy *Green, Royal, Red* in S 4, M 5-6, L 7.   0978912X   44.50
   Girl *Turquoise, Hot Pink, Red* in S 7-8, M 10-12, L 14.   10047122   49.50
   Boy *Green, Royal, Red* in S 8, M 10-12, L 14-16.   09790125   49.50

LANDS' END
DIRECT MERCHANTS
1 Lands' End Lane
Dodgeville, WI 53595

Bulk Rate
U.S. Postage
PAID
Lands' End, Inc.

■ ■ ■   *Notice how the product features are translated into customer benefits. Why did Lands' End do this?*

can organize product features in terms of the benefits each customer finds most important. Table 34–1 on page 440 shows the features of a nylon luggage set translated into customer benefits.

Adjusting the Presentation

An organized sales presentation is not a "canned" sales talk. That is, it is not a description of product features and benefits geared to such general audiences as newspaper readers or TV watchers whose needs are not considered.

Rather, an effective salesperson adjusts the presentation to fit each situation, amplifying or condensing certain benefits as necessary. The salesperson tries to stay aware of the prospect's needs and present the product in the way that best meets those needs. For one prospect, a simplified, three-minute talk may suffice. For another, a detailed discussion lasting much longer may be appropriate.

A good sales presentation, then, is flexible. It can be expanded or shortened to suit the sales situation. Its core consists of translating product features into customer benefits.

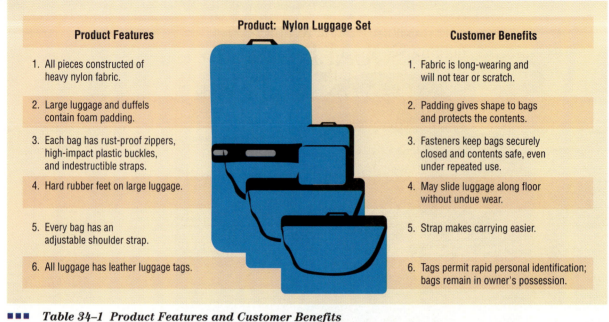

Product: Nylon Luggage Set

Product Features	Customer Benefits
1. All pieces constructed of heavy nylon fabric.	1. Fabric is long-wearing and will not tear or scratch.
2. Large luggage and duffels contain foam padding.	2. Padding gives shape to bags and protects the contents.
3. Each bag has rust-proof zippers, high-impact plastic buckles, and indestructible straps.	3. Fasteners keep bags securely closed and contents safe, even under repeated use.
4. Hard rubber feet on large luggage.	4. May slide luggage along floor without undue wear.
5. Every bag has an adjustable shoulder strap.	5. Strap makes carrying easier.
6. All luggage has leather luggage tags.	6. Tags permit rapid personal identification; bags remain in owner's possession.

■■■ **Table 34–1 Product Features and Customer Benefits**
The features of a nylon luggage set are translated into customer benefits. If the luggage featured many compartments, how might you translate this into a benefit?

Appealing to Sight and Hearing

It is estimated that people remember 20 percent of what they hear, 40 percent of what they see, and 80 percent of what they see and hear at the same time. For that reason, effective salespeople organize their presentations so that the prospect sees and hears the benefits at the same time.

They may do this by demonstrating the product. They may also use charts, posters, videos, or models to help the prospect see as well as hear the sales message. Visual aids allow salespeople to dramatize their presentations. Most prospects appreciate a factual and eye-catching presentation.

Bringing Prospects into the Presentation

Good sales presentations involve prospects as much as possible. This gives prospects a chance to sell themselves on the product. After they have seen and heard the product benefits, they have a natural urge to handle the product. This is why automobile salespeople often invite prospects to drive a car rather than simply look at it in the showroom. This is also why a manufacturers' representative may ask a store buyer to touch the fabric of his or her new line of winter coats. Some salespeople place a product in the prospect's home for a free trial period—sometimes up to 30 days—enabling the prospect to experience the feel of ownership.

Concluding with Extras

Most salespeople like to conclude their presentation with some "extras" that make a product more appealing. For example, to convince a prospect to buy a product that is totally new to him or her, the salesperson might say, "Best of all, Mr. Miller, these desks are guaranteed for one full year." To convince the prospect of the product's high quality, the salesperson might say, "An independent testing laboratory has given these desks an exceptionally high rating."

To reassure the prospect of the manufacturer's good reputation, the salesperson may point out, "The General Furniture Company will stand behind this product." Finally, the salesperson may use a testimonial as an extra by saying, "Ten other school districts in the area are using this school furniture."

Handling Objections

An **objection** is an honest difference between the customer and the salesperson. Suppose Mr. Miller tells the desk salesperson, "The desks look sturdy, but we don't know whether the school can afford them right now." His comment about the expense is an objection.

Experienced salespeople are prepared to answer objections. Objections tell the salesperson that the prospect is listening and is interested in the product. They give the salesperson a chance to judge how near the prospect is to committing to the sale.

Some sales executives think of objections as negative questions. After all, objections may be based on fear, uncertainty, or misunderstanding. In the case of fear or uncertainty, the salesperson will attempt to dispel any doubt that is causing the prospect to hesitate before buying. When Mr. Miller said, "I like your product, but I don't think the school can afford it right now," the salesperson could respond by stressing the benefits of immediate ownership. Then, he or she could explain the various credit plans by which the product could be purchased.

If the objection is based on a misunderstanding, the salesperson listens to the prospect carefully and repeats the objection to show that it is understood. Then, the salesperson proceeds to remove the misunderstanding.

For example, the prospect might say, "I like your product, but your delivery service is too slow." The salesperson could respond by mentioning the new warehouse that makes a faster delivery possible. The salesperson could even call the warehouse from the prospect's office and find out how soon the order could be delivered to the prospect.

The Close

The **close** is the completion of the sale. It is the main purpose of the selling process. Much has been written about the right psychological moment to close a sale. The experienced salesperson begins the close after thoroughly presenting the product and overcoming all objections. The salesperson can usually judge by the prospect's mood when it is the right time to close the sale. The close of the sale is often signaled by customer approval of the product benefits.

Avoid Pressure

Salespeople should avoid closing with a statement as blunt as "Do you want to buy?" This will make the prospect feel pressured. Instead, the salesperson should say, "I know you need and want this truck now, Mrs. Wood. I believe I can get you delivery next week if I can have your purchase order now."

In retailing, to help customers reach a decision, salespeople may ask, "Will you be charging this TV set or paying cash?" Or, with fashion goods, a salesperson could say, "How do you want these shirts monogrammed, Mr. Morgan?" This type of close assumes that the prospect wants to buy.

Call Again

The salesperson who is making a first call on an important prospect does not necessarily expect to close the sale on that visit. The chief purpose of the visit is to learn more about the prospect and his or her needs.

On the second and succeeding calls, the salesperson will be in a stronger position to present the product's benefits based on the prospect's needs. A salesperson who sells technical equipment such as computer systems may call on one company for several years before trying to close the sale.

Suggest Additional Purchases

After closing the sale, the efficient salesperson moves on to suggestion selling. **Suggestion selling** is the selling of related or additional items along with those items the customer has already purchased.

Suggestion selling increases sales while serving customers by calling attention to another needed item or special value. It is not uncommon for more to be sold in suggestion selling than in the original sale. Yet, many salespeople underestimate or overlook this important part of selling. Experts know that it is much easier to sell more to a person who is already a customer than it is to start a new sale. Customers, too, often appreciate additional items that will make the original purchase more useful. For example, a salesperson may suggest film to a customer buying a camera.

Principles into Practice

Hanson Galleries Follows Through

Nearly everyone has some discretionary income, that is, money they may spend as they please. Some people have a great deal of it and countless ways to spend it: more clothes, a larger home, antiques and art objects, travel or an expensive automobile are just a few possibilities.

The question is, how do salespeople capture that discretionary income? And more importantly, how do they keep that discretionary income continually flowing their way? Here is how one business, Hanson Galleries of Sausalito, California, does it.

Hanson Galleries sells $25 million in art a year from eight retail stores. The average sales slip amounts to around $4,200. The core of Hanson's selling strategy is to turn customers into art collectors. In doing this, clients become enthusiastic and knowledgeable about what they are doing, and collecting becomes a pastime.

In order to turn one-time customers into clients, Hanson Galleries focuses on attitude and follow-up. The gallery trains every salesperson to be an art consultant. Salespeople are informed of all of the artists' works and their backgrounds. They use this knowledge to interest customers in collecting art and create the attitude in customers that they can become knowledgeable collectors. In addition, salespeople are encouraged to learn as much as they can about their customers in order to determine each customer's buying needs.

All salespeople spend part of their time on the selling floor working with customers in the store. They spend the balance of their time following-up with customers on the telephone, informing them about new works of art. For this work, the average salesperson can expect to sell a half million dollars in art over the course of a year. Here's what Hanson Galleries gives its clients to help them become collectors:

1. *Education.* Salespeople tell clients who are interested in an artist's work, about that artist's other works, background, and ranking with other artists. Catalogs, videos, and conversations help clients become aware of art works. Education helps to increase customer interest in the works of art.

2. *Protection.* Buying a big-ticket item can be a risk. The gallery's guarantee to take back a work significantly lowers the buyer's fear of the investment. What is the risk of owning an artwork if the gallery will exchange it or take it back?

3. *Expectation.* People tend to buy in certain patterns. For example, a customer may expect to buy only one piece of art. When customers become collectors, their expectations change. They want to build their collections and become interested in acquiring more art.

4. *Satisfaction.* The customer must be pleased with the purchase and want to enjoy more art. The salesperson works to keep the customer satisfied by offering new information, invitations to gallery showings, and new works of art.

The selling strategy seems to work for Hanson Galleries. While new customers account for half of its business, the other half comes from its existing client collectors.[2]

1. How does Hanson Galleries get its clients to acquire art?
2. How does Hanson Galleries create repeat clients?

The Departure and Follow-up

When the sale is completed, the salesperson should thank the customer and leave. The departure should be neither too abrupt nor too drawn out.

Before leaving, the salesperson should give the customer assurance of rapid delivery, dependable service, and whatever else was promised. Even when no sale has been made, the salesperson should show appreciation for the prospect's time and attention.

A good salesperson is always interested in future business and sales. A customer can be a continuing source of business. So a salesperson should maintain good customer relations for future calls.

A good salesperson meets the terms of the sale. He or she does not promise the customer anything that cannot be delivered. When the salesperson concludes the sale, the job is not yet done. Details must be followed through so that the customer gets exactly what was ordered.

The departure and follow-up are the end of one selling process and the beginning of the next. Here, the salesperson concludes the sale and delivers the goods and services as promised.

After each call, the professional salesperson examines the reasons for success or failure. After all, the salesperson wants to return to the customer for future sales or to improve the chances of making an initial sale. This leads back to preapproach homework and starts another cycle of sales activity. With each of these cycles, the salesperson becomes more accomplished.

How the Telephone Is Used in Selling

A great deal of selling is done by telemarketing. In addition, salespeople use the telephone to inform customers about new products, price changes, special discounts, etc.

Wholesale salespeople call their retail customers to tell them certain merchandise is available or to find out how various goods are moving and whether they should be reordered. A manufacturers' representative may call customers to tell them about a successful product, inform them of a new one, or advise them of a special purchase offer.

Often, businesses hire telephone salespeople only to take customers' orders. These salespeople are responsible for accurately transmitting customers' requests, and for suggesting items they may have overlooked and unadvertised "specials" the organization may be promoting. (For example, Sears, Roebuck & Company markets service contracts on its washing machines and dryers over the telephone.) Obviously, the same principles of selling apply to order takers as they do to other salespeople.

Some stores, such as Nordstrom, encourage salespeople to keep card files on their customers and to call them when new merchandise arrives. Other stores encourage customers to use the telephone-shopping service—a form of inbound telemarketing—in which trained switchboard operators accept orders from customers who make selections from ads or catalogs.

The telephone is also used in selling for the following purposes:

- to build a strong prospect list;
- to make appointments;
- to service regular customers;
- to acknowledge orders;
- to close a sale;
- to revive old accounts;
- to notify customers of special events;
- to handle complaints;
- to take orders;
- to sell to new customers; and
- to follow up on customers after a sale to assure that they are satisfied with the purchase.

CHAPTER NOTES

1. Adapted from Ralph L. Woods, ed., *The Modern Handbook of Humor* (New York, 1967), pp. 34, 35.
2. Tom Richman, "Come Again," *INC.*, April 1989, p. 177

Chapter Summary

- Most sales follow a sequence of seven steps: prospecting, the preapproach, the approach, the sales presentation, handling objections, the close, and the departure and follow-up.

- Prospecting is the process of finding potential customers.

- The preapproach involves gathering and analyzing information about prospects and is useful in constructing the sales presentation.

- The approach is intended to get an interview and make a sales presentation.

- For in-store salespeople, the approach and preapproach are combined to welcome customers and discover their needs.

- The sales presentation is at the heart of the selling process. Skillful salespeople present the product features in terms of customer benefits; acknowledge objections as honest differences of opinion; and answer objections based on detailed product knowledge and insight into customer needs.

- The close of the sale is often signaled by customer approval of the product benefits.

- At the close of the sale, the salesperson makes use of suggestion selling. In addition, the salesperson is responsible for follow-up, arranging delivery if necessary, and determining customer satisfaction. Follow-up can lead to determining further customer needs and beginning the selling cycle again.

- Marketing businesses are using the telephone increasingly for selling, to build prospects, make appointments, and service customers.

Building Your Marketing Vocabulary

On a separate sheet of paper, define each of the following marketing terms. Then write a paragraph on personal selling for each group of terms below.

prospecting—endless chain method—
   cold canvass approach
preapproach—approach

greeting—service approach—
   merchandise approach
sales presentation—product features—
   customer benefits
objection—close—suggestion selling

Questions for Review

1. Name the seven steps of a sale.
2. Why is *prospecting* important in selling?
3. What are two methods of prospecting?
4. What is accomplished in the preapproach?
5. How does the service approach differ from the greeting?
6. What is the pattern of an effective sales presentation?
7. Why is it important for the salesperson to talk about customer benefits instead of product features?
8. What is an objection?
9. What is one way salespeople can judge when to close a sale?
10. Explain how a manufacturers' representative can use the telephone to increase sales.

Critical Thinking

1. Offering one good canned sales presentation would be much simpler and less costly than having to learn each customer's needs. Why can't salespeople use just one sales message for all customers?
2. With what types of products might you use the cold canvass approach to prospect for customers?
3. Suppose you see that a customer in your store is looking at a camera. What type of approach would you use with this customer? What exactly would you say to the customer?
4. You are selling a bicycle that features 12 speeds, mountain terrain tires, a padded seat, and instant-grip brakes. How might you translate these features into benefits?
5. After you have sold the bike, how might you employ suggestion selling?

Discussion Questions

1. Some say that customer objections signal the end of a sales presentation and that the salesperson might just as well give up. Do you agree or disagree? Why?

2. Salespeople sometimes find the close of the sales presentation difficult to handle. Give three examples showing a salesperson how to close a sale effectively.

3. All customers are important to a business and therefore all should be treated equally. Do you agree or disagree? Why?

4. How do you feel about telemarketing as a means of selling? Have you ever received a call from a telemarketer? Discuss reasons why you believe the call was or was not effective.

5. Discuss particular instances in which you were either encouraged or discouraged to buy something because of the salesperson. At what step in the selling process was the salesperson most encouraging or discouraging? If you were discouraged to buy, how would you suggest the salesperson improve his or her selling technique?

Marketing Project

Giving a Sales Presentation

Project Goal: Given a product requiring personal selling, define a customer's needs and tailor a sales presentation to highlight particular benefits. Give the presentation to your class.

Directions: Select a product such as a camera, radio, recorder, or toy. Prepare a form like the one that follows and list the product in the left column. In the center column, list the parts of the sales presentation: (a) organizing the story, (b) appealing to sight and hearing, (c) bringing the prospect into the presentation, and (d) concluding with extras. In the right column, list the key selling points for each part of the presentation. Use this material as the basis for delivering an oral sales presentation to your class.

Product	Parts of Presentation	Key Selling Points
Example: Camera	Organizing the story	Translate the camera's features into customer benefits.

Applied Academics

Language Arts

1. Develop a sales presentation rating sheet. List the seven steps of the sale. Next, visit three different stores in your community. Rate the salesperson on his or her sales presentation. Report on how the salesperson handled each step of the sales process.

Science

2. Choose a product such as a camera, computer, or printing press, and research how this product works. Prepare an illustration that shows how your product works. Using the illustration, describe your product to the class.

Marketing and Multiculturalism

Selling to multiethnic communities is a great challenge to marketers. A common misconception is that all those belonging to an ethnic group are alike. This is not true. Not all Hispanics share the same food preferences. Not all Asians share the same holidays, calendars, religions, or languages. In order to meet the needs of a wide variety of ethnic groups, salespeople must research carefully and never assume they know a market because they've interviewed one or two people from a specific ethnic group.

1. How could stereotyping an ethnic group harm a salesperson during the preapproach phase of the sales process?

2. How can a salesperson avoid stereotyping a customer?

445

The Walt Disney Company: Marketing a Mouse

Entertainment is a major industry in the United States. The Walt Disney Company is a pioneer and leader in the U.S. entertainment industry. Founded more than 60 years ago by Walt Disney, the company first became famous for its unforgettable cartoon characters Donald Duck, Goofy, Pluto, and Mickey Mouse. Throughout the 1940s, 50s, and 60s, the organization flourished. Nevertheless, in the 1970s after Walt Disney died, the company seemed to lose its strong direction and was almost sold. In the mid-1980s, however, a team headed by entertainment industry giant Michael Eisner took over the company and gave it new life.

Today, The Walt Disney Company is a diversified international organization that owns theme parks and resorts, produces films, and creates consumer products. Disneyland, Disney World, and the Tokyo Disneyland

are the most visited theme parks in the world. The Walt Disney Company produces films, television programs, and videos. Disney toys and clothing are available in retail stores and through mail-order catalogs.

Like most profitable businesses, a major economic goal of The Walt Disney Company is to increase the wealth of its owners (the stockholders, in this case) by increasing earnings and using capital wisely. Disney uses promotion to achieve its goal.

The original Disney theme park is Disneyland in Anaheim, California. Here, Disney celebrated Mickey Mouse's 60th birthday. Hollywood stars attended the birthday party on Main Street. For almost six months, daily parades and shows celebrated the occasion. Other Disneyland promotions included a send-off for the Olympic athletes, a celebration of '50s music, and a hula-hoop contest of 1,000 people "hooping it up" for a mention in the *Guiness Book of World Records*. Other birthday promotions included a visit by Mickey Mouse to the United Nations in New York; advertising supplements in *Time*, *Fortune*, and *People* magazines; and, with Delta Airlines, flying in 10,000 disadvantaged children from nine countries to Disneyland and Disney World as guests on Mickey's actual birthday.

The opening of the Disney-MGM Studios at Disney World in Orlando, Florida, was another major event. Hundreds of travel editors and journalists were invited to visit as guests of the Disney Company and were treated to previews of the new attractions. Their resulting articles described the new attraction and its features, such as rides through famous movie sets.

The Walt Disney Company now has theme parks in Japan and France. In Japan, 60 million people (half of Japan's population) visit the park annually.

The Disney Company produces and distributes film and television products for the theatrical, television, and home video markets. Some of its biggest film hits include *Who Framed Roger Rabbit?*, *The Little Mermaid*, and *Good Morning, Vietnam*. The company also produces original television shows for network and syndicated markets. "The Magical World of Disney," "The Golden Girls," and "Empty Nest" are perhaps some of its best-known programs. Its home video successes include *Cinderella*.

The company operates a pay television service called the Disney Channel. It has more than 4 million subscribers.

J.G. Hook creates and markets the Mickey & Co. line of designer clothing under a licensing agreement. Disney now represents about 12 percent of all licensed character merchandise in the world.

The Disney Company also uses direct-mail to sell more than 200 items, including toys, videos, and baby clothes. Disney licenses and distributes these products throughout the world.

Other recent endeavors include The Disney Stores. These stores are retail outlets for the company's merchandise. They also promote Disney film releases, sell tickets to the theme parks, and show activities of the entire company on television monitors. Shoppers can place orders with The Disney Channel and Disney Catalog on telephones conveniently located in the store.

1. From this case study, cite an example of each of the following promotional activities: advertising, publicity, sales promotion, and public relations.

2. Give an example of how one area of The Walt Disney Company can effectively promote other areas.

3. As a promotion manager for Disney, state a major promotional goal for the Walt Disney Company for the coming year and create three examples of promotional activities in a different area (advertising, publicity, sales promotion, and public relations) that would carry out this goal.[1,2,3,4,5,6,7,8]

CASE NOTES

1. The Walt Disney Company 1988 Annual Report.

2. Judith Graham, "Disney Wishes on Retail, Catalog Stars," *Advertising Age*, 28 November 1988, p. 46.

3. Wayne Walley, "Adman of the Year Michael Eisner," *Advertising Age*, 28 November, pp. 1 and 23.

4. Stephen Meye, "The New Frontier," *Advertising Age*, pp. 27—29.

5. Charles Leerhsen, "How Disney Does It," *Newsweek*, 3 April 1989, pp. 43–54.

6. Kenneth R. Clark, "The Battle for Dreamland," *Chicago Tribune*, 26 April 1989. sec. 5, pp. 1 and 2.

7. Jeffrey Schmalz, "Reinventing Hollywood at Disney World," *New York Times*, 4 June 1984, pp. 8 and 9.

8. Jeffrey Schmalz, "Movie Theme Park Fight: Nastiness Is Not a Fantasy," *New York Times*, 13 August 1989, pp. 1 and 15.

Marketing Management

Chapter 35

Managing the Marketing Mix

Terms to Know

marketing plan
situation analysis
   (SWOT)
marketing audit
management

planning
organizing
directing
controlling

Chapter Objectives

After studying this chapter, you will be able to:

- describe the activities and guidelines found in a marketing plan;
- explain how the marketing plan helps a company's success;
- identify and describe the four functions of management;
- discuss the responsibilities of the members of a marketing staff; and
- prepare a short-range marketing plan, including the goals to be achieved.

Case Study

Building a Marketing Plan

John Fenters began working at the Sun & Ski Sporting Goods Store during his junior year in high school. After graduation and a brief stint studying business at the local community college, John returned to Sun & Ski as a full-time sales associate.

Sun & Ski had been in business for about five years, successfully marketing sporting goods, trophies, some apparel (primarily athletic jackets, ski outfits, sweatshirts, and sweatpants), recreational equipment, and snow and water skis. After John had been working for about three months, the owners of Sun & Ski asked him to organize and manage a new department. To complement the current product mix, the owners decided to add an athletic shoe department.

To successfully establish and manage this new department, John had to answer these questions:

- What brands of athletic shoes should I carry?

- How many brands should I carry and in what quantities?
- What kinds of related merchandise should I offer (athletic socks? running shorts?)?
- What price ranges should I stock?
- Which vendors should I use?
- Where should the new department be located in the store? How should the shoes be displayed?
- How should the new department be advertised?
- How many additional employees should I hire?

In effect, John was asked to manage the marketing mix for a new department. To do so, he first developed a marketing plan for the new athletic shoe department. He then relied on his knowledge (and lots of help from the owner) of the functions of management to implement and evaluate the marketing plan.

The Marketing Plan

Marketing management involves much more than assembling the four parts of the marketing mix. The four Ps—product, place, price, and promotion—must be creatively blended so the firm develops the best mix for its target markets. Managers typically do this by developing a *marketing plan*. A **marketing plan** is a written statement of the marketing goals and strategies for a particular firm, department, or product line. It generally states the marketing goals that are to be achieved within a certain time period and the strategies that will be used.

The marketing plan usually identifies the amount of time each goal and strategy should take and the amount of money each will cost. Marketing plans also include strategies for measuring the plan's effectiveness. In short, a marketing plan typically tries to answer four questions (see Figure 35–1 on page 452):

- Where are we?
- Where are we going?
- How are we going to get there?
- How will we know we've arrived?

Importance of a Marketing Plan

Manufacturers, wholesalers, and retailers all need marketing plans. A company, a department, or even a specific brand such as Nike shoes cannot hope to succeed simply by putting its products on the market.

The company, for example, must know what customers want and what competitors are offering. It must develop new products and improve older products. It must seek out new markets for its products. It must also convince customers that these products will meet their needs. A marketing plan is the best way for a company to coordinate its activities and judge its progress.

Where are we?

Where are we going?

How are we going to get there?

Promotion? Price?

Place? Product?

How will we know when we've arrived?

■ ■ ■ *Figure 35–1 Four Questions of a Marketing Plan*
A marketing plan tries to answer four questions. Why are these questions important?

Elements of a Marketing Plan

A marketing plan consists of an organization's current situation, goals, strategies, and control or evaluation. As a first step in developing the marketing plan, managers typically assess the current situation. They provide data and information to serve as a basis for setting goals and developing strategies.

Managers use goals to describe where they want the company, the department, or the product line to be. Goals typically describe anticipated sales, profit expectations, and market share.

Strategies tell how the company will reach its goals. Strategies consist of specific activities the company or department plans to undertake. For example, strategies may include the specific market research to be conducted, the specific location in the store for a new product line, or the specific ad to be featured in the newspaper.

The plan is controlled by periodic progress checks. Are the strategies being carried out on time? Is the company approaching its goals? Usually the plan must be adjusted in response to marketplace results.

A marketing plan for a large business is nearly always a formal, written document. Every key executive, all members of the marketing department, and the key people in the company's advertising agency should know the plan. Only when the plan is written can everyone be completely informed of and participate in the strategies to follow.

For a small department like Athletic Shoes at Sun & Ski, a marketing plan is usually informal. It may not even be written out. However, the few people carrying out the plan know the details through frequent discussions and contact.

Situation Analysis

Situation analysis is usually the first section of the marketing plan. **Situation analysis**, or **SWOT**, involves the examination of a company's strengths (S), weaknesses (W), opportunities (O), and threats (T). SWOT provides data and information that underlie specific goals and strategies for the marketing plan.

Examples of a marketing unit's strengths (S) might include a good price, reasonable profit, and a well-trained sales force. An example of a weakness (W) might be an inconvenient location or the lack of a complete product line, such as Sun & Ski's situation in the Case Study at the beginning of this chapter. Opportunities (O) include areas for marketing possibilities in which the company could enjoy a competitive advantage. Sun & Ski's analysis showed a good opportunity for increased sales and profits by adding a line of athletic shoes. Finally, threats (T) include any activities that could have a negative effect on the business. Examples include strong competition that might cause the business or product to fail, a decline in potential consumers' purchasing power, or a misreading of consumer preferences for the product.

Statement of Goals

The next major section of the marketing plan establishes the goals. In large firms, the board of directors and chief executive generally set these goals or objectives. They usually base their decisions on the marketing staff's advice and suggestions.

Goals typically include specific figures and dates for completion. For example, a manufacturer of small appliances might set the following goals for the upcoming year:

- a 5 percent increase of the total market share, from 25 percent to 30 percent;
- a 10 percent increase in dollar sales;
- a 5 percent increase in the number of all products sold;
- a 10 percent increase in the number of blenders sold;
- a 15 percent increase in the number of coffeemakers sold; and
- a $200,000 profit on first-year sales of a new food processor.

Strategies

The next part of the marketing plan describes strategies for achieving the goals. It details the tasks and duties of the individuals or departments involved in the marketing effort and explains how each will contribute to the company's goals.

Like goals, strategies must have a completion schedule. The schedule gives the time in which the marketing plan will be put to work and says when the activities in it will take place. As you can see, a marketing plan provides the calendar for controlling a company's marketing activities and for measuring its progress.

There are both short-range and long-range marketing plans. A short-range plan covers a company's activities for a relatively short period of time— usually one year. It is the basis of day-to-day operations and may contain quite a bit of detail about the operations.

A long-range plan, however, covers a long time— often from five to ten years. Although the long-range plan is not as detailed as the short-range plan, it is often harder to come up with because market

Global MARKETPLACE

The Global Marketing Mix Makeup

Global marketing means managing the marketing mix in each of the nations to which you may sell products. Revlon International, the giant cosmetics manufacturer, switched in 1993 to one worldwide marketing campaign designed to give Revlon even more of a global identity. The same models and campaign slogans are used, thus standardizing print ads around the globe. Revlon is also expanding its worldwide distribution and pursuing former Soviet Union markets. Its goal is to increase worldwide sales.[1]

conditions are likely to change. Short-range marketing strategies for the appliance manufacturer mentioned earlier might include:

- surveying owners of coffeemakers to determine the most desirable features by June;
- developing a nationwide promotion and demonstration campaign for the company's new food processor by August;
- adding 20 new retail dealers in the Midwest in time for Christmas sales; and
- offering price reductions to new retail dealers nationwide this fall.

Long-term strategies might include:

- creating a line of fashionable coffeemakers, grinders, and accessories for sale in two years;
- establishing a catalog sales channel to introduce products in the West by next summer; and
- increasing prices to match a new advertised image over the next three years.

Evaluation

Marketers periodically evaluate their strategies and goals. In this process they can assess the performance of their company and their staff. Goals and strategies can be adjusted or changed. Mistakes can be corrected.

For instance, our appliance manufacturer might discover a booming demand for coffeemakers and speed up plans to introduce new products. Profits may be high enough to allow an extension of the discount to new retailers. The food processor campaign may have fizzled, leading the manufacturer to change its advertising agency.

Marketing goals and strategies can quickly go out of date. Thus, most companies periodically evaluate their marketing efforts as outlined on the marketing plan. Companies sometimes do this through a **marketing audit**—a comprehensive and systematic review of the various goals and strategies used in marketing.

The marketing audit covers all the major marketing areas of a business, not just trouble spots or those deemed unsuccessful. Marketing audits are usually conducted by an objective, experienced person or team of individuals outside the company. Auditors usually review sales figures, income statements, balance sheets, and other financial documents. They also interview customers, employees, managers, and vendors. Anyone or any data that helps auditors review marketing performance is usually fair game in a marketing audit.

A Sample Marketing Plan

After much discussion with the owners and customers at Sun & Ski, John decided to offer three brands of athletic shoes: Nike, Adidas, and Reebok. He also decided to offer athletic socks, gym shorts, and athletic shirts as related merchandise.

John then developed a marketing plan for his new department. A few items from the first draft of his short-range marketing plan are displayed in Table 35–1.

The Functions of Marketing Management

The owners of Sun & Ski asked John to implement and evaluate the marketing plan. They also gave him the title of manager for the new athletic shoe department.

Management is generally defined as the activities undertaken by one or more people to coordinate the activities of other people in order to achieve results. The primary purpose of all managerial work is the accomplishment of goals and strategies through the activities of other people. Thus, John can only achieve his goals by coordinating the activities of employees, vendors, advertising specialists, creditors, and others.

Successful managers typically engage in four management duties or functions: *planning, organizing, directing*, and *controlling*. Let's take a look at each function.

Planning

Careful planning is a key to effectively managing a company or a department. **Planning** involves setting goals and then choosing strategies that must be performed to attain the goals. Through their

	Goals	Strategies
Sales	1. Sell $100,000 of athletic shoes during the year. 2. Sell $15,000 in related merchandise by end of year.	1. Establish the new department, including three brands of shoes and selected socks, athletic shirts, and running shorts by July 1. 2. Locate stock in right, center area of store with large department sign. Post six related signs throughout the store. 3. Create three raised platform displays around department. 4. Create two window displays by July 1 with signs.
Market Share	1. Obtain 3 percent of the area's market by December 31; 5 percent by the end of one year of operation. 2. Obtain 20 percent of the age segment, 15-25, by the end of one year.	1. Obtain feature story for new department in local paper by July 15. 2. Run weekly ads in local and school newspapers; total ad allocation = $10,000. 3. Send direct-mail letter to all area schools' track and cross country teams, members of health clubs, and store's current charge customers.
Profitability	1. Obtain an 8 percent profit on all shoe sales by the end of the year. 2. Obtain a 6 percent profit on the sale of all related items by the end of the year.	1. Keep retail reductions at 10 percent. 2. Control expenses to 30 percent of sales. 3. Avoid markdowns, but offer 10 percent discounts to all school-sponsored athletic teams and the store's current charge customers.

■ ■ ■ *Table 35–1 Athletic Shoes Marketing Plan for Sun & Ski*
This table lists the short-range marketing plan for Sun & Ski. What is one way Sun & Ski plans to obtain an 8 percent net profit on all shoe sales by year's end?

plans, managers outline exactly what the company or the department must do to be successful.

Good marketing managers typically spend considerable time and effort in planning for the future. In fact, some experts indicate that as much as one-third of a manager's time at work should be devoted to planning.

Organizing

Organizing is the process of assigning the tasks developed during planning to various individuals or groups within the company or department. Through careful organization, managers decide when, how, and by whom the activities are to be completed.

People within the firm or department are given work assignments that should help achieve the goals outlined during planning. Tasks are organized so that the work of these individuals helps achieve the goals.

In John's situation, he will need to work with his co-workers to outline their duties. He will need to assign tasks to employees such as checking in the new stock, putting the athletic shoes on display, creating merchandise signs, developing advertisements, and selling the shoes.

Principles into Practice

Managing for Excellence

One of the best-selling business books is *In Search of Excellence—Lessons from America's Best-run Companies*. The authors, Thomas J. Peters and Robert H. Waterman, Jr., wrote about 50 American firms that they considered to be excellent, well-managed companies. The companies included such familiar names as McDonald's, Delta Airlines, Marriott Corporation, IBM, Texas Instruments, General Foods, Frito-Lay, Kmart, and Disney Productions.

From studying the literature on these companies and from personal interviews with key managers in each firm, Peters and Waterman identified eight basic principles of management and marketing that were fundamental in helping these companies achieve their goals.

1. *A bias for action.* Excellent companies share a "do it, try it, fix it" preference for action to accomplish goals and strategies and to help solve customers' problems quickly and efficiently.

2. *Staying close to the customer.* Excellent companies listen to and analyze customers, learn their preferences, and cater to them. They are committed to customer service, product quality, and dependability.

3. *Autonomy and entrepreneurship.* Excellent companies break the big company into smaller "companies" and encourage managers and employees to think independently and competitively. Leadership and innovation are rewarded in excellent companies.

4. *Productivity through people.* Managers know how to motivate employees. They believe in their employees and create in them the awareness that their best efforts are essential and will be rewarded.

5. *Hands-on, value-driven leadership.* Top management understands what the company is all about and strives to create an exciting work environment through personal attention, persistence, and direct intervention.

6. *Stick to the knitting.* Excellent companies stick with the essential mission of the company and focus on the goods, services, and markets they know best.

7. *Simple organization form and a lean staff.* Organization structures tend to have few administrative layers and relatively few people at top management. These companies thereby trust all employees to make good decisions.

8. *Simultaneous dedication to company values and tolerance for employees who accept those values.* Excellent companies foster a climate where there is dedication to the central or core values of the company (for example, customer service and product quality) combined with tolerance for all employees who uphold those values.[2,3]

Are there companies in your community—perhaps even the company at which you work—that seem to adhere to some or all of Peters and Waterman's eight principles for excellence? Describe the firm and tell how the company adheres to one or more principle.

■■■ *As manager, John constantly observes customer interest in the products. What type of management function is he engaging in?*

Directing

Directing is the process of guiding people's activities to accomplish the goals. Sometimes this management function is referred to as leading, motivating, or influencing. Managers direct activities by issuing assignments, helping people break down major jobs into smaller tasks, training their employees on new products and procedures, and motivating people to accomplish the goals.

Controlling

Controlling, the evaluation function of management, is measuring performance and comparing it to expected standards. Controlling is an ongoing process.

Managers constantly gather and assess information. They then modify the goals or strategies. They correct mistakes. They retrain employees. They take any other necessary corrective action.

In John's situation, he will constantly check sales figures and compare actual sales with projected sales. He may observe the apparent interest in his shoes from prospective customers as they look at his displays. He will probably observe his sales staff as they assist with customer purchases. He may find that he needs to modify his sales projections. He may want to rearrange his shoe displays. Or, he may need to train his salespeople in suggestion selling.

In effect, then, marketing managers manage the marketing mix. They plan, organize, direct, and exercise control over product, place, price, and promotion. They accomplish all of this by coordinating the activities of other people. This concept is illustrated in Figure 35–2.

■■■ *Figure 35–2 Managing the Marketing Mix*
Marketing managers manage the marketing mix. What aspects of the marketing mix must they manage?

CHAPTER NOTES

1. Pat Sloan, "Revlon Eyes Global Image," *Advertising Age,* 11 January 1993, p. 1.

2. Thomas J. Peters and Robert H. Waterman, Jr., *In Search of Excellence* (Warner Books, 1982).

3. P. "Rajan" Varadarajan, "Pathways to Corporate Excellence in Retailing," *Retailing Issues Letter,* Texas A & M University, College Station, February 1989.

Chapter Summary

- Effective marketing managers blend all elements of the marketing mix by creating a marketing plan.

- The marketing plan consists of the current situation, goals, strategies, and evaluation activities to answer such questions as: Where are we? Where are we going? How are we going to get there? and How will we know we've arrived?

- Successful managers achieve their goals through the activities of other people by planning, organizing, directing, and evaluating (or controlling) those activities.

Building Your Marketing Vocabulary

On a separate sheet of paper, define each of the following marketing terms. Then use each term in a sentence on how to manage the marketing mix.

marketing plan	planning
situation analysis (SWOT)	organizing
	directing
marketing audit	controlling
management	

Questions for Review

1. What is a marketing plan?
2. What four questions does a marketing plan typically try to answer?
3. What is usually included in the marketing plan?
4. Why should a marketing plan be in written form? Are marketing plans always written?
5. What does situation analysis involve?
6. Explain the difference between a short-range and a long-range marketing plan.
7. What is the purpose of a marketing audit?
8. Identify and describe each of the four functions of marketing management.

Critical Thinking

1. How does a marketing plan help a company practice the marketing concept?
2. How can a marketing plan help control a business?
3. Why is it so important for marketing managers to spend considerable time in planning?
4. As a marketing manager for an ice cream company, state two goals you would include in your marketing plan for the upcoming year.
5. State the strategies you might use to achieve the goals you named in question 4.
6. Explain how your goals and strategies named in questions 4 and 5 might be adjusted during the evaluation stage.

Discussion Questions

1. Discuss why a marketing plan helps companies to succeed.
2. Discuss why a marketing plan alone will not guarantee success.
3. Discuss what skills and traits are needed to make a good marketing manager.
4. Discuss questions you would have to get answered in order to successfully manage a children's clothing store.
5. What do you think are the key principles that make an excellent company? Which of these principles do you find most important? Why? Cite examples of companies that adhere to these principles.

Marketing Project

Organizing a Marketing Plan

Project Goal: Given a business that markets a specific product, develop a marketing plan for the business. Describe the situation and specify your goals, strategies for achieving the goals, and evaluation methods. Provide specific details as appropriate.

Directions: Assume that you manage a compact-disc store. Your chief competitors are the CD departments in six department and discount stores. Your present share of the market is 25 percent. Marketing research has indicated that you need to aim your promotions at the teenage market segment. There are about 10,000 teenagers in your market area. Your present expenses and profit rate are satisfactory. Your major goal is to have 35 percent of the market one year from now.

Prepare a marketing plan for your compact-disc store, including the following elements: situational analysis, which includes the above information and any other information you can gather on the teenage market for CDs in your community; your goals, including expected share of the market and anticipated sales volume, expenses, and profit; your marketing strategies for achieving these goals, including a completion schedule; and your evaluation methods. Your evaluation methods should include how you would monitor the effects of two strategies and how you would judge the achievement of two goals.

Suggestions: Re-study the chapter to refresh your memory on what a marketing plan contains and why it is prepared. Here are various types of actions to consider in gathering data for your marketing plan.

1. Send a questionnaire to or interview teenagers in your market area. Find out what CDs they buy, how much they pay for them, and where they presently shop.
2. Check out your competition. What threats are posed by competition? What's missing that might provide a marketing opportunity?
3. Review your prices and price lines to see if a change in prices would appeal to teenagers.
4. Run advertisements with coupons to be turned in for CD discounts. Ask market information questions to be answered on the coupons.
5. Decide on special promotions that would appeal to teenagers, such as sponsoring a dance at school or giving away free CDs to introduce other teenagers to your compact disc store.
6. Consider other actions you think would work.

Applied Academics

Language Arts

1. Interview an employed family member about his or her company or use your own personal work experience. Use SWOT analysis to find out about the company's marketing plan. Write a 250-word paper on your findings.

Math

2. If the goal of a marketing plan for a small gift shop is to increase its greeting card sales by 5 percent during the next year, what would the targeted dollar sales be if this year's total sales amounted to $54,000? How many more cards would need to be sold during the next year in order to reach the targeted dollar amount if the average price of each greeting card is $1.25?

Social Studies

3. Interview a businessperson in your community to determine the goals that the company would like to acheive and the strategies his or her company will use to get there. Report your findings to the class.

Marketing and Multiculturalism

Bunuelitos, the first cereal designed for the Hispanic market in the United States, will also be the first product conceived and developed by the General Mills Special Markets group. This new unit was established to work with all General Mills brands on ethnic products. General Mills developed this idea based on research that showed that 75 percent of Hispanic households buy cold cereal and found that they prefer presweetened products. Bunuelitos will be similar to the already popular Kix but will be sweetened with cinnamon and honey.

1. Why would a marketing plan help General Mills undertake marketing this new product?
2. Would you expect General Mills to have a formal or informal marketing plan for this new product? Why?
3. How will General Mills know whether this cereal was a good idea or not?

459

Chapter 36

Managing Human Resources

Terms to Know

human resource
  development
business philosophy
communications
motivation
equity

Equal Employment
  Opportunity
  Commission
total quality management
orientation

Chapter Objectives

After studying this chapter, you will be able to:

- describe the role people play in marketing;
- explain the importance of human resource development;
- tell how the elements of a work environment contribute to an organization's effectiveness;
- describe the major principles of total quality management; and
- explain how a marketing supervisor's actions can enhance the effectiveness of the workplace.

The 100 Best Companies

If you want to work for a company that treats you well, you might check out a book entitled *The 100 Best Companies to Work for in America* by Robert Levering and Milton Moskowitz. According to the authors, these 100 companies were selected because they treat employees with respect and provide excellent work environments.

These 100 companies provide good salaries and benefits and offer employees opportunities to share in company profits. Most of the companies offer great job security. There have been few layoffs, even in difficult periods. There are good relationships between employees and managers, good opportunities for advancement—especially for women and minorities—and more employee involvement in company decision making and goal setting. The companies are also sensitive to family and health issues. Many offer health facilities and on-site day-care for children.

The authors reviewed employee handbooks, benefit packages, newsletters, and annual reports to determine an initial list of companies that seem to treat their employees well. Then they interviewed thousands of employees, CEOs, and managers at 400 companies. Questions they typically asked were: Do you enjoy working here? Why? How does it compare with other places you worked? They then narrowed their list of 400 to the "best 100." These companies ranged in size from Wal-Mart, with 390,000 employees, to Great Plains Software, Inc. (headquartered in Fargo, North Dakota), with 397 employees.

The authors further identified ten companies that they considered among the best of all. Here, listed in alphabetical order, are the top ten best companies and their headquarters:

- Beth Israel Hospital, Boston, MA
- Delta Airlines, Atlanta, GA
- Donnelly Corporation (maker of glass parts for cars), Holland, MI
- Federal Express Corporation, Memphis, TN
- Fel-Pro, Inc. (gasket maker), Skokie, IL
- Hallmark Cards, Inc., Kansas City, MO
- Publix Super Markets Inc., Lakeland, FL
- Rosenbluth International (travel agency), Philadelphia, PA
- Southwest Airlines Company, Dallas, TX
- USAA (insurance and financial services), San Antonio, TX [1,2,3]

One key to becoming one of the "best" companies is effective human resource management. In this chapter you will take a closer look at managing human resources.

The People Component of the Marketing Mix

The 100 "best" companies discussed in our opening case study share some crucial common elements. Customers are treated with respect. Vendors and suppliers are highly regarded. But, most importantly, employees are well treated by managers.

Loyal, pleasant, productive employees are a company's greatest asset. Unhappy, negative, unreliable employees are a company's greatest problem. Employees can make or break a company. That's why people are an important part of the marketing mix.

The Importance of People in Marketing

People with good attitudes and good work habits are especially important in marketing. The vast majority of marketers have face-to-face contact with customers, vendors, and media representatives. The quality of these personal contacts has an important effect on the outcome of the transactions. Often the impression the customer or vendor has of the company is based on the contact with the employees. Well-trained, friendly, knowledgeable marketers can earn repeat business for years to come. Rude, indifferent, or poorly trained employees can ruin a business by sending customers running to competitors.

Management often considers people (or personnel) when planning its marketing activities in terms of product, place, price, and promotion. Look at the following comments from managers who recognize the importance of people to the profitability of their companies.

- Larry McVey, president of Thom McAn, attributes its success to people, product, and presentation. "While product and presentation are essential to our business," says McVey, "it's the people of Thom McAn who service the customers (that) make the difference."[4]

- Tom Monaghan, chief executive officer of Domino's Pizza, says "Business is nothing but people. Most important are your customers, and the job is to fulfill their expectations." Next come employees. "The lower the level of employees, the more important, because they are the ones who do the work. Most new ideas come from them."[5]

Human Resource Development

Today, most companies spend considerable time and effort on **human resource development**—a process that includes planning and managing all activities that hopefully result in employee satisfaction and productivity. Human resource development usually includes:

- recruiting and selecting employees;
- training employees;
- creating an effective work environment;
- motivating employees;
- counseling employees;
- evaluating employees; and
- helping employees with career planning and development.

Building an Effective Work Environment

If we were to ask ourselves what we want out of a job, we would probably all say about the same thing. We want to feel good about our work. We want a boss who values our work. We want a fair wage. We want to like our work. We want to be treated fairly.

Studies also consistently show that the quality of the work environment is important to a person's job satisfaction. This includes pleasant surroundings, friendly and cooperative co-workers, and harmonious relationships between supervisors and employees.

If our bosses were asked what they wanted out of their jobs, they would probably respond in much the same way. They, too, want to feel good about their work, their earnings, and their work environment. In addition, they want their employees to be dependable, cooperative, loyal, responsible, and helpful to customers.

A good work environment doesn't just happen. It is created by good management and based on principles and practices from both management and marketing studies. We learned about some of these in Chapter 35. In this chapter, we will take a more detailed look at some solid management principles that guide human resource development efforts.

Believing in People

Management begins at the top of any company or organization. The chief executive officer, the president, the owner, the store manager, the department head—all must sincerely *believe* that the company's employees make a difference and *practice* those beliefs through their actions.

Business management experts believe that a good *business philosophy* is perhaps the key point in effectively managing a business or a department. A **business philosophy** is a particular set of beliefs or guiding principles for the way in which business is to be conducted with the public and through employees.

Peters and Waterman, in their book entitled *In Search of Excellence*, describe a business philosophy of people management: "Treat people as adults. Treat them as partners; treat them with dignity; treat them with respect. Treat them—not capital spending and automation—as the primary source of productivity gains. These are fundamental lessons from excellent companies' research."[6]

Staying Close to the Customer

Effective companies understand that managers and employees must listen to and communicate with prospective and actual customers. They study customer buying habits. They inform customers of additions and deletions to product lines. They research customer needs and wants. All of these company activities reinforce the philosophy that the customer must be well served.

Here are the rules of customer relations from one company—Nordstrom—that perhaps summarize this principle the best.

- Rule 1—Our customers are our reason for existence. They are to always receive priority attention.
- Rule 2—There are no other rules.

Communicating Clearly

Communications is the transfer of information, including feelings and ideas, from one person to another. Good communications are basic to interpersonal relations. They are essential for the coordination of business activities.

Communications can take place orally through informal conversations, meetings, small group discussions, or at training sessions. Communications also can occur through written letters or memorandums; bulletin board notices; newsletters; reports; and notes of appreciation, congratulations, or reprimand.

There are other ways we communicate. We can do this through our attitudes and moods. We can communicate through such body language as smiling or nodding the head. We can even communicate through inference, such as appearing to compliment someone but using a sarcastic tone of voice.

Effective communications are not easy. We often unintentionally send the wrong message. Or the person receiving the message fails to correctly understand what we have to say. Either way, our message is unclear.

Some people have a hard time expressing their feelings or ideas. Some people talk so much that we tune them out without hearing their message at all.

Effective managers and employees constantly work on their communication styles. They write and

■ ■ ■ *The same words can communicate different feelings, depending on our body language and facial gestures. What does the body language of these people suggest?*

speak clearly. They say what they mean. They try to promote understanding by asking those to whom they are communicating if they understand the message. "Do you understand what I'm saying, Mary?" "Here, Dave, see if you can now do this." "Tell me, Luis, how does this fit in with what you had planned?"

Taking Pride in Work

People's *self-concept*—the way in which they see themselves and the way in which they think others see them—is identified with their jobs and their companies. They may say they are supervisors, salespersons, cashiers, or computer programmers. They may say they work for Wendy's, Lowe's Hardware, U.S. Air, or 7-Eleven.

It is important for managers and supervisors to recognize that people identify themselves with their jobs and their companies. If employees are proud of their work and the products they sell, the firm and its employees have a greater chance of success.

Building Teamwork

Studies tell us that teamwork produces high productivity and profitability. When the operation of a business is structured as a team effort, each person typically knows the total job that must be completed. Each person may have some input into how the work should be completed and who will do each task at what time. Sometimes all team members are cross-trained so they can perform some or all of the job tasks.

Many successful restaurants develop employee teams for their busy times. For example, Subway sub shops usually have several people employed "on the line" during their busy lunch hour. One person takes orders. Another fills drink orders. One puts the meats and cheeses on a sub roll. A fourth heats the sandwiches and gets chips and salads. A fifth finishes making the sandwich by adding lettuce, mayonnaise, and mustard. And a sixth bags the sandwich, totals the sale, and collects the money.

Each day, the team members decide who will do what job. All can do each other's tasks, and all pitch

■■■   *Subway creates employee teams to help productivity. What is needed for teamwork to work well?*

in if someone is getting behind or needs a break. The team members communicate constantly with each other and their customers. They enjoy what they are doing and enjoy working together.

Motivating Employees

Motivation is the internal drive to accomplish a particular goal. People are motivated by many different needs. Some people are interested in money, trendy clothes, or a new car. Some are motivated by social acceptance and recognition. For others, basic needs such as food and clothing are strong motivators. To make matters more complicated, people are motivated by different needs at different times in their lives.

Motivating employees is interesting and challenging for managers. Understanding an individual's motivation to work, and integrating the firm's goals with that person's motivation, usually result in good employee productivity and morale.

As we saw from the 100 best companies at the beginning of this chapter, some ways managers motivate employees are with good pay, good benefits, and job security. They also motivate employees by training them well to do their jobs, providing them with opportunities to advance, and involving them in decisions affecting their work.

Treating People Fairly

Equity involves the fair and equal treatment of employees in the work environment. Work environments are much more harmonious, productive, and effective when all managers and employees are treated fairly. They are also more harmonious and productive if employees are trained for all jobs for which they are qualified, promoted when they are qualified, and paid equally according to performance.

Unfortunately, prejudice, discrimination, and harassment sometimes occur on the job. Fairness in employment should be a basic principle underlying all personnel discussions in the workplace.

Today, businesses are forbidden by law to discriminate against any employee on the basis of his or her race, religion, gender, national origin, marital status, and age. Various laws have been passed to help some minority groups gain access to adequate education, employment, training, and promotion.

The **Equal Employment Opportunity Commission** (EEOC) processes charges of individual or group discrimination and develops guidelines to help businesses avoid it.

Fostering Careers

Effective companies today work with employees through their human resource departments to establish career goals and develop programs to help employees attain them. It costs a lot of money to train new employees correctly. It is a good business practice to continue to work with them to help them advance within the firm and to further develop their careers. This includes providing them with training and promotion opportunities, and making their present jobs more interesting and challenging by increasing their responsibilities.

All people at the firm benefit from career development opportunities. The company has an experienced, well-trained, and productive employee. The employee feels good about his or her job, knows the firm's products, and feels secure in his or her career growth.

Total Quality Management

Many American companies have recently implemented relatively new management principles and strategies known as **total quality management** (TQM). TQM is based on the work of W. Edwards Deming, a statistician and management specialist who is given much credit for helping to make Japan's industries so successful. Many other business specialists have built on Deming's work. Today, TQM is the management system used in companies such as Xerox, Motorola, Federal Express, and Harley-Davidson, to name a few. In addition, TQM is increasingly being used as a management formula for government agencies, hospitals, social organizations, and schools.

Essentially, the fundamental philosophy behind TQM is that individuals want to do their best. It is management's job to enable them to do so by constantly improving the system in which they work.

Federal Express: A Quality Company

You may easily recognize it by its distinctivly colored fleet of trucks and aircraft. You may know it for its overnight package delivery service that delivers letters and packages anywhere in the United States by the next day. But what you may not know is that it is viewed by corporate America as being one of the top-quality companies in the United States.

Federal Express was founded in Memphis, Tennessee, in 1973. This high-tech service company—a rapid distributor of packages and information—has grown to $7 billion annually in sales. It has 400 aircraft, some 30,000 trucks, and 94,000 employees who deliver in excess of 2.95 million packages and letters a day to 127 countries. The fact that the company has been able to gather such assets in such a short period of time is amazing. It's even more astounding that the company can deliver that many packages anywhere in the United States in less than 24 hours!

The company has been so successful that in 1990 it won the coveted Malcolm Baldrige National Quality Award. This award was created by Congress to recognize the achievement of companies that improve significantly the quality of their products.

What did it take for Federal Express to become a Baldrige National Quality Award winner? Here are just a few examples of management practices that helped it to succeed.

- *Planning and direction.* The company stands by its statement to do "the *right* things right the first time…every time." Careful strategic planning is implemented to help try to get things right…the first time.

- *Passion for quality.* The company's mission statement highlights phrases such as to "provide totally reliable, competitively superior global air-ground transportation of high-priority goods and documents that require rapid, time-certain delivery…."

- *A strong focus on customer satisfaction.* The mission statement further states, "We will be helpful, courteous, and professional to each other and the public. We will strive to have a satisfied customer at the end of each transition."

- *A goal of 100 percent customer satisfaction and nothing less.* This was a result of asking customers what they thought quality meant. The answer: on time delivery every time.

- *Setting additional clear goals and reinforcing them by word and action.* Such goals dealt with providing 100 percent accurate information to customers and employees, conducting annual customer surveys, improving profit margins, and reducing failures.

- *Focus on technology.* The company uses unique electronic tools to gather data on each package as it moves through the Federal Express process of pick-up, transport, sort, and delivery. It also uses interactive video instruction combining computer technology and audiovisual capability to train employees, keep personnel records, keep track of job applicants, and help employees prepare for job-knowledge tests.

- *Training for all employees.* Six classes are offered through the Federal Express Quality Academy. Emphasis is on quality job performance. Classes are also regularly held on leadership training and effective coaching for company managers.

- *Employee involvement and recognition.* This includes a host of activities and benefits that recognize and help employees. Over 3,000 employee quality action teams are in place to work on continuous improvement problems. Cash awards, dinners, letters of recognition, theater tickets, etc., are regularly given to reward a particularly outstanding job by employees.

So, does the company achieve its goal of 100 percent customer satisfaction? It comes close. Overall customer satisfaction ratings have averaged more than 95 percent on domestic service and 94 percent on international. Federal Express continues to score well above its competition on customer service surveys. Its domestic market share is 43 percent. Its nearest competitor holds 26 percent of the market. For these and many other reasons, Federal Express became the *first* company in the service industry to be recognized with the Malcolm Baldrige National Quality Award. [1,2,3,4,5]

1. List one example from Federal Express that illustrates each of the four functions of marketing management you learned about in Chapter 35.

2. Cite examples of how Federal Express implemented total quality management.

3. Describe ways in which Federal Express seems to have built an effective work environment.

4. Why do you think Federal Express was cited as one of the nation's outstanding quality companies?

CASE NOTES

1. Robert Haavind, *The Road to the Baldrige Award* (Boston: Butterworth-Heinemann, 1992), pp. 71-80.

2. Christopher W. L. Hart and Christopher E. Bogan, *The Baldrige*, (McGraw-Hill, Inc., 1992).

3. David Jamieson and Julie O'Mara, *Managing Workforce 2000*, (San Francisco: Jossey-Bass Publishers, 1991), p. 105.

4. Larry W. McMahan, "Federal Express Corporation," *Baldrige Winners on World-Class Quality*, (New York: Conference Board), pp. 16–18 and 26–28.

5. Marion Mills Steeples, *The Corporate Guide to the Malcolm Baldrige National Quality Award*, (Milwaukee: ASQC Quality Press, 1992), pp. 287–292.

UNIT 10

Business Management and Entrepreneurship

Chapter 38

Entrepreneurship

Terms to Know

small business   franchising agreement

guaranty loans   business plan

Chapter Objectives

After studying this chapter, you will be able to:

- discuss the economic impact of small businesses on our economy;
- describe the common traits of successful entrepreneurs;
- explain the advantages and disadvantages of running a small business;
- discuss the role of the Small Business Administration;
- explain the advantages and disadvantages of four forms of business ownership; and
- identify the elements in a business plan for a small business.

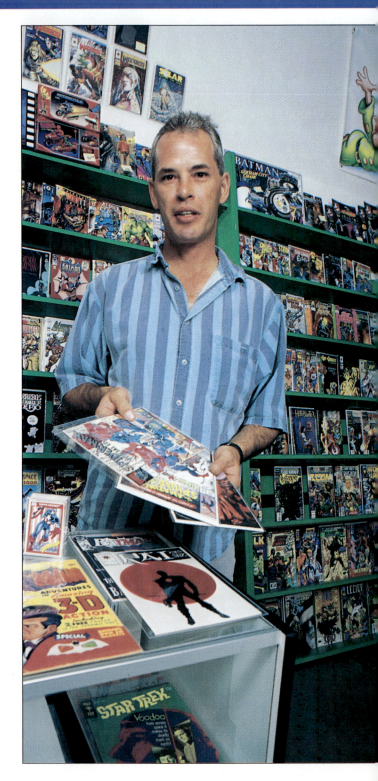

Case Study

Artful Entrepreneurs

Most artists don't think of themselves as entrepreneurs. Perhaps that's because they feel more skilled with their paintbrushes or chisels than in business practices. Regardless, many artists are entrepreneurs because they take the risk of opening and operating a business for a profit.

For centuries Native Americans created pottery, jewelry, paintings, baskets, and carvings. Until recently, many of these works of art sold for less than $20 each. The cost of the raw materials alone often left the artists with little profit.

Today, however, many Native American artists use modern marketing and business practices. By creating cooperatives and other retail businesses, they now sell their art worldwide. Some of it commands up to $40,000 per piece.

As a result, some Native Americans are earning incomes of $100,000 or more. Their businesses, which the artists usually own and operate, are playing a pivotal role in marketing Native American art.

The artists who own these cooperatives and other retail businesses don't just sell art. They also stockpile raw materials, collect key data on prices and market trends, and act as auditors and bookkeepers. They organize workshops to help fellow artists with new design ideas and media. Initially, some even regulated the production and the quality of the art in order to maintain high prices.

In Cherokee, North Carolina, Qualla Arts & Crafts sells the works of more than 300 Eastern Cherokee artists and craftspeople. Art sells through a retail store and a mail-order catalog. The company annually sells more than 10,000 items from its catalog. By utilizing the marketing concept, the artists of Qualla Arts & Crafts and other Native American businesses are benefiting not only themselves but the public as well.[1]

Entrepreneurship and Small Business

As you know from Chapter 3, people who assume the risk and provide the capital to start and operate their own business are known as entrepreneurs. Most businesses start out small. You may remember your first entrepreneurial experience. Perhaps you started a neighborhood lemonade stand or a lawn-cutting service. You may have participated in student business programs such as DECA or Junior Achievement. Or you may have sold candy or holiday wrapping paper to earn money for your school or athletic team. In any of these situations, you likely experienced challenges and frustrations similar to those faced by millions of small business owners throughout the country.

Small ventures often mature into large enterprises. For example, in 1977 Vernon Buchanan founded his printing business with five centers in Michigan. Today, his business, American Speedy Printing, oversees more than 600 print center franchises. It is the largest quick-printing operation in this country.

For Buchanan, thinking like an entrepreneur began early. With an appetite for work and its rewards, he delivered newspapers for the *Detroit News* at the age of 12 and bagged groceries 30 hours a week in high school. By the time Vernon Buchanan turned 33, the Harvard Business Club of Detroit was honoring him with its Entrepreneur Award.[2]

An increasing number of Americans are turning toward entrepreneurship. Between 1970 and 1988 the number of self-employed people in the United States doubled.

Among the many trends affecting people's decisions to become entrepreneurs are the downsizing of corporations, government support, and a global economy. The downsizing of large corporations has meant fewer jobs and growth opportunities within these corporations. As a result, many people have turned from corporations toward self-employment.

In addition, government agencies have encouraged new business ventures. They have provided increased assistance to minorities and women to help them begin their own businesses. Finally, as trade barriers loosen and we move toward a global economy, more global opportunities will arise for entrepreneurs.

What Is a Small Business?

We commonly think of local service stations, print shops, appliance stores, restaurants, and video stores as small businesses. Indeed, these types of businesses do follow a common small business pattern. A **small business** is an independently owned and managed business that serves a limited geographic area and is not dominant in its industry.

The following facts about small businesses will help us understand their economic impact:

- Ninety-nine percent of nonfarm businesses are considered small.

- Approximately 50 percent of small businesses are classified as full-time operations.

- Small businesses employ about 60 percent of the private work force. Moreover, small businesses contribute about 40 percent of all sales and are responsible for approximately 40 percent of the gross national product. In the period between 1986–1988, small businesses employed an additional estimated 4.5 million people.[3]

- Two-thirds of new jobs are created by businesses that employ fewer than 500 people and that are less than five years old.[4]

- Most young people learn their basic job skills working for small businesses.

Figure 38–1 shows the industry concentrations of small businesses. As you might expect, the service and retail industries dominate the small business arena, while the production sector plays an important but less significant role. Since the service sector is the fastest-growing part of the U.S. economy, the number of small businesses is likely to grow.

Entrepreneurial Traits

Studies on the personal characteristics of entrepreneurs show that successful entrepreneurs are usually high achievers, with enough drive to meet

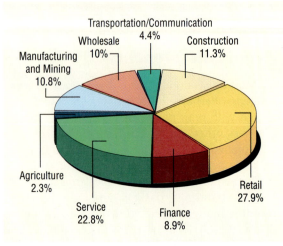

Source: *Small Business Primer*, National Federation of Independent Businesses, 1989.

■■■ *Figure 38–1 Small Business Employers by Industry*
There are small businesses found in all industries. In what two industries are more than half of the small businesses found?

the daily challenges and frustrations of running small firms. Most entrepreneurs are willing to assume moderate risks and are aware of potential failure. Successful entrepreneurs are goal-oriented. This is important because a new business requires a high degree of planning.

Many entrepreneurs start their own businesses because their jobs with other firms do not allow for enough individual creativity. In addition to thinking creatively, small business owners must communicate effectively with customers and employees. The crucial link in the communication process is the ability to empathize—to put yourself in someone else's position. Of course, this customer orientation is a key to marketing the successful business.

Finally, successful entrepreneurs understand their goods and services. They must constantly study the latest technologies, trends, and markets if they wish to remain technically competent.

Advantages of Small Business Ownership

There are many advantages to owning your own business. Let's take a look at the most important of them.

Key Decision Maker

Most small businesspeople cherish the independence of being their own boss. In an ownership role, entrepreneurs can implement new ideas with a minimum of red tape. Feedback on their decisions is usually fast.

Control of Profits

It is up to each business owner to decide how profits will be used. Entrepreneurs can either reinvest in their businesses or keep the profits as earned income.

Customer and Employee Contact

To many customers, businesses seem impersonal. Entrepreneurs can often motivate and lead their employees. By creating a "family" atmosphere, the entrepreneur shows employees and customers how they can go to the owner for assistance.

A well-run business often has a warm and friendly feeling. Small business owners who recognize the value of greater personalization can enhance the success of their businesses.

Pride and Status

Entrepreneurs can take great pride in owning their own business. Owning and operating a business is often the fulfillment of a dream. This achievement is the result of considerable personal sacrifice and hard work. Entrepreneurship can bring them status as someone who has made it on his or her own.

Work Satisfaction

Few entrepreneurs say money is their primary motive in owning their businesses. Many could actually earn more working for someone else. Instead, they work because they thrive on the challenge of controlling their destiny and turning their ideas into reality. Their work enriches them and provides them with great satisfaction.

Disadvantages of Small Business Ownership

There are certain limitations that owners of small businesses must be aware of. Here are some of the key ones.

Customer Satisfaction Demands Long Hours

Some entrepreneurs soon learn that the independence they sought in establishing their own business is lost to a demanding public. Studies show that most entrepreneurs spend more than 50 hours per week working. Many spend 70 to 80 hours on the job.[5] Business owners may find themselves wishing they were back to secure, 40-hour-a-week jobs.

Lack of Specialization

Large businesses have the luxury of hiring specialists in such areas as marketing, accounting, production, law, safety, and human resources. Entrepreneurs, however, wear many hats. Often they assume so many roles that they become preoccupied with short-term planning. This can trap a business owner into solving one crisis after another instead of planning for the future.

Sole Responsibility for Decisions

Since entrepreneurs are often limited to relying on only their own skills and information, it is difficult to make sound decisions. If a decision is good, the owner gets all the recognition. If a decision is bad, the owner takes the blame. Regardless, an entrepreneur's decisions determine the fate of the enterprise.

Competition with Big Business

Because large firms can produce, distribute, and sell mass quantities of products, they often have the advantage of being able to offer products that are priced lower than products produced by small businesses. For example, the owner of a local drugstore in Texas will be hard-pressed to compete on the basis of price with a new Wal-Mart. In order to be successful, the local druggist must recognize this competitive environment and stress nonprice variables such as service, expertise, and friendliness.

Risk of Failure

The ultimate risk of any business is failure or bankruptcy. The survival statistics for new businesses are less than encouraging. Analysts agree that the newer and smaller the business, the more likely it is to fail. For example, 55 percent of the firms that go out of business annually have been in existence for five years or less. Nearly 98 percent of those business failures involve poor management.

Help from the SBA

The Small Business Administration (SBA) is an independent federal agency founded by Congress in 1953 as an advocate for small businesses. In this supportive role, the SBA provides both prospective and established entrepreneurs with financial assistance, management counseling, and training. Furthermore, small businesses owned by minorities and Vietnam veterans are given special opportunities to bid for government contracts. The SBA makes small businesses aware of their eligibility in such programs.

The SBA has helped launch many of today's thriving corporations. Some firms that received help from the SBA include Nike, Apple Computer, Federal Express, Winnebago Industries, T. J. Cinnamons, and Compaq Computers.

Financial Programs

The SBA offers a wide variety of loan programs to small businesses. The purpose of these programs is to help small businesses that are unable to borrow money at reasonable interest rates from conventional lenders without government help.

Most SBA financial assistance has been in the form of **guaranty loans**—loans made by banks or other private lenders that are guaranteed up to 90 percent by the SBA. By underwriting loans the SBA assumes much of the risk. Thus, lenders are more willing to make money available to entrepreneurs. Guaranteed loans carry a maximum of $750,000, and maturity (the time in which a loan must be paid) may run as high as 25 years. The average loan is approximately $175,000, and the average maturity is eight years.

Business Development

Many businesses fail due to poor management. Thus, the SBA places special emphasis on improving the management ability of small business owners and managers. SBA staff specialists, known as management assistance officers, are located at more than 100 offices nationwide to provide free advice and consultation on specific problems.

One responsibility of the management assistance officer is to plan and organize various business management courses. These seminars and workshops are cosponsored by the SBA in cooperation with educational institutions, chambers of commerce, and trade associations. These courses cover such topics as cash management, business forecasting, and marketing. Pre-business workshops and more than 100 inexpensive "how to" publications are also offered.

Additional assistance is available from two other groups: the *Service Corps of Retired Executives (SCORE)* and the *Active Corps of Executives (ACE)*. Both groups are SBA-sponsored volunteer groups. SCORE consists of more than 13,000 retired executives who give advice and consultation to small businesses. There are about 400 SCORE chapters in some 750 locations across the United States. ACE is a group of active business executives that gives advice and consultation to small businesses.

A closely related program is the *Small Business Institutes (SBI)*. This SBA- and university-sponsored program allows qualified seniors and graduate students in business schools the opportunity to provide on-site managerial counseling to small businesses. Students are usually assigned to a consulting team and are supervised by faculty advisors and SBA personnel. More than 500 universities and colleges participate in the program.

Another campus-centered program, located at 52 universities, is *Small Business Development Centers (SBDCs)*. These centers draw from resources of local, state, and federal government; the private sector; and university facilities. They provide managerial and technical assistance, research studies, and other types of specialized assistance to small business. SBDCs in 45 states use faculty members to support and nurture these activities.

Contract Assistance

Each year the federal government contracts with private companies for billions of dollars in goods and services. The government's procurement specialists want to give small businesses their share of government contracts, as required by law. The SBA counsels businesses on how to prepare bids, secure government contracts, and get their companies on bidders' lists.

To help match small businesses and federal contracts, the government developed a computerized system called the *Procurement Automated Source System (PASS)*. It lists more than 130,000 businesses and their capabilities. Federal procurement officers use PASS to find small businesses capable of providing necessary goods and services.

Business Ownership Opportunities

Once you have decided to run your own small business, you need to consider ways in which to obtain a business. There are four ways in which you may do this: enter the family business, start your own business, buy an existing independent business, or buy an existing franchise. Let's take a closer look at these ownership opportunities.

Entering the Family Business

Many people become entrepreneurs by entering their family business. The majority of small businesses are family owned. Often family members are brought up working in the family business and are prepared to take over when older family members retire or die.

Advantages

Family business members have the advantage of knowing each other's strengths and weaknesses. There is often a feeling of loyalty and trust among family members. This togetherness creates teamwork which can often help the business to function more efficiently.

Disadvantages

One of the biggest disadvantages of family businesses is that the owner cannot get away from the business. It is often hard to separate family matters from business matters. Emotions can overrule objective decisions. Knowing each other too well can cause family members to overlook the strengths and weaknesses of the business and its employees.

Starting Your Own Business

One way in which to become an entrepreneur is to start a new firm from the ground up. Beginning a new business allows an entrepreneur the freedom to create the business of his or her choice. However, starting from scratch also has its drawbacks.

Advantages

There are several major advantages to starting a business from scratch. The entrepreneur can decide how the business will be set up. Starting a new business means you do not inherit previous unhappy customers, bad debts, obsolete equipment, or an inconvenient store location. It also means you do not have to deal with someone else's poor marketing and organization or weak management.

Disadvantages

Starting a new business can also have its disadvantages. Starting a new business often involves more time and effort than other means of starting a business. Everything from facilities, employees, and stock must be attended to. In addition, you must create relationships with suppliers and with consumers.

Buying an Existing Independent Business

Buying an existing independent business is a popular method of going into business. The first step in buying an existing independent business is to find

■ ■ ■   *Anita Roddick of The Body Shop became an entrepreneur by starting her own business. What is one advantage to starting your own business?*

Workers' Compensation Insurance

Every state in the United States has passed laws setting up systems of workers' compensation insurance to cover job-related injuries and diseases. As a rule, employers must buy insurance that will pay the sums for which they may become liable under these laws.

The employers are thus relieved of liability in cases where there has been no negligence on their part. However, most states allow workers to sue employers for negligence. So, workers' compensation insurance does not relieve employers of their duties to provide a safe place to work and to train workers how to perform their work safely.

In a few states, this insurance must be bought from a state insurer called a workers' compensation fund. In a large number of states, the employer can buy insurance protection only from a private insurer. In most states, qualified employers may insure the company against employee risks.

Legal liability is based on the law of negligence. In other words, the company that practices poor safety and maintains hazardous working conditions can be legally liable in addition to the insurance claims.

The laws of most states provide coverage for injuries arising by accident out of and in the course of employment. Cash benefits to covered workers are computed as a percentage of the worker's wages. They are usually less than half the wages the injured worker would have earned.

Crop Insurance

Crop insurance can help cover crop losses caused by natural hazards such as drought, floods, insects, and hail damage, but it does not insure profit. Of course, it does not cover losses due to negligence or failure to observe appropriate farming practices.

Umbrella Insurance

Umbrella insurance covers extra liability that might result in a major loss of hundreds of thousands of dollars. For example, consumers now actively file lawsuits to recover damages caused by poor or faulty products such as automobiles, food, home appliances, and machinery. Sometimes a large number of customers are able to collect from a company that sold a faulty product. Umbrella insurance covers the risk of such a loss.

Cost of Insurance

When a firm applies for insurance, the insurance company's agent figures out the amount of risk involved. The cost of insurance is based on the insurance company's estimate of risk amount.

Insurance costs are hard to figure out because every case is slightly different. For example, two applicants—ABC Company and XYZ Company—may have identical store buildings with identical values. After investigation, however, the insurance company may charge ABC Company a slightly higher rate than XYZ Company because XYZ has a better sprinkler system. The sprinkler system makes the risk involved in insuring XYZ less than the risk for insuring ABC.

Small firms select the separate insurance coverage they want. However, insurance companies also offer contracts that include all the major kinds of insurance that a business might want. The cost of complete coverage is very high, and such contracts are usually of interest only to large firms.

Reducing Risks Through Good Management

The best way to reduce losses from risks is to prevent trouble. Insurance companies emphasize risk prevention in order to cut down on business losses and insurance claims.

For example, an insurance agent looking at a building whose owner wants fire insurance might point out what could be done to reduce the risk of fire. If the owner follows the agent's suggestions, the insurance company might offer a lower rate.

Good management in a company also reduces risks. Although it is impossible to eliminate risks, careful planning and quick action can avoid some kinds of trouble and reduce the impact of others. (See Table 41–1.)

Type of Risk	Methods of Reducing Risk
Economic	• Anticipate risks and be prepared for them by studying market conditions and general economic trends.
Natural	• Watch the weather and take measures against the forces of nature such as building irrigation systems against possible drought.
Human	• Bond employees that handle cash and other valuables. • Treat employees well and set an example of honesty for them. • Allow employees to own stock in the company. • Keep employees well-informed and trained. • Operate safe, healthy facilities.

■■■ **Table 41–1 Reducing Risks**
Why should management work toward reducing risks?

Reducing Economic Risks

Economic risks can be hard to minimize. The businessperson cannot prevent a national depression or skyrocketing costs due to inflation.

However, a marketer can anticipate these risks and be prepared for them. This means studying market conditions and general economic trends. The marketer must keep up to date on local conditions—political events, population shifts, traffic patterns, new real estate developments, and competition—in order to reduce risks.

Reducing Natural Risks

Losses from natural risks often can be reduced by careful prevention measures. For example, citrus growers in Florida know that frost is hazardous to crops. Thus, they watch the weather closely to see whether wind machines will be needed to heat the orchards.

Reducing Human Risks

Human risks can often be reduced through careful management. Four ways human risks can be reduced are bonding, improving management-worker relations, changing security policies, and removing hazards.

Bonding

Theft is a major risk in any business that deals in merchandise or keeps cash on the premises. Businesses lose millions of dollars a year from pilferage and shoplifting. One way to protect against pilferage is to place employees who handle cash and other valuables under bond. **Bonding** means the employer buys insurance on employees to protect against possible employee theft.

A *fidelity bond* protects an employer against dishonesty on the part of employees. If a theft is discovered, the employer can claim compensation from the insurance company.

A *surety bond* guarantees that the principal is honest and has the necessary ability and financial capacity to carry out the obligation for which he or she is bonded. (The principal is a person or business named in the insurance contract.)

Management-Worker Relations

If employers treat employees well and set an example of honesty for them, employees are less likely to steal. When employees see themselves as members of a team working for the success of the business, they will tend to perform honestly.

Many employees can own stock in their companies. When employees are stock owners, they see dishonesty on the job as taking money from their own pockets.

Where employees are kept well informed and trained by management, the risk of accidents on the job or careless work is kept to a minimum. For example, Federal Mogul, an automotive aftermarket business, sets the following operating objectives for itself:

- operate safe, healthy facilities;
- maximize employee morale by utilizing an employee participation approach;

Principles into Practice

Car Manufacturers Risk Marketing Electric Cars

Car manufacturers are taking the risk of introducing electric cars onto the market. General Motors pledges that it will be the first big auto manufacturer to mass-produce electric cars. Both Ford and Chrysler are developing battery-powered vans. Overseas, Fiat is working on an urban two-seater called Elettra. And at a Tokyo Auto Show, Japanese manufacturers displayed six different electric vehicles.

The risk of introducing the first mass-produced electric car and marketing is considerable. The research needed to develop an electric car costs millions of dollars. People are slow to accept drastic changes such as a move from gasoline-powered cars to electric cars. They may not like the style of the electric cars produced.

Before mass marketing the cars, all manufacturers must improve battery performance. For example, GM's electric car, the Impact, runs out of energy after 120 miles. It takes an hour to recharge the car's batteries. The Impact's lead-acid cells have to be changed after 20,000 miles at a cost of about $1,500. This would make it too costly for many owners. However, GM thinks the urban commuter would provide adequate market potential to make its car profitable.

To GM's advantage, its battery-powered Impact meets air standards as well as commuter needs. It can out-accelerate many cars now on the road, and its aerodynamic lines are especially stylish.

Stricter clean air legislation enhances the market potential for the electric car. The electric car does not emit the air pollution that gasoline-powered cars do.

Will electric cars succeed? If car makers are willing to risk investing millions of dollars in research and production, they must think it's worth the risk.[5,6,7]

1. What type of risk is involved in producing and marketing electric cars?
2. How can car manufacturers reduce the risks involved with marketing electric cars?

- provide "best in class" customer services both internally and externally;
- maximize order filling by 93 to 95 percent; and
- meet or exceed financial objectives.

These objectives are posted in the workplace and discussed in regular meetings between the managers and workers.

Changing Security Policy

Another way of reducing losses from pilferage and shoplifting is to tighten security policies. Retailers can do this by using security guards, television monitors, security devices on merchandise, and electronic sensors on store doors.

Some losses result from people issuing bad checks, forged checks, altered checks, and counterfeit money. A bad check is one for which there is not enough money in the bank to cover the amount of the check. A forged check is one signed or endorsed by someone other than the legal owner of the money drawn on by the check. An altered check is one on which the amount has been illegally changed. Counterfeit money is illegally made coins and bills.

These losses can be reduced by setting definite policies as to who can accept checks and by instructing those who handle cash how to detect counterfeit money. Credit risks may be reduced by carefully screening those who apply for credit and by following up on accounts that are past due.

Removing Hazards

Business owners guard against on-the-job accidents by providing safe working conditions. Accident risks can be reduced by making sure that defective electrical equipment and wiring are repaired, by having their premises inspected at regular intervals, by discouraging careless smoking, and by providing special storage for flammable liquids. Equipment such as vehicles, elevators, escalators, and high-speed machines should be inspected often.

Management asks that employees listen carefully during safety training sessions or when a supervisor is telling how to prevent job-related accidents. They should pay attention to safety warning signs and follow safety rules.

THE FUTURE IS NOW

Hot-Site Recovery Programs

What may be the latest on the list of prevention possibilities are hot-site recovery programs. These programs provide subscribers with "hot sites" or office sites where businesses can relocate in the event of a natural disaster such as a fire or an earthquake. Some also offer fully equipped mobile trailers. As part of the program, subscribers can send their data to be backed up and stored at the hot site on a monthly, daily, or minute-by-minute basis. The building may burn, the earth may shake, but the information and business will be safe!

In cold weather, stores and other businesses should keep walks and outdoor passageways free from ice and snow. Many firms employ safety directors who keep a constant watch to prevent and eliminate accident hazards. They also set up training programs to teach employee safety.

The federal government has an agency called OSHA (Occupational Safety and Health Administration). Its inspectors visit businesses to see that safety and health protection rules are being followed. Moreover, OSHA encourages company employees and unions to report health and safety hazards.

■ ■ ■   *Accidents can be very costly to a business. However, good management can reduce hazards. What type of business risk is an accident? How can the risk of accidents be reduced?*

CHAPTER NOTES

1. G. DeGeorge, "Andrew Leaves Behind Bills in the Billions," *Business Week,* 7 September 1992, pp. 29–30.

2. M. J. O'Brien, "Hurricane Destroys One Bookseller's Store, Home," *Publisher's Weekly,* 7 September 1992, p. 11.

3. "The Two Edges of Andrew's Sword," *Time,* 21 September 1992, p. 17.

4. S. A. Forest, "The Uneven Twists of a Killer Hurricane," *Business Week,* 14 September 1992, p. 29.

5. William J. Cook, "Jump-start to the Future," *U.S. News & World Report,* 30 April 1990, p. 48.

6. "Can the Big Three Get Back in Gear?" *Newsweek,* 22 January 1990, p. 43.

7. General Motors Annual Report, 1989.

- marketing;
- restaurant marketing;
- sales;
- transportation and travel marketing; and
- vehicle/petroleum marketing.

Each of these occupational areas contains jobs that can be organized according to the level of skills, education, and experience required.

Levels of Marketing Occupations

In each occupational area in marketing you could work at one of five levels. These five levels include entry level, career sustaining, marketing specialist, marketing supervisor, and manager/ owner. Figure 42–1 lists some career-sustaining jobs in each of the occupational areas of the marketing cluster.

Occupations at the entry level are jobs that involve limited decision-making skills and routine activities. Usually, no previous marketing education is required to do these jobs well. For example, cashiering is an entry-level job whether it is in food marketing, apparel and accessories marketing, or fast-food restaurant marketing.

Career-sustaining level occupations involve per-forming more complex duties that require some decision-making skills. Individuals who have reached this level typically are thinking of mar-keting as a career. These occupations also allow some individual control of the work environment. Examples of career-sustaining occupations include sales representative, head cashier, or customer ser-vice representative.

Occupations at the marketing-specialist level involve frequent use of decision-making and lead-ership skills, and mastery of marketing skills. A buyer, for example, must make daily decisions regarding purchases for his or her store.

At the marketing supervisor level, occupations require mastery of marketing skills and higher-level decision-making and leadership skills. Responsibili-ties at this level include supervising, planning, and coordinating. Department store managers and sales managers are jobs at the marketing supervisor level.

Finally, the manager/owner level is the high-est career level of the marketing occupations. Individuals who attain this level have achieved mastery in a variety of areas related to owning or managing a business. Marketers at this level are largely responsible for the success or failure of the organization. Examples of jobs at this level include store manager, sales vice president, marketing manager, and owner.

Planning for Your Marketing Career

A marketing career can bring lasting rewards and many hours of job satisfaction if it suits your inter-ests and abilities. You can begin now while you are still in school to explore occupational areas and pre-pare for a marketing career that is right for you. Successful preparation for a marketing career requires four steps.

1. Analyze your interests, abilities, and values.
2. Recognize the competencies (skills) needed in marketing jobs.
3. Explore the career opportunities in marketing that appeal to you.
4. Translate your special interests and abilities into a career plan.

Let's take a look at each of these steps.

Analyzing Your Interests, Abilities, and Values

The first step to take when thinking about potential careers is to look at your interests, abili-ties, and values. This will help you select a career that is both interesting and challenging. To start, answer these questions:

- What kinds of work do you enjoy?
- Do you express yourself well?
- Are you good at dealing with people?
- What special skills do you have?
- Do you have particular knowledge about goods or services?

Apparel/Accessories Marketing

Salesperson
Responsible for presenting merchandise, handling customer inquiries, and ringing up purchases.

Stock Clerk
Responsible for controlling the flow of merchandise in and out of the stock room, keeping track of the amount of merchandise in stock, marking the merchandise with proper codes and prices, and stocking the shelves.

Entrepreneur
Responsible for setting up and operating a business. Involves planning, money management, and marketing.

Finance/Services Marketing

Customer Service Representative
Responsible for handling customer inquiries and resolving customer complaints.

Bookkeeper
Responsible for keeping financial records for businesses.

Bank Teller
Responsible for handling customer deposits and withdrawals and recording the transactions.

Food Marketing

Cashier
Responsible for totaling customer purchases and handling payment for food.

Food Broker
Responsible for assisting food manufacturers and producers by selling their food products to stores.

General Merchandising/Retailing

Store Salesperson
Responsible for presenting merchandise, handling customer inquiries, and ringing up purchases.

Merchandise Receiver
Responsible for receiving incoming merchandise.

Hospitality and Recreation Marketing

Hospitality Cashier
Responsible for taking payments from customers, making change, and giving receipts.

Hotel Desk Clerk
Responsible for checking guests in and out of rooms and providing hotel information.

Marketing

Copywriter
Responsible for writing the text of print or radio ads or the storyboards for television ads.

Marketing Assistant
Responsible for assisting marketing manager in analyzing, planning, and supervising the marketing of a company's products.

Marketing Research Assistant
Responsible for assisting marketing researchers in gathering and analyzing marketing information needed to make business decisions.

Restaurant Marketing

Caterer
Responsible for planning, preparing, and serving food to customers, usually for select occasions.

Host and Hostess
Responsible for making reservations and greeting and seating guests.

Waiter and Waitress
Responsible for serving food to customers.

Sales

Telemarketer
Responsible for selling products and handling customer relations by phone.

Sales Demonstrator
Responsible for demonstrating products to customers in order to get them to purchase the product or product line.

Transportation and Travel Marketing

Airline Reservation Agent
Responsible for checking available flights and making reservations for customers.

Car Rental Agent
Responsible for renting cars to customers and handling payment.

Vehicle/Petroleum Marketing

Auto Salesperson
Responsible for selling cars to customers.

Truck Terminal Manager
Responsible for overseeing operations in the terminal where trucks load and unload their freight.

■■■ *Figure 42–1 Career-sustaining Jobs in the Marketing Career Cluster*
Here are some common career-sustaining marketing jobs in each of the occupational areas that you might consider pursuing. Pick one or two jobs and tell what position you might move into from this job.

economic competency. This text discusses the purposes and goals of business in the United States. As you know, businesses operate to make a profit by producing or distributing products that people and organizations need and want. You have acquired an economic competency when you understand that, as an employee, you are part of the team that will enable the company to serve its customers and make a profit.

A company's success depends on how efficiently all of its employees do their work. As you continue gaining economic competency, you will see how forces in the economy, such as consumer spending patterns and federal laws and regulations, affect the marketing of goods and services.

Exploring Career Opportunities in Marketing

After you have determined your interests, abilities, and values and have begun to recognize the competencies needed in marketing jobs, your next step is to match them to specific areas of marketing. Start at your school. Your marketing teacher, librarian, and guidance counselor all have information on marketing jobs. Most libraries have copies of four valuable references: *The Career Directory* series, the *Dictionary of Occupational Titles*, the *Occupational Outlook Handbook*, and the *Encyclopedia of Careers and Vocational Guidance*. These books give thousands of job descriptions, as well as more sources of information about your job interest.

Many libraries also maintain a special reference shelf of pamphlets that describe various jobs and list sources to contact for more information. Look through the card catalog or computerized database for books in your area of special interest. Also, check with the librarian, who may be able to give you information about job opportunities.

If you know people who work in your specific area of interest, talk with them about their jobs. Find out how they prepared for the field, what they like and dislike about their job, and the long-range employment opportunities in the area. If you do not know anyone who works in your specific area of interest, your marketing teacher or marketing education coordinator may know someone you can contact.

Translating Your Interests, Abilities, and Values into a Career Plan

Once you have an idea of the marketing career you would like to pursue, it is time to develop a career plan. First, think of yourself as a product with many benefits. Ask yourself how you can make yourself attractive to an employer. Think about the educational requirements of the career. Consider whether further education will increase your chances of getting the job of your choice. Plan now to attend a business school, community college, or university to further prepare you for your chosen career.

Second, develop a plan to package and label yourself so potential employers will see you as a competent, enthusiastic person. How can you do this? One good method is to use information about a career that you studied and match the job requirements to your special interests and abilities. You can do this by writing a resume and a job application letter. (See Figure 42–3 and Figure 42–4.)

A **resume** is a personalized data sheet that describes your career goal, education, work experience, extracurricular activities, and reference information. A **job application letter** is a formal letter of introduction to a potential employer that usually accompanies a resume. In a job application letter, you state your qualifications, discuss the contributions you can make to the company, and ask for an interview.

Global
MARKETPLACE

Jobs Around the World

Will you be on the Wanted List? Four hundred million workers will answer the call for "Help Wanted" worldwide in the 1990s. As companies expand into the global marketplace, employers will be seeking marketing professionals who can handle international promotion and distribution. So get your resume *and* passport ready.

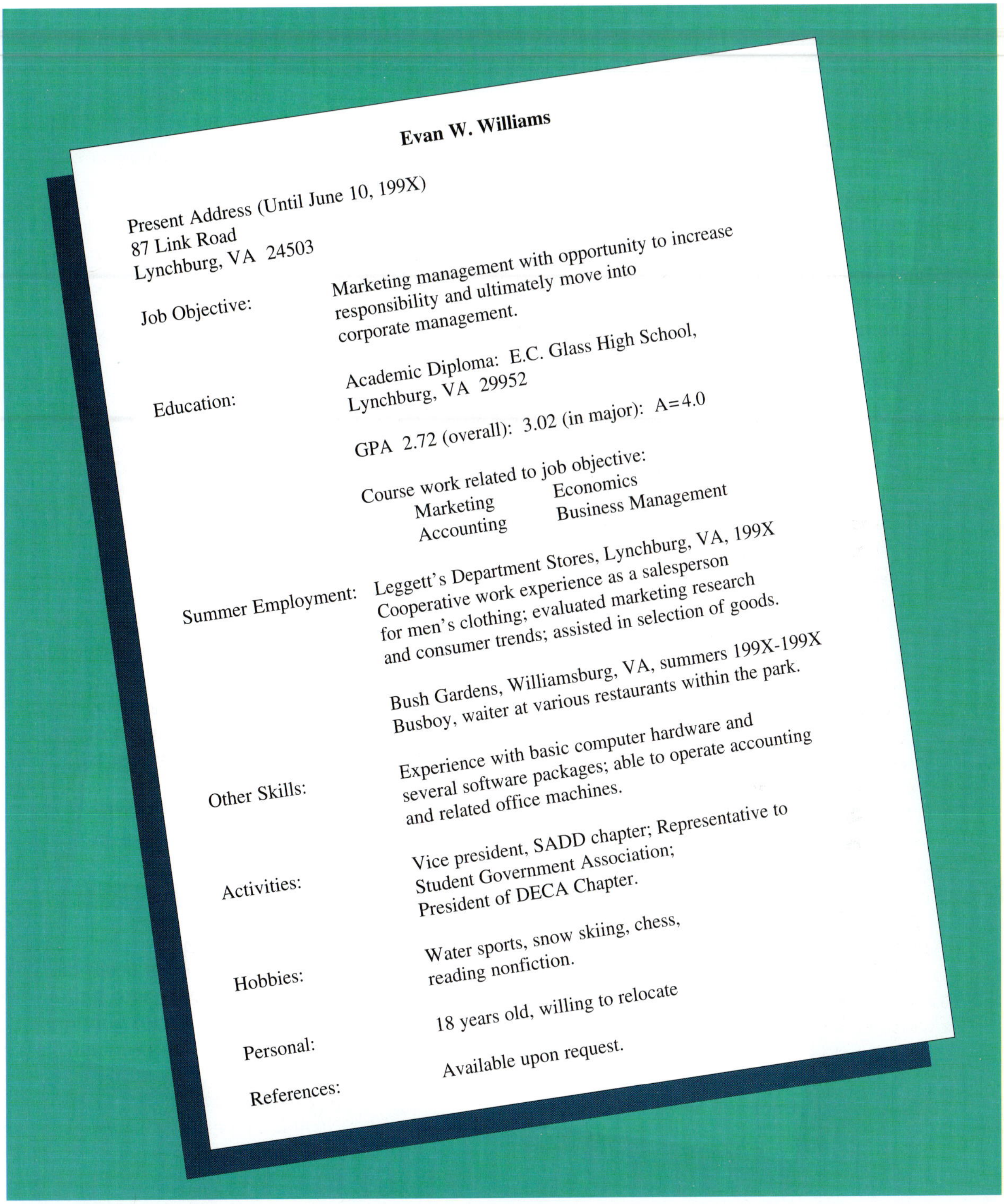

Evan W. Williams

Present Address (Until June 10, 199X)
87 Link Road
Lynchburg, VA 24503

Job Objective: Marketing management with opportunity to increase responsibility and ultimately move into corporate management.

Education: Academic Diploma: E.C. Glass High School, Lynchburg, VA 29952

GPA 2.72 (overall): 3.02 (in major): A=4.0

Course work related to job objective:
Marketing   Economics
Accounting   Business Management

Summer Employment: Leggett's Department Stores, Lynchburg, VA, 199X Cooperative work experience as a salesperson for men's clothing; evaluated marketing research and consumer trends; assisted in selection of goods.

Bush Gardens, Williamsburg, VA, summers 199X-199X Busboy, waiter at various restaurants within the park.

Other Skills: Experience with basic computer hardware and several software packages; able to operate accounting and related office machines.

Activities: Vice president, SADD chapter; Representative to Student Government Association; President of DECA Chapter.

Hobbies: Water sports, snow skiing, chess, reading nonfiction.

Personal: 18 years old, willing to relocate

References: Available upon request.

■■■ *Figure 42–3 Resume*
A resume describes your career goal, education, work experience, extracurricular activities, and references. What career goal would you state on your resume?

credit The ability to obtain goods, services, or money in exchange for a promise to pay later.

credit period The length of time for which mercantile credit is extended.

current assets Cash or other property that can be quickly converted to cash.

current liabilities Debts owed by a business and due within a limited period of time, such as a year.

customer Anyone who buys or rents goods or services.

customer benefits Desirable effects of product features; they show how a product will serve a customer's needs.

D

data processing The activity of organizing facts into information.

debt capital Funds raised through various forms of borrowing that must be repaid.

debit cards Cards that withdraw money from a customer's account.

decline stage The period in a product life cycle during which sales slow down.

demand The amount of a product that consumers are willing and able to purchase at a given price.

demographics Statistics about population patterns such as age, income, education, and occupation.

department store A retail establishment that employs 25 or more people; it offers clothing, home furnishings, gift items, and services.

depression An extended recession with high unemployment.

derived demand A demand that comes from the demand for consumer goods.

direct channel of distribution Marketing goods direct to the final user.

direct distribution channel Takes place when a manufacturer sells products directly to the final user.

direct mail Marketing goods and services directly through the mail by means of catalogs and other mailing pieces.

direct-mail advertising Advertising sent to prospective buyers through the post office; popular among large and small businesses.

directing The process of guiding people's activities to accomplish goals.

direct marketing Marketing by mail, telephone, or electronic marketing (with computers) or television to reach customers directly.

discretionary income The amount of money that people have left to spend as they choose after they have paid for the basic costs of living; disposable income minus the money spent for such necessities as food, shelter, clothing, transportation, and medical expenses.

dispensing closure A cap, lid, or seal through which the container contents can be dispensed in a controlled manner.

display advertisements   Ads that appear throughout a newspaper and use pictures, art, or different styles of type or print to attract attention.

disposable income   The amount of money that people have for spending and saving, it is the money they have left after paying taxes.

distribution center   The link between the supplier and the customer.

distributor   An independent intermediary who stocks the products of various manufacturers and sells them to industrial users.

drop shipper   An agent who makes arrangements for the direct shipment of goods from the manufacturer to the purchaser.

E

economic competency   An understanding of the purpose and goals of business in the United States and of the private enterprise system under which they operate.

economic goods   Goods that have utility and require human effort to bring them to market.

economic risks   Risks caused by changes in the market.

economic system (economy)   The way a nation chooses to use its productive resources to produce and market goods and services.

embargo   The total ban of a good from entering or leaving a nation.

emotional buying motives   Motives that are based on instincts, personal feelings, and emotions.

electronic vending   The use of computers in interactive vending machines.

endless chain method   A method of finding prospects in which the salesperson gets the names of prospects from customers who have already made purchases.

entertainment marketing   The use of entertainment business productions to promote products.

entrepreneurs   People who take the risk and provide the capital to start and operate their own business.

Equal Employment Opportunity Commission (EEOC)   Processes charges of individual or group discrimination and develops guidelines to help businesses avoid it.

equilibrium price   The price at which both the marketer and the customer make an exchange.

equity   Concerned with the fair and equal treatment of employees in the work environment.

equity capital   Money raised from within the firm or through the sale of ownership (equity) in the firm.

ethics   Guidelines for good behavior that benefit everyone in society.

ethnic group   All the people who have such characteristics in common as racial background, language, social customs, or physical traits.

impulse buying   Buying with little or no advance planning.

income   Money which is received or earned.

income statement   A summary of a firm's revenue and expenses over a period of time.

independent stores   Stores controlled and owned by one person or a family; usually managed by the owner.

indirect distribution channel   Occurs when the manufacturer uses an intermediary to act as a bridge between the seller and the user.

industrial advertisers   Promote goods, services, and ideas to the industrial market.

industrial distributor   Sells equipment, standardized parts, and operating supplies to industrial users.

industrial farm products   Products that reach the consumer having undergone a major change in form.

industrial goods   Tangible products bought by firms or organizations for business use rather than for personal use.

industrial market   The industrial market includes all the potential business customers for goods and services used in the production of other products, for use in daily business operations, or for resale.

industrial services   Services intended to satisfy the needs and wants of businesses by supporting business activities.

inflation   A general rise in prices.

information utility   The usefulness added to a product through communication.

installations   Buildings and major equipment used to produce goods or render services.

institutional advertising   The type of advertising that builds an image for a business organization without mentioning a specific product.

in-store salespeople   Those who sell inside a store; their main duties include serving customers, writing up the sale or processing it on the cash register, wrapping merchandise, making change, arranging and replenishing stock, keeping stock clean, and handling customer problems.

insurance   A contract between a subscriber and an insurance company in which the insurance company guarantees to cover certain losses or risks.

integrated distribution   The form of distribution in which manufacturers act as their own retailers or wholesalers.

intensive distribution   The form of distribution in which manufacturers distribute their product through any intermediary who wants it.

interactive electronic systems   Transmit information and pictures between a computer network and a consumer's computer screen.

intermediaries   Business organizations that perform buying and selling services which aid the flow of goods from the producer to the customer.

international marketing   Marketing activities performed to facilitate international trade.

international trade   The exchange of goods and services between nations.

in-transit storage   The process of storing manufacturers' goods in storage facilities provided by the railroad between their plants and the consumer until orders are received.

introduction stage   The first appearance of the product on the market.

J

job application letter   A formal letter of introduction to a potential employer that usually accompanies a resume.

L

label   An informative tag, wrapper, or seal attached to the product or the product's package.

leased dealership   A business that is owned by a particular company but is leased to someone else to operate.

liabilities   Amounts owed by a company.

licensed brand   A brand that is owned and trademarked by one firm and is licensed (rented) for use by other firms.

life-style   An individual's typical way of life.

limited-line retailer   A retailer that sells only one kind of merchandise, or several closely related lines of merchandise; includes apparel and accessories; home-furnishings; automotive dealers; food stores; service stations; and hardware and building-material dealers.

limited problem solving   Used to purchase an unfamiliar or a somewhat complex product that requires an information search before purchasing.

limited-service wholesaler   Unlike the full-service wholesaler, performs only certain services.

list price   The first price that customers are normally asked to pay for a product; sometimes called a base price.

local advertising   Advertising placed on local channels and aimed to an audience in a given geographic area.

long-term capital   Money used to purchase fixed assets.

M

macromarketing   The process of system that directs the flow of good and services in an economy.

mall intercept   A survey taken at a shopping mall or center.

mail questionnaire   A list of questions mailed to the survey group.

management   The activities undertaken by one or more people to coordinate the activities of other people in order to achieve results.

manufacturers' agent   An independent representative who handles part of the output of one or more manufacturers within a sales territory.

manufacturers' representatives   Salespeople who represent manufacturers.

market   All the potential customers and consumers for a product.

marketing   The process of planning and executing the conception, pricing, promotion, and distribution of ideas, goods, and services to create exchanges that satisfy individual and organizational objectives.

marketing competency   A general understanding of marketing concepts, practices, and processes.

marketing concept   The idea of efficiently fulfilling the wants and needs of customers at a profit (or other gain for a nonprofit organization).

marketing audit   A comprehensive and systematic review of the various goals and strategies used in marketing.

marketing ethics   Guidelines of behavior designed for organizations and their employees in their role as marketers.

marketing information system (MIS)   An organized way of continually gathering, sorting, analyzing, evaluating, and distributing information to marketing managers.

marketing mix   Product, price, place, and promotion—the core of any company's marketing system—known as the four Ps of marketing.

marketing plan   A written statement of the marketing goals and strategies for a particular firm, department, or product line.

marketing research   The gathering, recording, and analyzing of facts related to marketing goods and services.

marketing strategy   A marketing mix focused on certain groups of customers or a target market.

marketplace   Our commercial environment—the place where we make exchanges.

market position   A company's competitive standing based on its sales volume compared with that of other companies in the same industry.

market research   The study of the nature and characteristics of a market.

market segmentation   A process of subdividing the market according to customer needs and characteristics.

market share   A specific percentage of the sales volume of a total market.

markup pricing   Adding an amount or markup to the cost of goods to reach a selling price.

mass merchandisers   Stores that concentrate on selling a large number of consumer items at reasonable prices; they are often large, plain, and offer fewer services than department stores.

materials handling   The process of assembling, packing, weighing, and moving products from a producer to a warehouse, from a warehouse to a carrier, or from one carrier to another.

maturity stage   The period in a product life cycle when sales remain at a fairly even level.

merchandise approach   A type of retail sales approach used when customers are already focusing on merchandise; it deals directly with what interests the customer.

MDSS   An interactive communications network that links the decision maker with marketing information databases.

micromarketing   How products are conceived, promoted, priced, and distributed in individual marketing situations.

model display   A display in which merchandise is shown as it would look in actual use with related items.

monopoly   A market structure where one producer controls the industry.

mortgage   A written agreement between the borrower and the lending agency which gives property such as a building as security for payment of the debt.

motivation   The internal drive to accomplish a particular goal.

motive   An internal force that prompts a person to do something.

multipack   A special package design that groups two or more packaged products into a unit for easier display, carry-home utility, or user convenience.

N

national brand   The branded product of a manufacturer.

national advertiser   A manufacturer of consumer goods who advertises a product by its brand name.

national income   The money measurement of the annual flow of goods and services in a nation.

natural risks   Risks resulting from natural causes.

neighborhood shopping center   Contains an assortment of stores such as a grocery store, drugstore, dry cleaners, and barber, and is accessible to several thousand people within five minutes' travel.

net income   What a business has earned after taking income taxes into account; also called net profit.

network advertising   Carried across the country by the local stations owned and affiliated with one of the networks.

news releases   Articles about special events that are prepared and sent to the media.

nonprofit marketing   Consists of marketing activities conducted to achieve some goal other than profit-making.

nonstore retailing   The selling of goods and services direct to the consumer without the use of stores.

O

objection   An honest difference between the customer and the salesperson.

observation   The process of collecting information about customer buying behavior, product acceptance, and sales effectiveness by watching the actions of people without actually interviewing them.

obsolescence   Occurs when a product has become old and less useful.

occupational area   A category of jobs that involve similar interests and skills.

one-price strategy   The technique of offering the same price to all customers who purchase under similar conditions.

open display   A display in which merchandise is out in the open so customers can pick up articles and look at them.

operating ratio   The percentage of sales revenue represented by any value on a financial statement.

order taking   The process of filling the customer's purchasing requests; occurs throughout the channel of distribution and frequently at the retail level.

organization marketing   Those marketing activities that establish or change a target markets beliefs and/or behavior toward a particular organization.

organizing   The process of assigning the tasks developed during planning to various individuals or groups within the company or department.

orientation   An organized effort by the supervisor to get a new employee acclimated to the firm, the job, co-workers, and sometimes the customers.

outdoor advertising   Includes signs and posters displayed on billboards, building walls, and other rented outdoor spaces.

output   The results of computer processing.

owner's equity   The financial interest an owner has in a business.

P

packaging   The use of containers and wrapping materials to protect, contain, identify, promote, and facilitate the use of the product.

partnership   A business owned by two or more people.

patronage motives   Motives that are based on the customer's choice of a particular business.

peak prosperity   A period of high sales and income in the business cycle.

penetration pricing   A pricing strategy that means entering the market at a price low enough to reach as much of the market as possible.

person marketing   Includes those marketing activities that influence or change a target market's opinion about particular people.

personal care services   Services that help a person to be well-groomed.

personal code of ethics   A guide to one's own ethical behavior; our personal basis for judging whether a particular action is right or wrong.

personal income   The amount of money that a person earns or receives before any taxes are deducted.

personal selling   The direct effort made by a salesperson to convince a customer to make a purchase.

physical distribution   Total process of moving, handling, and storing goods on the way from the producer to the user.

physical motives   Motives that are based on physical needs such as the need to eat, avoid danger, and keep warm.

pilferage   Employee theft.

place marketing   Those marketing activities that establish or change a target market's beliefs and/or behavior toward particular places.

place utility   The increased usefulness of products because of location.

planned economy   An economy in which the government decides the economic questions.

planned shopping center   A shopping center that has been especially constructed for shopping.

planning   Involves setting goals and then choosing strategies that must be performed to attain the goals.

point-of-purchase promotion   Advertising and display material in and around a retail store; includes posters, counter cards, window-display material, and price cards.

possession utility   The ability of marketers to aid customers in owning goods.

preapproach   Gathering and analyzing information about the prospect and using it to construct the sales presentation.

preliminary research   The process of identifying a problem and devising a plan for solving the problem.

premium   Items given without substantial charge with the purchase of a product.

press kit   A folder containing a series of articles and photographs telling about the person, place, things, firm, or activity being publicized.

press releases   Articles about special events prepared and sent to the media.

price   The money value of a good or service.

price discrimination   Exists when prices for similar goods differ for different customers.

price fixing   Occurs when competitors get together to raise or lower prices.

price leader   A product of regular quality offered at a very low price for a limited time; sometimes called loss leaders.

price lining   Setting a limited number of prices for a line of products.

price-oriented promotion   Promotion that offers a special price reduction to the buyer.

primary data   Data gathered originally by researchers themselves for current use.

private brand   A product that carries the label of the middleman (wholesale or retailer) who sells it; also called middlemen's brands, retailers' brands, distributors' brands, and private label brands.

private carrier A transportation facility owned and used by a firm to transport its products.

private enterprise (capitalism) An economy in which the people—as consumers, business owners, or workers—make the economic decisions.

process materials Materials that come from raw materials and are used in manufacturing the finished product.

product All the physical features and psychological satisfactions received by the customer.

product advertising Advertising that stresses goods or services.

product features Unique characteristics of a product that make it different from every other product of its type.

product item A specific, physical product.

product life cycle An identifiable cycle in a product's life, which is represented by its sales history over a period of time and is usually divided into the four stages of introduction, growth, maturity, and decline.

product line A group of similar types of product items that are closely related because they satisfy a class of customer needs, are used together, or are sold to the same customer groups.

product mix The total of all product items and product lines offered for sale by a company.

product modification A planned change in a product or its packaging that may include changes in features, quality, or style.

product motives Motives that are based on the customer's choice of a particular product.

product planning The direction and control of all stages in the life of a product—from the time of its creation to the time of its removal from the company's product line.

product research The study of consumer reactions to a product.

product sample A small sample of an advertiser's product that is given away free.

production The process of creating or improving goods and services.

profit The difference between the amount of money a business brings in and the amount it spends.

program advertising Advertising that appears in church bulletins, school-play and athletic programs, and school yearbooks.

promotion The activities designed to bring a company's goods or services to the favorable attention of customers.

promotional goals Goals that state what the company wants to achieve through a particular promotion; based on the organization's goals and its marketing goals.

promotional mix The combination of different promotional elements used to promote a product.

prototype A model of a new product.

prospecting The process of finding potential customers who could benefit from and buy a good or service.

psychographics   Information about people such as their personality characteristics and life-style.

psychological motives   Motives that are based on the need for love and affection and prestige and recognition.

public relations   The total process of building goodwill toward a business organization.

public relations agencies   Firms that specialize in conducting public relations activities for their clients.

publicity   Unpaid promotion for a company or its products.

pull strategy   Promoting directly to consumers to encourage them to ask retailers and wholesalers to carry the product.

pump dispenser   A metal, plastic, glass, or combination container that releases its contents in spray or foam when a valve is pressed.

push strategy   Aiming promotional efforts directly at wholesalers and retailers to carry a certain product.

Q

quotas   Limitations on the amount of goods legally imported into a nation.

R

rack jobber   A limited service wholesaler that sells specialized lines of merchandise to certain types of retail stores.

rational buying motives   Motives that are based on the logical reasoning of the customer.

raw materials   Goods that are more or less in their original form and that need processing to become useful goods.

recession   A phase of the business cycle marked by a decline in the gross national product for six months.

regional shopping center   A planned shopping center that contains one or more department stores, a mass merchandiser, and many specialty shops. It draws more than 100,000 people from a radius of ten miles or more.

research plan   A step-by-step outline of everything that is to be done during a research project.

resources   The means to accomplish a goal.

response   The action taken to satisfy a need or want.

resume   A personalized data sheet which describes a career goal, education, work experience, extra-curricular activities, and reference information.

retail advertiser   A store or service organization whose advertising message encourages consumers to deal with its business.

retailers   Sell products directly to consumers.

retailing   Includes all forms of selling to the final consumer.

reverse marketing channel   Used when the goods to be reprocessed move from consumer to intermediary to producer.

risk   The possibility of loss or failure.

route drivers   Salespeople who travel an established route, selling products.

routine problem solving   Used to purchase frequently bought, low-cost items that require little research.

S

sales budget   A forecast of sales for a specific period of time.

sales presentation   At the heart of the selling process when the salesperson demonstrates or explains the product and attempts to build a desire for ownership within the prospect.

sales promotion   Any sales activity that supplements or coordinates advertising and personal selling.

sales promotion agency   An independent organization that specializes in sales promotion activities for other businesses.

sales research   The study of sales data.

sales support   Consists of creating goodwill by introducing new products and ways to promote them, and offering technical expertise to assist a customer in selecting the right product.

secondary data   Data already collected for another purpose, but which may be of use for the task at hand.

selective distribution   The form of distribution in which manufacturers carefully choose a number of intermediaries to market their product within a geographic area.

selling agent   An independent product specialist who sells the entire output of a line of goods for one or more manufacturers.

service approach   A type of retail sales approach that includes such questions to the customer as "How may I assist you?"

services   Benefits or satisfactions that improve the personal appearance, health, comfort, or peace of mind of their users.

shoplifting   The theft of merchandise from a store by a customer.

short-term capital   Capital needed to finance current operations; also called working capital.

shrink wrap   Package made by placing clear film around the product itself; it fits the contour of the product.

situation analysis or SWOT   Involves the examination of a company's strengths (S), weaknesses (W), opportunities (O), and threats (T).

skimming pricing   A pricing strategy that means entering the market at a relatively high price.

skin packaging Plastic film molded tightly over a product mounted on a card; the film keeps the product clean and protected, yet leaves it visible to the customer.

small business An independently owned and managed business that serves a limited geographic area and is not dominant in its industry.

social competency The ability to create a favorable impression and to work well with others.

social conscience A feeling of being responsible for one another.

social marketing Marketing practices that try to gain acceptance of a social idea, cause, or practice in a targeted group(s).

social responsibility The duty of an individual organization to the larger community.

socialism An economic system that depends heavily on the government to plan and make economic decisions and to own and control important economic resources and industries.

software Computer programs that give computers instructions.

sole proprietorship A business owned by one person.

specialty advertising Advertising on such useful things as matchbooks, address books, badges, and buttons.

specialty salespeople Salespeople who sell a particular product or line of products to customers at home or business; many sell door to door.

specifications An accurate description of the goods or services needed.

spending patterns The ways groups of people spend their money.

sponsor A company that pays for the advertising.

standards Limit the number of qualities, colors, sizes, varieties, and types of materials and commodities purchased.

statistical reporting area A geographic unit used to measure population characteristics.

stock turnover The number of times merchandise, or stock, is sold and replaced by new merchandise.

suggestion selling The selling of related or additional items along with those items the customer has already purchased.

supply The quantity of a product offered on the market at a specified price.

survey A method of collecting opinions by questioning a limited number of people chosen from a larger group.

T

target return A method of pricing that involves setting price levels according to the rate of profit that a company wants to earn from its sales.

target market The customers a business can serve best.

tariff A tax placed on imported goods.

Index

F

T

U

X

Y

Z

Photography Credits

Cover photo: Bill Ross/Westlight

3M Company 207; 7-Eleven 419; Mark Adams/Westlight 486, 487; Advantage Media Group 164; Larry Aiuppy/FPG International 365; Apple Computers Inc. 101; Association of Collegiate Entrepreneurs 130; AIDS Project Los Angeles 141; AT&T 210, 258, 288; Cradoc Baghaw/Westlight 357; Stephen Bauer/Tony Stone Worldwide 40; Beef Industry Council 139; Best Foods 277; Blue Diamond Almond Growers 120; Body Shop 493; Boston Globe 158; Robert Brenner/Photo Edit 8; Brookfield Zoo 137l; Budget and Credit Counseling Services, Inc. 248; G. B./The Stock Market 448, 449; BPI Communications 395; Jim Caldwell/FPG International 527; Jim Cambon/Tony Stone Worldwide 193; Campbell Soup Company 264; Canon U.S.A., Inc. 192b; Chrysler Corp. 87; Cineplex Odeon 389; Dennie Cody/FPG International 427; Cross Colours 542; Bob Daemmrich/Tony Stone Worldwide xi, 252; Dennis Degman/Westlight vi, 54, 55, 68t; Mary Kate Denny 25; Disney Publishing Group 222; Domino's Pizza Inc. 52; Amy C. Etra/Photo Edit 102, 105; Fannie May Candies 302; Federal-Mogul Corp. 301; Lois Ellen Frank/Westlight 134; Tony Freeman/Photo Edit 6, 56, 96, 188b, 190, 236; Gerald L. French/FPG International xviii, 520; Bud Freund/Westlight 370, 371; Frito-Lay, Inc. 211; Fukuhara, Inc./Westlight 114; FPG International 446; General Mills, Inc. 220; General Motors 526; David Getlen/FPG International xv, 414; Gillette Company 167; Robert W. Ginn/Photo Edit 47; Glencoe Stock 349, 401; Jeff Greenberg/Leo de Wys 28; Jeff Greenfield/Photo Edit 188t; Guide Dog Foundation 137r; Hanson Galleries 442; Harley-Davidson UK Ltd. 378; Walter Hodges/Westlight 68b, 82; Holiday Inn Corp. 62; Arnulf Husmo/Tony Stone Worldwide 18; Hyatt Hotels Corp. 72; Index Stock 160, 161; David Joe/Tony Stone Worldwide 316; Kawasaki Motors USA 221t; Chuck Keelor/Tony Stone Worldwide 19; Kentucky Fried Chicken Corp. 151; Kmart Corp. 400; Lands' End 439; Robert Laudau/Westlight viii, 146; Peter Le Grand/Tony Stone Worldwide 522; Leo de Wys 94; Levi Strauss & Co. 294; R. Ian Lloyd/Westlight xiii, 352; Dick Luvia/FPG International 296, 297, 530; Maxwell Mackenzie/Tony Stone Worldwide 116; Macy's 385; Magnavox 49; Marion Merrel Dow, Inc. 129; Marriott Corp. 468; MasterCard International 479; Bruce Matlock 362; Maybelline 36; Mayhaw Tree, Inc. 368; Art Monte de Oca/FPG International xii, 312; D. Murawski/Tony Stone Worldwide xiv, 372; Nabisco Foods Group 216 ; National Business Incubation Association 516; Nestlé USA Inc. 221b; John Neubauer/Photo Edit 33; Nielsen Media Research 180; Richard Nowitz 11; Richard Nowitz/FPG International 424; Nutri Pet, Inc. 364; Alan Oddie/Photo Edit 37, 172; Greg Pease/Tony Stone Worldwide 2, 3; Bob Perzel/Knotts Camp Snoopy 346; Photo Edit 23; Jim Pickerell/Westlight 266, 267; Ralph B. Pleasant/FPG International 200, 201; Proctor & Gardner Advertising 430; Rawlings Sporting Goods Company 224; Remedy 63; Remington Products Inc. 506; John Riley/Tony Stone Worldwide 484; Elena Rooraid/Photo Edit ix, 186; Rollerblade, Inc. 85; Bill Ross/Westlight 356; R.E /Tony Stone Worldwide 404; RPS Air 285; Andy Sacks/Tony Stone Worldwide 112, 119; Sara Lee Hosiery 230l; John Scheiber/The Stock Market 110, 111; Sony Corp. of America vii, 90; Superstock xvi, 30, 127, 162, 192t, 450; Stewart Tilger/Berkheimer Kline Golin/Harris v, 16; Titlelist & Foot-Joy 204b; Tony Stone Worldwide 166, 361; John Terence Turner/FPG International 298; United Airlines 382; United Parcel Service 359; United States Dept. of Agriculture/Forest Service 138; United States Gymnastics Federation 259; United States Postal Service 142; Valvoline Oil Company 477; VideOcart, Inc. 194; Walker Research & Analysis 165; Wal-Mart Stores, Inc. 46; Westlight 188c; Dana White/Dana White Productions x, xvii, 42, 74, 78, 91, 108, 124, 175, 198, 202, 219, 235, 268, 282, 295, 321, 324, 327, 328, 329, 332, 333, 334, 335, 337, 338, 428, 431, 434, 437, 456, 457, 460, 463, 464, 467, 474, 488, 494, 500, 510; Lee White Photography 4, 70, 109, 204, 212, 213, 228, 230r, 233, 234, 240, 244, 245, 271, 274, 276, 290, 291, 308, 309, 320, 342, 347, 348, 388, 392, 399, 409, 411, 417, 496, 539; World Cup Soccer 384; Young and Rubicam/United States Army 140; Zimmerman/FPG International 535